Radiocarbon and the Chronologies of Ancient Egypt

Edited by

Andrew J. Shortland and C. Bronk Ramsey

Assistant Editors
Michael Dee and Fiona Brock

Oxbow Books
Oxford and Oakville

Published by
Oxbow Books, Oxford, UK

© Oxbow Books and the authors, 2013

ISBN 978-1-84217-522-4

This book is available direct from:

Oxbow Books, Oxford, UK
(Phone: 01865-241249; Fax: 01865-794449)

and

The David Brown Book Company
PO Box 511, Oakville, CT 06779, USA
(Phone: 860-945-9329; Fax: 860-945-9468)

or from our website

www.oxbowbooks.com

A CIP record for this book is available from the British Library

Library of Congress Cataloging-in-Publication Data

Radiocarbon and the chronologies of ancient Egypt / edited by Andrew J. Shortland and C. Bronk Ramsey.
  p. cm.
 Includes bibliographical references.
 ISBN 978-1-84217-522-4
 1. Egypt--History--To 332 B.C. 2. Egypt--History--To 332 B.C.--Chronology. 3. Radiocarbon dating--Egypt. 4. Egypt--Antiquities. I. Shortland, Andrew J. II. Bronk Ramsey, Christopher.
 DT83.R194 2013
 932.01--dc23
                    2013011013

Cover image: *Part of a king-list from the Temple of Ramesses II at Abydos, 19th Dynasty.*
© *The Trustees of the British Museum, EA117, AN32689*

Printed in Great Britain by
Short Run Press
Exeter

Contents

Preface v

Acknowledgements vii

I. Introduction

1. Establishing Chronology in Pharaonic Egypt and the Ancient Near East:
   Interlocking Textual Sources Relating to c. 1600–664 BC... 1
   K. A. Kitchen

2. An Introduction to Egyptian Historical Chronology... 19
   A. J. Shortland

3. Using Radiocarbon Evidence in Egyptian Chronological Research................................ 29
   C. Bronk Ramsey

II. Radiocarbon Dating Methodology

4. Sample Selection for Radiocarbon Dating... 40
   F. Brock and M. W. Dee

5. Preparing Samples for AMS Radiocarbon Dating... 48
   F. Brock

6. Investigating the Accuracy of Radiocarbon Dating in Egypt:
   Checks With Samples of Known Age... 53
   M. W. Dee

III. The New Kingdom

7. A Radiocarbon-based Chronology for the New Kingdom... 65
   M. W. Dee

8. Antagonisms in Historical and Radiocarbon Chronology 76
   M. Bietak

9. Radiocarbon Data for Aegean Pottery in Egypt: New Evidence From
   Saqqara (Lepsius) Tomb 16 and Its Importance
   For LM IB/LH IIA 110
   F. Höflmayer, A. Hassler, W. Kutschera and E. M. Wild

10. Radiocarbon Calibration in the Mid to Later 14th Century BC
    and Radiocarbon Dating Tell El-Amarna, Egypt 121
    *S. W. Manning, B. Kromer, M. W. Dee, M. Friedrich, T. F. G. Higham
    and C. Bronk Ramsey*

11. The Ramesside Period: A Case Of Overstretch? 146
    Aidan Dodson

12. Garlands from the Deir el-Bahri Cache 153
    S. McAleely

13. New Radiocarbon Dates for the 21st Dynasty 167
    J. H. Taylor

IV. The Middle Kingdom

14. A Radiocarbon-based Chronology for the Middle Kingdom 174
    M. W. Dee

15. Correlating and Combining Egyptian Historical and Southern Levantine
    Radiocarbon Chronologies at Middle Bronze Age IIa Tel Ifshar, Israel 182
    E. S. Marcus

V. The Old Kingdom and Early Dynastic Period

16. A Radiocarbon-based Chronology for the Old Kingdom 209
    M. W. Dee

17. Radiocarbon Dates for the Old Kingdom and their Correspondences 218
    M. Bárta

18. Early Dynastic Egyptian Chronologies 224
    E. C. Köhler

19. Problems and Possibilities for Achieving Absolute Dates
    from Prehistoric and Early Historical Contexts 235
    J. M. Rowland

Appendix 250

Preface

The ideas behind this book have their origins in discussions held in the University of Oxford's Research Laboratory for Archaeology and the History of Art back in the 1990s. Due to the space constraints imposed by having a large university within an old city, with very high property prices, sharing offices was essential. In his wisdom, Mike Tite, then the Professor of Archaeological Science, thought it a very good thing that a radiocarbon scientist with a background in physics and a materials scientist with a strong interest in Egypt should be in the same room. And so it was, through the inevitably overheard conversations, and through discussion of issues, far from our usual research, we came to see that there was interesting research to be done in the application of radiocarbon in Egypt. It was some time, and only after we had moved offices and changed jobs, that we finally managed to do something with these ideas, thanks to a project funded by the Leverhulme Trust. The project's final form also owes much to the research coming from Manfred Bietak's SCIEM2000 project and to a radiocarbon dating project on papyri, conducted with the Oxford Radiocarbon Accelerator Unit which was led by Ezra Marcus.

Both the SCIEM2000 project and a major attempt by Georges Bonnani and colleagues to date monuments from Ancient Egypt, along with a whole series of projects looking at radiocarbon dating in relation to the Minoan eruption of Santorini, was that radiocarbon dating was not always in good agreement with prevailing archaeological interpretations of the chronology. It was far from clear whether this was due to problems with the chronologies, with the samples chosen for dating or indeed with radiocarbon dating itself.

Ezra Marcus brought to this the idea of using papyri from Egypt with known dates from the historical chronology to study this problem. By using many of these it should be possible to study the details of the radiocarbon record from Egypt. As it turned out this approach was, at that time, only possible for a very restricted timeframe. However, it was clear that the idea could be broadened out to looking at any radiocarbon dates that could be directly related to the political chronology of Egypt. By using the known order of kings, together with the new statistical methods now available for the analysis of radiocarbon dates, we could test the consistency of the radiocarbon measurements with the relatively well-known chronology of dynastic Egypt, especially in the New Kingdom.

The research project that provided the impetus to this book, was then primarily intended as a check of whether radiocarbon dating 'worked' in Ancient Egypt, and discovering if not, why not. As we conducted the research, however, and gained an appreciation of the issues surrounding the chronologies of dynastic Egypt, it became clear that, at least for some periods, radiocarbon might be reaching the stage where it can help resolve some of the chronological debates. It was with much needed humility that we approach this, since there is such a wealth and depth of scholarship in this field that we could never hope to understand in all its intricacy. We are very grateful to Kenneth Kitchen for summarising some of this at the start of this volume. Overall this book brings together both a summary of the findings of our research group and the perspectives of others on these and on related issues.

This book is not intended to address all of the issues that there are in the use of radiocarbon dating in Egypt. It could not possibly hope to do so. What we hope it does is to look at the underlying question of whether radiocarbon dating has the capability to resolve some of the chronological questions that need to be answered to properly understand the relationship of Egypt to the other civilisations in the region. While there are many problems, perhaps principally the recycling and curation of materials, and the disturbance of contexts by succeeding generations, we think that it does. The challenge for the future is to sort out how radiocarbon can be best applied in the region, and how the issue of access to accelerator-based radiocarbon dating within Egypt can be addressed.

It is perhaps ironic that a project borne of an overcrowded office should concentrate on Egypt, where many of the issues in radiocarbon dating seem to stem from the tight constraints of the Nile Valley meaning that people lived, not only close to each other, but also often on top of the remnants left by previous generations, leaving a complex agglomeration of material from different periods. Only by careful, almost forensic analysis can we use radiocarbon in such a situation. We have learnt a lot from both the research we have undertaken over the last few years and from the contributions of our colleagues to this volume.

C. Bronk Ramsey and A. J. Shortland

Acknowledgements

This book would not have been possible without the help of Michael Dee and Fiona Brock in helping to manage the editing, and in organising the symposium that led directly to it. The research project that underlies our contributions achieved what it did only because of the dedication of those involved: in particular, Michael Dee as the doctoral student in the project, stands out and this is reflected by his contributions to this volume. Another important contribution was that of Joanne Rowland who did so much to locate and identify samples that would be useful for dating from museums around the world. Tom Higham also provided intellectual input throughout the project, particularly in understanding the issues in choosing samples for radiocarbon dating and understanding the implications of their results. Stephen Harris ensured that we understood what we were dating from a botanical point-of-view and helped locate more recent known-age material from the Oxford University Herbaria and the Natural History Museum, London. Anita Quiles and Eva Wild provided important cross checking of results with the radiocarbon laboratories of Saclay and Vienna.

Given the nature of the research discussed here, our team has been totally dependent on many other people. Most obviously, because it is not possible to export material from Egypt for radiocarbon analysis, we have been reliant on museum material and so particular thanks are due to the staff of all of the museums who provided samples: Ägyptisches Museum und Papyrussammlung, Berlin; Ashmolean Museum, Oxford; Bolton Museum and Art Gallery; British Museum, London; City Museum and Art Gallery, Bristol; Cornell University, New York; Desert Research Institute, Las Vegas, Nevada; Kunsthistorisches Museum, Vienna; The Manchester Museum; Medelhavsmuseet, Stockholm; Metropolitan Museum of Art, New York; Musée du Louvre, Paris; Musées royaux d'art et d'histoire, Brussels; National Museums, Liverpool; The Petrie Museum of Egyptian Archeology, London; The Pitt Rivers Museum, Oxford; Royal Botanic Gardens, Kew; Staatliches Museum Ägyptischer Kunst, Munich; and the Victoria Museum of Egyptian Antiquities, Uppsala University, Sweden. The research would also not have been possible without generous funding by the Leverhulme Trust (grant no. F/08 622/A) nor without the infrastructure support for the Oxford Radiocarbon Accelerator Unit by the Natural Environment Research Council. The statistical methods essential for this kind of work were developed in collaboration with English Heritage and the background work performed with Ezra Marcus was made possible due to funding by the German-Israeli Foundation for Scientific Research and Development (grant no. I-2069-1230.4/2004) with preliminary background research aided by the SCIEM2000 project.

I. INTRODUCTION

CHAPTER 1

Establishing Chronology in Pharaonic Egypt and the Ancient Near East: Interlocking Textual Sources Relating to *c.* 1600–664 BC

K. A. Kitchen

1. Introductory

In any attempt to establish a viable chronology for ancient Egypt during the late second and early first millennia BC, it is absolutely essential to make full use of the data both from Egypt and from her Near-Eastern contemporaries – Egyptian data on their own are *not* sufficient to produce a sound and detailed chronology for pharaonic Egypt, *c.* 1600–664 BC. Before *c.* 1600, there is – still – a wealth of data reaching back to *c.* 3000 BC; but, at certain junctures, unsolved cruxes leave us with breaks in continuity, leading to approximations only, for the earlier epochs. To provide a firm foundation, and to avoid turning this paper into a book-length study, it must suffice us here to stay within the basic epoch (*c.* 1600–664) before which any earlier series of dates must in any case be located.

2. Basis for the early 1st millennium

Starting from Alexander III ('Great') of Macedon as a base-line (in Egypt, 332–323 BC/in Mesopotamia, 330–323 BC), we can move back in both lands to earlier fixed dates. The Achaemenid Persian empire took over Egypt from the 26th Dynasty in 525 BC, which line had ruled since 664 BC, before which Taharqa of the 25th Dynasty had ruled 26 years during 690–664 BC, taking good Egyptian dates back to 690. In the east, the Persians took over Babylon and its realms in 539 BC, from the Neo-Babylonian Dynasty founded in 626 BC. Both in Egypt and Mesopotamia, we have not only such compilations as Manetho for Egypt, and the Ptolemaic Canon for both Mesopotamia and Persia, but also regnal year-dates of kings in Egypt and the considerable series of dates-of-accession (from first-hand economic documents in cuneiform) of kings dominating Mesopotamia from 626 BC (Nabopolassar) down to 146 BC under the Seleucid Alexander Balas.[1] Before the accession of Taharqa in 690 in Egypt, its '25th Dynasty' was founded by Shabako (716–702 BC) when he took over Egypt in his 2nd year (715), to be followed in due course by Shebitku (702–690),[2] precursor to Taharqa.

Author's Address: **K. A. Kitchen**, School of Archaeology, Classics and Egyptology, 12–14 Abercromby Square, University of Liverpool, Liverpool L69 7WZ, UK

Returning to Mesopotamia, exact dates go far back beyond 626 to 910 BC, thanks to the preservation of a continuous sequence of annual eponym-officers (as maintained by the Assyrian state) during the years corresponding to 910–648 BC, as guaranteed by recognition of the solar eclipse of 763 BC in the eponymy of Bur-Saggilê in the reign of Assur-dan III.[3] From 747 BC down to the Seleucid period, we also have a series of year-by-year Neo- and Late- Babylonian chronicles through some six centuries, with gaps for which the relevant tablets have not yet been recovered.[4] So, dating for most of the 1st millennium BC is well-assured in Mesopotamia.

In Egypt, there are sound reasons to affirm good regnal dates within quite close limits for the period 945–715 BC, as covered by the continuous line of Libyan-origin kings that make up the 22nd Dynasty. Their sequence is: Shoshenq I (21 yrs), Osorkon I (32 to 35 yrs),[5] Takelot I (15 yrs), Osorkon II (30 yrs. min.), Takelot II (25 yrs.), Shoshenq III (39 yrs.), Shoshenq IV (13 yrs), Pimay (6 yrs), Shoshenq V (37 yrs), and Osorkon IV (14 or 15 yrs), a potential total of some 231 years, with possible plusses for Osorkons I, II and IV, and of possible minuses if Takelot II had coregencies with either his predecessor, successor or both.[6]

The foreign relations of the 22nd Dynasty at its beginning and end help to secure good dates for its accession and demise. Thus, as 'Shishak', Shoshenq I appears in the early Hebrew sources as invading Palestine in the 5th year of Rehoboam king of Judah, while pursuing his protégé Jeroboam king of Israel (whom he had in effect set up, to break up the former unity of the realm of Solomon who had died in 931/930 BC).[7] This synchronism can be combined with Egyptian data to set limits for the date of the accession of Shoshenq I. The 5th year of Rehoboam (on the autumn/autumn calendar of Judah) encompassed 926/925 BC. As ancient Near-Eastern kings commonly went to war in spring/summer, to seize their foes' harvests,[8] Shoshenq's campaign can thus be set in that phase of 925 BC. At some time following his victorious return to Egypt, he launched a massive programme of temple-building-works in Egypt's three major centres: at Thebes above all (as a sop to its innately hostile hierarchy), plus Heliopolis and Memphis. At the start of his 20 years' reign (so far) he already had two adult sons, mature enough for the younger (Iuput) to be put in charge of both a hostile Thebes and the governorship of all Upper Egypt. So, by the time of his Levant campaign, he would already have reached his 50s; thus, the execution of propagandistically immense works at Thebes (and while he still lived) was an urgent necessity. Thus the decree of Year 21 for quarrying at Silisila[9] cannot long have followed his victory abroad, especially if loot from Jerusalem (or anywhere else) had enhanced his resources. This is why the campaign is best dated to the summer of his Year 20 (and certainly not earlier than Year 19). Once home in the autumn of 925, he could then plan his great building-projects, and set in motion the quarrying of stone, and during that winter (925–924) hasten deliveries to Thebes and beyond, and get the works started. One may thus date the stela (of 2nd Shomu <1>, Year 21) to around December/January of 925/924 BC; and his accession, consequently, to 945 BC, or 944 at the very latest. At his death in an incomplete *Year 22, the Theban works were well-begun – but manifestly unfinished: the great colonnades were left in the rough (with neither texts nor décor), the planned pylon left unbuilt, and even (it seems) his figure in the vast triumph-scene was perhaps hastily finished-off in plaster for final painting. Thus, it is unwise in the extreme to lower the starting-date of the 22nd Dynasty more than a year below 945 BC, on extant evidence.[10] Which is close enough for most purposes.

Some 80 years or so later, we have a now-fragmentary presentation vessel of Osorkon II that was dug up in the excavations at Samaria. In 853 BC, most of the petty kings of the Levant banded together to oppose the invasion by Shalmaneser III of Assyria, leading to a non-victory for both sides at the battle of Qarqar; among his opponents, Shalmaneser includes mention of a contingent of 1000 troops from Egypt (*Musri*), an identification supported by the depiction and mention of African animals as tribute on his 'black obelisk'. Thus, this Musri should be accepted as Egypt in these cases, and not some imaginary shadow-land elsewhere.[11] Chronologically, if the Samaria vessel is a trace of an Egypto-Israelite alliance on the eve of Qarqar (854/853 BC), then we have an implicit synchronism for Osorkon II, agreeing with a rough date for him of *c.* 875–845 BC (on our figures of our list of 22nd Dynasty regnal figures given above) albeit not needfully precise to a year.

Much more useful is the little batch of links for Osorkon IV who ends this Dynasty. In his own 2nd year, in 715 BC, Shabako definitively swept through Egypt, removing all other would-be kings (in practice, Osorkon IV of the 22nd Dynasty. Iuput II of the 23rd Dynasty, Bakenranef of the 24th Dynasty and any other local pretenders). So, Osorkon IV did not reign after that date. But before it, we do have other clear correlations. First, he was undoubtedly the trembling kinglet (U)shilkanni (for '<O> silkon' < 'Osorkon') who presented Sargon II with 12 large horses as a 'sweetener' to stay away, in 716 BC,[12] just a year before Shabako did for him. Second, he was equally clearly the 'So, king of Egypt' appealed-to by Hoshea, last king of Israel, in 726/725 BC (2 Kings 17:4). The abbreviation to 'So' or 'Sa' is now known to be commonplace in Egypt around this epoch, as in proper names like Tentsa for *Tent-Osorkon, as Yoyotte long since pointed out,[13] while such drastic abbreviations are well-known in various other cases, such as Sesse for Ramesses, Mose for Amenmessu, Shosh for Shoshenq (especially on scarabs), and innumerable abbreviations of non-royal names in the New Kingdom. And even earlier, Piye from Nubia encountered our Osorkon (IV) as from Bubastis, during his own epic campaign through Egypt. Piye certainly reigned 24 years and (with near certainty) 30 years, and in fact up to 32 or even 34 years, setting his invasion of Egypt at *c.* 730/729 or 728/727 BC. On these dates, we would then have a reign of (maximally) 15 or (minimally) 13 years, for Osorkon IV. Thus, all the intervening kings of the 22nd Dynasty from Osorkon I to Shoshenq V inclusive will have reigned within *c.* 924–730 BC, allowing about 194 years for: Osorkon I (32 years minimum), Takelot I (15), Osorkon II (32), Takelot II (± 20, and ± 4 for co-regencies), Shoshenq III (39), Shoshenq IV (13), Pimay (6), and Shoshenq V (37).[14]

Finally for this epoch, the 21st Dynasty. Here, most things are simpler, if we stick to the real essentials. In Manetho, seven kings are named: Smendes, Psusennes (I), Neferkheres; Amenophthis, Osochor, Psinakhes; and another Psusennes (II).

This equates extremely well with the kings known from original sources: (Ne)subanebdjed (I), attested up to an attributable Year 25 (cf. Manetho, 26 years); one Neferkare Amenemnisu, no definitive dates [unless Years 1–5 of the Banishment Stela are his], but ephemeral (cf. Manetho, Neferkheres, 4 years; but placed after next); Psusennes I, Years 48, 49 (cf. Manetho, 46 years [var., 41]); Amenemope, Year 5 and possibly Year 10 (cf. Manetho, 9 years; Osorkon the Elder, Year 2 (cf. Manetho, 6 years [var., 9]); Siamun, Year 17 (cf. Manetho, Psinaches, 9 years); and Psusennes II, probably Years 5 and 13 (cf. Manetho, 14 years [var. 35 *<15 years]). In terms of the original regnal figures just given, we have: 25 + 5 + 49 + 5/10 + 2 + 17 + 13 = 121 or 116 years; Manetho reports 130 years' total, but his Africanus figures only total 114 years; the Eusebian variants subtract 5 years from Psusennes I, and add 21 years for Psusennes II, end additional balance = 16 years. Added to the Africanus 114 years, 114 + 16 = the standard Manethonic 130 yrs.

To reach a real chronology, one must sift the total data. Smendes I's Year 25 clearly supports Manethonic (M) 26; the years 1–5 of the Banishment Stela might be adduced to support a Manethonic 4-year reign [5th year incomplete] for Amenemnisu; Psusennes at 46 years (M) but Years 48, 49 in original data may – as others have suggested – imply a 48-year reign (Psusennes dying in Year 49), including a 2-year coregency with his successor. Amenemope's known Year 9 (and possibly 10) agree well with Manetho; so, if a co-regency be allowed, Amenemope may either be allowed a total of 11 years, 2 as co-regent and 9 solo, or merely 9 total, 7 solo. Osochor may be allowed his M 6 years, only 4 above the epigraphic Year 2 date. On placement, the 9-year rule of Psinaches has to correspond with Siamun, known up to a 17th year; again, one may (as often suggested) amend Manetho to 19 years here. Finally, the probable Year 13 of Psusennes II agrees well with 14 years that could thus be accorded to him; the 35 is best taken as an error for *15 (by compounding with an otiose 20).

If we take the minimum series (Smendes 26, + Neferkare Amenemnisu 4, + Psusennes I 46 [& 2 CR] + Amenemope 9 [including 2 as coregent], + Osorkon the Elder 6 + Siamun 19, + Psusennes II, basic 14 [mean of 13 and 15 opposites], then the 21st Dynasty total would be 124 years, giving – when added to 945 BC for start of the 22nd Dynasty – a starting-date of 1069 BC for the 21st Dynasty, as is commonly used. (If one prefers a nice round figure like 1070, then of course, one could simply allow a full *15 years (< 35) for Psusennes II, and adjust the intervening reigns back to Smendes to fit. It matters little!) Thus, the end of the New Kingdom (the 18th, 19th, and 20th Dynasties) and start of the post-New-Kingdom epoch for Egypt occurs close to 1069 BC (or 1070 if preferred).

3. Moving back into the late 2nd millennium

Egyptian basics for the 18th, 19th and 20th Dynasties

Here, first, we will gather just the essential Egyptian 'nuts and bolts' that are the nucleus for this period, without reference to the bracketing that links with the contemporary Near East MUST necessarily impose. Then, the state of the latter can be ascertained, the cross-links with Egypt be established, – and finally, such adjustments to the Egyptian "minimal" dating as may prove necessary can be made, hopefully to provide us with an essential working chronological framework from soon after 1600 BC down to 664 BC, from our textual sources, that will be a fit tool to compare with the findings of the radiocarbon commission – and, hopefully, leading to a happy chronological marriage twixt the two disciplines! But business first.[15]

Regnally, the 18th Dynasty comprises: Ahmose I, 25 years; Amenhotep I, 21 years; Thutmose I, 12 years (8 attested); Thutmose II, 13 or only 3 years (1 attested); Thutmose III, 54 years (including the 21 years of Queen Hatshepsut); Amenhotep II, 26 years (1 year overlap with Thutmose III); Thutmose IV, 9/10 years; Amenhotep III, 38 years; Amenhotep IV (Akhenaten), 16 years; Smenkhkare, 2 years; Tutankhamun, 9 years; Ay, 3 or 4 years; Horemheb, 28 years.[16] The maximum total, 257 years, unless Thutmose II is only 3 years, and Ay only 3 years = reduced total (by 11) of 246 years. The improbable reduction of Horemheb by 14 years would give an absolute minimum of 232 years.

In turn, the 19th Dynasty comprises: Ramesses I (1 full year); Sety I, 11 years attested; Ramesses II, 66 years; Merenptah, 9 years; Amenmessu, 3 years; Sety II, 6 years; Siptah plus Tausret, 8 years. Total, 104 years. The supposed inclusion of Amenmessu's reign within that of Sety II has now to be abandoned, as the known 3 ¾ years of Amenmessu will *not* fit inside the 2 ¼ years' 'gap' around Year 3 of Sety II.[17]

Finally, the 20th Dynasty comprises: Sethnakht, 3 years (a Year 4 is now known); Ramesses III, 31 years; Ramesses IV, 6 years; Ramesses V, 4 years; Ramesses VI 7 years minimum; Ramesses VII, 7 years minimum.; Ramesses VIII, 1 year. (so far); Ramesses IX, 18 years. minimum; Ramesses X, 3 years, possibly 7; Ramesses XI (incl. *whm-mswt* era), 29 years. This gives us a minimum total of some 109 years overall. If Ramesses VI and VII had completed their respective 8th years, and Ramesses IX his 19th, then the total would reach 112 years – and up to 114, if Ramesses VIII be allowed 2 more years. A disputed Year 8 possibly for Ramesses X would add 4 more years (not favoured by most), up to 116/118 years. So, a range of 109 to 118 at extremes.

In theory, therefore, on minimum totals, before 1069, the 20th Dynasty at 109 years would date minimally to *c.* 1178–1069 BC. On that basis, minimal figures for the 19th Dynasty (104 years) would set it at *c.* 1282–1178 BC (Ramesses II at 1270–1204). In turn, best minimal figures for the 18th Dynasty (3 years each for Thutmose II and Ay, but still 28 for Horemheb) would cover 1282 + 246 = 1528–1282 BC (if 13 years for Thutmose II and 4 for Ay be allowed, then the 18th Dynasty would be a basic 257 years, during 1539–1282 BC). In contrast, the 14 years-for-Horemheb theory would reduce the dates running from 1528ff. down to 1514–1282 for the 18th Dynasty.

But mere theory in splendid isolation, as we shall now see, risks being unmasked as pure self-delusion, if vital correlations from independent Near-Eastern data are not put into practice. 'The Egyptian Chronology' (to cite a well-meaning but unfortunate phrase…) simply does not exist before 664 or at best 690 BC, as the variety of recent treatments shows to the full.[18]

4. The late 2nd millennium contd.

Mesopotamian basics, c. 1400–900 BC: Assyria first.

Therefore, we now turn again to the Near East, and especially Mesopotamia (but not exclusively) for the late 2nd millennium, for which rich resources are available, beginning with the Middle-Assyrian kingdom, within the 14th to 10th centuries. To keep things concise, we tabulate the essential data as follows, embodying: (1) modern sequence number, (2) reign-length (from the king-list and allied data), (3) dates pre-910 based on the attested reign-lengths, (4) the kings' names, (5) known data on the eponyms' sequence (by reign), and (5) personal/monumental attestations of kings as main-line rulers [not as rivals thereto!] at Assur and elsewhere.

Table 1.1: Kings of Assyria.

KG NO.	REIGN	DATES BC	KINGS	DATA ON EPONYMS	ATTESTATIONS
72	27	1391–1364 (1381–1354)	Eriba-Adad I	Sp,[19] 33–36/44.	Assur
73	36	1364–1328 (1354–1318)	Assur-uballit I	Sp. 44–55.	Assur, Nineveh, etc.
74	10	1328–1318 (1318–1308)	Enlil-nirari	Sp. 56.	Assur
75	12	1318–1306 (1308–1296)	Arik-den-ili	Sp. 56.	Assur
76	32	1306–1274 (1296–1264)	Adad-nirari I	Mentioned in texts; Sp. 57–61.	Assur, Nin(eveh), etc.
77	30	1274–1244 (1264–1234)	Shalmaneser I	trs. in Ep(onym) lists; and Sp. 72–99.	Assur, Nin., etc.
78	37	1244–1207 (1234–1197)	Tukulti-Ninurta I	trs., in Ep. Lists; and Sp. 76, 99, 114–129.	Assur, Nin., etc.
79	4[20]	1207–1203 (1197–1193)	Assur-nadin-apli	trs., Ep. Lists; and Sp. 130–131.	Assur
80	6	1203–1197 (1193–1187)	Assur-nirari III	Sp. 131–132.	as the king, in letters
81	5	1197–1192 (1187–1182)	Enlil-kudur-usur	–	king in Synchr. King-list and in Sync Hist.
82	13, var. 3	1192–1179 (1182–1179)	Ninurta-apil-Ekur	Sp. 143, 147–8.	Assur
83	46	1179–1133	Assur-dan I	cf. Sp. 133–146.	Assur, etc.
84	–	(x–1133)	Ninurta-tukulti Assur	– (*tuppi-shu*)	letter(s), etc.
85	–	(1133)	Mutakkil-Nusku	– (*tuppi-shu*)	also in Synchr KLs
86	18	1133–1115	Assur-resh-ishi I	–	Assur, Nin, etc. SKL
87	39	1115–1076	Tiglath-pileser I	trs. Ep. lists; Sp.	Assur, Nineveh
88	2	1076–1074	Ashared-apil-Ekur	trs., Ep. lists	Synchr KL
89	18	1074–1056	Assur-bel-kala	Eps in docmts	Assur, Nineveh; SKL
90	2	1056–1054	Eriba-Adad II	–	Assur, Nineveh; SKL
91	4	1054–1050	Shamshi-Adad IV	Ep., in documnt	Assur, Nineveh; SKL
92	19	1050–1031	Assur-nasir-pal I	Ep. lists.	Assur
93	12	1031–1019	Shalmaneser II	Ep. lists	Assur
94	6	1019–1013	Assur-nirari IV	Ep. lists	Assur
95	41	1013–972	Assur-rabi II	Ep. lists	Assur; Synch KL
96	5	972–967	Assur-resh-ishi II	– ; S(ynchr) KL	Assur and Bel-Erish text
97	32	967–935	Tiglath-pileser II	Ep. lists	Assur, Nineveh
98	23	935–912	Assur-dan II	Ep. lists	Assur, etc.
99	21	912–891	Adad-nirari II	Ep. lists	Sync. Hist and KL +
100	7	891–884	Tukulti-Ninurta II	Ep. lists	Assur, Nineveh, etc.
101	25	884–859	Assur-nasir-pal II	Ep. lists	Assur, Nineveh, etc.
102	35	859–824	Shalmaneser III	Ep. lists	Calah, etc.

Subject to minor caveats, this list provides a clear, reliable sequence of kings of Assyria who in hard fact did rule in direct succession as shown here. Assur was the highly-traditional point-of-origin of the Assyrian realm, and centre-point of its kingship. The real chronology of Assyria (beginning already in Old-Assyrian times, by the 19th century BC) was vested in the unbroken succession of years each named after an individual (including the reigning king) who held office as name-person for that year (thus, 'eponym'), and continued down to 612 BC, on the eve of the final extinction of that kingdom (609/608 BC).

As our list shows, virtually every single king is known from activity in Assur (and often elsewhere), or from traces of their eponym-lists, or both, as well as in a series of 'cross-references' in documents that synchronised sets of kings of Assyria and Babylon as contemporaries in their respective reigns. Exceptions are virtually zero, and in no case chronologically significant. The Assyrians subsumed Assur-dan I's would-be successors (Nos. 84–85) as a merely ephemeral pair, to be included under his official timespan; hence, we can do no different, unless fresh data prove otherwise. Going back earlier, to No. 80, rude letters to Assur-nirari III as *de facto* king of Assyria by his Babylonian contemporary in fact guarantee his role in that office. At that time, Assur-nirari III's contemporary as Governor of Hanigalbat, one Ili-ipaddu,[21] was also at times given the honorary title of 'King' of Hanigalbat, to satisfy local sentiment – Hanigalbat was the last version of the former great kingdom of Mitanni, its eastern half that first was backed (under Artatama II and Suttarna III) by Assyria (against the Hittites); but its later rulers then resisted Assyria until conquered by the latter. Such local honorary 'kingships' for key governors of local stock are known in later times also, and served local political purposes likewise.

Thus, despite the efforts of some chronologers to shorten Near-Eastern chronology artificially by denigrating the Assyrian king-list, and attempting to pull kings out of it at random to suit their reductionist ends, the basic list and datings listed above for Assyria stand firm, and cannot be tampered with in any such arbitrary fashion. The only serious point-at-issue is whether Ninurta-apil-Ekur reigned for 13 years (as in our oldest version [Nassouhi copy] of the Assyrian king-list) or only 3 years (as in the later version, in the SDAS/Khorsabad copies).[22] Hence we give dates on both options here, for convenience.

5. The late 2nd millennium contd.

Mesopotamian basics, c. 1400–900 BC: *Babylonia next*

Thus, given the close political interrelationships between Assyria and Babylonia, and the links of both with Egypt in the 14th and 13th centuries, we need here to measure the Babylonian input, specifically for the Kassite period, second half (*c.* 1400–*c.* 1157 BC).[23] The link with Egypt is first visible in the Amarna letters, with Kadashman-Enlil I and Burnaburiash II, and then not again until Kadashman-Turgu in the 13th century (cf. below, for these). The Babylonian king-lists are badly damaged and incomplete, preserving some reign-lengths but many are lost; however, we do have both a Synchronistic King List (SKL)[24] and a Synchronistic History[25] (plus 'Chronicle P'[26]) equating the reigns of ostensibly mutually contemporary kings of Assyria and Babylon – which helps to anchor such known Babylonian reigns as we do have. But first, we tabulate the Babylonian (Kassite) kings for our period (Nos. 19–36 of that Dynasty) with their lengths of reign as discernible so far:[27]

Table 1.2: Babylonian (Kassite) Kings for our period.

No	King	YRS	No	King	YRS	No	King	YRS
19	Burnaburiash II	27	25	Kadashm Enl II	9	31	Adad-shum-iddin	6
20	Karahardash	1	26	Kudur-Enlil	9	32	Adad-shum-usur	30
21	Nazibugash	0	27	Shagarakti-Sh	13	33	Meli-shipak	16
22	Kurigalzu II	25	28	Kashtiliash IV	8	34	Merodachbaladan I	13
23	Nazimarutash	26	29	Enlil-nadin-sh	1	35	Zababa-shum-id	1
24	Kadashman Turgu	18	30	Kadashm Kh II	1	36	Enlil-nadin-ahi	1

Next, we need to link up the Babylonian series with the Assyrian dates, with (in theory) two options corresponding to the two options for Assyrian dates, deriving from the alternate reign-lengths of 13 or 3 years for Ninurta-apil-Ekur, and subject to comparison with the long series of recorded synchronisms of kings of Assyria and Babylonia at this epoch. Here we turn to one particular episode that permits a close synchronism of the two series, namely the very close overlap between the reigns of kings Assur-uballit I of Assyria (36 years) and Burnaburiash II of Babylon (27 years).

We learn that Assur-uballit married-off a daughter to Burnaburiash II, who bore two sons to the latter, namely Karahardash and Kurigalzu 'the younger' (later, Kurigalzu II). In due course, Burnaburiash II died, and Karahardash succeeded him. The new king was old enough to wage a full military campaign (against the Suteans), and to institute a series of public works, namely the digging of wells and the building of fortresses. Conceivably, needing up to a year's activity. Then, the Kassite populace rebelled, the young king was murdered, and a purely Kassite usurper, Nazi-bugash, enthroned in his place. Enraged at the death of his grandson Karahardash, the veteran Assyrian king Assur-uballit marched his troops into Babylonia, disposed of the would-be usurper, and installed his younger grandson Kurigalzu (II) instead, who in due course reigned for up to 25 years.[28] Thus, in Babylonia, we have most likely a time-sequence of 27 years of Burnaburiuash II + 1 year for the brief but active reign of Karakhardash, his murder, the usurpation by Nazi-bugash, and invasion by Assur-uballit, eliminating Nazi-bugash and installing Kurigalzu II; total, 28 years between the accessions of Burnaburiash II and Kurigalzu II.

But when? Here, we may invoke ancient usage; Assur-uballit was surely already a reigning king when he sent his daughter to marry in Babylon; a mere crown-prince would have no authority to do this. Nor is it likely that he sent her to a king in Babylon to be married to his heir rather than to the reigning Babylonian king himself. So, both Assur-uballit and Burnaburiash would both have been reigning kings when the match was enacted. Three possible dates can be offered for the 28-year sequence set out in the preceding paragraph. A *minimum date* (option C): namely, that Assur-uballit I crushed the murderers of his elder grandson, eliminated Nazibugash, and installed Kurigalzu II all within his 36th and final year, shortly before his own decease. On that basis, from our §4 Table above, the year 1329–28 (or, alternatively, 1319–18) would have witnessed (at latest) the death of Burnaburiash II, an almost one-year reign by Karahardash, and the brief irruption by Nazi-bugash, and Assur-uballit's final campaign before his own decease. In which case, the 27-year reign of

Burnaburiash II would at latest have run during 1356–1329 (or, 1346–1319), and the reign and aftermath of Karahardash, 1329–28 (or, 1319/18), plus 25 years of Kurigalzu II during 1329–1304 (or, 1319–1294).

Or, we can have, in contrast a *maximum date* (option A): namely, that soon after the new (young?) king Burnaburiash II's accession in Babylon, his neighbour Assur-uballit (also a new ruler, already 'veteran' of a full year's reign?) saw his chance of extending his power and influence by befriending his new neighbour, and giving him a daughter in marriage who (within a year or so) bore him one grandson – putative heir to the Babylonian throne! – and later a second. So, from about Assur-uballit's Year 1 (at earliest?), 1363, the accession and ensuing 27 years of Burnaburiash II would have run during *c.* 1363–1336 (or, 1353–1326), the year of two kings (Karahardash and Nuzibugash) in 1336/35 (or, 1326/25), and the reign of Kurigalzu II the ensuing 25 years, 1336–1311 (or, 1326–1301).

Or, to complete our series (option B), we might more realistically assign the dealings with Burnaburiash II to a 'middle zone' within Assur-uballit's 36-year reign; one may begin the 27 years of Burnaburiash II at around, for example, the 6th year of Assur-uballit, and run the Babylonian's 27 years through to the latter's Year 33, equating the years 1–27 of the latter with Years 6–33 of the Assyrian king, – with 5 years' space at the start, and 4 at the end, of the latter's reign, and giving a much smaller margin-of-error than the 9 years (too much?) on the maximal and minimal options. The Years 6 and 33 of Assur-uballit I = Years 1 and 27 of Burnaburiash II fall maximally in 1358 (or, 1348) and 1331 (or, 1321); the year of Karahardash and turmoil would then be 1358/57 (or, 1348/47), with Kurigalzu II ruling thenceforth 25 years, 1358–1333 (or, 1348–1323) BC.

Thus, on any of options A, B, C, one may then proceed to calculate the fall of the Kassite Dynasty's remaining 204 years from the accession of Kurigalzu II to its end with the death of Enlil-nadi-ahi. Of our options A, B, C, on both high and low Assyrian dates, we tabulate the "final" choice of options as follows:

Table 1.3: Based on reign of Assur-uballit I, c. 1364–28 (High) or c. 1354–18 (Low); three options for Burnaburiash II of Babylon.

OPTION A (max.)	OPTION B (mid.)	OPTION C (min.)
1363–1336 (high)	1358–1331 (high)	1356–1329 (high)
1353–1326 (low)	1348–1321 (low)	1346–1319 (low)

Thus, one may in turn give three high/low dates for the end of the Kassite Dynasty, as follows:

Table 1.4: High/low dates for the end of the Kassite Dynasty.

OPTION A (Max.):	OPTION B (Mid.):	OPTION C (Low):
1363/1353 – 204 =	1358/1348 – 204 =	1356/1346 – 204 =
1157/1147 BC.	1154/1144 BC.	1152/1142 BC

Or, a maximum range of *c.* 1157–1152, or 1147–1142 BC overall, for the end of Kassite rule.

An important point to be made here is that this result is a calculation made *wholly independently* of any calculation based on any figures for the post-Kasssite dynasties from the beginning of the 2nd Dynasty of Isin until the accession of Nabopolassar in 626 BC. The two overall options, just 10 years apart (thanks to the 13-/3-year options on the Assyrian Ninurta-apil-Ekur) show a narrow band of only 5 years' margin in each case (1157/52; 1147/42). The higher option is almost identical in result with the calculations based on the data for the 1st-millennium dynasties; the lower overall option here may indeed be too low, unless an overlap of up to a decade with the last Kassite kings and the new Isin dynasty were allowed for. This may be deemed unlikely. Our old estimate *c.* 1157/52 may be about right after all! Regardless of whether there was (*a*) an interval (with or without Elamite intervention) between the fall of the Kassites and assumption of rule in Babylon by the 2nd Isin dynasty; or (*b*) the latter followed directly upon the fall of the former around 1157/52 BC; or (*c*) the founder of the new Isin line was already claiming rule within Babylonia before the last Kassite reign had finally come to an end.

The last test for the Near-Eastern side of our quest is to verify the dates here for Assyria and Babylon against the reported synchronisms in our cuneiform documents. The latter (the Synchronistic King List and Synchronistic Chronicle) are not free of error, but hitherto, their data have been correlatable with the received chronologies; ours, too, must necessarily pass this test, before – at last – we finally come back to Egypt, to attempt at last to integrate Egypt and the East into one viable overall scheme, so far as the written sources are concerned.

Mesopotamian integration, c. 1400–1100 BC.
Here, we tabulate as concisely as possible the two sets of kings, dates and links.

Table 1.5: Comparing the two sets of kings.

Assyrian Datings	Assyria: Kings	Babylonia: Kings	Babylonian Datings
1391–1364 (1381–1354)	Eriba-Adad I (27 y.)		
1364–1328 (1354–1318)	Assur-uballit I (36)	Burnaburiash II (27)	A: 1363–1336 or -10 C: 1356–1329 or -10
		Karahardash (± 1)	A: 1336/35 or -10 C: 1329/28 or -10
		Nazi-bugash (0)	A: 1335/C: 1328/-10
1328–1318 (1318–1308)	Enlil-nirari (10)	Kurigalzu II (25)	A: 1336–1311 or -10 C: 1329–1304 or -10
1318–1306 (1308–1296)	Arik-den-ili 12)	Nazi-maruttash (26)	A: 1311–1285 or -10 C: 1304–1278 or -10
1306–1274 (1296–1264)	Adad-nirari I (32)	Kadashman-Turgu (18)	A: 1285–1267 or -10 C: 1278–1260 or -10

		Kadashman-Enlil II (9)	A: 1267–1258 or -10 C: 1260–1251 or -10
1274–1244 (1264–1234)	Shalmaneser I (30)	Kudur-Enlil (9)	A: 1258–1249 or -10 C: 1251–1242 or -10
		Shagarakti-Shuriash (13)	A: 1249–1236 or -10 C: 1242–1229 or -10
1244–1207 (1234–1197)	Tukulti-Ninurta I (37)	Kashtiliash IV (8)	A: 1236–1228 or -10 C: 1229–1221 or -10
		Enlil-nadin-shum (1)	A: 1228–1229 or -10 C: 1221–1220 or -10
		Kadashman-Kharbe II (1)	A: 1229–1228 or -10 C: 1220–1219 or -10
		Adad-shum-iddina (6)	A: 1228–1222 or -10 C: 1219–1213 or -10
1207–1203 (1197–1193)	Assur-nadin-apli (4)	Adad-shum-usur (30)	A: 1222–1192 or -10 C: 1213–1183 or -10
1203–1197 (1193–1187)	Assur-nirari III (6)		
1197–1192 (1187–1182)	Enlil-kudur-usur (5)		
1192–1179 (1182–1179)	Ninurta-apil-Ekur (13 or 3)		
1179–1133 x–1133	Assur-dan I (46) + Ninurta-tukulti-Assur	Melishipak (15)	A: 1192–1177 or -10
			C: 1183–1168 or -10
1133	Mutakkil-Nusku (2 × *tuppi-shu*)	Merodachbaladan I (13)	A: 1177–1164 or -10 C: 1168–1155 or -10
		Zababa-shum-iddina (1)	A: 1164–1163 or -10 C: 1155–1154 or -10
		Enlil-nadin-ahi (1)	A: 1163–1162 or -10 C: 1154–1153 or -10

As will be clear from the foregoing table, people, links and regnal years all seem to form a consistent whole, with good correlations virtually throughout. The options for the end of the Kassite kings (1162 or -10, and 1153 or -10) cover all possibilities – the highest would leave a brief time-space for any Elamite intervention; the middle dates are close to a direct succession from the last Kassite to a grasping new chief; the lowest would allow of a theoretical overlap of the last Kassite kinglets in Babylon losing the country at large to the new Isin leaders. It would difficult in the present review to offer any final solution (and probably premature, in the state of the documentation). Going back all the way to Burnaburiash II and Assur-uballit I, and the triple-option link-up proposed for them, one is justified in remarking that – so far – it stands up to such tests as the scrutiny of their successors currently allows.

It is now time, at last, to return to Egypt, and to compare notes between our Egyptian minimal dates, wholly theoretical as they are for anything before *c.* 1070 BC (cf. §3, above).

6. The late 2nd millennium contd.

Possibilities for Near-East-integrated Egyptian dating, c. 1400–1100 BC

Here, we finally bring two worlds into harmony or collision (!) so far as the purely historical sources are concerned. The vital links between Egypt and Mesopotamia during this epoch were those attested in the famous Amarna correspondence, late in the reign of Amenhotep III, throughout those of Amenhotep IV [Akhenaten] and the ephemeral Smenkhkare, and finally in the first year or two of Tutankhamun.

After Kadashman-Enlil I's letters (E[l] A[marna] 1–5) to Amenhotep III, we have his successor Burnaburiash II writing successively to Amenhotep III (EA 6), then much more to Amenhotep IV/Akhenaten (EA 7–8, 10–11, 14), and once to Tutankhamun (EA 9). Assuming only a last year or two with the aged Amenhotep III, then we have a 16-year reign of Akhenaten, probably 2 years of Smenkhkare [not represented], then only an initial year or two of Tutankhamun before he and the court moved back to Memphis, Egypt's normal administrative capital. In other words, a correspondence that lasted about 20 of Burnaburiash's 27 years as king. The turmoil after his death, of the accession and murder of his successor Karahardash, usurpation by Nazibugash, and intervention by Assur-uballit I of Assyria to restore the royal line in Kurigalzu II, – all this could not be later than the last (36th) year of Assur-uballit, as indicated above), but may have been anything from 2 to 7 years earlier (cf. Tables 1.3–4, A, B, C options above).

As already established above, one may set the 36-year reign of Assur-uballit I at 1364–1328 or a decade later; within that reign, the Assyrian's intervention in Babylonia *could* have occurred in his very last year, such that he got safely home, celebrated with a quick flagon of wine – and dropped dead immediately! This is a purely minimum dating for technical reasons [lowest-conceivable date]; it is rather more likely that (much less dramatically) he in fact survived the exertions of that campaign at least a while, making our option B (Tables 3–4) a more realistic one.

If this be best, then (option B) on the normal high option for Assur-uballit I, based on 13 years for Ninurta-apil-Ekur, we can set Burnaburiash II's reign at *c.* 1358–1331 (a decade less, on the 3-year figure for N.) This would mean that Tutankhamun in Egypt had to be on the throne there for at least a year or more before the death of Burnaburiash II. In other words, minimally, he became king in about 1332 at *latest* (*1322 on the Assyrian 3-years-for-N. option). Then, one may in turn set minimum dates for his predecessors and successors, subject to correction. Thus, we may further tabulate (retrograde groups) in theory as follows:

Table 1.6: Near East integrated Egyptian dating.

BC	Kings	BC	Kings
1353–1337:	Amenhotep IV/Akhenaten (16)	1479–1425:	Thutmose III (54)
1337–1335:	Smenkhkare (2)	1426–1401:	Amenhotep II (26, 1 coregent)
1335–1326	Tutankhamun (9)	1401–1391:	Thutmose IV (10)
1326–1323/2:	Ay (3 or 4)	1391–1353:	Amenhotep III (38)

Here, we count downwards, from Thutmose III, set at 1479 by lunar data, combined with total regnal years for the 18th Dynasty. The result, if we count down to Tutankhamun, is to raise his date by 3 years above the utter minimum (on Assyrian dating) at 1332 for his accession. This is no problem: Burnaburiash II could as easily have written to him in 1335 or 1334, as in 1332/1. What should be noted is the closeness of the margin (only 3 years).

We may now count down still further. Horemheb at 28 years would follow Ay (3 years) c. 1323–1295. For the 19th Dynasty, Ramesses I at 1 year would come at 1295–1294, and his son Sethos I at 1294, 11 (or 15) years at 1294–1283 or 1294–1279, the latter bringing us precisely to the lunar-functional date of 1279–1213 for Ramesses II, as is widely admitted.[29] The result is then a sensible and rational chronology for the entire New Kingdom, allowing (at its beginning) the normal 25 years for Ahmose I, and likewise 21 years for Amenhotep I, then 12 years (7 or 8 attested) for Thutmose I; only Thutmose II remains in contention, as to whether he be allowed a full 13 years, or be cut back to 3, merely because of the current lack of dated items from his reign. Hence, a span of 1550–1479 BC, or of 1540–1479 BC, depending on use of 13 or 3 years for Thutmose II. Queen Hatshepsut's 21 years are wholly coeval with the initial 21 years of Thutmose III's reign (1479–1458), and hence do not affect the main chronology at all.

7. The Hittite contribution

The Hittite Empire (based in Anatolia) was the third major player in the power-contests of the late 2nd millennium. Its kings' annals and international treaties contain a considerable (if at times fragmentary) contribution of chronological/historical data, which serve as an additional check upon the Egyptian and Mesopotamian sequences and interrelationships. Thus, the first major, truly imperial king, Suppiluliuma I, is known from the Amarna letter EA 41, addressed to an Egyptian king, 'Khuriya'. None such exists, giving rise to speculation over who was intended. In the Akkadian texts of these letters, the missives were always addressed 'to' such-and-such, by their official prenomen where pharaohs were concerned. The simplest solution so far (and the best) is to identify here a haplography – *ana khururiya* is an easy slip for *ana Anakhururiya*, 'to (king) Anakhururiya' – a good cuneiform Akkadian format for Ankhkheprure, the prenomen of the pharaoh Smenkhkare, immediate predecessor of the more famous Tutankhamun. Scribes did not like *ana* twice, where once was expected, failing to note that the second *ana* was the beginning of the proper name – hence the written *ana <Ana>khururiya*. As Smenkhkare is (in Table 1.6) datable to about 1337–1335 BC, this letter from Suppiluliuma I is closely datable within those two years. We have no other letters to earlier pharaohs from him – possibly owing to the mere chances of (non?)-preservation, or simply because he had come relatively late into this circle of international diplomacy.

Suppiluliuma I next appears just over a decade later when, as he was besieging Carchemish (a key city in North Syria), he received not only the news of the death of Tutankhamun of Egypt but also his widow's plea to supply a suitable groom for her, to be the next pharaoh of Egypt – so around 1326 in our Table 1.6. The son sent was murdered, leading to war between the two states. Having then captured Carchemish, Suppiluliuma then spent the next 6 years subduing Syria and in effect neutralising the nearby (hostile) realm of Mitanni into becoming essentially a vassal, before dying of a plague, thus in *c.* 1320 BC. His reign may have begun not too long before he wrote to Smenkhkare (*c.* 1337/1335), perhaps 1345, giving him a 25-year reign. His immediate successor was the eldest son, Arnuwandas II, who died barely a year later (also of the plague), thus reigning only *c.* 1320–1319 BC.

He in turn was followed by a younger brother, Mursil II, whose career (from his annals) lasted most of 28 years, thus during *c.* 1319–1291 BC. Early on, his North-Syrian vassals rebelled, in Year 7, including the wealthy seaport of Ugarit. Finds made there include a presentation-vessel from the pharaoh Horemheb (who reigned also 28 years, *c.* 1322–1294, as Tutankhamun's second successor). The Year 7 of Mursil II would coincide with 1313–1312 BC, and so with Year 10 of Horemheb. From *c.* 1291, Mursil II's son Muwatallis II, reigned through in time to almost defeat Ramesses II (1279ff. on our dates so far) at the Battle of Qadesh, in the latter's Year 5, 1275 BC. Then, 16 years later, the pharaoh finally (in his Year 21) signed a peace-treaty with the next-but-one Hittite king, Hattusil III (younger brother of Muwatallis II). In between, about 4 years after Qadesh, the latter was followed by a lesser son, Urhi-Tesub [officially, Mursil III] for reputedly 7 years (*c.* 1271–1264), until his uncle Hattusil threw him out of office. Hattusil III reigned long enough to marry-off his eldest daughter to Ramesses II in the latter's Year 34 (in 1245 BC), and a second daughter about a decade later, by about 1235 BC (Year 44/45). So, probably, Hattusil III lived to reign about 30/35 years (*c.* 1264–1234/30 BC).

After Ramesses II (died, 1213), his successors Merenptah to Tausret inclusive reigned some 26/27 years, giving place to a new (20th) Dynasty in *c.* 1186 BC. After which, by Years 7–8 of Ramesses III (*c.* 1180), the 'Sea Peoples' had swept around the East Mediterranean, changing the face of its polities and politics, while by about that time, other (land-based) forces finally ended the central-Anatolian Hittite power forever. Thus, the last three Hittite emperors – Tudkhalia IV, Arnuwandas III and Suppiluliuma II – fall into the time-space around 1234–1180 BC, some 54 years. Of these, Arnuwandas III was ephemeral (about 4 or 5 years), leaving about 30 years for the major reign of Tudkhalia IV, and 20 years for Suppiluliuma II before his kingdom crashed or was swept away.

The point of this Hittite survey is that we have here a further series of major rulers, nine in all, covering (during *c.* 1340–1180) at least 160 years of continuous rule alongside both Egypt in the deep south-west and Mesopotamia's twin kingdoms to the east and south-east, in a major, mainly stable monarchy of 9 monarchs in this period, belonging to 6 continuous generations through about 160 years, averaging some 26/27 years per generation – widely recognised as not untypical in many regions and cases. Thus, even with less time-span or amounts of statistical data to go on than in Egypt or Mesopotamia, the Hittite Empire is still a valid confirmatory witness to the consistency of the scale of the chronological/historical picture of the course of ancient Near-Eastern civilisation to be gained from careful analysis of our historical sources from that world.

8. A sobering postscript on the abuse of chronology

Finally, here, a brief note on the repeated attempts to reduce dates (too often, with scant regard for the evidence). As will be evident from the foregoing, it is superfluous. If we go the whole distance (as some would), pushing Ramesses II to 1268ff., or 1265ff. (lunar reduction by 11/14 years), this will then shrivel all later Ramesside dates to very tight minimum figures, liable to be contradicted instantly by any future finds of higher date-lines than now accessible. In fact, on 109 years absolute minimum for the 20th Dynasty (*1078–1069 BC), the 66 years of Ramesses II if set at *1265–1199 BC would leave only 21 years between him and Setnakht (*1078ff), to contain the 26 years for Merenptah (9), Amenmessu (3), Sety II (6), and Saptah-plus-Tausret (8); even the suggestion of slipping the 3 years of Amenmessu into 2 central years of Sety II is impossible, as 23 years cannot be fitted within the 21 year gap between Ramesses II and Setnakht.

The idea of cutting Horemhe's 28 years in half down to 14 is not new (Helck tried it, once), and would merely cause other inconsistencies. Dropping other reigns by 14 years to match would set Tutankhamun's accession down from 1335/1332 to 1321/1318 – which is after the death-date of Burnaburiash II, or has him writing from his death-bed, if we go for the most extreme, and very unlikely, 'low' dates for his reign. Alternatively, one would have to raise the Ramesside dates artificially (Ramesses II, back to 1290 on old lunar options now long discarded; or *20 years for Merenptah; or some other such shift with no supporting evidence)

And the idea of making all three kings Ramesses IX, X, XI into contemporaries? (So, Thys). By this means, the 18 + 3 (min) + 29 years for Ramesses. IX–X–XI in normal succession, totalling 50 years minimum could be slashed to Ramesses. XI's basic 29 years, cutting overall dates before him by 21 years. Alas, this makes no sense as the 20th Dynasty would begin (minimally) in *1057 BC, leaving a huge gap of 42 years, even using a *1265–1199 date for Ramesses. II, which cannot be filled with merely the 26 years of Merenptah to Tewosret inclusive (even *20 years for Merenptah would not be enough to account for this).

In short, the 'squash-dates-down at any cost' mania (in any form) is a sheer waste of everybody's time. We simply need dates to be as accurate as possible – not pushed lower and lower merely out of a misplaced search for novelty. Nobody is helped that way. Instead, the content and approach of this paper is offered as a possible step forward, for comparison with whatever practical help our radiocarbon scientists may now be able to provide, with the enhanced techniques now developing.

Abbreviations used in the notes

ANET	J. B. Pritchard (ed.), *Ancient Near Eastern Texts relating to the Old Testament,* Princeton: UP, 1950 and later eds.
CdE	*Chronique d'Égypte.*
CRIPEL	*Cahiers de Recherches de l'Institut de Papyrologie et d'Égyptologie de Lille.*
HdO	*Handbuch der Orientalistik,* series, Leiden: E.J. Brill.
IEJ	*Israel Exploration Journal.*
JNES	*Journal of Near Eastern Studies.*
OIC	Oriental Institute of the University of Chicago, Chicago.
RLA	(Various editors), *Reallexikon der Assyriologie und Vorderasiatischen Archäologie,* 1ff., Berlin: W. de Gruyter, 1928/32 to the present.
SBL	Society of Biblical Literature, Atlanta.
UP	University Press (of each centre named).

Notes

1. For Manetho, see conveniently W. G. Waddell, *Manetho* (Loeb Classical Library), Cambridge Mass.: Harvard UP/London: Heinemann, 1940, reissued 1948. The Ptolemaic Canon is compactly excerpted in J. von Beckerath, *Chronologie des pharaonischen Ägypten* (Münchener Äg. Forschungen, 46), Mainz: Ph von Zabern, 1997, 230–231. For the Mesopotamian documentary datelines, see R. A. Parker, W. H. Dubberstein, *Babylonian Chronology 626 B.C.–A.D. 75*, Providence: Brown UP, 1956, 10–24. The Egyptian 28th–30th Dynasties functioned chronologically as merely 'breakaway' regimes within the period of the Persian empire.
2. The Tang-i-Var text of the Year 706 under Sargon II of Assyria was inscribed well AFTER Sargon's message to 'Shapataka' (= Shebitku), which occurred at the time of his clearly earlier capture of Ascalon, *c.* 711 BC; cf. already, Kitchen in M. Bietak (ed.), *The Synchronisation of Civilisations in the Eastern Mediterranean in the Second Millennium BC,* [I], Vienna: Austrian Academy, 2000, 50–51, and more fully in *Ägypten und Levante* 16 (2006), 293–294, §§2–5; and in *Libyan Period*, (n. 6 below), 162–164, §§3–8. It should be stressed that in 706 Shebitku was simply Shabako's deputy in Nubia, NOT a royal co-regent; and likewise Taharqa in 701 for Shebitku in Egypt.
3. See A. R. Millard, *The Eponyms of the Assyrian Empire 910–612 BC* (State Archives of Assyria, Studies, II), Helsinki: Neo-Assyrian Text Corpus Project, 1994, 2.
4. Basic publication, A. K. Grayson,, *Assyrian and Babylonian Chronicles* (Texts from Cuneiform Sources, V), New York: Augustin, 1975.
5. Including the brief coregency (and no known sole reign) of Shoshenq II Heqakheperre, perhaps into a 3rd year; data, see Kitchen, *Third Intermediate Period in Egypt*, Warminster: Aris & Phillips [now Oxbow imprint, Oxford], 1996, 308 n. 368, and 545.
6. Cf. dates and discussion, Kitchen, in G. P. F. Broekman, R. J. Demarée, O. E. Kaper (eds), *The Libyan Period in Egypt*, Leiden/Louvain: NINO/Peeters, 2009, 161–201 *passim*, and list, 202.
7. See 1 Kings 14:25–26 (plus 2 Chronicles 12:2–10). It should be noted here, that the chronology for the Hebrew rump-kingdoms in 1–2 Kings is extremely well-preserved, operates on well-established Near-Eastern principles, and synchronises consistently well with external sources; it is thus appropriate to draw upon it with considerable confidence; Mesopotamian chronicles and the Ptolemaic Canon are well-transmitted, the Hebrew likewise. The basic work here remains that of E. R. Thiele, *Mysterious Numbers of the Hebrew Kings*, Chicago: UP, 1951, and especially the 2nd (and improved) ed., Winona Lake: Eerdmans 1965/Exeter (UK): Paternoster, 1966; nothing subsequent is any better, so far.
8. Cf. biblical 2 Samuel 11:1 on this, plus external source-examples; under Thutmose III of Egypt (mid.–15th century BC), one finds such allusions in his April/May Levant campaigns (cf. refs., in J. B. Pritchard (ed.), *Ancient Near Eastern Texts rel. to OT*, Princeton: UP, 1950 (and later), 238a top (Year 23); 239a top (Year 29), 240a below (Year 33, 8th campaign), timings, cf. 238 n.1.
9. Latest translation, see R. K. Ritner, *The Libyan Anarchy* (Writings from the Ancient World, 21), Atlanta: SBL, 2009, 187–193, esp. 190–191.
10. A supposed lunar date (Dakhleh stela) for 943 BC is illusory; there is no mention of either the term *pesdjentyu* or of any other distinguishing term to indicate a lunar dating. Kings of Byblos are inscriptionally known as contemporaries of Shoshenq I and of Osorkon I and II; but they are not independently datable (except in very wide epigraphic terms), beyond their links with their Egyptian contemporaries.
11. On Musri as Egypt here and in other cases, see H. Tadmor, *IEJ* 11(1961), 145–147.
12. See references, Kitchen, *Third Intermediate Period in Egypt*, 1996 ed., 376.
13. See refs., Kitchen, *op. cit.*, 374, n. 751; and (on So), J. Yoyotte, *CRIPEL* 11 (1989), 123 and n. 64, including other abbreviations of 'Osorkon'.

14 See full dates-table, Kitchen, in *Libyan Period* (n. 6 above), 202. The 23rd, 24th Dynasties and sundry local dynasts are of no independent chronological significance because they operated entirely within the overall period of the 22nd Dynasty.
15 For what follows, see in far more detail Kitchen, in M. Bietak ed., *Synchronisation,* [I] as in n. 2 above, 42–44.
16 And not just 13/14 years, on misconstrued data from a few pots – mere reused items.
17 See Kitchen, in *CdE* 81/Fascs. 161–162 (2006), 148 on ODM 889 (not '886', as there printed).
18 Compare the variety of Egyptian chronologies (for pre–664) offered by: J. von Beckerath, *Chronologie,* 1997 (cf. n. 1, above), by various authors in E. Hornung, R. Krauss and D. A. Warburton (eds), *Ancient Egyptian Chronology* (HdO I, Vol. 83), Leiden: Brill, 2006, and also (Broekman, Kitchen, Krauss, *et al.*), in Bietak's Vienna series (cf. n. 2 above), *Synchronisation...* I–III, 2000–2007, to name no others.
19 Sp. = C. Saporetti, *Gli eponimi medio-assiri* (Bibliotheca Mesopotamica, 9), Malibu: Undena Publications, 1979, with page-references.
20 And variant, 3 years; scholars opt for the '4 years' reading.
21 Whose son Ninurta-apil-Ekur (No. 82) supplanted Assur-nirari III's successor, Enlil-kudur-usur (No. 81); as son of Ili-ipaddu, the new man was, in fact, a distant cousin of the senior line, going back in ancestry to Assur-uballit I, just as they did. On Ili-ipaddu, etc., see briefly A. K. Grayson, *Assyrian Royal Inscriptions*, I, Wiesbaden: Harrassowitz, 1972, 137, §889, with fuller references to Borger and Weidner. Reading Ili-ipaddu instead of Ili-Hadda, cf. Grayson, in *RLA* 9, 7–8, 2001, 524 and refs.
22 Full transliteration of all three King List copies in parallel, see A. K. Grayson, in *RLA*, VI, 1–2, Berlin: de Gruyter, 1980, 101–115, §3.9 (King List 9); special paragraphs are also translated; Full English version of parallel SDAS/Khorsabad copies, see I. J. Gelb, *JNES* 13(1954), 209–230.
23 For post-Kassite dynasties, *c.* 1157 down to Nabunasir, 747 BC, dates in the standard histories will suffice (e.g. in A. L. Oppenheim, *Ancient Mesopotamia*, Chicago: UP, 1964, 339–340.
24 Transliteration, Grayson, n. 22 above, 126–121; in English, cf. in Pritchard, *ANET,* 272–4 (but misleadingly termed a chronicle).
25 Termed 'Chronicle 21' in full edition by Grayson, *Assyrian and Babylonian Chronicles* (Texts from Cuneiform Sources, V), New York: Augustin, 1975, 157–170.
26 Full edition, Grayson, *op. cit.*, previous note, 170–177, as 'Chronicle 22'.
27 Cf. (e.g.) J. A. Brinkman, *Materials and Studies for Kassite History*, I, Chicago: OIC, 1976, 21/31.
28 The two narrative sources, the Synchronistic History and Chronicle P, exhibit variations in detail. Thus, Karahardash is termed Kadashman-Kharbe (I) in Chronicle P; the latter confuses Nazibugash with the later Shuzibugash, and intercalates a (spurious?) Karaindash, making Assur-uballit the grandfather of Karahardash/Kadashman-Kharbe. In contrast, the Synchronistic History confuses its Karahardash with a Karaindash *post-mortem*, but avoids turning the latter into a (spurious?) middle generation. In both documents, there seems to be confusion of a spurious (second) Karaindash with the contemporary of Puzur-Assur III (a pair wrongly down-dated by the Synchronistic History). In short, the Synchronistic History gives the more believable account, but commits one error (of mentioning Karaindash in a wrong sequence [as it did, earlier] instead of Karahardash). While Chronicle P inserts a probably spurious 'extra'-generational Karaindash, changes the name of Karahardash to Kadashman-Kharbe, and confuses Nazibugash with the later Shuzibugash. Our account seeks to extract the most likely original situation, by eliminating the seeming confusions and probable generational error.

29 It is fashionable to use the minimal datum of 11 years for Sety I, but which is not finally proven. The 4 years over from *15 would go one more for Ay (4, not 3), and admission of a Nefer-nefuru-aten reign (over and above Smenkhkare), also after Akhenaten, would easily account for the remaining three years. The various twin 'Acherres' (and variants) wrongly located after Tutankhamun (Ratothis) in Manetho at {1}2 years and 1/3/5 months (for 2 years and x months) may be a reflex of Smenkhkare and a second ephemeral ruler (female or otherwise?)

Chapter 2

An Introduction to Egyptian Historical Chronology

A. J. Shortland

Introduction

This paper aims to provide an elementary background of how the Egyptian historical chronology has been constructed over the many centuries that it has been studied. It is aimed at those who have little or no knowledge of the chronology itself, perhaps having come to this book from the sciences or archaeology. It is not intended for the specialist in Egyptian chronology, who will notice that there are simplifications used and complexity glossed over. It tries, however, to point out the strengths and weaknesses of the reconstructions, some of the competing arguments used, and show where further reading might be obtained.

The primary source used in the Egyptian historical chronology are king-lists. The most important of these is the list drawn up by Manetho and copied by later authors, but this can be complimented with other lists on temples and stelae. After the lists of kings, other evidence has also been used including archaeological evidence for the order of tombs and buildings. This has been supplemented by synchronisms with other chronologies in the Near East and the Aegean, where Egyptian objects or king's names occur in datable contexts abroad and *vice versa*. However, all these lists 'float' in absolute time. They all involve adding up the reigns of kings and counting back from a relatively modern, known point in time to the more distant past. The problem is, of course, that the further away from the fixed point one goes, the higher the error in the date is likely to be. A very few 'pins' are available, all of them connected with astronomical observations, that might help fix particular points in the past to absolute time, and these are hugely significant, but also debated.

Each of these sources of evidence is now considered in more detail.

In the beginning...

Any discussion of Egyptian historical chronology has to start with the most important single source of all, Manetho (Manetho 1940). Manetho was a priest working in the Delta of Egypt in the early third century BC. He produced a work written in Greek called *Aegyptiaca*, probably drawing sources in temple libraries which as a priest he had access to. He dedicated his work to Ptolemy II (285–246 BC). Unfortunately, the autograph copy of his work has

---

Author's Address: **A. J. Shortland**, Centre for Archaeological and Forensic Analysis, DEAS/CDS, Cranfield University, Shrivenham, SN6 8LA, UK

not survived. Instead we have copies or partial copies of it in the works of other authors (Manetho 1940). Josephus, a Jew writing in the late first century AD, preserves some extracts of the Manethonian text plus other parts of his works that are clearly drawn directly or indirectly from Manetho. An *Epitome* of Manetho's work was produced early on, although probably not by him, and this lists kings and reign lengths and key events. This work is partially preserved in the writings of three later chronographers. The first is Sextus Julius Africanus, in around 220 AD, who seems to accurately transmit the detail. The second is Eusebius of Caesarea in around 326 AD, who inserted some changes into the original text. The final source is George the Monk, known as Syncellus, in around 800 AD, who was trying to use Manetho to establish the date the birth of Christ (Manetho 1940).

As can be seen, the text of *Aegyptiaca* is only available from later authors, all of whom where using Manetho's work to forward their own political and/or religious views. They are also more or less accurate in what they record. However, there is no doubt that the work of Manetho, transmitted through these authors, forms the backbone of the reconstruction of the Egyptian chronology even until this day. Manetho drew up thirty dynasties of Egyptian kings, ranging from Menes, the first king of the 1st Dynasty, through to the last of the 30th Dynasty. In the nineteenth century AD, these dynasties were grouped into Kingdoms and intermediate periods and it was shown that some of the dynasties ran concurrently rather then sequentially, as shown on Table 2.1 (Shaw and Nicholson 1995).

Within each dynasty a variable amount of information is given by Manetho. Some dynasties consist only of a number of kings and the years, for example the 10th Dynasty

> *"the Tenth Dynasty consisted of 19 kings of Heracleopolis, who reigned for 185 years"* (Manetho and Waddell 1940, 63)

However, for other dynasties there is much more information. One of the better examples is the 18th Dynasty, shown in Table 2.2. Here individual kings (and occasionally queens) are named, with their relationships to each other, the reign lengths and occasionally some significant events that occurred during the reign. However, comparison of the different accounts of the 18th Dynasty reigns by the different authors who were drawing on Manetho show some obvious problems, especially when compared to the modern very well accepted list of names for the 18th Dynasty (the last column). Some of the names are wrong (Tuthmosis is listed for the first king, when it should be Ahmose), the order of the kings is in places wrong (Amenophis II should be before Tuthmosis IV), there are kings missing (Tuthmosis I and all the Amarna period kings) and some of the reign lengths are different from the different authors. The picture that can be drawn up from the Manetho material is that it is patchy and there are errors; however, it does give a very good starting point from which to work.

King-lists

Working from the Manetho starting point, several other sources can be used to refine and improve the sequence of kings (Redford 1986). The most important of these are king-lists that can be found on the walls of temples and chapels, or probably associated with them, of which five are perhaps key (Kitchen 1991):

2. An Introduction to Egyptian Historical Chronology

Table 2.1: Manetho's Dynasties grouped into Periods and Kingdoms

Dynasty	Period
1	Early Dynastic
2	
3	OLD KINGDOM
4	
5	
6	
7 and 8	First intermediate
9, 10 and 11	
11	MIDDLE KINGDOM
12	
13 and 14	Second Intermediate
15, 16 and 17	
18	NEW KINGDOM
19	
20	
21	Third Intermediate
22, 23 and 24	
25	Late Period
26	
27	
28	
29	

1. Palermo Stone, 5th Dynasty (*c.* 2400 BC)
2. Hall of the Records, Temple of Amun, Karnak (Tuthmosis III, *c.* 1450)
3. Temple of Abydos (Seti I, *c.* 1250 BC)
4. Turin Royal Canon (*c.* 1250 BC)
5. Tomb chapel of Tjunuroy, (official of Ramesses II) at Saqqara

These are probably the same kind of sources that Manetho himself was using. They are closer in date to the actual events than the Manetho text, so there is reason to hope that they might be more accurate. Some of them provide just a list of kings' names in order; others provide more detail of the reign lengths and occasional details of the reign. They very largely support the Manetho account, but add more details of certain dynasties where Manetho was brief, and other kings that were missed by the Manetho text.

As a negative point, king-lists tend to simplify what can be a more complicated picture. There are several factors that can cause problems, perhaps the most important being the idea of co-regencies, where more than one king rules at the same time. The most common way this might work is for a son to reign alongside his father, the aim being to ensure on the death of the father a smooth transition to the son. An example from a hypothetical king list might say that the father reigned for 20 years and the son for ten. The modern scholar would add this up to be 30 years in total for reckoning up the length of the dynasty. But if the son was co-regent for five years of his reign, then while the two kings did indeed reign for 20 and ten years, the total length of time represented is only 25 years. Identifying the existence and length of co-regencies can be difficult and is often debated, and causes some of the variation in the reconstruction of the chronology.

Table 2.2: Manetho's 18th Dynasty

JOSEPHUS	THEOPHILUS	AFRICANUS	EUSEBIUS	CURRENT
Tethmosis 25/4	Tethmosis 25/4	Amos ?	Amosis 25	Ahmose 25
Chebron 13	Chebron 13	Chebros 13	Chebron 13	
Amenophis 20/7	Amenophis 20/7	Amenophthis 24	Ammenophis 21	Amenophis I 21
Amessis 21/9	Amessis 21/1	Amensis 22		Hatshepsut 22
Mephres 12/9	Mephres 12/9	Misaphris 13	Miphres 12	Tuthmosis II 12
Mephramuthosis 25/10	Mephrammuthosis 20/10	Misphragmuthosis 26	Misphragmuthosis 26	Tuthmosis III 54
Thmosis 9/8	Tuthmosis 9/8	Tuthmosis 9	Tuthmosis 9	Amenophis II 27
Amenophis 30/10	Amenophis 30/10	Amenophis 31	Amenophis 31	Tuthmosis IV 10
Orus 36/5	Orus 36/5	Orus 37	Orus 36	Amenophis III 38
Acencheres 12/1	? 12/1	Acherres 12	Achencherses 12	
Rathotis 9	[ ]	Rathos 6	Athoris 39	
Acencheres 12/5	[ ]	Chebres 12	Cencherres 16	
Acencheres II 12/3	Jencheres [ ]12/3	Acherres 12	Acherres 8	
			Cherres 15	
Harmais 4/1	Harmais 4/1		Armais 5	Horemheb 28
Ramesses 1/4	Ramesses 1/4	Ramesses 1		Ramesses I 1
		Amenophath 19		Seti I 15
Harmesses 66/2	Ramesses 66/2		Ramesses 68	Ramesses II 66

Other Genealogical lists

In addition to king-lists, there are other genealogical texts that can be used to supplement those above. These include the lists of priests and viziers under certain kings, the dates of the burial of the Apis bulls and other lists of family histories that can be linked in to royal reigns. They tend to be reasonably short in time range, but can be very detailed. Their study in itself tends to be complex, but they can give rewarding detail and confirmation. See several papers in (Bietak 2007) for more detail.

Archaeology and objects

The lists provide by far the most important source of information for the royal reigns. However, there is always the chance, and this is obviously the case in some lists, that a mistake might be made or the truth deliberately 'manipulated' by the scribe for political ends. It is important therefore to have an independent source of evidence and here archaeology is predominant. The standard archaeological techniques of the interpretation of stratigraphy and superposition can give sequence to remains, which, if they are associated with kings names in the form of inscribed artefacts, can give order to the kings and sometimes some evidence of length of reign.

While not strictly archaeological, other objects can be inscribed with the king's name and a regnal year, for example papyri or stelae. This gives an indication that if the text is correct, the king must have reigned at least this many years. This is only a minor piece of information, but there can be relatively large numbers of these individual pieces, which support other evidence and give very good reassurance that reign lengths might be accurate. A good example of these stelae, often cited are those set up by Akhenaten in the fifth and eighth years of his reign to mark out the boundaries of his new city at what is now known as Amarna (Murnane and Van Siclen 1993; Aldred 1988; Kemp 1989).

Synchronisms

Synchronisms are when it is possible to link two different and independent chronologies together. This might happen when a datable object from one culture is found in a datable context in another. Ceramics from the Aegean being found in Egyptian tombs and temples are examples of this. However, while important indicators, they do not often give the level of precision required to give anything more than an indication the chronology is broadly correct. More important is where there are records of two kings having contact. An example of this occurs in the Amarna letters, where Tushratta, King of the Mitanni, is in correspondence with Akhenaten, clearly showing that they were contemporaries (Moran 1992). This allows links into king-list systems of other states, most notably perhaps Assyria, which have been reconstructed in a similar way to the Egyptian king-lists. These provide support and clarification for the Egyptian records, where such links can be made. Other lists of Assyrian officials can also be used, such as the eponym lists (Hunger 2008). In the Assyrian records that survive the early second millennium BC and for first half of the first millennium BC, each year was given the name of the Magistrate for that year. These names can be linked into other events forming an especially strong chronology, especially for the first half of the first millennium BC (Roux 1992; Oppenheim 1964), which can be linked into the Egyptian chronology.

An important synchronism occurs in 664 BC, when the Assyrian king Ashurbanipal sacks Thebes and founds the 26th Dynasty, putting Psamtek I in control of Egypt. This event is very well dated in Assyrian records, supported by Egyptian texts and can confidently and relatively uncontroversially be assigned to that particular year. This therefore provides the earliest date that can be firmly fixed, and a point for 'dead reckoning' back into deeper history (Kitchen 1986).

Dead reckoning

From this fixed point of 664 BC, the Egyptian historical chronology counts back though history by summing up reign lengths and dynasties. It takes into account the complexities of co-regencies, unknown kings, contemporaneous dynasties and so forth and works back by 'dead reckoning' to the beginning of the 1st Dynasty in around 3100 BC (Shaw and Nicholson 1995). As mentioned above, in general the further back from the fixed point the history goes, the more the error – so the errors in absolute dates for reigns in the New Kingdom are less than the Middle Kingdom which in turn are less than the Old Kingdom. What is needed is something that enables one to pin the history to absolute time at other points in its length, particularly the second and third millennium BC, where the distance from the fixed point of 664 BC begins to grow large and the potential error correspondingly high.

Astronomy

The only way of pinning the historical chronology to absolute time (other than the use of scientific dating techniques, specifically radiocarbon) is by linking it to rare astronomical events (Parker 1974). These can be broadly speaking split in three types depending on the celestial body involved: solar, lunar and astral. The principle for all of these is the same. Certain celestial events are rare, occurring only once every tens or even hundreds of years. If these events are recorded in ancient texts, the text can be dated to a king's reign or even a year of that reign, and the record can be positively fixed to one particular event of known absolute date, then this creates a pin between the historical chronology and the absolute date, that can be used as a new fixed point. However, there are often uncertainties involved in all of the stages linking the recorded event to absolute time.

Solar eclipses

The first of these rare events to be discussed is the solar eclipse. Solar eclipses occur when the moon passes in front of the sun. Between two and five eclipses occur on the Earth each year, but many of these are partial eclipses, where some but not all of the Sun is obscured and these are not always very evident to the observer only a maximum of two full eclipses are possible in any one year, and these are only visible from the relatively small parts of the Earth's surface which pass directly under the Moon's umbra, or the darkest part of its shadow. This means that only every few decades does any part of the Earth's surface have a total solar eclipse. Not only that, but because the motions of the Earth and Moon are so well understood, the precise day when this would have happened in the past can be calculated (Kudleck and Mickler 1971; de Jong and Van Soldt 1989).

Unfortunately, there are very few mentions of solar eclipses in relevant ancient records (Hornung 1965). One is mentioned in a papyrus and immediately followed the death of Psammetic I. This eclipse occurred on 30th September 610 BC (Hornung 1965 38–9) and can be precisely correlated, but unfortunately this is after the 664 BC point about which there is little doubt, so it is of no help with earlier history. A second eclipse is recorded in the Neo-Assyrian Eponym list which can be dated to the 15th June 763 BC:

"In the eponymy of Bur-Saggilê the sun became eclipsed in the month of Simanu"

This is again a well-established pin, but is only a century after the fixed point of 664 BC, so again does not really help with the deep history of the second and third millennium BC. There are no records of eclipses in earlier periods in Egypt (although there are for the Near East (de Jong and Van Soldt 1989), so solar observations are not a great deal of help to the reconstruction of the early chronology.

Lunar observations

Lunar observations have the potential for use in exactly the same way as solar eclipses (Krauss 1985; Hornung *et al.* 2006; Parker 1957; Krauss 2006). Once again, it necessary to know the name of the king and his regnal year. However, unlike the solar eclipses, moon observations recur quite regularly. The Egyptian lunar month relied on observation, and the observation that the Egyptians were looking for, was the disappearance of the last part of the Moon's crescent. If the crescent was visible just before sunrise, then this was the last day of the month. The next day, just before sunrise, the crescent would be invisible, and this would be the first day of the lunar month. The Moon orbits the Earth every 29.53 days, so some months would have 29 days and some 30 (Parker 1957, 39). Parker states that while in the Julian calendar, lunar observations cycle on a 19 year periodicity, because the Egyptian calendar had no leap year (see below), "a lunar date is likely to repeat itself every 25 years" (Parker 1957, 39). In other words, every 25 years the first day of the lunar month fell on the same day in the Egyptian civil calendar. It is heavily reliant on no mistakes being made with observations and that bad weather does not obscure the picture. It is not known what might have been done should this have been the case. The repeat of the observation roughly every 25 years means that it is necessary to know reasonably precisely what period the observation is likely to be in. Lunar observations can only fine-tune the historical chronology; it cannot establish it in the first place.

This method is of some limited help in dating the 12th Dynasty in the nineteenth and eighteenth centuries BC. Later, such an observation for Year 52 of Ramesses II helps to set his accession in 1279 BC, less likely in 1290 BC. Just 200 years earlier, more lunar dates similarly would indicate the accession of Tuthmosis III in 1479 BC, less likely 1490 BC. Their dates then set limits for the reigns of most of the rest of the New Kingdom.

Sothic Dates

While lunar dates can fine-tune the chronology, their frequency means that they are of less use in fixing the chronology to the absolute timescale if the error in the dates is likely to be more than a few decades. What is needed is another event with a longer period. Such an event is the observation of the first appearance each summer of the star Sirius – Sopdet in Egyptian or Sothis in Greek (Parker 1976; de Jong 2006).

Alpha Canis Majoris, also known as Sirius or the 'Dog Star', is the brightest star in the sky after the Sun, with a magnitude of -1.46. Sirius lies close to the ecliptic, the plane on which the Sun appears to move through the sky. Circumpolar stars, such as Polaris, can be seen in the sky the whole year round. However, stars close to the ecliptic cannot be seen for part of the year, since for some period they lie close to the Sun's disc, are so are in the sky during the day, hence invisible due to the Sun's glare. At some point, these stars just become visible at dawn in the eastern sky, moments before being whited out by the Sun. This is the heliacal rising of the star, which will then continue to be more and more visible and the weeks go on, until it is present in the sky throughout the night. The helical rising of Sirius was an important event for the Egyptian of two reasons (Parker 1950). Firstly, this bright, very visible star was important in its own right, its reappearance therefore worthy of note. However, there is a second more important reason. The heliacal rising of Sirius occurs in early summer and, entirely by coincidence, corresponded with the Nile flood. Thus Sirius appeared to be a forerunner or marker for the flood, the most important event in the Egyptian year. Due to this importance, the Egyptian civil New Year started on the day of the heliacal rising of Sirius. The year then had three seasons, *Akhet*, *Peret* and *Shemu*, each of four months of 30 days (Parker 1950). Five extra epagominal days were then added to make up a total of 365 days. However, significantly the Egyptian civil year had no concept of a leap year, so the Egyptian year was 0.24224 days short of a true solar year (365.24224 days).

This lack of a leap year has interesting consequences, because it means that the Egyptian year progresses through real time. If on year 1, the heliacal rising of Sirius corresponds to the first month of *Akhet*, day 1 (I *Akhet* 1), then in four years, this will have slipped by one day – i.e. the helical rising of Sirius will day be first month of *Akhet*, day 2 (I *Akhet* 2). In 120 years, it will have slipped by an entire month, in 480 years by a whole season and in 1,480 years it will be back to where it started. This is sometimes known as the Sothic cycle. If there is an observation of which day the heliacal rising of Sirius occurred on, then this has the potential to be used as a dating tool, providing several conditions are met. Firstly, it is necessary to know when one of these great cycles began. Fortunately, there is very good evidence for this. The Roman author Censorinus says Sothis rose on New Years day by the Egyptian calendar on 20th July 139 AD and this is supported by good archaeological evidence. By this, Censorinus means that the helical rising of Sirius occurred on I *Akhet* 1 in 139 AD, giving us the beginning of one of these cycles (de Jong 2006; Parker 1976). Any other observation of the heliacal rising could therefore by absolutely dated against this point, potentially an immensely powerful dating tool.

Unfortunately, there are problems. Firstly, the latitude of the observation and the presence of climatic effects can affect the observation and make a few years difference to the date derived from it. These need to be taken into account. However, by far the most important problem is simply a lack of observations that have survived into the record – there are, in fact, only two, and both of these are not as clear as might have been hoped. Just one of them is considered here (the better one) to give some idea of the complexity involved.

The best Sothic observation is found in Papyrus Berlin 10012 (Parker 1976), which is the diary of the funerary temple of Senuseret II. It states that "… the going forth of

Sopdet will happen on IV *Peret* 16". The papyrus is dated to year 7, but of which king is not stated. Working on a study of the scribe's handwriting on Papyrus Berlin 10012 and comparing it to other papyri, it is very likely that the king concerned is Senusret III. The helical rising of Sirius would have occurred on IV *Peret* 16 in 1871 BC, dating year 7 of Senuseret to that year. This is widely considered to be the earliest independently verified absolute date in recorded history. However, the text appears to be a prediction, the future tense is used, not an actual observation. And the precise location of where the prediction is valid for is also not known. This adds once more to the uncertainty. It is also very difficult to reconcile the Sothic date with contemporary lunar dates (Krauss, 1985), which means one of them must contain an error in observation or interpretation. However, having said all this, the date is widely regarded as reliable, and marks a very important pin for the chronology.

Conclusions

The Egyptian historical chronology is based on a very wide range of range of sources and evidence, each with their own advantages and disadvantages, strengths and weaknesses, proponents and opponents. The result is extremely complex and somewhat variable by period, with in general the older periods being less precisely dates than the younger. However, what results from this complexity is an extremely precise and accurate chronology for most periods of Egypt – not perfect and certainly not free from debate, but nevertheless useful and reliable. However, the huge range of sources and evidence types, some of which flatly contradict each other, means that there are multiple ways that the chronology could be reconstructed, each more-or-less likely, depending on the individual's point of view and the evidence stressed. Some of these verge on the outlandish and are not taken seriously by any modern scholar. However, others have merit. Two reconstructions have particular relevance for this volume, and form the main two ideas for the reconstruction of the chronology. These are the High Chronology (Shaw 2000; Shaw and Nicholson 1995) and the Low Chronology (Hornung *et al.* 2006), each of which has its adherents. The High Chronology is longer, meaning that its accession dates for most kings are earlier and older than the Low Chronology. The difference is at its maximum of around 100 years at the start of the Old Kingdom, but by the 18th Dynasty the two chronologies basically agree. Slightly confusingly, by the 20th Dynasty the High Chronology dates are actually slightly younger than the Low Chronology. See the charts in later chapters and the appendices for illustrations of this.

The Egyptian Historical Chronology is perhaps best summed up by Professor Kitchen (1991) in his classic paper:

> "*Historical and archaeological chronologies of Egypt... have long provided a backbone for establishing timescales... in world history and archaeology... However, they do not provide that backbone easily or with uniform exactitude*"

References

Aldred, C. 1988, *Akhenaten, King of Egypt*, London.
Bietak, M. (ed.), 2007, *Ägypten und Levante* **16**, Wien.
De Jong, T. 2006, Sothic dates, In *Ancient Egyptian Chronology* (eds R. Krauss and D. A. Warburton), 432–437, Brill, Leiden and Boston.
De Jong, T. and Van Soldt, W. H. 1989, The earliest known solar eclipse record redated, *Nature*, **338**, 238–40.
Hornung, E. 1965, Die sonnenfinsternis nach dem tode Psammetichs I, *Zeitschrift fur Aegyptische sprache*, **92**, 38–9.
Hornung, E., Krauss, R. and Warburton, D. A. 2006, *Ancient Egyptian Chronology*, Brill. Leiden and Boston.
Hunger, H. 2008, Zur datierung der Neuassyrischen eponymenliste. *Altorientalische Forschungen*, **35**, 323–5.
Kemp, B. J. 1989, *Ancient Egypt: Anatomy of a Civilization*, Routledge, London.
Kitchen, K. A. 1986, *The Third Intermediate Period in Egypt*, Aris and Phillips, Warminster.
Kitchen, K. A. 1991, The chronology of ancient Egypt, *World Archaeology*, **23**, 201–8.
Krauss, R. 1985, Sothis-und Monddaten, Gerstenberg Verlag. Hildesheim.
Krauss, R. 2006, Lunar dates, In *Ancient Egyptian Chronology* (eds R. Krauss and D. A. Warburton), 395–431, Brill, Leiden and Boston.
Kudleck, M. and Mickler, E. H. 1971, *Solar and Lunar Eclipses of the Ancient Near East from 3000 BC–0 with Maps*, Butzon and Bercker Kevelaer.
Manetho, 1940, *Aegyptiaca*, Heinemann Ltd London; Harvard University Press, Cambridge.
Moran, W. L. 1992, *The Amarna Letters*, The Johns Hopkins Press, Baltimore.
Murnane, W. J. and Van Siclen, C. C. 1993, *The Boundary Stelae of Akhenaten*, Kegan Paul International, London and New York.
Oppenheim, A. L. 1964, *Ancient Mesopotamia*, Univeristy of Chicago Press, Chicago.
Parker, R. A. 1950, *The Calendars of Ancient Egypt*, University of Chicago Press, Chicago,
Parker, R. A. 1957, The lunar dates of Thutmose III and Ramesses II, *Journal of Near Eastern Studies*, **16**, 42–42.
Parker, R. A. 1974, Ancient Egyptian astronomy. *Philosophical Transactions of the Royal Society of London*, **274**, 51–65.
Parker, R. A. 1976, The Sothic dating of the 12th and 18th Dynasties, In *Studies In Honour Of George R Hughes*. (eds J. H. Johnson and E. F. Wente), Chicago University Press, Chicago.
Redford, D. B. 1986, *Pharaonic King-lists, Annals and Daybooks*, Benben Publications, Missisauga.
Roux, G. 1992, *Ancient Iraq*, London, Penguin.
Shaw, I., (ed.) 2000, Oxford History Of Ancient Egypt, Oxford Univeristy Press, Oxford.
Shaw, I. and Nicholson, P. T. (eds) 1995, *British Museum Dictionary of Ancient Egypt*, British Museum Press, London.

Chapter 3

Using Radiocarbon Evidence in Egyptian Chronological Research

C. Bronk Ramsey

When we measure radiocarbon dates we measure isotope ratios. In order to use these isotope ratios to learn about chronology we must assess them in relation to environmental information. The most important information we have is measurement of radiocarbon in known-age samples, which we can use to calibrate our isotope measurements into 'dates'. Other environmental information might be relevant to specific regions but it is important that such information is collected systematically and is not assumed from anecdotal information and that we realise the limitations in the possible range of regional variability. In addition to the environmental information, we must also consider how the radiocarbon results can be related to their context and to all of the other relative chronological information we have at our disposal. By using Bayesian modelling techniques it is possible to integrate all of this information together into models that help us interpret chronology in the light of radiocarbon evidence. In this volume we use this approach to assess the relationship between the dynastic chronologies of ancient Egypt and the radiocarbon evidence from samples attributed to specific reigns and dynasties. Other approaches, such as the construction of site or cultural chronologies are also possible ways to incorporate scientific dating into the routine repertoire of Egyptological research and should be the subject of future research in this region.

Introduction

Radiocarbon dating is the most widely used scientific dating method for the study of the archaeology of the last fifty thousand years. It is primarily used for the study of prehistoric periods but increasingly also being applied to the study of historical periods, either where the linkage between individual sites or artefacts to the historical chronology is weak, or where the historical chronology itself has uncertainties to be resolved. The study of ancient Egypt has areas of research that fall into both of these categories. For the Old and Middle Kingdoms, and also for the Intermediate Periods, the chronologies have uncertainties that are greater than a century, and therefore potentially resolvable by the radiocarbon technique. In the New Kingdom the uncertainty in the chronology itself is certainly less, but of course much of the archaeology cannot be directly tied to the reigns of specific kings and so relating archaeology on the ground to the historical chronology

---

Author's Address: **C. Bronk Ramsey**, RLAHA, University of Oxford, Dyson Perrins Building, South Parks Road, Oxford OX1 3QY, UK

is something where radiocarbon could have a significant role to play. Radiocarbon has not been used as much as it might have been to address these issues for two reasons: firstly, the regulatory arrangements in Egypt preclude the radiocarbon measurement of samples from new excavations in laboratories outside Egypt and yet there is no radiocarbon laboratory within Egypt with an Accelerator Mass Spectrometer that can measure the kinds of small samples needed for high resolution chronology; secondly, there have been problems in reconciling the radiocarbon dates from some sites with the chronology assigned to them by more traditional archaeological means (see for example Chapter 8) and this has led to a postulation among some sections of the Egyptological community that radiocarbon does not work in Egypt – or more generally in the Eastern Mediterranean – for particular periods.

The Radiocarbon Method

In order to understand the issues involved it is necessary to have at least a broad understanding of the way in which radiocarbon dating works, the underlying mechanisms, the assumptions that are made and what can go wrong in the application of the technique (Bronk Ramsey 2008). Here we will look at this, with particular reference to the issues surrounding the use of radiocarbon in Egypt.

Radiocarbon is the unstable radioactive isotope of carbon and, in the natural environment, is primarily produced in the upper atmosphere in the cascade of reactions caused by high-energy cosmic rays. The radiocarbon atoms formed quickly oxidise to carbon dioxide and mix into the lower atmosphere. Much slower exchange of carbon dioxide with the surface oceans, and mixing with deep water, results in surface ocean waters that have a lower component of radiocarbon (by on average about 5%). Rapid transport of air masses by the trade winds and weather systems lead to a well-mixed atmosphere with a fairly homogeneous isotope ratio within each hemisphere. The greater ocean surface in the southern hemisphere results in level of radiocarbon that is about 0.5% lower than that of the northern hemisphere (McCormac *et al.* 2004). During the annual cycle of seasons, the changes in ocean surface temperature and biological activity result in a fluctuation in radiocarbon levels with an amplitude of about 0.4% (Kromer *et al.* 2001, Levin and Kromer, 2004) – the Northern hemisphere being lower in the winter. The atmospheric transport of radiocarbon is amenable to modelling using global climate models (Braziunas *et al.* 1995) and has been studied experimentally in detail for the current climate (Hua and Barbetti, 2004).

Once radiocarbon from the atmosphere becomes incorporated into plants by photosynthesis, exchange with the atmosphere ceases. Thus plants hold a snapshot record of the radiocarbon levels when the plant was growing. Because the radiocarbon is gradually decaying away this level falls with a half life of just over five thousand years – so for the oldest samples we will be dealing with here, there is about half the amount of radiocarbon in the samples as you would expect for modern material. Animal remains can also be analysed for radiocarbon since they ultimately get their carbon from plant material via the food chain, but a full understanding of the food chain is required, especially if there is the possibility of food from aquatic environments.

The cosmic rays responsible for production of the radiocarbon impinge on the solar system at a fairly constant rate. However, fluctuations in the Earth's magnetic field and in solar activity result in variations in the fluxes into the upper atmosphere. For this reason the production of radiocarbon does fluctuate over time. The same can be said for the carbon cycle itself, and in particular for the rates of ocean circulation and the consequent exchange of carbon dioxide between the atmosphere and the ocean. The implication of this for us is that the levels of radiocarbon in the atmosphere do vary from year to year, in addition to the seasonal variation already discussed. Fortunately because tree-rings provide an archive of this radiocarbon variation and can also be precisely dated by dendrochronology, we have a complete record of the levels for the Northern Hemisphere (Reimer *et al.* 2004) based on trees from mid-latitudes (Northern Europe and N America), which can be used to allow for these variations.

The method of radiocarbon dating is then essentially a comparative one. We measure the radiocarbon levels in samples and compare these to levels in known-age tree rings in a process called calibration. In doing so we make two critical assumptions: firstly, that the measurements of radiocarbon in the samples and tree rings are accurate (see Brock, this volume, for a discussion of the chemical pre-treatment which is most critical to this), and secondly that the original levels of radiocarbon where the known-age wood was growing was the same as the levels where our sample grew. Any systematic problem with radiocarbon dating in a whole region would have to imply that the radiocarbon in that region was anomalous in some way. For Egypt, a test of known-age preindustrial plant samples indicate a slight difference in radiocarbon (*ca.* 0.25%) from the Northern Hemisphere consensus values (Dee *et al.* 2010) as do the measurement of New Kingdom samples (Bronk Ramsey *et al.* 2010). These are consistent with the annual variability under the assumption that the growth season in Egypt is more concentrated in the winter whereas that for the Northern European and North American trees is primarily in the spring and summer. Similar effects have previously been postulated for wood from Gordian in Anatolia (Kromer *et al.* 2001) but in this case, for most periods there is no discernable difference from the Northern hemisphere tree ring consensus values (from Reimer *et al.* 2004). The measurements from Miletus (Galimberti *et al.* 2004), albeit over a shorter timescale, similarly show consistent radiocarbon variation in Anatolia too.

There are still those (see e.g. Bietak, Chapter 8, for a discussion) who postulate periods where the radiocarbon levels in certain regions were consistently anomalous over a significant period. This theory is based primarily on a mismatch between the chronologies, in particular for the eruption of Santorini (Friedrich *et al.* 2006, Manning *et al.* 2006) and of Tel el-Daba in the Nile Delta. Such a hypothesis would imply a mechanism that operated over a limited time period (*c.* 1700–1500 BC), and given the other evidence we have, over a limited geographical range (Aegean Sea and Nile Delta, but not Anatolia). No plausible physical mechanism has been proposed which could produce such an effect. Any deviations due to volcanic activity, for example, should be much more localised, both temporally and geographically. To be convincing, this hypothesis requires some direct evidence of anomalies in, for example Aegean marine cores, and a demonstration that, within a global atmospheric model such an extended regional offset is feasible.

Assuming that we trust our radiocarbon analyses, and that we understand the environmental variations that have taken place in radiocarbon over the period of interest,

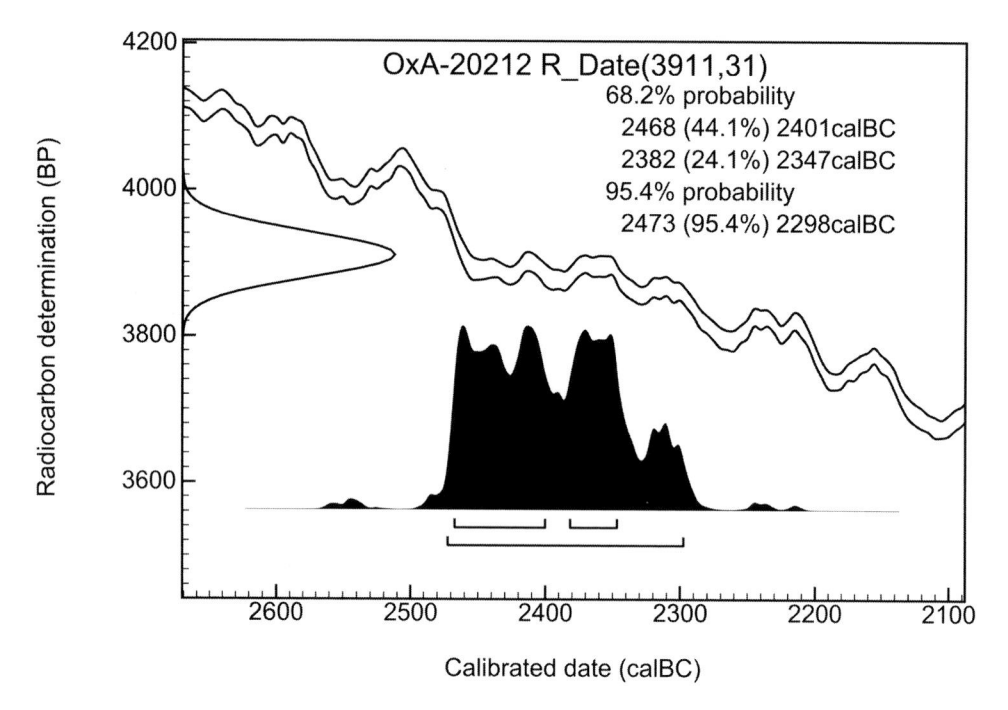

Figure 3.1: This shows a typical calibrated date. This particular sample is from a papyrus dating to the reign of Djedkara. The Normal distribution on the left hand side shows the radiocarbon measurement and its associated uncertainty. The two curved lines across the plot represent measurements on known-age tree-rings from this period (± one standard error). The black probability distribution is derived from these two and shows how likely the sample is to be any particular age. This distribution can be summarised by probability ranges: the most likely date for the sample lies in the 68% probability range, which is either 2468–2401 cal BC or 2382–2347 cal BC; a more conservative estimate, with 95% probability, is that the sample's age lies somewhere in the range 2473–2298 cal BP. It is unlikely that the true age lies outside the 95% probability range

we are in a position to generate calibrated radiocarbon dates for our samples (Figure 3.1). These give us the time at which the organic material in those samples fixed the carbon dioxide from the atmosphere. To use these calibrated radiocarbon dates to study the chronology of a region, however, requires further stages of inference.

Beyond Radiocarbon Dates

The first thing we need to do is to consider the nature of the sample itself. For example, if the sample is on wood or charcoal, the radiocarbon date relates to the year of growth of the part of the tree from which the wood was taken. This could be some decades or even centuries before the tree was felled. For this reason we can see that, in general, radiocarbon dates on wood only provide a *terminus post quem* for the death of the tree. The same is true, but to a much lesser extent, for bone in long-lived animals. This limitation can be overcome if we restrict our samples to those of short-lived materials (including single-year samples, such as seeds, grains and grasses). We can see immediately that for precise use of radiocarbon in chronology, we need to restrict the types of samples that we consider, and this in turn makes the use of Accelerator Mass Spectrometric methods, which work on smaller samples, very important in this process. This is not to say that it is impossible to use *terminus post quem* data, but you cannot build a chronology on such data alone.

Equally important to the sample itself is its context and its relationship to the events that are really of interest to us. We are rarely interested in the growth of organic material *per se*. In some cases there might be a direct functional relationship: for example, dates on cereal grains from a site to give a date at which cereal was being grown. One stage removed from this, we might infer that cereals deposited within a tomb are likely to be fresh on deposition and so, within the resolution of the technique, directly date the tomb (or more specifically the offering deposited in the tomb, where there is the possibility that that might be later). Most often radiocarbon dates either provide a *terminus post quem* (TPQ) or a *terminus ante quem* (TAQ) for the events that might be of interest. You can see from this that dates cannot be meaningfully interpreted in isolation we need to include in our analysis the matrix of events which we infer must have taken place in our archaeological context.

In order to get beyond single radiocarbon dates on organic samples we need models, and if we are going to get quantitative information from our models, those models must be mathematically formulated. The most flexible framework for such models is Bayesian statistics (see for example Buck and Millard 2004, Bronk Ramsey 2009).

Modelling Radiocarbon Dates

We need modelling for three reasons: firstly, we need to make use of information other than radiocarbon dates in our analysis; secondly, we are often interested primarily in the dates of events that are not themselves directly dated; thirdly, when we are analysing a large number of calibrated radiocarbon dates it is impossible, even for the experienced practitioner, to correctly infer the likely range of a set of radiocarbon dates by eye. Mathematical models provide a way to get around this problem and to generate quantitative results. The types of information that can be dealt with in these models vary widely. However, the most frequently used models are multi-phase models (Buck *et al.* 1991, Bronk Ramsey 2009) where sets of events are grouped in phases, each phase having a start and end date, or phase 'boundaries' between which the events within the phase occur. In most cases, the start and end event are not directly dated but can be inferred from the distribution of dated events with the phase. This type of model is most effective at delivering high precision when there is a series of phases since it provides both TAQ and TPQ for most of the phase boundaries.

In addition to information about the grouping of events into phases, we can also include other types of information: prior information about the length of the phases, and the certainty with which samples can be assigned to specific phases.

Having ascertained that we need to use models, we need to ask what kind of model is most appropriate for any particular situation and here there are a number of different approaches that can be taken. Each has its strengths and uses, and each has its own dangers:

Site-based models

These are perhaps the easiest to understand, and also potentially the most robust. If you have a well-excavated site with well-stratified remains then, if you understand the relationship between the samples and the site stratigraphy properly, it is possible to construct a model which defines the timing of the different phases of activity on the site, and provides dates for destruction and construction events, for example. In a single-phase site, the start and end boundaries are simply the start and end of activity on the site. In multi-phase sites the order of the phases is clear from the stratigraphic sequence of contexts. Because the relationship between the samples and the events being studied is physical, this type of model is easier to justify than some of the others we will consider here and, with carefully chosen samples, the certainty of the context can often be high. Site-based models give site chronologies and this is an approach that has been used to great effect, for example, in understanding the British Neolithic (Whittle *et al.* 2011). It is possible in this way to understand sites at the resolution of individual human generation; and by considering many sites in a region it also enables you to understand the dynamic of cultural change across a region. Such an approach would be very valuable in Egypt. However, in the current circumstances, where dating of freshly excavated material on this scale is not feasible, this approach is something we must leave as an aspiration at present.

Models of political change

Exactly the same mathematical models can be applied when considering political rather than site chronologies. In this case, in place of the main events on a site that characterise the transition from one phase to another, we have political events that lead to changes apparent in the archaeological record. In this context, we can for example see a succession of kings in Egypt, or a succession of dynasties as phases in our chronological model. The phase boundaries in this example become the succession dates of each new ruler. Such a model is just as valid as the site-based one, but it presents the problem that it is usually much harder to relate directly datable events (that is radiocarbon dated samples) to the reign of individual kings. We need to be aware that there is significant opportunity for misidentification of samples to individual reigns and this uncertainty needs to be built into our models. Such a model also requires us to have a clear framework within which we can construct our models, something which, for example, makes their use difficult for the Intermediate Periods of Egypt. This consideration, along with the requirement to work entirely with museum material, is one reason why we operate with a rather restricted dataset in the studies discussed in this volume. One advantage of this type of model is that we often have some prior information about the length of the phases (reigns) and this is also information that can be included in our models. The result of such a political model is a political chronology even though it may also indirectly give us information about specific sites.

Models of cultural change

In many cases, and certainly when you move to the prehistoric period, it does not make sense to try to relate dated events directly to political events and processes of change but rather to changes in cultural activity and practice. One important method used in building traditional archaeological chronologies is seriation. This is based on the assumption that certain types of artefact are only used for a limited period of time and are subsequently replaced by new types, or the associated activity ceases altogether. It is of course possible to build mathematical chronological models around such assumptions. In such cases there are a number of difficulties: firstly, we have to be confident in our attribution of artefacts to different classes, and there must always remain some uncertainty in such an attempt. Secondly, we need to think about what the most appropriate model is for such a situation. We can simply use the same phase model we might for a site, or for political change. If we do so we are assuming that types of object come into use at a specific time and go out of use at another time, which might be considered rather simplistic. We have a choice about whether we assume in our model that one type of artefact goes out of use at the same time as another comes in. In practice a different kind of model might be more appropriate where we allow a period of transition from one type to another (Karlsburg 2006, Lee and Bronk Ramsey 2012). With this type of cultural sequence, it is well worth considering a number of different possible formulations of the information and also to consider the outputs of the different models in the light of the specific assumptions made. This approach to modelling has been taken, for example, for the dates on British Bronze Age axes (Needham *et al.* 1998).

In all model types there are common considerations. We need to take account of the fact that our information included in the models is always to some degree uncertain. This can be dealt with in two ways: firstly by considering several different models that can be used to explore different interpretations of the data and secondly, on a more detailed level, outlier analysis can be used to allow for the inclusion or exclusion of individual data-points that might otherwise have an excessive influence on our conclusions. We also need to balance model complexity with clarity. It is possible, for example, to include every detailed piece of information in a model and in doing so create a model that is so complex it is hard to visualise exactly what assumptions have been made when we come to look at the output. In undertaking modelling of this kind it is important to remember at all times that modelling is part of the interpretative process, different interpretations are always possible and it is better to explore several of these rather than endeavour to come up with a single 'right answer'.

Models for the Egyptian Dynastic Period

The models presented in this volume and in Bronk Ramsey *et al.* (2010) are all similar in nature. They are models of political sequences and are directed at investigating the chronology of the dynastic periods of Egypt. We assume that the order of the kings is known which gives us the order of the phases in our model. The boundaries between subsequent phases are the accession dates of the kings on the assumption that, within the sequence, there is always one king on the throne. There are of course some periods where we need to make use of our knowledge of co-regency and these will be discussed where this is relevant. The accession dates themselves are treated as an unknown and are inferred as part of the output of the model. The absolute dating information that we do have comes from the calibrated radiocarbon dates for samples associated with particular

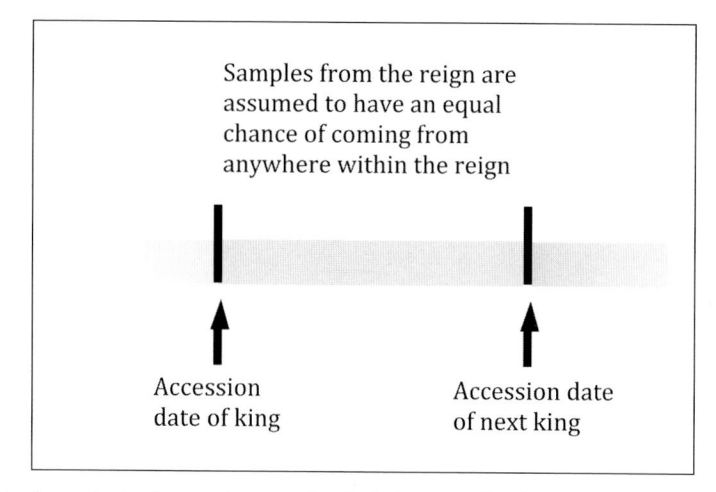

Figure 3.2: This shows the fundamental assumption built into a multi-phase model of the type discussed here. Where we have samples that are related to a particular king's reign we assume that they are equally likely to have come from anywhere within this reign. The actual accession dates are almost never dated directly by radiocarbon but the samples from different reigns provide constraints for them.

reigns (or in some cases a number of different reigns or a specific dynasty). These dated samples provide TAQ and TPQ constraints on the accession dates. We make some other specific assumptions about the samples which are necessary to fully specify the model: within each reign we assume that the samples are equally likely to come from any period within the reign (Figure 3.2) and that there is a probability (normally set at 5%) that any sample might have been incorrectly assigned to a particular period.

In a basic multi-phase model we usually assume that any length of phase is equally likely. However, in the case of a historical chronology we can include much more specific information on the phase (reign) lengths. There are different approaches that we could take in doing this. If you look in detail at the archaeological evidence each reign length has different constraints, different in both nature and in certainty and it would be possible to construct a model that took all of this detail into account. However, you could never arrive at a consensus on these details and this is anyway something that would have to be done by an expert in each period. In addition, the information for one reign is not necessarily independent of that for others. To keep the models simple, we have instead chosen to take consensus reign lengths from publications that provide a summary of the work of many scholars. In the chapters by Dee in this volume you will see how the radiocarbon data can be interpreted in different ways by using different possible interpretations of reign length. Of course with any estimate of reign length there is an uncertainty and we have chosen to use a student t-distribution to express this (rather than, for example, a range or a Normal distribution). The reason for this choice is that it does give the highest probability to the expected value but also allows, albeit at lower probability, the reign length to be very different from that assumed (Figure 3.3) which increases the robustness of the models.

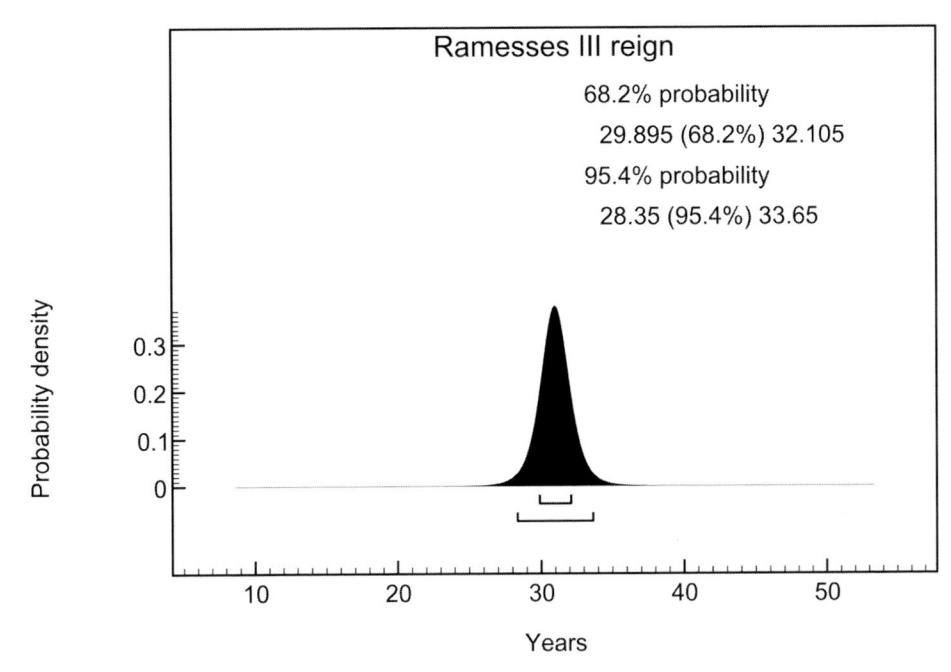

Figure 3.3: Here you can see the prior information provided for reign length, in this case for Ramesses III. In all cases we have tried models with different levels of uncertainty but the primary models for the New Kingdom assume an uncertainty of the scale indicated here. The uncertainty is based on a student-t distribution which is similar to a Normal distribution but with longer tails.

When trying to relate radiocarbon dates directly to the political chronology for Egypt there is considerable scope for uncertainty. Except for the case of royal tombs, there is always some question of the temporal linkage between the sample and the reign in question. Much of the material we have to deal with comes from old excavations and has been in museum collections for long periods. In addition, when the samples were excavated and first curated, no-one could have known how important the kind of materials most suitable for dating (such as plant fragments and grains) would be to future scientific study. For all these reasons, we need to keep in mind that any sample might be assigned to the wrong context in our models. We can deal with this possibility by the use of outlier analysis, which tests whether or not the model makes better sense if single samples are removed from the sequence. The resultant output of the model provides an average of model outputs, which both include and exclude individual samples from the analysis. Samples which are in disagreement with the other data are automatically down-weighted or even totally removed from the model output if their inclusion does not allow a consistent model to be generated.

The models discussed in the later chapters of this book then, are attempts at interpreting the available evidence in a quantitative way. The information included in each model is the same:

- Environmental data from the calibration curve (Reimer *et al.* 2004) and from the study of known age radiocarbon samples from Egypt (Dee *et al.* 2010).
- The radiocarbon measurements on samples attributed to particular reigns (Bronk Ramsey 2010) with an inbuilt possibility that these attributions may be wrong.
- Reign length information (but explicitly not the absolute date of reigns) with an allowance for uncertainty (from, for example, the consensus chronology presented in Shaw 2000).

Each model output should be considered as a possible interpretation of these available data, contingent on the assumptions made. The lengths of the chronologies produced are largely constrained by the inputs to the model, but the absolute placement of the chronology on the calendar timescale derives entirely from the radiocarbon dating constraints.

Discussion

The approach to using radiocarbon dates for the study of Egyptian chronology that has been explored in this volume and in Bronk Ramsey *et al.* (2010) is only one of many possible approaches. In this volume, we have attempted to look at how we can interpret the same data in different ways. What is certainly true is that radiocarbon does add another element to our armoury for addressing chronological issues in Egypt. For the New Kingdom our interpretation may depend on our standpoint: for many, the chronology of the New Kingdom is already well established and the fact that radiocarbon essentially corroborates the consensus view serves more to show that radiocarbon does work in this region, and confirms the small regional offset found in environmental samples (Dee *et al.* 2010). For others, radiocarbon might be important in showing that that consensus is indeed correct and that a major reassessment of the New Kingdom chronology does not make sense. For the Old and Middle Kingdoms the traditional chronologies are more uncertain and here it is clearer what radiocarbon has to offer. The precision achievable for the New Kingdom shows that, were we able to get a similar density of radiocarbon dates in the Middle and Old Kingdoms, we would gain a much higher precision in our absolute chronology for these periods than has hitherto been possible.

It is important to emphasise at that the work discussed here is only a start to this process. We have not yet explored the other types of modelling that might be applied to radiocarbon dating in Egypt. Both site-based and cultural chronological models have perhaps even more scope for transforming our understanding of the predynastic and dynastic periods of Egyptian archaeology and these must be the main focus for future research.

References

Braziunas, T. F., Fung, I. Y. and Stuiver, M. 1995, The preindustrial atmospheric14CO2 latitudinal gradient as related to exchanges among atmospheric, oceanic, and terrestrial reservoirs, *Global Biogeochemical Cycles*, **9**(4), 565–584.

Bronk Ramsey, C. 2008, Radiocarbon dating: Revolutions in understanding, *Archaeometry*, **50**(2), 249–275.

Bronk Ramsey, C. 2009, Bayesian analysis of radiocarbon dates, *Radiocarbon*, **51**(1), 337–360.

Bronk Ramsey, C., Dee, M. W., Rowland, J. M., Higham, T. F. G., Harris, S. A., Brock, F., Quiles, A., Wild, E. M., Marcus, E. S. and Shortland, A. J. 2010, Radiocarbon-based chronology for Dynastic Egypt, *Science*, **328**(5985), 1554–1557.

Buck, C. E., Kenworthy, J. B., Litton, C. D. and Smith, A. F. M. 1991, Combining archaeological and radiocarbon information – a Bayesian-approach to calibration, *Antiquity*, **65**(249), 808–821.

Buck, C. E. and Millard, A. 2004, *Tools for constructing chronologies: crossing disciplinary boundaries*, Springer, London.

Dee, M., Brock, F., Harris, S., Ramsey, C. B., Shortland, A., Higham, T. and Rowland, J. 2010, Investigating the likelihood of a reservoir offset in the radiocarbon record for ancient Egypt, *Journal of Archaeological Science*, **37**(4), 687–693.

Friedrich, W. L., Kromer, B., Friedrich, M., Heinemeier, J., Pfeiffer, T. and Talamo, S. 2006, Santorini eruption radiocarbon dated to 1627–1600 B.C., *Science*, **312**, 548.

Galimberti, M., Bronk Ramsey, C. and Manning, S. W. 2004, Wiggle-match dating of tree-ring sequences, *Radiocarbon*, **46**(2), 917–924.

Hua, Q. and Barbetti, M. 2004, Review of tropospheric bomb C-14 data for carbon cycle modeling and age calibration purposes, *Radiocarbon*, **46**(3), 1273–1298.

Karlsberg, A. J. 2006, *Statistical modelling for robust and flexible chronology building*. Unpublished PhD Thesis, University of Sheffield.

Kromer, B., Manning, S. W., Kuniholm, P. I., Newton, M. W., Spurk, M. and Levin, I. 2001, Regional (CO2) C14 offsets in the troposphere: magnitude, mechanisms, and consequences, *Science*, **294**, 2529–2532.

Lee, S. and Bronk Ramsey, C. 2012, Development and application of the trapezoidal model for archaeological chronologies, *Radiocarbon*, in press.

Levin, I. and Kromer, B. 2004, The tropospheric 14CO2 level in mid-latitudes of the Northern Hemisphere (1959–2003), *Radiocarbon*, **46**(3), 1261–1272.

Manning, S. W., Bronk Ramsey, C., Kutschera, W., Higham, T., Kromer, B., Steier, P. and Wild, E. M. 2006, Chronology for the Aegan Late Bronze Age 1700–1400 B.C., *Science*, **312**, 565–569.

McCormac, F. G., Hogg, A. G., Blackwell, P. G., Buck, C. E., Higham, T. F. G. and Reimer, P. J. 2004, SHCal04 Southern Hemisphere calibration, 0–11.0 cal kyr BP, *Radiocarbon*, **46**(3), 1087–1092.

Needham, S., Bronk Ramsey, C., Coombs, D., Cartwright, C. and Pettitt, P. B. 1998, An independent chronology for British Bronze Age metalwork: The results of the Oxford radiocarbon accelerator programme, *Archaeological Journal*, **154**, 55–107.

Shaw, I. (ed.) 2000, *The Oxford History of Ancient Egypt*, Oxford University Press, Oxford.

Whittle, A., Healy, F. and Bayliss, A. (eds) 2011, *Gathering time: Dating the early Neolithic enclosures of southern Britain and Ireland*, Oxbow Books, Oxford.

II. Radiocarbon Dating Methodology

Chapter 4
Sample Selection for Radiocarbon Dating

F. Brock and M. W. Dee

Obtaining reliable age data using radiocarbon dating requires a considered sampling strategy. It is first necessary to identify material suitable for dating, taking into account the availability of samples, the suitability of the sample material, and also how a sample is going to date the event in question. Before a sample undergoes chemical pre-treatment in the laboratory, it may have already been subject to processes that have reduced its suitability for dating. Such issues may relate to material use in antiquity, the integrity of the archaeological context, how carefully the object was excavated, or how it has subsequently been stored and preserved. In this chapter, we present a summary of key points to consider when choosing samples for radiocarbon dating, and also discuss suitable sampling procedures. To demonstrate the issues discussed, we give examples of the sampling strategy applied to the Oxford project.

Introduction to Sampling for Radiocarbon Dating

A radiocarbon date estimates the time at which a material ceased exchanging carbon with the reservoir in which it lived and grew. It is generally accepted that the death of an organism represents the start of the 'ticking' of the radiocarbon clock, the beginning of the decay of the ^{14}C isotope with the absence of any further replenishment. This is an oversimplification, however, since it ignores the complexities of the growth of certain organisms, such as wood.

A further difficulty is the way in which material interacts with the environment after deposition. Material in archaeological sites can be bioturbated, or mixed in other ways with residual or intrusive carbonaceous samples. Samples may become chemically contaminated with carbon of a different age too. Lake sediments are a good example: sometimes material washes into a lake and becomes incorporated with other carbon material of a different age within the sediments on the lake bottom. Dating homogenised material such as sediments, or even mixed assemblages of seeds or charcoal, can produce an average date, which may be in error. In early excavations, material was often collected poorly, and curated or treated in museums without due care. All of these influences serve to separate and blur the relationship between the radiocarbon age represented by the organic remains we select for dating, and the archaeological event we want to date.

Obtaining reliable age data using radiocarbon dating therefore requires a carefully considered sampling strategy. Waterbolk (1971) published a summary of all the pitfalls

---

Author's Address: **F. Brock and M. W. Dee**, RLAHA, University of Oxford, Dyson Perrins Building, South Parks Road, Oxford OX1 3QY, UK

that faced radiocarbon dating at the time. He examined a total of nine problem areas, and his guidelines on sample selection have become seminal. He introduced a twofold strategy to lessen the likelihood of selecting substances that would be asynchronous with their contexts.

The first was called the *Inbuilt Age* criterion. Inbuilt age is defined as the length of time between the death of the sample and the archaeological event being dated (McFadgen 1982). When inbuilt age arises naturally it is referred to as 'growth age'. A seed, for instance, is formed and isolated from atmospheric radiocarbon within weeks or months, while a tree will continue to grow and lay down tens or sometimes hundreds of tree rings over its entire life. Each tree will contain rings incorporating reduced amounts of radiocarbon as one goes towards the centre of the tree. Dating a tree ring and a seed from the same organism may therefore invite significant bias, with the former potentially much older than the latter. Similarly, there are potentially up to several centuries' difference between dates of pith and sapwood for slow-growing trees. Clearly, this problem is carried through to any charcoal that is selected for dating, particularly if it derives from long-lived wood. Inbuilt age may also occur where there is a delay between the death of the organism and the use of the material by people. This offset is known as 'storage age'. It encompasses, for example, occasions where woods were not used until they had fully dried out, or indeed, where materials were simply stockpiled as a matter of course. An additional consideration in ancient Egypt is the lack of native wood, and hence considerable time may have passed between the felling of a tree and its arrival and use in Egypt.

Although the age accrued during storage would certainly not be expected to be more than a decade or so, a related phenomenon can be far more detrimental to the dating process. It concerns the employment of materials that have lain unused for long periods of time, but not necessarily as a result of storage. A key example of this problem relates to the use of wood, if the material was selected some time after felling. Similarly, shells may be used many decades, if not centuries, after the death of the original organism. A further distinction is made between cases involving the passive ageing of material, and material reuse. Reuse relates to resources that were originally utilised in some way before they were later reclaimed, handed down or recycled for either the same or an entirely different purpose. In theory, reused items can be of any age greater than their context. In Egyptian archaeological sites, there is evidence for the reuse of organic material, such as in the rebuilding of monuments using pre-existing material. We can assume that sometimes monuments took a long time to construct, requiring us to think carefully about how to obtain material to date the beginning and end of a phase of building. Ultimately, the most problematic aspect of material reuse is how to identify whether it has occurred or not. In fact, such distinctions are sometimes impossible to make at the time of sample selection.

Waterbolk's second category was called the *Certainty of Association*. This test emphasized what a radiocarbon date actually represented and provided guidance on which samples were most likely to return dates commensurate with the event in question. For an individual item, such as a piece of fabric, Waterbolk advised that the best material would come from the object itself. The second level of association would be a functional one. If, for example, the weaving equipment associated with the fabric was made of datable material, it too could provide a trustworthy estimate. The third category was for items that did not display a direct functional connection with the material being dated, but whose abundance inferred an archaeological link. This might apply to nearby food remains or charcoal deposits. Finally, if poorly stratified material were found at a site, which also showed no sign of human agency, such as twigs or seeds, dates on these materials should be considered unreliable.

For dating in the historic era, it is necessary to employ these measures of 'chronometric hygiene' (Spriggs 1989) rigorously, in order to ensure that misassociation does not compromise the final dataset. Such concerns are particularly acute in Egypt, where reuse was commonplace and many monuments, cemeteries and habitation sites were revisited for centuries after their original construction.

The process of excavating, storing and analysing the sample material may also introduce uncertainty to the radiocarbon process. Currently, radiocarbon studies are dependent on collections long-housed in Western museums and galleries. Such sources are inferior to freshly excavated material for several reasons. Firstly, most of the artefacts held by museums were obtained by archaeologists prior to the Second World War. Sometimes these excavations were conducted without due care, or more with the antiquities market in mind than the documentation of Egypt's cultural heritage. As a result, many items are only partially supported by site-reports and other paperwork. Furthermore, some were irreversibly contaminated as a result of conservation and consolidation protocols in the years before the development of radiocarbon dating.

The type of organic material used for radiocarbon dating also needs to be considered carefully. For the reasons outlined above, short-lived plant materials are ideal, such as individual seeds (or stems, such as those used in basketry or wreaths) or textiles. Leather is best avoided as processes in its production may have added carbon from a different source (and potentially of a different age). Similarly, material from mummies may have been treated with various substances including resins and bitumen which are often extremely difficult, sometimes impossible, to remove and the presence of which may result in an erroneous age. Bones often play an integral part in dating archaeological sites, fitting Walterbolk's (1971) key certainty of association criteria. However, preservation of collagen (the organic component of bone used for dating) is poor in Egypt due to the hot, arid environmental conditions, and hence many bones from Egypt cannot be dated. However, screening the nitrogen content of bone can give a good indication of collagen content (Brock *et al.* 2010) prior to sampling and dating. This requires a minimum amount of material (~ 5mg bone powder) and can be measured quickly and cheaply, to determine whether or not destructive sampling of the bone can be justified. The suitability of different materials for dating is discussed in depth by Dee *et al.* (2012).

Sampling Protocols

Collecting samples from museums and galleries can be a time-consuming, often iterative process. For the Oxford project, we approached museums and galleries with a 'wish list' of samples that had been identified from museum and excavation records/archives as suitable for dating in terms of the material and historical context. A case to support the destructive analysis of each sample was often required by the museums, and in many cases we worked alongside curators before permission was obtained. As part of this project we were at times refused access to pieces we wished to sample due to their size, or because the historical value of the piece prohibited destructive analysis. Also, records don't always match up with objects, or they may not be as described (for example being poorly preserved, heavily conserved, or in some instances completely different from the records). On occasion objects could not even be located. Hence we frequently collected fewer samples than on our original wish lists.

Once a piece has been identified as suitable for dating and permission has been granted to sample it, there are several issues that need to be taken into consideration when sampling:

- Avoid handling the piece as much as possible, as this can add grease to the sample that needs to be removed before dating; wear gloves, use tweezers, scalpels, etc. The sample should preferably be wrapped in foil and stored in a plastic bag.
- The exact position to sample an object is often determined following discussion with the museum curator and/or conservator. Samples should be taken away from key features (for example, writing on papyri), and preferably on surfaces that would not normally be visible when the piece is on display (for example, on the underside of carvings). Samples should ideally be taken from the main body of the object (for example, from the ends of stems used in basketry rather than from broken off pieces). It is important to note the location from which the sample was taken, either in writing or, ideally, photographically. If sampling wood, it is useful to pay attention to any visible tree rings, and if possible to sample from the outermost rings in order to date the felling of the tree.
- When sampling bones, the surface should be cleaned either by shot-blasting or by drilling away a thin layer of the surface. Bone powder should be drilled from a small hole located away from key structural or archaeological features. At ORAU, we routinely use 500–600 mg of bone powder to radiocarbon date a bone specimen, but where material is limited we can work with as little as ~ 200 mg.
- When sampling, potential contaminants such as glues or varnishes and areas of repair or retouching should be avoided. Careful consideration of museum records is critical, but one also needs to be aware of visual clues such as 'shiny surfaces' when sampling which alert to the potential of unrecorded treatments. If it is impossible to avoid potential conservation treatments, then it is imperative to provide as many details to the laboratory as possible so that chemical treatment can be designed to remove contaminants (see Chapter 5). Dust and other surface dirt should also be removed if possible, either with compressed air if available, or by just scraping surface material away with a scalpel. The storage conditions of the object being sampled should also be considered (for example, if the piece has been kept on cotton wool, as many textiles we encountered were, all fibres should be removed and the laboratory made aware of the storage conditions).
- When sampling seeds or small plant remains, single entities should be collected where possible (to avoid erroneous dates caused by mixed assemblages).
- Sample size is key: while it is obviously preferable to take minimum amounts of material to avoid the unnecessary destruction of valuable historical material, it is important to ensure that a sufficient amount is taken to provide a reliable date. One of the advantages of the development of AMS radiocarbon dating over the last 20 years or so is that dates can be produced from much smaller samples than conventional decay-counting techniques. For

plant material (e.g. seeds, textiles, basketry, papyri), we routinely work with 10–20 mg of material at Oxford. Single seeds obviously can have very low mass, and realistically it is difficult to work with samples weighing less than ~ 5mg. We found it useful to take a 'demo kit' of samples (e.g. seeds, linen, wood) of known weights with us when sampling to reassure curators and for our own information.
- Most good radiocarbon laboratories will be very happy to advise on sampling strategies, or even to assist with sampling. Some museums may require any unused (and sometimes pre-treated but not dated) material to be returned.

Samples Selected for the Oxford Project

A breakdown of the samples selected for the Oxford project is given in Figure 4.1. All were either scraps of plant remains or items fashioned from plant material. This avoided the potential complexity of dietary effects on bone and other animal tissues (for an example, see Cook *et al.* 2001). A great majority of the samples were from short-lived plant species, although a small number of comparatively short-lived woody species were also chosen. No charcoal was dated on this project.

The choice of sample material had a significant effect on the accuracy of the dates obtained. For example, excluding one contaminated papyrus (Berlin specimen 10038 b + c, see Bronk Ramsey *et al.* 2010), all but one of the remaining 17 papyrus documents produced calibrated dates that overlapped with the historical estimates given in Shaw (2000, 479). On the other hand, scraps of unworked *Cyperus papyrus* plant remains produced some of the least accurate dates of the entire study (see Figure 4.2). But in this case, it was clearly the misassociation of the sample that resulted in the error. Indeed, short-lived

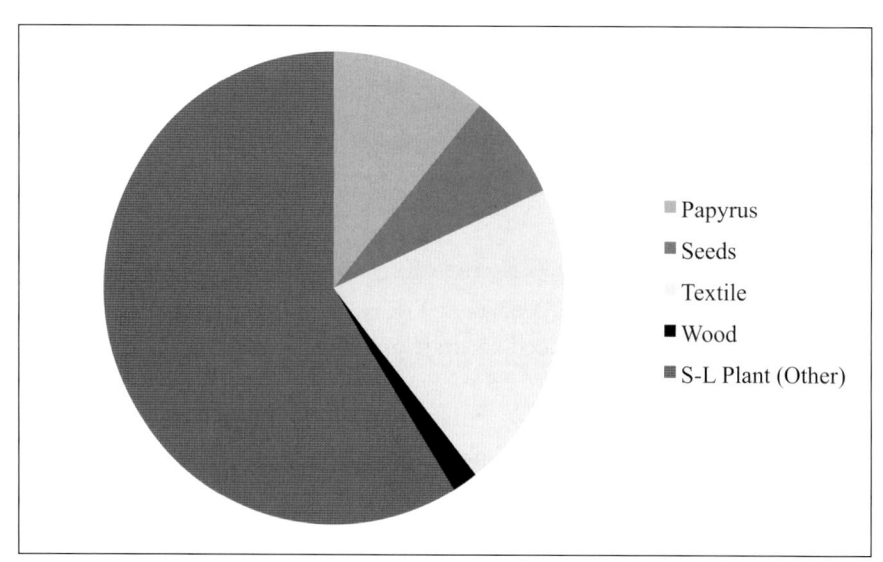

Figure 4.1: The different sample types chosen for the Oxford project. All were plant-based materials with the majority falling into the category of S-L (Short-lived) Plant remains.

plant material remains preferable because it reduces the problem of inbuilt age to just material reuse and storage. If a sample is unlikely to have experienced either of these two complications, then the amount of inbuilt age is likely to be negligible. However, short-lived plant remains are also frequently light, flimsy and easily transportable by environmental or human agency. Therefore, there is a heightened possibility that such samples will be intrusive at an archaeological site or even in a museum collection (see Figure 4.2). This is reflected in the persistence of younger-than-expected outliers in the Oxford project. Nonetheless, in our experience, it is certainly advisable to prioritise short-lived plant materials (and objects fashioned from them). If the item in question cannot be connected with a specific archaeological event (such as an authentic papyrus document) then it is always possible the date will be errant.

An excellent example of the importance of both context and sample material, and the close-relationship between the two, was demonstrated by a group of four short-lived plants obtained from the Royal Botanic Gardens, Kew, UK. The provenance of these samples was undoubtedly secure, with each of the four specimens being connected with Tutankhamun's tomb by Howard Carter's own excavation numbers. As the samples were all seeds they could be considered to contain no inherent inbuilt age, either by means of natural or storage processes. And finally, the tomb of Tutankhamun was the only royal tomb of the high New Kingdom known to have remained undisturbed after initial ancient robberies, right up to its systematic excavation by Carter in the 20th Century. Hence it would be virtually impossible on archaeological grounds to explain younger-than-expected results. As shown in Figure 4.3, all the dates obtained for Tutankhamun's reign were in good agreement with historical estimates.

Summary

When choosing samples for radiocarbon dating, a wide range of factors need to be taken into consideration, in particular: how securely is the object going to date the context or event under investigation, and has the piece been subject to any contamination at any stage that may result in an erroneous date? Short-lived material must be selected for AMS dating, and plant remains offers the most trustworthy and ubiquitous sample type for Egypt. This reduces the number of variables to consider in understanding outlying results (offsets to older ages are usually caused by inbuilt age). The complexities of the site formation processes in Egypt make completely error-free sample selection impossible; reuse and post-depositional interference are the main culprits. Despite these problems, the vast majority of AMS dates in this project produced accurate and reliable results.

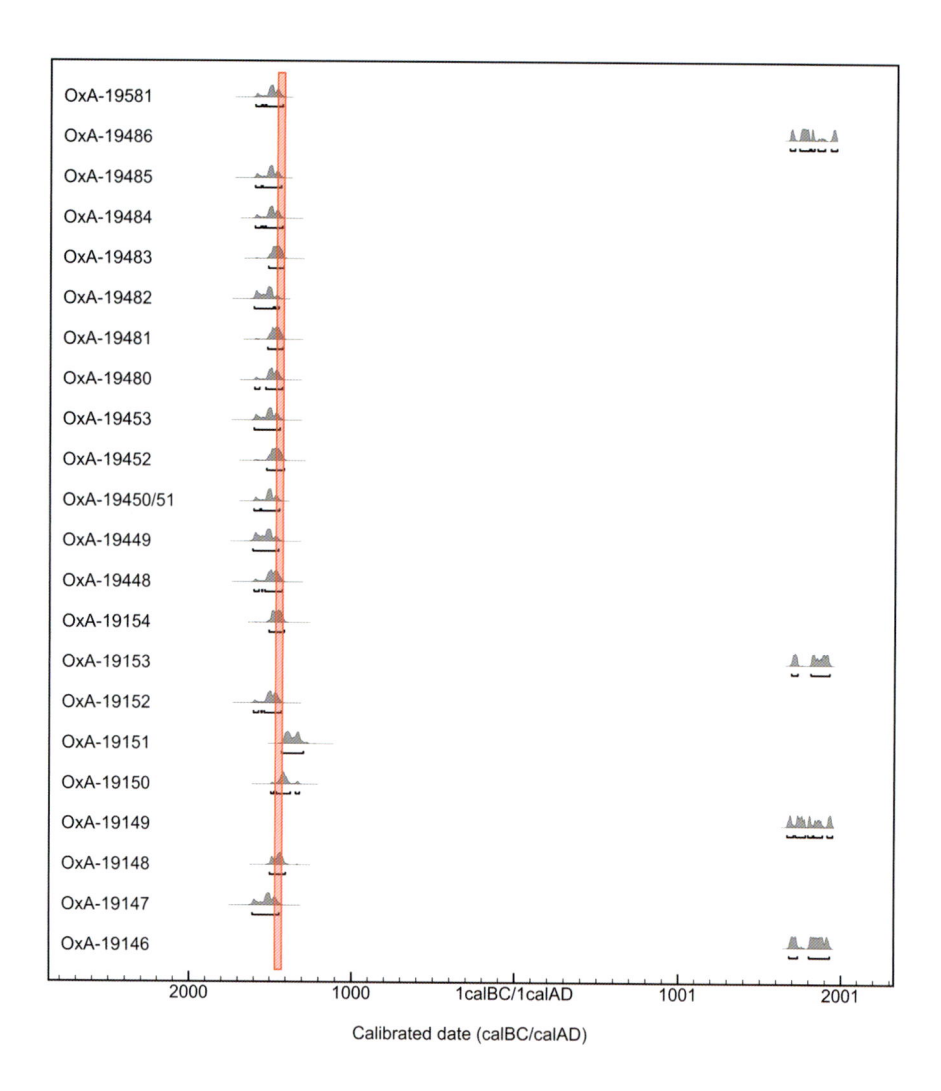

Figure 4.2: Calibrated radiocarbon dates (95%) made by ORAU for the Oxford project on various short-lived plant remains from the Musée du Louvre, Paris. All were associated with the reign of Thutmose III shown in red [1479–1427 BC including coregency with Hatshepsut (Shaw 2000, 479)]. The four samples to the right of the figure were the only Cyperus specimens in the group. Clearly, these fragments were added in modern times.

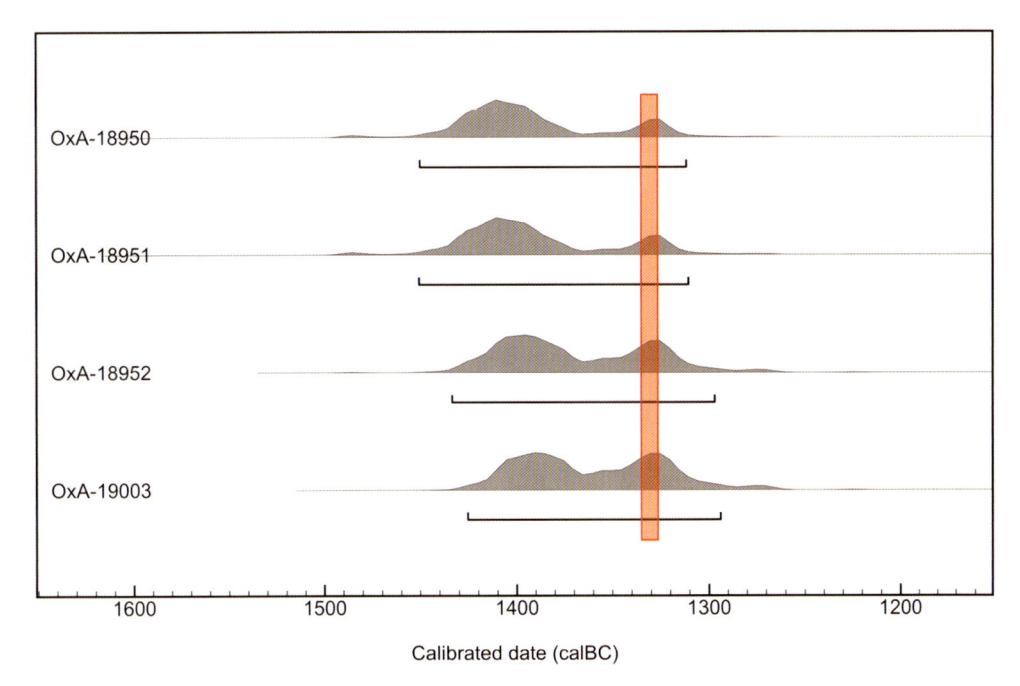

Figure 4.3: The calibrated radiocarbon dates (95%) obtained on seeds excavated by Howard Carter from Tutankhamun's tomb. In red are the historical estimates for the reign of Tutankhamun (Shaw 2000, 479).

References

Brock, F., Higham, T. F. G. and Bronk Ramsey, C. 2010, Pre-screening techniques for identification of samples suitable for radiocarbon dating of poorly preserved bones. *Journal of Archaeological Science* **37**, 855–865.

Bronk Ramsey, C., Dee, M. W., Rowland, J. M., Higham, T. F. G., Harris, S. A., Brock, F., Quiles, A., Wild, E. M., Marcus, E. S. and Shortland, A. J. 2010, Radiocarbon-based chronology for dynastic Egypt, *Science*, **328**(5985), 1554–1559.

Cook, G. T., Bonsall, C., Hedges, R. E. M., McSweeney, K., Boronean, V. and Pettitt, P. B. 2001, A freshwater diet-derived C-14 reservoir effect at the Stone Age sites in the Iron Gates Gorge, *Radiocarbon*, **43**(2A), 453–460.

Dee, M. W., Rowland, J. M., Higham, T. F. G., Shortland, A., Brock, F., Harris, S. and Bronk Ramsey, C. 2012, Synchronising radiocarbon dating and the Egyptian historical chronology by improved sample selection. *Antiquity*, **86**, 868–883.

McFadgen, B. G. 1982, Dating New Zealand archaeology by radiocarbon, *New Zealand Journal of Science*, **25**, 379–392.

Shaw, I. (ed.) 2000, *The Oxford History of Ancient Egypt*, Oxford University Press, Oxford.

Spriggs, M. 1989, The dating of the island southeast Asian Neolithic: an attempt at chronometric hygiene and linguistic correlation, *Antiquity*, **63**, 587–613.

Waterbolk, H. T. 1971, Working with Radiocarbon Dates, *Proceedings of the Prehistoric Society*, **37**, 15–33.

CHAPTER 5
Preparing Samples for AMS Radiocarbon Dating

F. Brock

Prior to a sample being radiocarbon dated, any contamination (the presence of which may alter the age of the sample) needs to be removed and the original organic material extracted. Contamination can arise via the depositional environment of the sample, subsequent chemical conservation treatments, and general handling of the specimen during curation, sampling, and pre-treatment. Careful sampling can filter out samples known, or thought to be at risk of, such contaminants, as discussed in Chapter 4, and techniques such as SEM (scanning electron microscopy) can be employed to look for signs of contamination where it is suspected. Samples then undergo a chemical pre-treatment procedure prior to dating. If a chemical contaminant is known, or thought, to be present, a sample will initially undergo a solvent extraction to remove this material. This solvent wash can be tailored to remove a specific contaminant, or can consist of a more general sequence of solvents if the contaminant is unidentified. An acid-base-acid (ABA) sequence is then used to treat each sample. ABA treatments performed at the Oxford radiocarbon laboratory are similar to those used in many other radiocarbon laboratories. The three main steps are designed to remove sedimentary and other contaminant carbonates, organic acid contaminants such as humic and fulvic acids, and dissolved atmospheric carbon dioxide that may have been absorbed during the base wash, respectively. Sturdier plant remains and woody tissues are also subjected to a bleach wash. The concentrations, temperatures, and length of treatments are altered for each sample according to the amount of material available and its fragility. The samples then are freeze-dried before being combusted at 1000°C using a combustion elemental analyser coupled to an isotope ratio mass spectrometer. This provides valuable elemental and stable isotopic information about the carbon and nitrogen content of each individual sample, and can be used as quality control to check for the presence of contaminants. The carbon dioxide released during combustion is cryogenically distilled before being converted to graphite for AMS (accelerator mass spectrometry) radiocarbon-dating.

Introduction

Prior to radiocarbon dating, samples need to be subjected to pre-treatment chemistry to isolate the original carbon-containing compounds of the living organism and to remove any contaminants that may contain ^{14}C of a different age to that of the original material, which would result in an erroneous radiocarbon age. There are four key requirements for successful radiocarbon pre-treatment: i) successful sampling; ii) identification of the presence of potential contaminants; iii) thorough pre-treatment chemistry to remove contaminants, and; iv) quality control throughout the dating process. The requirements for careful sample

---

Author's Address: **F. Brock**, RLAHA, University of Oxford, Dyson Perrins Building, South Parks Road, Oxford OX1 3QY, UK

selection have already been discussed (Chapter 4); the procedures required for identifying contaminants, pre-treating samples for dating, and quality assurance protocols are described in this paper.

Substances which can contaminate samples for radiocarbon dating can be divided into two main categories: those which are added to, or incorporated into, the sample from the depositional environment, and those which are added during excavation, curation and conservation. Environmental contaminants are commonly carbonates present in sediments, or dissolved in water, and which are usually 'old' (i.e. beyond the detectable range of radiocarbon), or humic and other organic acids. Humic acids are formed by the breakdown of plant material. Their presence within a sample may either be due to the internal degradation of the piece itself or, because they are soluble and therefore mobile, from the decay of plant material of a different age to the sample and its diffusion through the depositional environment. Such contaminants are not regularly problematic for samples of interest to the Egyptian Historical Chronology project as many samples have been stored in tombs or similar contexts where sedimentary or dissolved carbonates and humic acids would not have been an issue, rather than being buried in soil, and have not been subjected to a fluctuating water table. The exception is in the case of specimens of plant material collected from within mud-bricks or jar-seals that may have sedimentary matter adhered to their surfaces.

Contamination may also be introduced either deliberately, for example by the application of varnishes or glues, or accidentally via the presence of packing materials (e.g. cotton wool, sawdust), or hair, skin cells or grease added during handling and storage. These latter contaminants are often the same age as, or younger than, the sample itself, but glues and varnishes may be modern, 'old' if they are petroleum-based, or potentially anywhere in between, depending on the origin of their constituent chemicals.

The effect of contamination on the age of a piece depends on the age of the sample, and the age and amount of the contaminant present. For example, the presence of small amounts of modern contamination within a sample with an age of 900 years BP will be relatively small: 1% contamination would shift the date to ~890 BP, and 5% to ~850 BP (Gupta and Polach 1985). Conversely, the presence of the same amounts of 'old' contamination would result in dates that are significantly too old, at ~980 BP and ~1320 BP respectively (Gupta and Polach 1985).

Therefore, it is important to have an understanding of the potential presence of contamination prior to preparing a sample for radiocarbon dating. A range of processes and techniques can be applied to determine the presence of potential contaminants. In the first instance, museum records should be consulted to check for any mention of conservation treatments. The samples can then be visually inspected for the presence of packing materials (for example, threads of cotton wool or other packing fibres) and shiny surfaces that may indicate the presence of glues or varnishes. Optical microscopy and scanning electron microscopy (SEM) can be useful for identifying the presence of rogue fibres or of glues. Both techniques were used extensively during the course of the Egyptian Historical Chronology project, and samples were discarded prior to dating when substances such as rogue fibres, fungal spores and glues or varnishes were observed. Fourier Transform Infrared Spectroscopy (FTIR) is another useful tool for detecting the presence of chemical contaminates, including carbonates, humic acids, and glues, although it wasn't used within this project. These methods can not only be used before pre-treatment to detect the presence of contaminants, but can also be applied after pre-treatment, and prior to dating, to confirm that contaminants have successfully been removed.

If contaminants are detected, it doesn't necessarily mean that the sample cannot be successfully pre-treated and a reliable date obtained. Fibres can potentially be picked out by hand, and if conservation treatments have been applied to specific areas of a sample they can be avoided by sampling away from these areas (e.g. away from specific cracks or tears which have been glued). The majority of sediments stuck to samples taken from within mud-bricks and jar seals can be removed by careful scraping with a clean scalpel and/or blowing with compressed air. Routine pre-treatments (see below) are designed to remove carbonates and humic acids, and if identifiable glues or conservation materials are detected then an additional solvent step may be added to the pre-treatment process to remove them. If, however, contaminants are detected in large quantities (e.g. samples coated thoroughly in glue or varnished), or if additional fibres appeared interwoven into pieces, the likelihood of successfully removing the contaminant needs to be carefully considered before deciding whether or not to destructively sample the piece. Due to the necessity of high precision dates for this project, the majority of samples known or suspected to be contaminated were discarded prior to pre-treatment.

Methodology and Discussion

Standard routine pre-treatment protocols are adopted by radiocarbon preparation laboratories around the world. Although minor details may vary, most pre-treatments for cellulose-based materials (e.g. seeds, twigs, wood, textiles etc.) such as the ones dated in this study are based on an acid-base-acid (ABA, sometimes referred to as acid-alkali-acid or AAA in the literature) sequence. The initial acid step removes sedimentary and dissolved carbonates, and the base wash removes humic acids and other organic acids. The base wash absorbs modern carbon dioxide (CO_2) from the atmosphere and so the treatment time must be kept to a minimum (whilst ensuring that all humic acids are removed) and followed by a second acid wash to eliminate the dissolved CO_2 from the sample. Woodier plant samples may also then be treated with a bleach wash to break down some of the larger organic biomacromolecules such as lignins. After each step the samples are washed thoroughly with ultra pure water until neutrality. The general conditions used at ORAU are described in detail by Brock *et al.* (2010), but briefly consist of sequential washes as follows:

- 1 M hydrochloric acid, 80°C, 20 mins
- 0.2 M sodium hydroxide solution, up to 80°C, 20 mins
- 1 M hydrochloric acid, 80°C, 1 hour
- 2.5–5.0% sodium chlorite bleach at pH3, 70°C, up to 30 mins (if required)

Exact conditions, such as temperature, concentration, and length of wash are varied for each sample, depending on the degree of preservation and the fragility of the piece. Pre-treatment chemistry needs to be strong enough to remove a contaminant effectively, but not unnecessarily harsh to avoid the destruction of some or all of the sample. In some cases, however, samples are lost during pre-treatment which ever technique is chosen.

If the presence of a chemical contaminant is known or suspected, the ABA pre treatment can be preceded by a solvent wash. If the exact contaminant is known, the solvent wash can be tailored to remove it, otherwise the sample can be subjected to a more generic sequence of washes involving acetone, methanol and chloroform (Brock *et al.* 2010).

After the chemical pre-treatment, samples are freeze-dried to remove any remaining water and weighed to calculate the sample yield. Ideally, 0.8–1.8 mg carbon is needed for the sample to be dated, so those with very low yields may be failed after pre-treatment and not dated. Samples are then combusted at 1000°C in an elemental analyser linked to a continuous flow isotope ratio mass spectrometer. This cleans up the sample (for example, removing any additional sulphur-containing compounds), and allows measurement of elemental (% carbon and nitrogen and CN ratio) and stable isotopic (δ^{13}C, δ^{15}N) data. The remaining CO_2 released during the combustion is collected cryogenically, distilled, and graphitised in the presence of an iron catalyst before being AMS dated. For more details refer to Brock *et al.* (2010).

Throughout the pre-treatment, combustion and graphitisation processes, care is taken not to add any additional carbon to the sample. To do this, samples are treated in glassware (rather than plastic), which is thoroughly washed and baked out at 500°C. The water used for rinses and to make up the acid and base solutions is ultrapure MilliQ™ water. We also undertake a range of quality assurance procedures throughout the dating process. For example, alongside every batch of samples treated we also treat a standard which may be modern, background (i.e. sufficiently old to contain virtually no radiocarbon) or of known age. Most of the samples dated in this project were treated alongside tree rings that had already been dendrochronologically dated. These standards are combusted and dated alongside the samples, and can indicate when contamination has been introduced during laboratory procedures. The elemental and stable isotopic data measured when the samples are combusted can also be useful for quality assurance – values which fall out of expected ranges may indicate the presence of contaminants which have not been removed during pre-treatment.

Inter-laboratory comparisons, whereby different radiocarbon laboratories pre-treat and date sub-samples of the same pieces, can also be very useful for quality assurance. During such comparisons, slight variations in pre-treatment and dating techniques still tend to result in the same radiocarbon ages. While the majority of the samples dated within the Egyptian Historical Chronology Project were dated at the Oxford Radiocarbon Accelerator Laboratory (ORAU) at the University of Oxford, some samples, including some repeats of those dated at ORAU, were pre-treated and dated at the Vienna Environmental Research Accelerator (VERA) at the University of Vienna, Austria, and the Laboratoire de Mesure du Carbone-14 (LMC-14) at CEA-Saclay, University of Paris, France. The pre-treatment methods used by these laboratories are described in the supplementary information of Bronk Ramsey *et al.* (2010).

To ensure that the pre-treatment processes used for dating the samples in this study were both removing contaminants and also not adding any extraneous carbon, tests were run using a carbon-free substance called Chromosorb® which acted as a proxy for sample material. Although Chromosorb® does not completely mimic organic matter such as plant material and charcoal by cross-linking with contaminants, it is absorbant and is hence a very useful substance for measuring the effectiveness of our pre-treatment processes. Tests were run to establish i) that standard ABA procedures used at ORAU were not introducing any additional carbon to the samples and ii) that standard procedures (including solvent washes) were successfully removing contaminants. Firstly, Chromosorb® was subjected to routine pre-treatment procedures, and the amount of carbon on the Chromosorb® after each stage was measured. This successfully demonstrated that at no stage in our pre-treatment processes was extraneous carbon added (except during the base wash, as expected, after which it was fully removed by the subsequent acid wash). Separate aliquots of Chromosorb® were then contaminated with a range of substances, including hard water (to mimic dissolved carbonates), humic acids, and a selection of glues that were artificially aged onto Chromosorb®. Pre-treatment procedures were followed, and the carbon content of the Chromosorb® measured at the end of the processes. This demonstrated that while carbonates and humics were, in the main, completely removed, many glues were very difficult, or impossible, to remove. Further details of this study will shortly be published in Dee *et al.* (2011).

References

Brock, F., Higham, T. F. G., Ditchfield, P. and Bronk Ramsey, C. 2010, Current pretreatment methods for AMS radiocarbon dating at the Oxford Radiocarbon Accelerator Unit (ORAU), *Radiocarbon*, **52**(1), 103–112.

Bronk Ramsey, C., Dee, M. W., Rowland, J. M., Higham, T. F. G., Harris, S. A., Brock, F., Quiles, A., Wild, E. M., Marcus, E. M. and Shortland, A. J. 2010, Radiocarbon-based chronology for Dynastic Egypt, *Science*, **328**(5985), 1554–1557.

Dee, M. W., Brock, F., Higham, T. F. G., Bowles, A. D. and Bronk Ramsey, C. (2011), Using a silica substrate to monitor the effectiveness of radiocarbon pre-treatment, *Radiocarbon*, **53**(4), 705–711

Gupta, S. K. and Polach, H. A. 1985, *Radiocarbon dating practices at ANU*, Handbook, Radiocarbon Dating laboratory, Research School of Pacific Studies, ANU, Canberra.

CHAPTER 6

Investigating the Accuracy of Radiocarbon Dating in Egypt: Checks with Samples of Known Age

M. W. Dee

The agreement of radiocarbon dates with the Egyptian historical chronology was fundamental to the verification of the scientific technique. However, the two dating methods have at times been inconsistent. One of the objectives of this project was to check the accuracy of radiocarbon dates obtained on Egyptian materials. In order to achieve this, a collection of known-age organic samples was required. However, the absolute ages of historical artefacts could not be independently substantiated to the level of accuracy required. Fortunately, permission was granted to analyse a corpus of botanical specimens from the University of Oxford Herbaria and the herbaria of the Natural History Museum, London. The samples consisted of short-lived plant materials collected in Egypt between 1700–1900 AD. Crucially, this period was prior to the damming of the Nile and the major changes that ensued for the local environment. The collection dates or 'true ages' of the samples were all known to within ± 2 calendar years. A total of 77 dates were produced on 66 samples. In all but 2 cases, the 95% probability ranges of the radiocarbon dates included the known date of collection. The average difference between the radiocarbon measurements and expected values, taken from the international calibration curve, was 19 ± 5 radiocarbon years. This small but significant variation has been ascribed to a local growing season effect.

Introduction

The accuracy of radiocarbon dating in Egypt has remained a source of contention for many decades. Egypt is exceptional because its written records are precise enough to challenge the scientific method as far back as the 3rd millennium BC. Indeed, such testing ensures that the performance of radiocarbon dating in Egypt has important resonances for the method as a whole.

The Egyptian historical chronology was integral to the establishment of the radiocarbon method. In the 1940s, there were few independently dated items available to Willard F. Libby of sufficient age to verify his hypothesis. Of the handful of items he chose, the majority were historically dated Egyptian artefacts. The results fitted correctly within a continuum of items ordered by radiocarbon content. This result, published by Arnold and Libby (1949), provided the first verification of the radiocarbon method.

Over the subsequent decades, the process of resolving discrepancies with the Egyptian historical chronology has led to an improved understanding of the factors that govern the performance of the scientific technique. Key examples include the discovery that

---

Author's Address: **M. W. Dee**, RLAHA, University of Oxford, Dyson Perrins Building, South Parks Road, Oxford OX1 3QY, UK

radiocarbon dates needed to be calibrated onto the calendrical time-scale (see de Vries 1958; Suess 1965), and the elucidation of the 'old wood' effect (Save-Soderbergh and Olsson 1970; Waterbolk 1971). However, the continual adjustment of the scientific method on account of its incompatibility with established historical records undermined its appeal to Egyptologists. Moreover, in a few cases serious divisions have emerged between established historical positions and radiocarbon results. Currently, the scientific and historical dates of the Bronze Age eruption of Santorini differ by about a century (see Bietak and Hoflmayer 2007; Manning 2007). Another example is the Old and Middle Kingdom Monuments project published by Bonani *et al.* (2001). Many sites of the Giza plateau and other Memphite locations were radiocarbon dated for the study, but the results were generally older than expected, often by as much as 200–300 years.

As part of this project, a database was compiled of all the published radiocarbon measurements made on Egyptian items. Known as the Egyptian Radiocarbon Database (ERD), it is available now at: https://c14.arch.ox.ac.uk/egyptdb/db.php.

The prevalence of outlying results in the database illustrated the unsatisfactory level of agreement between the radiocarbon record and the historical chronology. The problem was relatively consistent across all dynasties, and included data offset to both older and younger ages. It was clear that a research programme was required to determine whether there was a systematic fault with the application of the radiocarbon method in Egypt.

Methodology

Several factors were taken into account when developing the research programme. The primary concern was obtaining a set of Egyptian organic materials that were of exact known age. The aim was then for the samples to be analysed using the radiocarbon technique, thereby revealing the nature and magnitude of any discrepancies. The main problem was that no collection from Dynastic times could be independently dated to the levels of accuracy required. Further, it was also considered preferable for the samples to be representative of the most common types in the Egyptian radiocarbon record. This essentially meant plant material, as more than 90% of the ERD archive is made up of charcoal, grasses, reeds, and wood. Plant matter is the most prevalent because bone collagen preserves poorly in the sandy soils and arid climate of Egypt. In addition, in terms of the accuracy of radiocarbon dating, bone collagen is subject to a variety of additional complications that do not affect plant material. For example, strongly riverine or marine diets (see Hogg 1998; and Bonsall *et al.* 2004) may significantly change the isotopic composition of bone and result in spurious radiocarbon dates. Although such effects were not thought to be responsible for the discrepancies in the Egyptian record, it was clear that bone was not the best material for this study. The final constraint was a temporal one. Since the completion of the first Aswan dam (1902) and more especially the High Dam (1970), the annual inundation of Egypt by the Nile has ceased and the local environment has been completely transformed. As a result, the natural environment of modern Egypt does not provide a good proxy for the growing conditions and hydrology of the country in antiquity. Therefore, it was also necessary to obtain samples that were grown prior to the 20th century.

The two sources of material that remained were short-lived (preferably annual) plants or a tree core with discernable annual rings. The latter was soon eliminated because the long-lived trees of Egypt are not known to produce such rings. Fortunately, short-lived plant specimens can be found in herbaria and permissions were obtained to sample the collections in the University of Oxford Herbaria (OXF) and the Natural History Museum, London (BM). Crucially, these herbaria included specimens collected before the damming of the Nile. The OXF held specimens collected by Augustine Lippi in Egypt at the turn of the 18th century, as well as a number obtained by various collectors between 1820 and 1880 AD. Permission was granted by the BM to sample some specimens that were brought back to London in the mid 18th century but no samples were available for the beginning of the 19th Century, because of the region's involvement in the Napoleonic wars. In all cases, the date of collection (i.e. the 'true age') was known to within ±2 calendar years and often the dating records were even more precise than that.

An added advantage of using 18th and 19th century plants was that there were several significant plateaux in the calibration curve over this period (see Figure 6.2). Plateaux are usually considered problematic for radiocarbon dating, but for this study they ensured minimal variability in the expected radiocarbon data, thereby providing clear reference levels against which any shifts to older ages (higher determinations) could be identified. In addition, it also allowed for some leeway in the historical dating of the samples, as the expected radiocarbon determinations did not vary much from year to year.

A central notion of this study was that the natural processes underlying any reservoir effect in antiquity would have continued right up until damming of the Nile. However, this assumption was not predicated on the riverine environment remaining static over that period. The Nile certainly fluctuated between periods of high and low flow (Bell 1970; Rampino *et al.* 1987), but throughout the Holocene its origin and course has remained essentially unchanged (Hassan 1997). Nonetheless, to ensure the rigour of the programme, the sample set was kept as broad as possible in terms of taxa, geographic location, and preferred habitat. Those plants naturally found close to the river were prioritised, although the availability of wholly aquatic plants was unfortunately extremely limited. Materials that were routinely utilised by the Egyptians themselves were also favoured and fortunately three samples of the quintessential Nilotic resource, *Cyperus papyrus*, were obtained. A summary of the diversity present in the sample set is shown in Table 6.1, and a detailed list of all the specimens is included in Table 6.2.

In general, the botanical specimens had been stored on paper mounts using glue or adhesive strips. Care was taken to obtain samples that were free of such contamination. Additionally, mercuric chloride ($HgCl_2$) had been applied as a preservative to some specimens but, being carbon-free, this posed no problem for radiocarbon dating. Images of two typical samples from the OXF are shown in Figure 6.1.

Sections approximately 40 mg in size were taken for each specimen, and the treatments done in batches of 15–20 samples. In order to ensure that any non-polar additives were removed, a solvent wash was conducted on all samples, even if such contamination was not suspected. This consisted of the following three steps: acetone (45 min, 45 °C), methanol (45 min, 45 °C) and chloroform (45 min, RT). After the solvents had been applied, the samples were left to thoroughly dry (1–2 days) in a fume hood. The cellulosic fraction was extracted using Oxford Radiocarbon Accelerator Unit's (ORAU) routine pre-treatment

Table 6.1: The diversity of locations, environments and taxa in the set of 66 botanical specimens obtained from the University of Oxford Herbaria and the Natural History Museum, London.

Category	Detail	Count
Location	Cairo (Greater)	21
	Alexandria	5
	Sinai	4
	Luxor	3
	Rosetta	2
	Other 'Near Nile, Egypt'	5
	Other 'Egypt'	26
Natural Environment	Terrestrial (wild)	57
	Riverbank	4
	Terrestrial (wild or cultigen)	3
	Terrestrial (cultigen)	1
	Aquatic	1
Plant Family	Asteraceae	17
	Fabaceae	10
	Apiaceae	4
	Cyperaceae	4
	Zygophyllaceae	4
	Geraniaceae	3
	Amaranthaceae	3
	Rutaceae	3
	Aizoaceae	2
	Malvaceae	2
	Molluginaceae	2
	Tamaricaceae	2
	Other	10

process, outlined by Brock *et al.* (2010). Approximately 5 mg samples were then combusted in an elemental analyser coupled to a mass spectrometer, which measured the stable isotope values ($\delta^{13}C$ and $\delta^{15}N$). The CO_2 produced was collected cryogenically, graphitized and dated at ORAU's AMS facility (see Bronk Ramsey *et al.* 2004).

Results

The conventional radiocarbon ages (CRAs) obtained for the 66 plant specimens are shown in Figure 6.2 and Table 6.3. The calendar dates were taken from the herbaria records, although on occasion supporting references were required, in particular Forskaal's catalogue (Hepper and Friis 1994). Where there was any doubt over the exact year of collection, an appropriate error was assigned. However, as discussed above, this uncertainty was ultimately negligible, as the data set straddled the early-modern plateaux in the calibration curve (Figure 6.2). In fact, the consistency expected in the radiocarbon measurements was clearly evident in the results obtained. Multiple results on the same samples were combined, and then averages were obtained for individual calendar years. Both these procedures were achieved using the R_Combine command in OxCal (Bronk Ramsey 1995), a function regulated by

Figure 6.1: Images of two known-age specimens (OxA-16724, OxA-16742, Table 6.2) from the OXF collection sampled as part of the investigation into environmental effects.

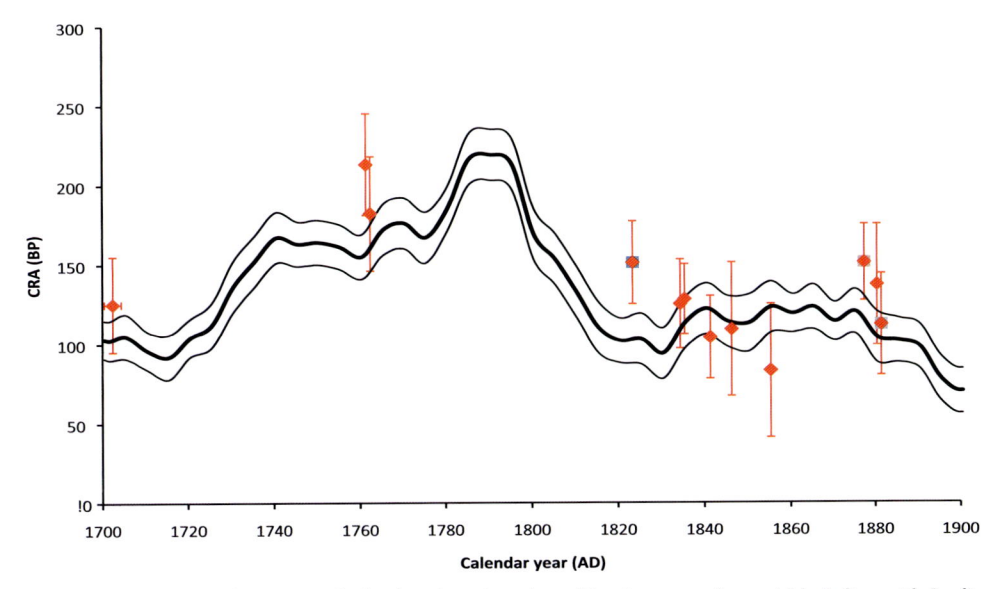

Figure 6.2: The 2σ yearly averages (red) plotted against the calibration curve (central black line with 2σ lines shown above and below). Where the red error bars cross the calibration curve the corresponding 95% probability distribution will include the true date of collection.

Table 6.2. *Herbarium Sample Details and Radiocarbon Measurements: Provenance and Taxa Details of the Plant Specimens.*

Sample No.	Herbarium	Collector	Family	Genus	Species	Site	Habitat[1]
1	OXF	Lippi, A.	Poaceae	Desmostachya	bipinnata	Nile riverbank	3
2	OXF	Lippi, A.	Cyperaceae	Cyperus	alopecuroides	-	2
3	OXF	Lippi, A.	Asteraceae	Senecio	coronopifolius	-	3
4	OXF	Lippi, A.	Fabaceae	Trigonella	laciniata	-	3
5	OXF	Lippi, A.	Plantaginaceae	Kickxia	aegyptiaca	-	3
6	BM	Forsskal, P.	Amaranthaceae	Atriplex	coriacea	Alexandria	3 or 4
7	BM	Forsskal, P.	Amaranthaceae	Kochia	muricata	-	3
8	BM	Forsskal, P.	Amaranthaceae	Salicornia	macrostachya	Alexandria	3
9	BM	Forsskal, P.	Brassicaceae	Anastatica	hierochuntica	Cairo	3
10	BM	Forsskal, P.	Zygophyllaceae	Zygophyllum	album	Alexandria	3
11	BM	Forsskal, P.	Boraginaceae	Lithospermum	callosum	Cairo	3
12	BM	Forsskal, P.	Asteraceae	Pulicaria	crispa	Cairo	3
13	OXF	Sieber, F.	Tamaricaceae	Tamarix	gallica	Cairo	3
14	OXF	Sieber, F.	Zygophyllaceae	Tribulus	pentandrus	Cairo	3
15	OXF	Sieber, F.	Asteraceae	Cotula	pratensis	-	3
16	OXF	Sieber, F.	Tamaricaceae	Tamarix	gallica	Cairo	3
17	OXF	Sieber, F.	Rutaceae	Haplophyllum	tuberculatum	-	3
18	OXF	Sieber, F.	Apiaceae	Deverra	tortuosa	Giza	3
19	OXF	Sieber, F.	Asteraceae	Anthemis	scoparia	Cairo	3
20	OXF	Sieber, F.	Apiaceae	Daucus	glaber	Giza	3
21	OXF	Sieber, F.	Asteraceae	Senecio	aegyptius	-	3
22	OXF	Sieber, F.	Fabaceae	Rhynchosia	minima	Thebes	4
23	OXF	Schimper, W. and Wiest, A.	Rhamnaceae	Ziziphus	spina-christi	Gephr Belscheft	3
24	OXF	Schimper, W. and Wiest, A.	Asteraceae	Conyza	aegyptiaca	Atfe	3
25	OXF	Traile, J.	Cyperaceae	Cyperus	dives	Alexandria	2
26	OXF	Traile, J.	Cyperaceae	Scirpus	tuberosus	Nile riverbank	2
27	OXF	Traile, J.	Cyperaceae	Cyperus	?longus	Alexandria	2
28	OXF	Schimper, W.	Zygophyllaceae	Tribulus	pentandrus	Turra	3
29	OXF	Schimper, W.	Aizoaceae	Aizoon	canariense	Cairo	3
30	OXF	Schimper, W.	Cleomaceae	Cleome	africana	Turram	3
31	OXF	Wiest, A.	Zygophyllaceae	Zygophyllum	simplex	Cairo	3
32	OXF	Wiest, A.	Molluginaceae	Glinus	lotoides	-	3
33	OXF	Wiest, A.	Apiaceae	Ammi	majus	Cairo	3
34	OXF	Wiest, A.	Apiaceae	Ammi	majus	Cairo	3

6. Investigating the Accuracy of Radiocarbon Dating in Egypt

Sample No.	Herbarium	Collector	Family	Genus	Species	Site	Habitat[1]
35	OXF	Wiest, A.	Geraniaceae	*Erodium*	*neuradifolium*	Kankam	3
36	OXF	Wiest, A.	Asteraceae	*Pulicaria*	*crispa*	–	3
37	OXF	Schimper, W.	Fabaceae	*Lotus*	*arabicus*	Wadi Hebran	3
38	OXF	Wiest, A.	Asteraceae	*Chrysocoma*	*mucronata*	–	3
39	OXF	Wiest, A.	Geraniaceae	*Erodium*	*glaucophyllum*	Cairo	3
40	OXF	Wiest, A.	Asteraceae	*Anthemis*	sp.	–	3
41	OXF	Wiest, A.	Molluginaceae	*Glinus*	*lotoides*	–	3
42	OXF	Traile, J.	Malvaceae	*Abutilon*	*fruticosum*	Cairo	3
43	OXF	Traile, J.	Rutaceae	*Haplophyllum*	*tuberculatum*	–	3
44	OXF	Traile, J.	Asteraceae	*Conyza*	sp.	–	3
45	OXF	Traile, J.	Asteraceae	*Senecio*	*aegyptius*	Near Nile	3
46	OXF	Traile, J.	Asteraceae	*Senecio*	*aegyptius*	Near Nile	3
47	OXF	Traile, J.	Rosaceae	*Potentilla*	*stipina*	Near Nile	3
48	OXF	Pinard	Asteraceae	*Conyza*	*aegyptiaca*	–	3
49	OXF	Pinard	Fabaceae	*Lotus*	*lalambensis*	–	3
50	OXF	Schimper, W.	Fabaceae	*Sesbania*	*sesban*	Abuzabel	3 or 4
51	OXF	Schimper, W.	Fabaceae	*Sesbania*	*sesban*	Abuzabel	3 or 4
52	OXF	Ball, J.	Asteraceae	*Achillea*	*fragrantissima*	Suez	3
53	OXF	Ball, J.	Geraniaceae	*Erodium*	*glaucophyllum*	Mokattam Hill	3
54	OXF	Ball, J.	Asteraceae	*Pulicaria*	*crispa*	Cairo	3
55	OXF	Ball, J B.	Rutaceae	*Haplophyllum*	*tuberculatum*	Rhamses	3
56	OXF	Ball, J.	Asteraceae	*Pulicaria*	*crispa*	Rhamses	3
57	OXF	Letourneux, A.	Aizoaceae	*Aizoon*	*canariense*	Suez	3
58	OXF	Ball, J.	Fabaceae	*Lotus*	*arabicus*	Cairo	3
59	OXF	Ball, J.	Onagraceae	*Ludwigia*	*repens*	Rosetta	2
60	OXF	Letourneux, A.	Fumariaceae	*Fumaria*	*densiflora*	Thebes	3
61	OXF	Letourneux, A.	Malvaceae	*Sida*	*alba*	Cairo	3
62	OXF	Letourneux, A.	Fabaceae	*Trifolium*	*fragiferum*	Ramlo	3
63	OXF	Letourneux, A.	Asteraceae	*Nauplius*	*graveolens*	Suez	3
64	OXF	Letourneux, A.	Nymphaeaceae	*Nymphaea*	*nouchali*	Rosetta	1
65	OXF	Letourneux, A.	Fabaceae	*Tephrosia*	*apollinea*	–	3
66	OXF	Letourneux, A.	Fabaceae	*Lotus*	*arabicus*	Luxor	3

Note
[1] The habitats were defined as follows: 1 = wholly aquatic, 2 = riverbank, 3 = terrestrial wild, 4 = terrestrial cultigen.

Table 6.3: The full set of 75 ^{14}C measurements. The yearly groups are indicated by the dashed lines.

Sample No.	Calendar Date Year	±	^{14}C Measurement Date (BP)	±	$\delta^{13}C$ (‰)	Lab No. (OxA-)
1	1702	2	104	27	-9.5	16345
2a	1702	2	141	27	-9.0	16346
2b			129	23	-8.8	18470
3	1702	2	144	31	-25.9	16347
4	1702	2	121	28	-27.9	16721
5	1702	2	117	29	-28.0	16722
6	12/1761	-	209	23	-9.8	17983
7	1761	1/2	190	24	-24.9	17984
8	1761	1/2	226	28	-9.4	18046
9	1761	1/2	239	28	-23.7	18047
10	01/04/1762	-	157	29	-23.3	18048
11	1762	-	203	24	-26.7	17982
12	1762	-	175	31	-25.2	18049
13a	1823	1	171	24	-23.5	16661
13b			103	25	-25.1	16970
14	1823	1	152	27	-10.8	16741
15	1823	1	122	25	-25.2	16987
16	1823	1	60	25	-23.8	16989
17	1823	1	126	25	-21.2	17158
18	1823	1	55	25	-22.0	17311
19	1823	1	180	25	-22.6	17535
20	1823	1	146	25	-22.0	17537
21	1823	1	160	26	-25.9	17538
22	1823	1	145	30	-22.3	16724
23	04/12/1834	-	172	26	-25.7	17540
24	30/12/1834	-	116	27	-28.5	16675
25a	1834	-	112	26	-8.3	16342
25b			144	25	-8.8	16512
26	1834	-	75	26	-24.3	16343
27	1834	-	126	27	-8.2	16344
28	06/01/1835	-	117	25	-9.1	16662
29	07/01/1835	-	99	25	-26.2	17315
30	17/01/1835	-	180	26	-18.9	17422
31	01/1835	-	91	27	-11.0	16742
32	01/1835	-	140	26	-22.8	17314
33	01/1835	-	116	25	-25.4	17536
34	01/1835	-	134	25	-24.9	17753
35	15/03/1835	-	119	25	-24.9	16972
36	29/03/1835	-	121	29	-25.6	16725
37a	03/04/1835	-	93	26	-21.3	16734
37b			136	26	-21.9	16735
38	1835	-	138	25	-20.8	16986
39	1835	-	130	23	-24.7	17156
40	1835	-	169	25	-22.2	19491
41a	1835	-	239	27	-25.0	19492
41b			150	26	-25.6	17539
41c			223	28	-26.9	18034
42	1841	1	71	30	-26.0	16726
43	1841	1	106	26	-24.1	16738
44a	1841	1	329	24	-28.2	16988

44b			91	26	-28.0	17016
44c			111	24	-27.3	17157
45	1841	1	73	26	-26.0	17309
46	1841	1	110	25	-26.4	17313
47	1841	1	156	26	-25.0	17424
48	1846	-	117	26	-27.5	16737
49	1846	1	101	26	-21.1	17425
50	06/01/1855	-	103	29	-25.8	16723
51	06/01/1855	-	68	25	-25.9	16984
52	10/04/1877	-	145	26	-26.0	17421
53	04/1877	-	124	27	-24.4	16740
54	04/1877	-	158	22	-23.9	17419
55	1877	-	134	27	-24.0	16736
56	1877	-	128	26	-25.6	16739
57a	1877	-	122	25	-23.1	-
57b			365	31	-22.8	-
57c			212	24	-23.7	-
58a	1877	1	189	25	-25.5	19490
58b			170	26	-25.4	16971
59	1877	1	170	26	-25.1	17310
60	1877	1	145	26	-23.3	17423
61	06/1880	-	113	24	-25.5	16660
62	1880	-	161	24	-22.7	17159
63	05/1881	-	133	25	-23.1	17312
64	1881	1	88	27	-22.7	16727
65	1881	1	119	25	-25.7	16985
66	1881	1	103	27	-24.7	17426

the Ward and Wilson test (Ward and Wilson 1978). The details of the treatment of the data are given in Dee et al. (2010). The final results per calendar year are given in Table 6.4.

The CRAs of the plant samples selected for this study were on average 19 ± 5 years higher than the reference values. The error of ± 5 years is an estimate of the variability of the observed shift. In fact, the yearly offsets given in Table 6.4 are not quite consistent enough to pass the Ward and Wilson test as a group, which indicates that the shift may indeed not be constant. Hence, 19 ± 5 years should be seen as a best estimate of the mean value of the observed shift. In fact, a range of methods of summarising the data were carried out, and the offsets obtained were consistently between 16 and 21 years.

Discussion

The data presented here show radiocarbon dating is accurate in Egypt. Offsets an order of magnitude greater would have been required to account for the major disparities present in the ERD record. Even though the results do exhibit a 19-year shift towards elevated radiocarbon ages, when the uncertainty in any given date is taken into account, as well as the irregularity of the calibration record itself, the impact of this uplift is almost imperceptible. This is most clearly illustrated in Figure 6.2, where there is little sign of a variance. However, although the impact of the offset on a single calibration is essentially negligible, it becomes relevant for very high-precision models that include tens of dates.

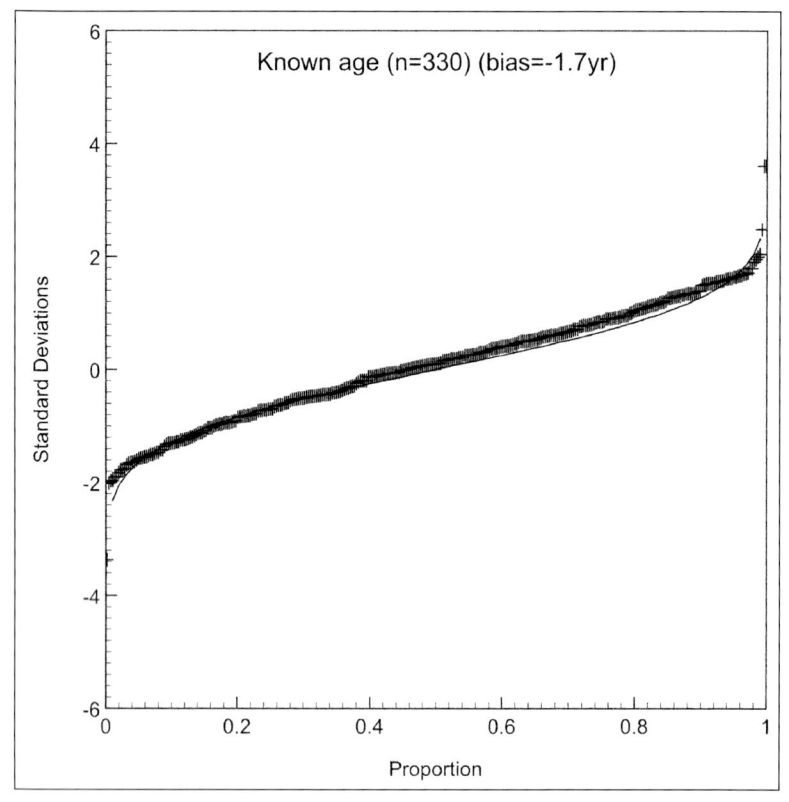

Figure 6.3: The known-age tree-rings measured at ORAU for the 3 years up to March 2010. Of the 330 samples dated, the spread of the results closely follows the ideal normal distribution curve and show an overall bias of just -1.7 (^{14}C years).

Thus, the 19 ± 5 estimate of the average offset from the IntCal09 values was used for the standard models detailed elsewhere in this volume.

The robustness of the 19-year variance is strongly supported by the comprehensive nature of the dating programme. Indeed, more than 10 separate samples were analysed for some individual calendar years. Further, the ORAU laboratory conducts routine known-age sample measurements as part of its quality assurance programme. Dendrochronologically dated tree-rings, predominantly grown at high latitudes, provide the main source of reference data. More than a dozen such tree-ring sections from across the Holocene are regularly employed. As shown in Figure 6.3, the average offset from the IntCal calibration curve over the 3 years prior to the symposium (330 measurements) was just -1.7 (^{14}C years).

The mechanisms that might be responsible for the 19-year offset are detailed in Dee *et al.* (2010). The pathway determined to be most likely was a growing season effect. This relates to the annual variation in atmospheric radiocarbon activity of about ± 16 ^{14}C years (see Kromer *et al.* 2001). Plants that grow in the early spring tend to absorb their CO_2 close to the minimum annual level and the reverse is true of trees that produce their wood in late

Table 6.4: Comparison between the yearly averages obtained by this study and the reference values obtained by interpolating the calibration curve. Where the calendar year included an error, the calibration curve values were also averaged.

CALENDAR YEAR		AVERAGE CRA		CALIBRATION CURVE VALUE		OFFSET	
YEAR (AD)	ERROR (YEARS)	YEARS (BP)	ERROR (1σ)	YEARS (BP)	ERROR (1σ)	YEARS (BP)	ERROR (1σ)
1702	2	125	15	103	9	+ 22	17
1761	0.5	213	16	157	7	+ 56	18
1762	0	182	18	161	7	+ 21	19
1823	1	151	13	103	10	+ 48	16
1834	0	125	14	109	8	+ 16	16
1835	0	128	11	113	8	+ 15	14
1841	1	104	13	121	10	- 17	16
1846	1	109	21	113	10	- 4	23
1855	0	83	21	123	8	- 40	22
1877	1	151	12	114	11	+ 37	16
1880	0	137	19	104	8	+ 33	21
1881	1	112	16	103	10	+ 9	19
AVERAGE OFFSET						+ 19	5

summer. The hot arid climate of Egypt is typical of the former case, and the temperate trees used for the calibration curve typical of the latter. An offset of 19 years in Egypt would be highly congruent with this explanation; and being seasonally driven, it should also have been present in antiquity.

If a natural process is not responsible for the considerable offsets found in the Egyptian radiocarbon record, then an alternative cause must be proposed. Only a small proportion of the dates in ERD database are made on items where contamination might have been possible. Indeed, most are on charcoal, structural wood, reeds and grasses – not the sorts of items likely to have been exposed to contamination in antiquity or for the purposes of preservation in modern times. Indeed, only a handful of the archaeological samples obtained for this work were suspected of contamination, and yet the problem of outlying results still persisted. This research team believes that issues relating to the selection of samples for radiocarbon dating are mainly responsible for the discrepancies in the Egyptian record. This matter is the subject of discussion in Chapter 4.

Conclusion

In this study, 66 short-lived plant samples of precise known age were radiocarbon dated to determine whether any inaccuracies were evident in the measurements. The results showed no significant problem in the application of the radiocarbon method in Egypt. A small average offset of 19 ± 5 (^{14}C years) was found between the known-age samples and the expected values from the calibration curve. This was interpreted as a growing season effect and is subsequently accounted for in all the high-precision radiocarbon-based chronologies constructed for this study.

References

Arnold, J. R. and Libby, W. F. 1949, Age determinations by radiocarbon content: checks with samples of known age. *Science*, **110**(2869), 678–680.
Bonsall, C., Cook, G. T., Hedges, R. E. M., Higham, T. F. G., Pickard, C. and Radovanovic, I. 2004, Radiocarbon and stable isotope evidence of dietary change from the Mesolithic to the Middle Ages in the Iron Gates: new results from Lepenski Vir, *Radiocarbon*, **46**(1), 293–300.
Bell, B. 1970, The oldest records of the Nile floods, *The Geographical Journal*, **136**(4), 569–573.
Bietak, M. and Hoflmayer, F. 2007, Introduction: high and low chronology, In *The Synchronisation of Civilisations in the Eastern Mediterranean in the Second Millennium BC III* (eds M. Bietak and E. Czerny), 13–24, Austrian Academy of Sciences Press, Vienna.
Bonani, G., Hass, H., Hawass, Z., Lehner, M., Nakhla, S., Nolan, J., Wenke, R. and Wolfli, W. 2001, Radiocarbon dates of Old and Middle Kingdom monuments in Egypt, *Radiocarbon*, **43**(3), 1297–1320.
Brock, F., Higham, T. F. G., Ditchfield, P. and Bronk Ramsey, C. 2010, Current pre-treatment methods for AMS radiocarbon dating at the Oxford Radiocarbon Accelerator Unit (ORAU), *Radiocarbon*, **52**(1), 103–112.
Bronk Ramsey, C., Higham, T. F. G. and Leach, P. 2004, Towards high-precision AMS: progress and limitations, *Radiocarbon*, **46**(1), 17–24.
Bronk Ramsey, C. 1995, Radiocarbon calibration and analysis of stratigraphy: the OxCal program, *Radiocarbon*, **37**(2), 425–430.
Dee, M. W., Brock, F., Harris, S. A., Bronk Ramsey, C., Shortland, A. J., Higham, T. F. G. and Rowland, J. M. 2010, Investigating the likelihood of a reservoir offset in the radiocarbon record for ancient Egypt, *Journal of Archaeological Science*, **37**(4), 687–693.
Hassan, F. A. 1997, The dynamics of a riverine civilisation: a geoarchaeological perspective on the Nile Valley, Egypt. *World Archaeology*, **29**(1), 51–74.
Hepper, F. N. and Friis, I. (eds) 1994, The plants of Pehr Forsskal's 'Flora Aegyptiaco-Arabica': collected on the Royal Danish expedition to Egypt and the Yemen, 1761–63. Royal Botanic Gardens, Kew (in association with the Botanical Museum, Copenhagen), London.
Hogg, T. 1998, C-14 dating of modern marine and estuarine shellfish, *Radiocarbon*, **40**(2), 975–984.
Kromer B., Manning, S. W., Kuniholm, P. I., Newton, M. W., Spurk, M. and Levin, I. 2000, 14CO2 offsets in the troposphere: magnitude, mechanisms, and consequences, *Science*, **294**(5551), 2529–2532.
Manning, S. W. 2007, Clarifying the 'high' v. 'low' Aegean/Cypriot chronology for the mid second millenium BC: assessing the evidence, interpretive frameworks, and current state of the debate. In *The Synchronisation of Civilisations in the Eastern Mediterranean in the Second Millennium BC III* (eds M. Bietak and E. Czerny), 101–138, Austrian Academy of Sciences Press, Vienna.
Rampino, M. R., Sanders, J. E., Newman, W. S. and Konigsson, L. K. (eds) 1987, *Climate: History, Periodicity and Predictability*, Van Nostrand Reinhold, New York.
Save-Soderbergh, T. and Olsson, I. U. 1970, C14 dating and Egyptian chronology, In *Radiocarbon Variations and Absolute Chronology* (ed. I. U. Olsson), 501–511, Almquist and Wiksell, Stockholm.
Suess, H. E. 1965, Secular variations of the cosmic-ray-produced carbon 14 in the atmosphere and their interpretations, *Journal of Geophysical Research*, **70**(23), 5937–5952.
de Vries, H. 1958, Variation in the concentration of radiocarbon with time and location on Earth, *Koninklijke Nederlandse Akademie van Wetenschappen*, Series B, **61**, 94–102.
Ward, G. K. and Wilson, S. R. 1978, Procedures for comparing and combining radiocarbon age determinations: a critique, *Archaeometry*, **20**(1), 19–31.
Waterbolk, H. T. 1971, Working with radiocarbon dates, *Proceedings of the Prehistoric Society*, **37**, 15–33.

III: THE NEW KINGDOM

CHAPTER 7

A Radiocarbon-based Chronology for the New Kingdom

M. W. Dee

The New Kingdom chronology is one of the best understood of the Dynastic era. For this period, the historical record is supported by a wealth of both archaeological and documentary evidence, including several king-lists. However, the positioning of the floating chronology on the absolute time-scale is still a matter of conjecture. By taking advantage of the detailed information available for the New Kingdom, it was possible to prepare a radiocarbon-based chronology for this period of unprecedented precision. Specifically, this involved the construction of Bayesian statistical models using 128 new radiocarbon dates that were obtained on short-lived plant materials from items such as basketry, textiles, seeds and papyri. Most of the samples were connected with an individual king's reign, or a short series of reigns. The models were calculated using king-list order as a known constraint, as well as assumptions about the lengths of individual reigns. Variations of the models that employed different interpretations of the historical evidence were also run. The outputs were all highly consistent and resulted in absolute date estimates for every accession year of the New Kingdom.

Introduction

The New Kingdom is the latest of the periods of political unity addressed by this study. Largely because of this fact, it is supported by the most archaeological and textual information (see Chapter 1). Indeed, Kitchen (1991) claims that historical dates for the New Kingdom are reliable to within a decade or two. Nonetheless, no one version of the chronology is universally accepted. Primarily due to differences in the years allocated to some kings (see below), two main configurations exist. For this project, consensus versions of each were used as basic frames-of-reference. The first, taken from Shaw (2000, 479), is referred to as a 'high' chronology, as it is longer by 18 years and begins the New Kingdom at an earlier date. The 'low' chronology given by Hornung *et al.* (2006, 490) was taken as the principle alternative.

Despite the considerable amount of evidence related to the chronology of the New Kingdom, it was not the aim of the scientific programme presented here to exploit such information to its maximum extent. On the contrary, the following chronological models were reliant on only the most secure knowledge established *a priori*, and such information was always expressed conservatively.

Author's Address: **M. W. Dee**, RLAHA, University of Oxford, Dyson Perrins Building, South Parks Road, Oxford OX1 3QY, UK

Methodology

The Samples

The selection of samples for this project was undertaken with much care and rigour. The criteria taken into account are discussed in Chapter 4. For the New Kingdom, the outcome was a corpus of 114 samples that consisted almost exclusively of short-lived plant remains or items fashioned from them, such as baskets, textiles and papyri. The full list is given in the Appendix, Table 2, which is equivalent to that published in the updated Supporting Online Material by Bronk Ramsey *et al.* (2010). In the main, the samples were associated with particular reigns, but in some instances insufficient information was available for such precise attributions. In such cases, the constraints placed on the samples in the models were adjusted to reflect the increased uncertainty.

The temporal coverage of the sample set, although extensive, was somewhat uneven. For the early 18th Dynasty, only one specific reign prior to Thutmose III was directly dated. However, the reign of Thutmose III itself, including the co-regency (CoR) period with Hatshepsut, yielded 47 samples. Another dense concentration of dates was obtained for the Amarna Period, with 18 samples from the reigns of Akhenaten and Tutankhamun. A final cluster of 8 samples was obtained for Amenemnisu of the 21st Dynasty, whose reign is believed to have only lasted for 4 years. The 21st Dynasty, like the 17th Dynasty, is not considered part of the New Kingdom *per se*, but for the modelling process it was important to obtain samples for them in order to restrict the estimates for the 18th–20th Dynasties.

Absolute chronological information: the radiocarbon data

From the full set of 114 samples, a total of 13 were excluded from all the chronological models. The first 7 of these were from the Common Era, more than 1000 years after the end of the New Kingdom. Although the model was designed to deal with minor outliers, results as divergent as these prevented it from even running. Secondly, a group of samples from the Tomb of Nefertiri was also rejected. The curators of the Staatliches Museum Ägyptischer Kunst in Munich had interpreted them as belonging to either the reigns of Ramesses I or Sety I. However, all of the radiocarbon measurements supported a much earlier date (see Figure 7.1). In addition, with the exception of sample OxA-20210, which was actually identical in age to an accompanying set of samples from Munich, the dates were all highly consistent. These findings were reported to the museum along with a query as to whether the context might actually be mid 18th rather than early 19th Dynasty. However, no confirmation of this possibility was received. In the end, on account of the compelling uniformity of the measurements, the historical interpretation was deemed to be uncertain; the only occasion upon which such a judgement was made on this project.

For quality assurance purposes, 25 of the New Kingdom samples were dated more than once. Both the duplicate measurements made at Oxford and the inter-laboratory comparisons returned highly satisfactory results (see the Appendix, Table 3).

Relative chronological information: king-list order and reign lengths

Bayesian modelling proceeds in an iterative fashion. For each iteration or pass, calendar dates are selected for each sample that are both consistent with the calibrated ranges of the individual measurements and the stated prior assumptions. The two main assumptions employed in this study related to king-list order and reign-length information.

A conventional order for the kings of the 18th–20th Dynasties has been established for many years (see the Appendix, Table 1). Key ancient resources include the Abydos king-list of Sety I, the Turin Canon of the Kings, and the chronology of Ptolemaic historian Manetho (see Waddell 1940; Gardiner 1961, 48; Kitchen 1991). All the outcomes of this study are predicated on the correctness of this sequence.

The modelled ranges were also constrained by the incorporation of prior knowledge about the lengths of individual reigns. Like king-list order, the lengths of reigns of the New Kingdom have been determined to a high degree of precision, often to within a couple of years. This has been accomplished by the painstaking analysis of a variety of textual and archaeological sources, with particular emphasis on highest attested regnal years. By using a Bayesian modelling approach, differing archaeological interpretations of the reign-length evidence could be tested (see below). In fact, the reign-length prior actually helped to restrict the range of possible solutions available to the New Kingdom models and without such information they failed to compute.

Model configuration and specifications

The building blocks of the chronological models were the reigns, each of which was represented by an OxCal Phase (see Bronk Ramsey 1995). The Phases were first populated with all the radiocarbon dates for that ruler and then placed in Sequences, wherein they were required to comply with king-list order. A parameter calculated by the program itself, representing the most probable transition point between one Phase and the next, proved the most informative for this study. Known as Boundaries, these parameters had a direct historical interpretation. By marking the transition point between one reign and the next they clearly correlated with accession years. An important clarification, though, is that the Boundaries were taken to refer to the beginning of the rule of each king. On several occasions co-regencies occurred, in which the first years of the incoming king overlapped with the last years of the outgoing king; in such cases, the year the new king became co-regent is the one described as his 'accession year'.

Reign-length information was modelled by including a command called an Interval in each Phase. Where no measurements were available for a given reign, empty Phases were employed that still included Interval estimates. A certain degree of flexibility was also allocated to each Interval. This was achieved by employing a Student's t-distribution with 5 degrees of freedom, or T(5). This function takes the 'bell' shape of the Normal curve but has longer tails (see Figure 7.2). The T(5) distributions can be thought of as being centred at the end of each reign (see Figure 7.3). Specifically, they placed a 95% prior weighting on the selection of reign lengths within ± 2.65 calendar years of the historical estimates. This comparatively small degree of reign-length uncertainty reflected the robustness of the historical information for the New Kingdom. Nonetheless, the iterative process still allowed reign lengths that were within ± 20 years of these values. Other default settings included the

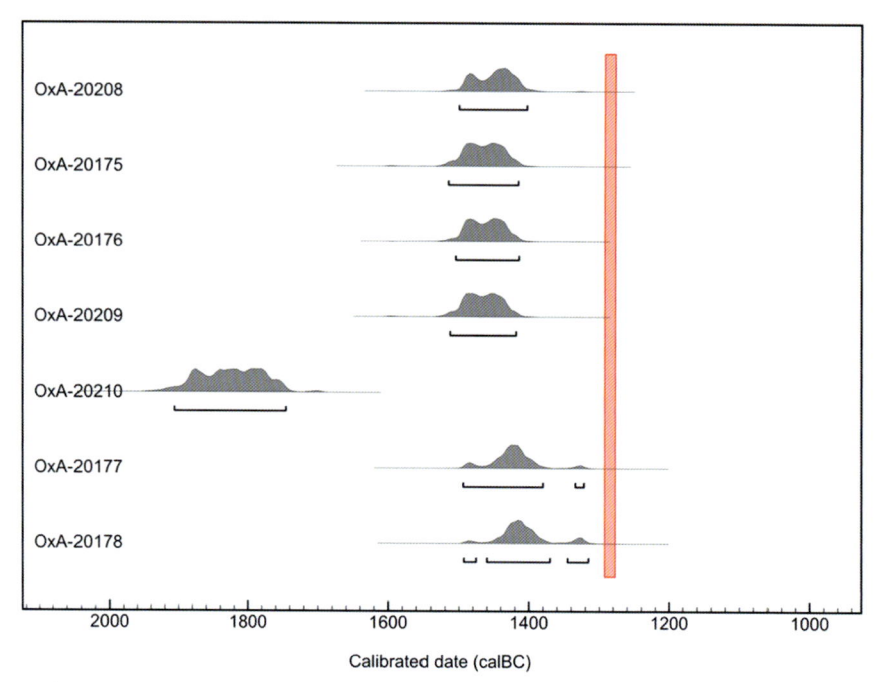

Figure 7.1: The 7 calibrated dates from the Tomb of Nefertiri. Results OxA-20177 and OxA-20178 were duplicate measurements on the same sample. The red bar indicates a consensus positioning of the consecutive reigns of Ramesses I and Sety I (Shaw 2000). The historical attribution was challenged on account of the chronometric evidence.

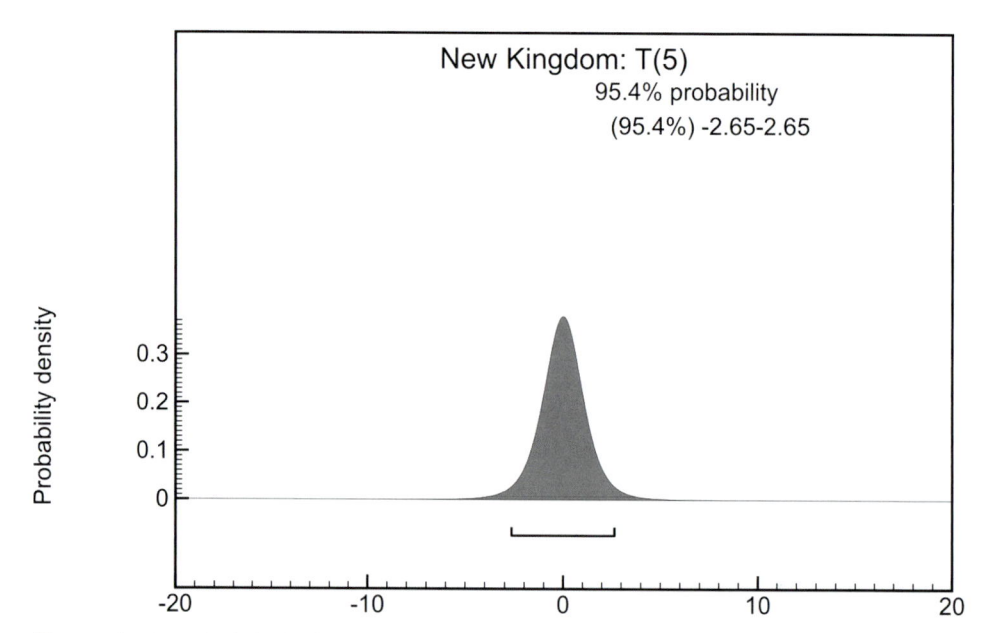

Figure 7.2: A graph of the Student's t-distribution with 5 degrees of freedom. This function was used to model the lengths of the reigns in the New Kingdom. Where greater uncertainty is present the distribution may be scaled.

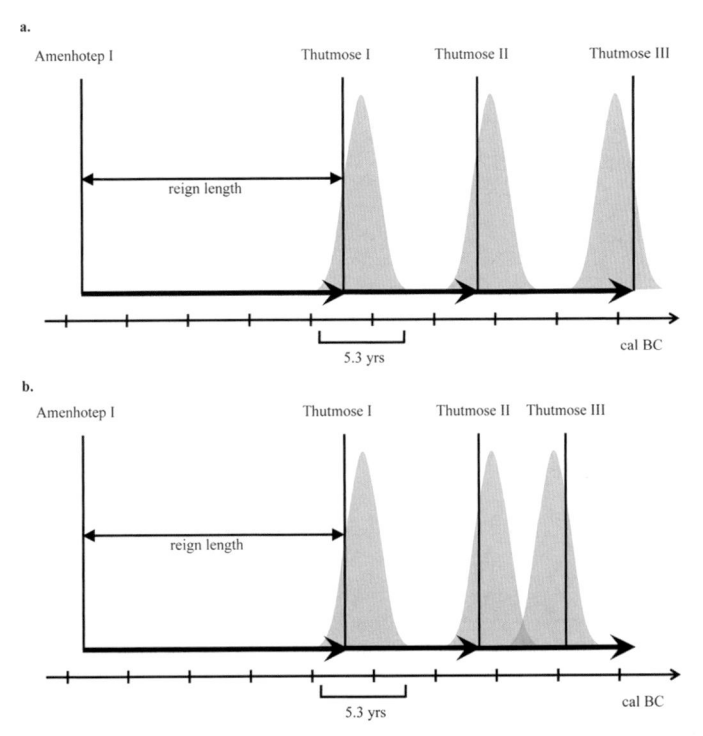

Figure 7.3: Incorporating reign-length information in the chronological models. The grey T(5) distributions ensure 95% of the spans selected for each ruler lie within ± 2.65 years of consensus values. The length of the reign of Thutmose II is the most disputed of the New Kingdom and necessitated the construction of 2 separate models (shown schematically in a and b).

allocation of a 5% prior outlier probability to every date and the allowance for a localised offset in radiocarbon values of 19 ± 5 (^{14}C years) with respect to the Northern Hemisphere calibration curve (see Dee *et al.* 2010 and Chapter 6). All such modelling parameters were extensively tested. The impact of different outlier probability values, the omission of the localised offset, and doubled reign-length constraints were all published previously (Bronk Ramsey *et al.* 2010; Supporting Information). For this publication, the intention was to examine the impact of different historical interpretations on the results obtained.

The standard New Kingdom model (NKM1) utilised the series of reign lengths in the historical chronology published by Shaw (2000, 479). The first variation (NKM2) used the reign lengths of Hornung *et al.* (2006, 490), and for this volume a third variation (NKM3) was also trialled that used those of Kitchen (2000). Although the reign-on-reign differences between each of these chronologies was generally encompassed by the T(5) function (see the Appendix, Table 1), on a few occasions the discrepancies between them were more significant. For such cases, the reign is usually considered to be either one of two lengths and not some value in between. For the New Kingdom, the quintessential example of this dilemma relates to Thutmose II. Advocates of a longer reign generally allocate 13 years to the king on the basis of circumstantial evidence (see Hornung 2006).

Table 7.1: Specifications for the set of New Kingdom models. The outputs for each model are given in the Appendix, Table 5.

MODEL NAME	REIGN LENGTHS	DESCRIPTION
NKM1	Shaw 2000	High or standard configuration
NKM2	Hornung *et al.* 2006	Low chronology configuration
NKM3	Kitchen 2000	Alternative reign lengths
NKM4	Shaw 2000	Shortened reign of Horemheb
NKM5	Shaw 2000	100% outliers eliminated
NKM6	Shaw 2000	Alternative 21st Dynasty configuration

Other chronologists reduce Thutmose II's reign to 3 years, as only his first year has been directly attested in the archaeological record. The former option is favoured by Shaw (2000, 479) and the latter by Hornung *et al.* (2006, 490) and Kitchen (2000). A similar change was incorporated in a further model (NKM4) for the reign of Horemheb. Although all the historical chronologies mentioned above specify either 27 or 28 years for Horemheb's reign, an alternative value of just 14 years has long been considered plausible. Wine jar labels recently discovered at the tomb of Horemheb strengthen the possibility of a shorter reign (see van Dijk 2008). Apart from this single change, NKM4 was identical to NKM1.

The final two models examined the possibility that sample contexts had been misinterpreted. In NKM5, the 13 samples allocated a 100% posterior outlier probability by NKM1 were eliminated before the model was run. These results had been identified by the program as being particularly incompatible with their assigned position in the sequence. Lastly, NKM6 involved the modification of two 21st Dynasty allocations. On the advice of John Taylor, sample OxA-18960 was moved from the reign of Amenemope to that of Siamun; and the constraint on the samples from the mummy of Horemkenesi (OxA-20060-67 and OxA-20201) was broadened from just the reign of Amenemnisu to the period from Smendes to Psusennes I.

All the New Kingdom models were run for at least five million iterations and the average convergence consistently passed 95%. The specifications for each model are summarised in Table 7.1 (see the Appendix, Table 4, for NKM1 program code).

Results and Discussion

The Radiocarbon-based Chronologies

By including Interval constraints at the outset, the approach taken here waived the right to draw conclusions about reign lengths from the results. In many ways, this reduced the task to one of positioning the relative chronology on the absolute time-scale. However, such an achievement is still of considerable value in itself, and the ultimate goal of any absolute dating study. Moreover, the reign-length information was the main reason for the exceptional levels of precision achieved. In fact, it was this feature that enabled the outputs to be treated as radiocarbon-based *chronologies*, and allowed the first detailed comparisons to be made between radiocarbon results and historical records.

Figure 7.4 shows the results of the standard configuration of the New Kingdom model (NKM1) for a selection of royal accession dates. The full set of calendar ranges is given in the Appendix, Table 5. The high precision of the results and their close agreement with the historical estimates are immediately apparent. In fact, the precision attained by NKM1 was unprecedented for any science-based chronology from this historical period. The average 95% calibrated range for each accession year of the New Kingdom was 29 years. This level of confidence is virtually on a par with historical estimates. As discussed above, the precision was mainly due to the strong internal correlation caused by the reign-length restrictions. NKM1 was also exceptionally accurate. As indicated in Figure 7.4, the modelled calibrations are congruent with both the high and low chronologies. It is worth re-emphasizing at this point, that no absolute information or restrictions were placed on NKM1 or any other model; the calendar dates produced by the models are solely the product of the radiocarbon determinations and the relative information described above. In comparison with the historical chronologies, the radiocarbon probability densities peak at slightly older ages, especially towards the start of the sequence. The inference is that the radiocarbon data support a slightly higher chronology than that of Shaw (2000, 479). Such evidence may inform future debate over the exact length of New Kingdom reigns and co-regencies.

Figure 7.5 shows the outputs for NKM2 against the same selection of accession dates as Figure 7.4. The tightened reign-lengths produced 95% probability ranges that averaged a remarkable 18 years for the New Kingdom (see the Appendix, Table 5). Although the shorter overall length of the low chronology 'pulled' the sequence to slightly younger ages, the calibrated ranges (95%) still show little support for the low chronology 1539 BC start date for the New Kingdom. In fact, the most obvious effect of employing the shorter reign lengths was an almost uniform shift of the 'low chronology' to a higher position. Such a change may be most problematic for the end date of the New Kingdom, as the model implies the 21st Dynasty had to begin before 1080 BC – a position at odds with all of the historical chronologies consulted in this study. Despite the further modifications built into models NKM3-NKM6, they also showed very little variation from the results produced by NKM1 and NKM2 (see the Appendix, Table 5 and Model Results, for data and figures). As expected, the shortened reign length for Horemheb in NKM4 caused the latter half of the New Kingdom to shift back in time by about a decade; otherwise the results were comparable to NKM1. Moreover, the removal of the extreme outliers for NKM5, and the modifications to the 21st Dynasty assignments for NKM6, both resulted in date ranges that were almost indistinguishable from NKM1. In summary, the most obvious feature of the results of all the models was their striking consistency.

The Historical Implications

The precise starting date of the New Kingdom is of particular importance to Eastern Mediterranean history, in part because of its connection with the eruption of Santorini (see Bietak and Hoflmayer 2007; Manning 2007). The reign of Ahmose, first ruler of

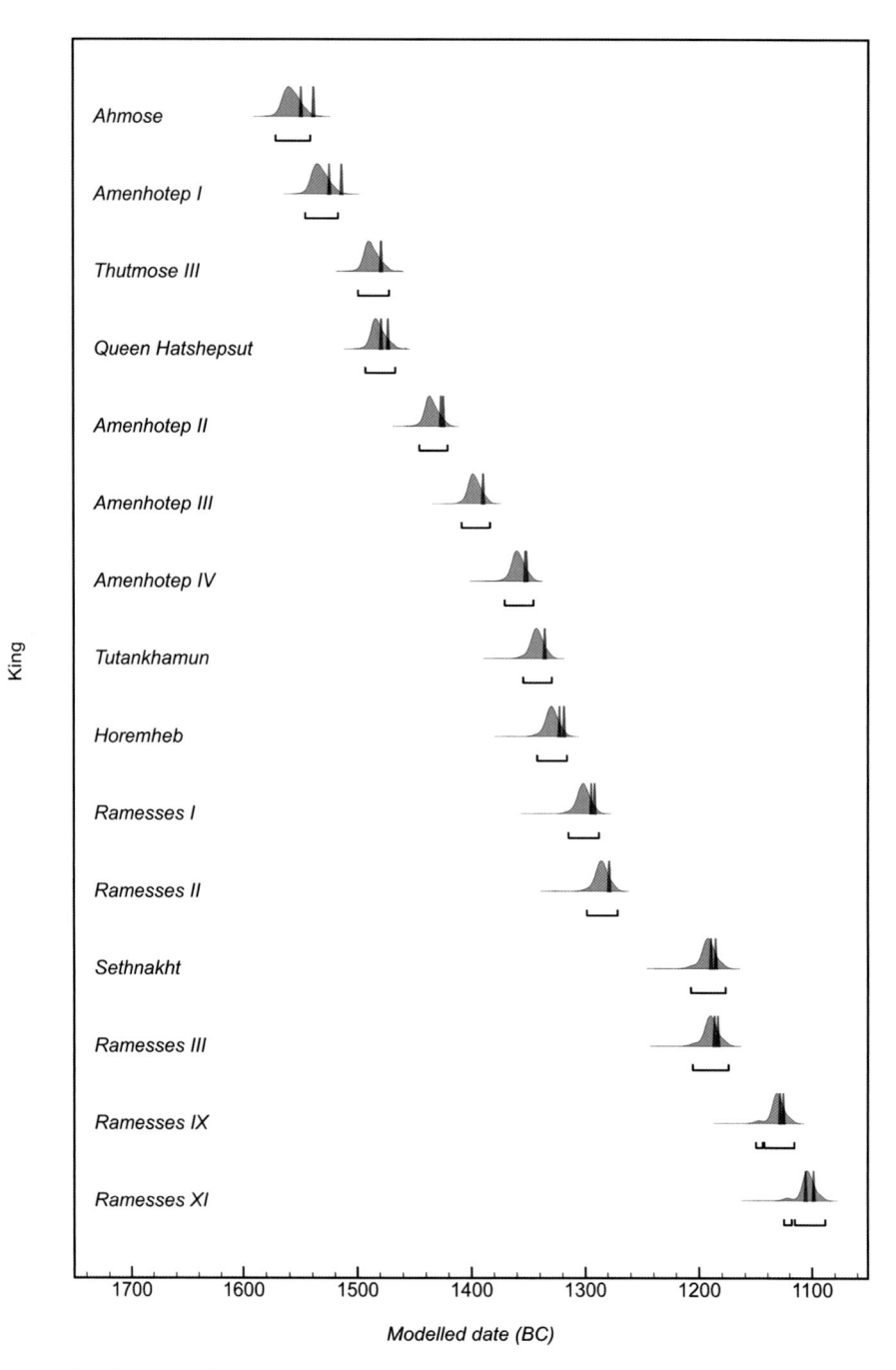

Figure 7.4: Selected accession dates from NKM1. The high chronology estimates are shown in red; low chronology in blue; modelled radiocarbon dates in grey. The calibrated ranges (95%) given by the square brackets are listed in the Appendix, Table 5.

7. *A Radiocarbon-based Chronology for the New Kingdom* 73

Figure 7.5: Selected accession dates from NKM2. The high chronology estimates are shown in red; low chronology in blue; modelled radiocarbon dates in grey. The calibrated ranges (95%) given by the square brackets are listed in the Appendix, Table 5.

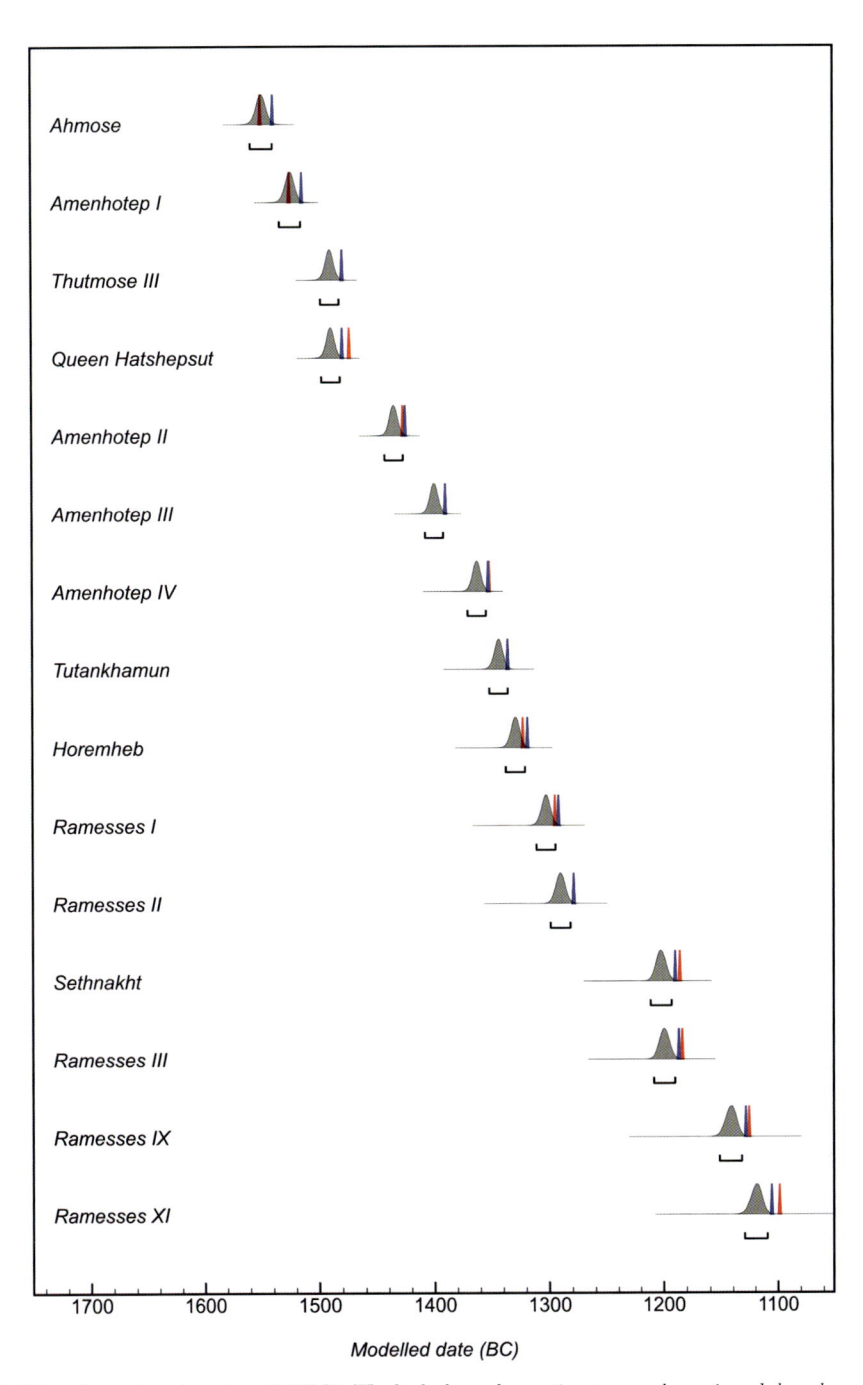

the New Kingdom, has been linked with the Late Minoan IA period in the Aegean. One such connection involves the similarity of frescos at Akrotiri, buried beneath the ash of Santorini, and those of Ahmose's royal palace at Tell el-Daba. Egyptian archaeologists strongly defend a mid 16th century BC date for the start of the New Kingdom, but scientific analysis has consistently supported a 17th century BC date for the eruption. The dates obtained by this study strongly support the hypothesis that New Kingdom began in the mid 16th century and certainly no earlier than 1573 BC. Although this result appears to back the historical standpoint, it also strengthens the scientific argument, as it was achieved by exactly the same means as the studies that place the eruption of Santorini in the 17th century BC. As previous work has identified, this calls into question the reliability of the links between Ahmose and Late Minoan IA; one solution to the controversy might be that the king's reign relates to a later, post-eruptive period called Late Minoan IB. Although largely lost from the archaeological record, this period may have been characterised by very similar cultural and aesthetic styles (see Manning 2007, for details).

The Amarna Period has been a key source of synchronicity between radiocarbon dating and the historical chronology. This project was no exception. As mentioned above, a large number of dates were produced for this period and, aside from one or two outlying results, the raw measurements all overlapped the historical dates for Akhenaten, and the rule of Tutankhamun, which followed soon after. All six of the models generated estimates for the coronation of Tutankhamun (which took place at Amarna) peaked about 6–8 years earlier than both the high and low estimates for this event.

Despite the improvements made in this work, some historical questions remain beyond the capability of the technique. The results are unable to directly inform debate on individual co-regencies such as have been suggested for Thutmose III and Amenhotep II; and Amenhotep III and Amenhotep IV. Unfortunately, the coronation date of Ramesses II, another source of dispute, could also not be resolved by this analysis. The historical evidence provides two main possibilities for Rameses II's accession: 1279 or 1290 BC. By pure coincidence, the probability density function produced by NKM1 for the accession of Ramesses II peaks between the two, offering both dates approximately equal probability. However, the short chronology of NKM2 and the truncation of Horemheb's reign for NKM4 result in accession date estimates that do not encompass 1279 BC (at 95% probability). Although this may provide useful information for future analyses, it is unlikely that reusing the New Kingdom model with more dates will allow for these issues to be categorically resolved. This is mostly because the model is already highly populated and it represents the limits of what can be achieved before the reliability of the calibration curve itself is called into question.

Conclusions

By combining radiocarbon dates on short-lived plant material with relative information obtained from historical analysis, this study has produced the first radiocarbon-based chronology for the New Kingdom. The high precision of the results and their close agreement with historical estimates not only validates the use of radiocarbon in Egypt, but also shows the technique has the capacity to directly inform chronological debate in the field. The standard New Kingdom model (NKM1) presented here was closest to the high chronology compiled for Shaw (2000, 479) in which the New Kingdom starts in 1550 BC. Furthermore, it was possible to alter the standard model to express differing historical assumptions, although in this case the outputs remained remarkably consistent.

References

Bietak, M. and Hoflmayer, F. 2007, Introduction: high and low chronology. In *The Synchronisation of Civilisations in the Eastern Mediterranean in the Second Millennium BC III* (eds M. Bietak and E. Czerny), 13–24, Austrian Academy of Sciences Press, Vienna.

Dee, M. W., Brock, F., Harris, S. A., Bronk Ramsey, C., Shortland, A. J., Higham, T. F. G. and Rowland, J. M. 2010, Investigating the Likelihood of a Reservoir Offset in the Radiocarbon Record for Ancient Egypt, *Journal of Archaeological Science*, **37**(4), 687–693.

Bronk Ramsey, C. 1995, Radiocarbon calibration and analysis of stratigraphy: the OxCal program, *Radiocarbon*, **37**(2), 425–430.

Bronk Ramsey, C., Dee, M. W., Rowland, J. M., Higham, T. F. G., Harris, S. A., Brock, F., Quiles, A., Wild, E. M., Marcus, E. S. and Shortland, A. J. 2010, Radiocarbon-based Chronology for Dynastic Egypt. *Science*, **328**(5985), 1554–1559.

Gardiner, A. 1961, *Egypt of the Pharaohs: An Introduction*, Clarendon Press, Oxford.

Hornung, E. 2006, The New Kingdom, In *Ancient Egyptian Chronology* (eds R. Krauss and D. A. Warburton), 197–217, Brill, Leiden and Boston.

Hornung, E., Krauss, R. and Warburton, D. A., (eds.) 2006, *Ancient Egyptian Chronology*, Brill, Leiden and Boston.

Kitchen, K. A. 1991, The chronology of ancient Egypt, *World Archaeology*, **23**(2), 201–208.

Kitchen, K. A 2000, Regnal and Genealogical Data of Ancient Egypt (Absolute Chronology I) The Historical Chronology of Ancient Egypt, A Current Assessment. In *The Synchronisation of Civilisations in the Eastern Mediterranean in the Second Millennium BC I* (ed. M. Bietak), 39–52, Austrian Academy of Sciences Press, Vienna.

Manning, S. W. 2007, Clarifying the 'high' v. 'low' Aegean/Cypriot chronology for the mid second millenium BC: assessing the evidence, interpretive frameworks, and current state of the debate. In *The Synchronisation of Civilisations in the Eastern Mediterranean in the Second Millennium BC III* (eds M. Bietak and E. Czerny), 101–138, Austrian Academy of Sciences Press, Vienna.

Reimer, P. J., Baillie, M. G. L., Bard, E., Bayliss, A., Beck, J. W., Blackwell, P. G., Bronk Ramsey, C., Buck, C. E., Burr, G. S., Edwards, R. L., Friedrich, M., Grootes, P. M., Guilderson, T. P., Hajdas, I., Heaton, T. J., Hogg, A. G., Hughen, K. A., Kaiser, K. F., Kromer, B., McCormac, F. G., Manning, S. W., Reimer, R. W., Richards, D. A., Southon, J. R., Talamo, S., Turney, C. S. M., van der Plicht, J. and Weyhenmeyer, C. E. 2009, IntCal09 and Marine09 radiocarbon age calibration curves, 0–50,000 years cal BP. *Radiocarbon*, **51**(4), 1111–1150.

Shaw, I., (ed.) 2000, *The Oxford History of Ancient Egypt*, Oxford University Press, Oxford.

van Dijk, J. 2008, New Evidence on the Length of the Reign of Horemheb, *Journal of the American Research Center in Egypt*, **44**, 193–200.

Waddell, W. G. 1940, *Manetho*, Heinemann, London.

CHAPTER 8

Antagonisms in Historical and Radiocarbon Chronology

M. Bietak

Increasingly, scientific evidence is being used in an uncritical way to support many specific views and arguments. This may serve its purpose for a while, but it is highly doubtful whether such a procedure advances progress in research. In a similar way, it has in some circles become a crime to cast doubt on the reliable accuracy of radiocarbon dating. A critical attitude of itself becomes a casus belli instead of reflecting if and where there could be complications. These remarks are, however, not directed at the Oxford Laboratory, which is perfectly aware of the limitations of radiocarbon dating but is, at the same time, innovative in creating greater accuracy (Bronk Ramsey 2006; Bronk Ramsey et al. 2010; Dee et al. 2009). The VERA Laboratory in Vienna has also always shown an open understanding of the scientific difficulties in achieving accuracy and precision in dating. This article tries to explain why from archaeological-historical point of view the high Aegean chronology, based on radiocarbon chronology, does not work out and that a date of the Thera eruption in the late 17th century BC seems not at all to be possible.

Introduction

The results of the project 'Radiocarbon-based Chronology for Dynastic Egypt' of the Research Laboratory for Archaeology and the History of Art, University of Oxford, under Christopher Bronk Ramsey (Bronk Ramsey *et al.* 2010. See some criticism by Hagens, in press) in co-operation with other laboratories and institutions seem to be right in line with the high Egyptian historical chronology, especially for the era of the New Kingdom. This positive result merits comment.

It seems that the Oxford research project can be regarded as ushering in a breakthrough in the endeavour to weld together historical and scientific dating. Numerous short-lived plant remains which could be assigned to the reign of a specific king were evaluated. The final results were obtained by using historical information such as the range and length of reign of the pharaohs together with ^{14}C dates for a Bayesian model.

It is also a very positive step to incorporate into the Bayesian statistical model the offset of 19.5 years observed from more recent plants from Egypt obtained from Kew Gardens with recorded historical dates. The offset is explained by the fluctuation of radiocarbon in the atmosphere during different growing seasons of plants, especially of wheat-growing in Egypt during the winter season. The offset might be slightly larger if sufficient quantities of winter and summer growing plant remains could be examined separately.

Author's Address: **M. Bietak**, Austrian Academy of Sciences and Vienna Institute of Archaeological Science of the University of Vienna

The results of the Oxford project receive support from the revision of the historical chronology of the SCIEM 2000 research program which postulates a high chronology for the Middle and the New Kingdoms[1] (several data in the meantime have to be revised, but this, however, will have only a small influence on the result of this Bayesian statistic). King Horemheb most probably reigned for only 14 years and not 28 years according to the dates on the wine dockets in his tombs (van Dijk's lecture at the Rhodes Conference 2008; van Dijk 2008; Krauss and Warburton 2009, 128–9). King Seti I probably reigned for only 8–9 years, judging from a vast number of wine dockets in his tomb (Aston, in press), none of which extend beyond his 8th year. Sethnakht may have reigned over 3, perhaps 4 years, instead of the 2–3 years attributed hitherto (Boraik 2007; 2008/09. See also http://weekly.ahram.org.eg/2007/827/hr1.htm). Some adjustments have to be made at the end of the 20th Dynasty (Schneider 2003; overview: Schneider 2010, 394–395).

It is important that the radiocarbon chronology of the Oxford project seems to rule right out the low chronology of Hornung et al. (2006), starting with the New Kingdom at 1524 BC; which is something of a paradox as one of the authors has defended the radiocarbon chronology against the historical-archaeological chronology from Tell el-Dabʿa (Warburton 2011).

The radiocarbon dates of the Oxford project, though numerous, still feature large lacunae. Samples are missing from the Second Intermediate Period and the early 18th Dynasty. The Oxford series first large group of dates in the New Kingdom is from the reign of Thutmose III after which the gap between the historical and radiocarbon chronology begins narrowing down again. It would be very useful to have many more dates from the earlier New Kingdom. The period in question is covered by samples from a stratigraphic series at Tell el-Dabʿa. Direct connections between phases and specific reigns are, however, with the exception of Phases K (Sesostris III), late E/1/early D/3 (Khayan) and C/2 (Thutmose III and Amenhotep II) not possible. The results have just been published (Kutschera et al. 2012) but, in marked contrast to the Oxford dates, the radiocarbon results from Tell el-Dabʿa show an average offset of 120 years (Figure 8.2). The dates are too high. As they are short-lived samples, mainly wheat seeds, the 'old wood effect' can be ruled out. The offset could be scaled down if we were to remove the high terminal data from 'Ezbet Helmy at the end of the series from the reign of Thutmose and before (suggestion from Ezra Marcus). Furthermore, if we deduct the 19.5 years offset of plants, as observed from the Kew garden samples, we would still be left with an offset of $c.$ 80 years.

As a matter of fact, offsets of samples from Ancient Egypt, also apart from Tell el-Dabʿa, are an old problem of radiocarbon research (S. Bonani et al., 2001). Nevertheless the results from Tell el-Dabʿa have caused Warburton and Manning to doubt the reliability of the archaeological dating at Tell el-Dabʿa and the reliability of its stratigraphy: 'the anomaly is the archaeological dating' without offering any serious professional archaeological argument.[2] They insist that the phases in Tell el-Dabʿa have to be dated according to the radiocarbon results and not according to pottery or seals (Warburton 2011, 16–19). Logically, this would mean dating contexts with seals of the Thutmoside Period up to Amenhotep II (Phase C/2) to the Hyksos Period and the Palace of Khayan with seals of this king (Phases late E/1/early D/3) to the time of the late Middle Kingdom. The reader may decide by himself if this is a useful approach for chronology.

Principally, the results of the radiocarbon dates from Tell el-Dab'a endorse the reliability of the stratigraphy as they represent, in toto, a continuous series by itself (Figure 8.2). This shows that the stratigraphy has not caused the problems of the offset. On the dating of the individual phases it is important to explain the link between the stratigraphy of Tell el-Dab'a with the history and chronology of Egypt, as far as this is possible in a conference paper (see already Bietak 2002).

Tell el-Dab'a is a site with a stratigraphy from the start of the 12th Dynasty until the Thutmoside Period, more precisely up to the reign of Amenhotep II and covers a time-span of 600 years (c. 2000–1400 BC). After an interruption, the stratigraphy continues from the Amarna Period to the end of the Ramesside Period. The site was a harbour town and as such can be identified with Avaris, the capital of the Hyksos (15th Dynasty, see Bietak 1975; 1996; Habachi 1954; 2001; van Seters 1966), furthermore with Peru-nefer (Habachi 2001; Bietak 2005; 2009a; 2009b; 2010a; 2010b, 167–170), the naval base of Thutmose III and Amenhotep II and, finally, with the southern part of Piramesse, the Delta Residence of the Ramessides (Habachi 1954; 2001; van Seters 1966; Bietak 1975; 1981; 1996; 2001; Bietak and Pusch, in press).

The whole stratigraphy cannot be assessed in a single excavation area but in several excavation areas which overlap considerably (see Figure 8.1) as is normally the case with Tell excavations. The links are forged by pottery seriation and by recurring architectural features such as building material, house types, tomb types plus a combination of all of them.

Substantial studies on the statistical evaluation of the ceramics have been published (Bader 2009; Kopetzky 2004; 2010; Müller 2008), as has the evaluation of tombs and offering deposits from stratigraphic contexts (Kopetzky 1993; Forstner-Müller 2008; Müller 2008; Schiestl 2010) and typological corpus studies (Aston 2004). There is no other site in the Near East where similar quantitative evaluations have been undertaken and published. As anticipated, statistical evaluation of the pottery collected from settlement layers shows that the percentage of ceramic classes and types has a repetitive pattern in each phase of the settlement of Tell el- Dab'a which reflects the market situation at the relevant time. This is a well-known phenomenon since the evaluation of archaeological materials by seriation started decades ago in prehistoric archaeology (see Bader 2009; Kopetzky 2004; 2010; Müller 2008). The method even works when assessing the linkage of non-stratified sites using a time overlap. The ceramic assessment at Tell el-Dab'a as a historical site linked to wide trading networks is more effective as we possess not only Egyptian, but also Levantine and Cypriot pottery in large quantities which add to the diversity and accuracy of the phasing. The evaluation is based on the knowledge of complete shapes, together with collected fragmentary ceramic material. The percentages were assessed on large quantities of authentic stratigraphic settlement material[3] at Tell el-Dab'a and then compared with the material from other stratigraphies at other parts of the same site, reaching further back in time, whilst showing a significant overlap. On Tell A, however, complete stratigraphies covering the late Middle Kingdom to the end of the Hyksos Period were documented with more than a hundred recorded sections, the bulk of which has not yet been published as the processing of large excavations takes a long time, but the development of ceramic materials has been made available through publication see Bader 2009; Kopetzky 2004; 2010; Müller 2008). The stratigraphy of Area F/I covering the period of the early 12th Dynasty to the early Hyksos Period is in the process of publication (Czerny 1999; Bietak

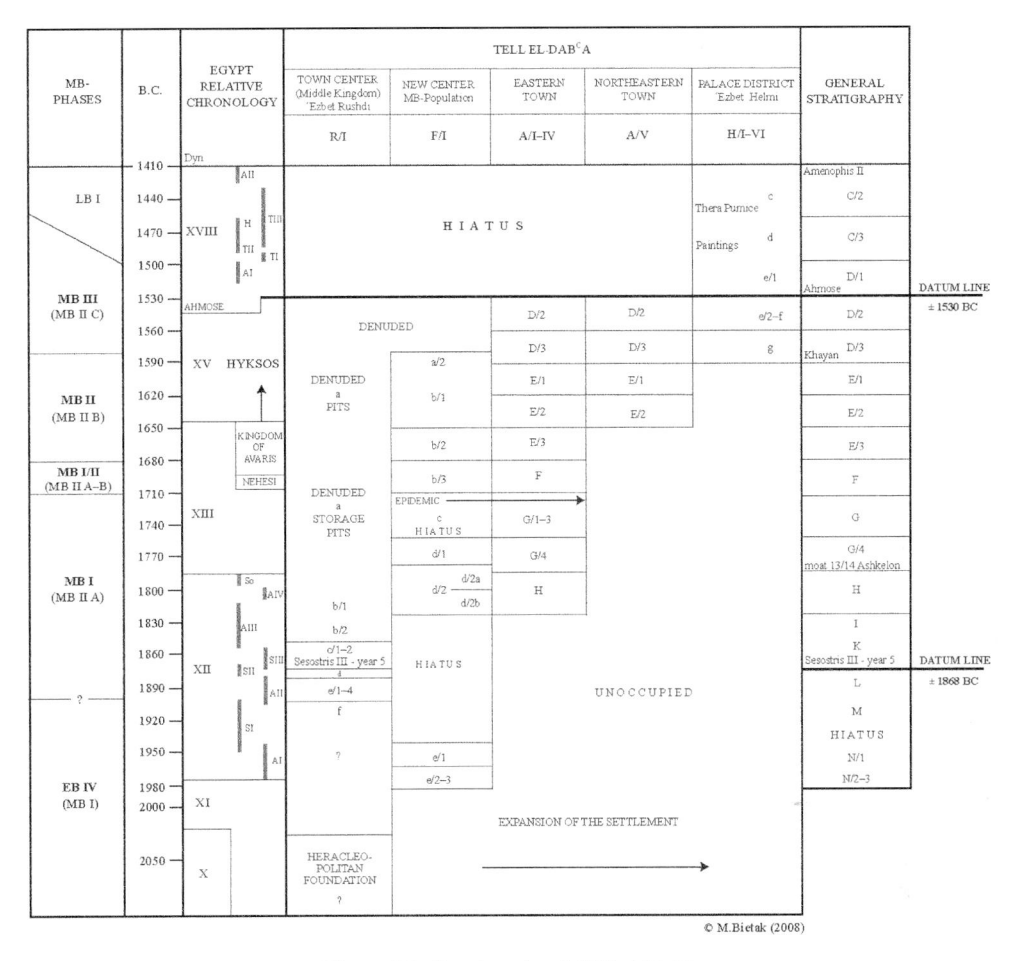

8. Antagonisms in Historical and Radiocarbon Chronology

Figure 8.1: Stratigraphy of Tell el-Dab'a.

et al. in preparation). So are the stratigraphy and material culture of 'Ezbet Rushdi (Area R/I) with a succession of strata from the middle of the 12th Dynasty until the early Second Intermediate Period (Czerny, in press).

In addition to the ceramic assessment and its seriation, which add to the accuracy of stratigraphic excavation over vast expanses, other criteria for compiling evidence for individual settlement phases were also employed, such as follow-up of architectural units and their relationship to adjacent buildings. This also spawned the observation that there are phases in which specific building material and specific house types were introduced for the first time. The discovery of emergency graves surfacing at the end of a specific phase (G/1-3) late in the 13th Dynasty and in two different excavation areas was an observation which confirmed the ceramic and architectural connection of the two stratigraphies. As a result, the stratigraphy and the dating of the phases of Tell el-Dab'a is highly reliable and was confirmed repeatedly by site-to-site comparisons with other excavations (Bietak *et al.* 2008; Bader 2009).

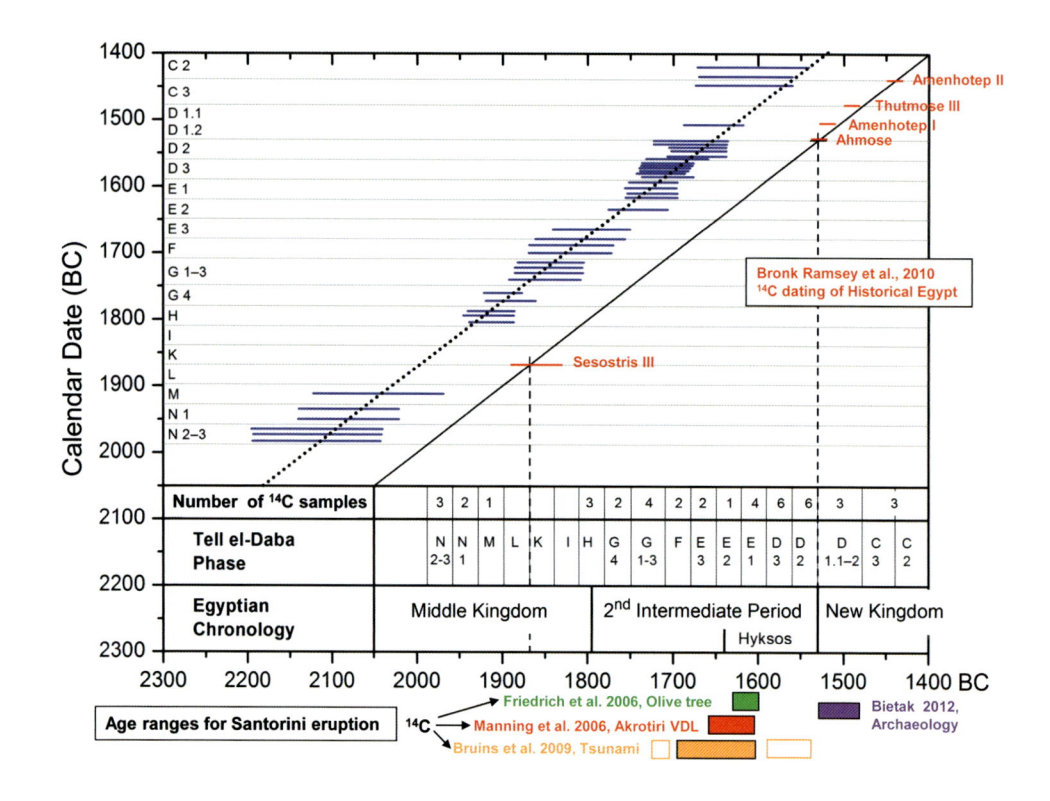

Figure 8.2: The offsets of the Tell el-Dab'a series of radiocarbon dates (after Kutschera et al. 2012, fig. 7).

The ceramic dating was obtained by thorough study of the material culture of the Middle Kingdom, the Second Intermediate Period and the New Kingdom not only at Tell el-Dab'a but also at other sites in Egypt. Combinations of shapes which appear also at other well-dated sites, such as the royal complexes at Dahshur (Arnold 1977; 1982) or Memphis (Bader 2009), were usable for cross-dating.

Besides ceramic dating of the stratigraphies in which at least ten specialists were engaged who compete with and supervise each other, the dating of the stratigraphy at Tell el- Dab'a and its phases rests also on datum lines such as the 5th year of Sesostris III on a stela (1868 BC after von Beckerath 1997 and Kitchen 1990 and to *c.* 1879 according to Schneider 2008) at the start of Phase K, which is tied to the construction of the temple of 'Ezbet Rushdy; furthermore the construction of a palace of the Hyksos Khayan[4] during late Phase E/1/early Phase D/3 and the conquest (abandonment) of Avaris by Ahmose at the end of Phase D/2 (*c.* 1530 BC). In addition Phase C/2 has turned up numerous scarabs from the 18th Dynasty with the latest from Thutmose III and Amenhotep II at the upper end (Bietak *et al.* 2001, 37–38). The datum lines and the cross-links to other well-dated sites create a tight framework for the chronology of the Tell el- Dab'a stratigraphic series.

The median time-span for a phase between the two datum lines of Sesostris III and the conquest of Avaris comprises 31–32 years, between the datum line of the fall of Avaris (c. 1530 BC) and the end of the reign of Amenhotep I. (c. 1400 BC) c. 32.5 years each. Of course we have to understand that some phases, which show sub-phases lasted slightly longer, such as D/2 and G/1-3, but it is significant that the two parts of the stratigraphy in Tell el-Dab'a result in nearly the same statistical median time-span of just over 30 years – which represents roughly the equivalent of a generation. This is the result of applying historical dating to the phasing, based on the stratigraphy, not *vice versa*, by dating the accumulation of the stratigraphy by adding time-spans of 30 years each, as implied by Manning (Manning 1999, 35) although the procedure has been explained repeatedly (e.g. Bietak 2002; 2007).

The Tell el-Dab'a stratigraphy incorporates Egyptian material culture of the Middle Kingdom, the Second Intermediate Period and the New Kingdom. It also incorporates, through imports and locally manufactured copies of Near Eastern pottery types, links to the Middle Bronze Age of the Levant with all its subtle changes. This allows the synchronisation of the two cultures and, by the project *stratigraphie comparée,* close comparison of the superimposed cultural assemblages of Tell el-Dab'a with sites in the Levant (Bietak 2002; 2007). Especially significant was the repetitive pattern of the first appearance of Kamares ware and Middle and Late Cypriot wares in the stratigraphy of a series of sites studied so far (Figure 8.3). This enabled the export of the Egyptian chronology to the Levant and to Cyprus by establishing timelines. The exporting happened, however, not only via the stratigraphy of Tell el-Dab'a and its dating but also via other sites which are connected to each other in a comparative stratigraphy. For example, Phase 14 at Ashkelon with an advanced phase of MB IIA comprising the same combination of artefacts as Phase G/4 at Tell el-Dab'a (among it Kamares Ware of MM IIB) can be dated by 40 Egyptian seal imprints of the late 12th and the 13th Dynasty.[5] This is an independent and very cogent crosslink between Egypt and the Levant which not only thoroughly endorsed the reliability of the Tell el-Dab'a chronology but also helped in finally scaling down the high and middle Chronology of the Middle Bronze Age which had been propagated for years by William Dever.[6] There is also a series of other sites involved in the comparative chronology network. For the time being, see Figure 8.3.

The comparative chronology also made it possible to make a link of Phase F[7] at Tell el Dab'a via the site of Hazor Phase 4/XVII to Mesopotamian chronology which represents the undisputed transition of Middle Bronze IIA to IIB (MB I/II, see Ben-Tor 2004). This link opens up the possibility of comparing the relationship of the historical chronologies of both civilisations (Figure 8.4).

Hazor, an enormous Tell of 80 ha, is mentioned at least 19 times in connection with trade and diplomatic emissaries on an equal level with Mari, Qatna, Aleppo, and even Babylon in the Mari archives which date back to the last decades before the town was conquered in the 32rd year of Hammurabi. It is significant that Egypt seems not to be mentioned in the archives with any certainty, as Egypt did not play a significant role in the Near East at that time which still predated the Hyksos Period. According to the present excavator of Hazor Amnon Ben-Tor, the correspondence referred not to the small Hazor in the late MB IIA period, but must be referring to the larger-scale Hazor of the MB II B period. Although the construction of the enormous ramps started as early as during the MB IIA–B transitional period, it must have taken one or two decades to finish off the vast enlargement of the town. This would take us into Hazor Phase 3/XVI, fitting within

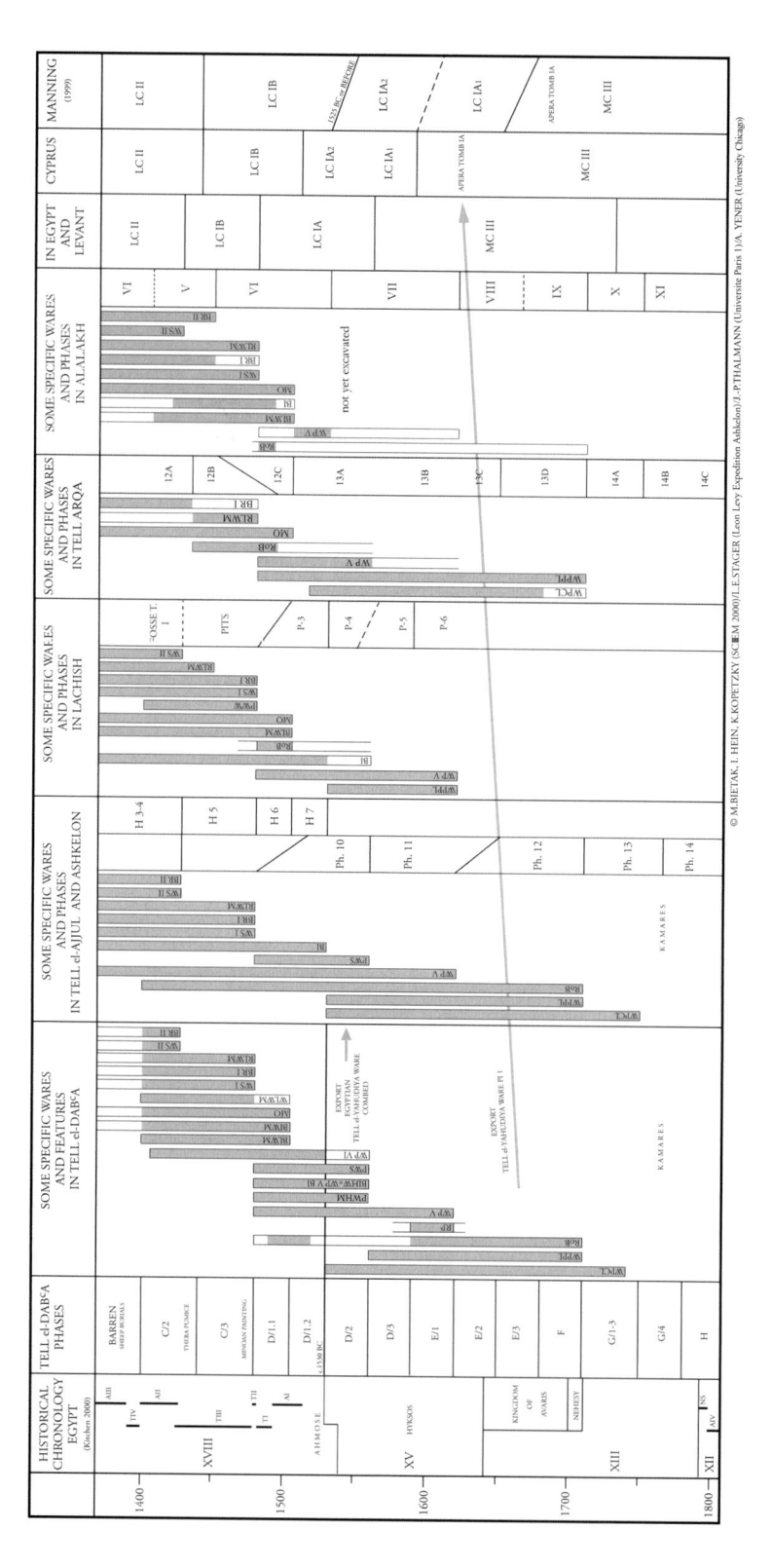

Figure 8.3: Stratigraphie comparée, *showing the first appearances and the time-spans of specific ceramic families in a site to site comparison.*

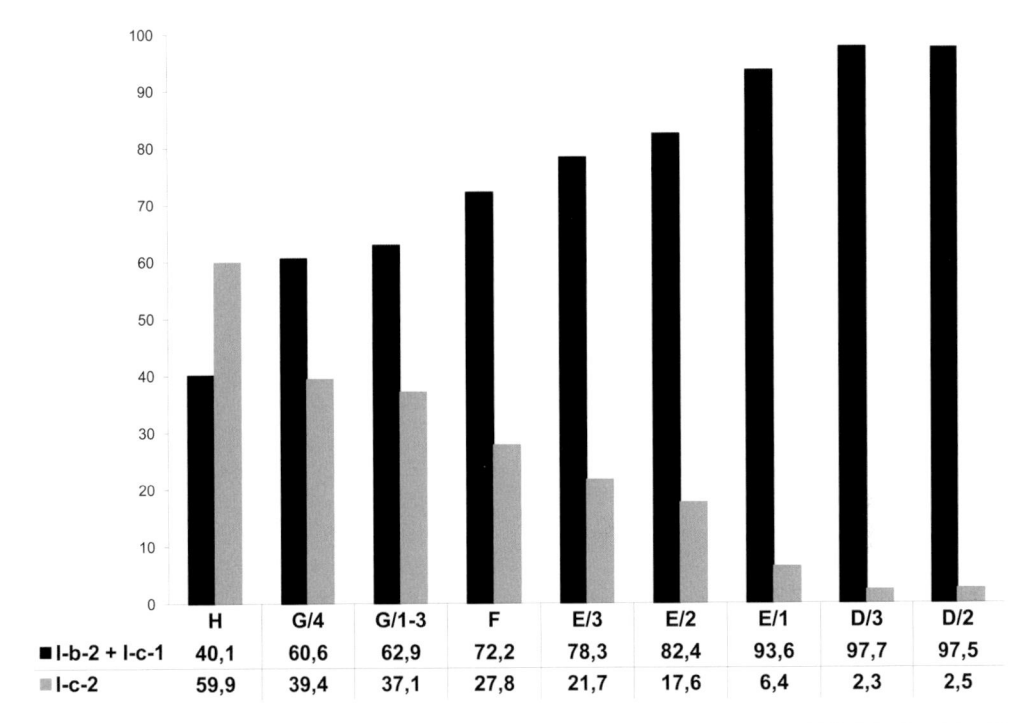

8. Antagonisms in Historical and Radiocarbon Chronology

	H	G/4	G/1-3	F	E/3	E/2	E/1	D/3	D/2
■ I-b-2 + I-c-1	40,1	60,6	62,9	72,2	78,3	82,4	93,6	97,7	97,5
■ I-c-2	59,9	39,4	37,1	27,8	21,7	17,6	6,4	2,3	2,5

Figure 8.4: Percentage proportion between chaff tempered and dung tempered ware in Tell el Dab'a (after K. Kopetzky 2010, fig. 35).

MB IIB. As the transition between MB IIA/B (Hazor 4/XVII) progressed, according to the synchronism with Tell el-Dab'a, at around 1700 BC or slightly before, we would arrive at the first half of the 17th century for the Hazor (3/XVI) of the Mari correspondence (Ben-Tor 2004). This puts strong downward pressure on the Mesopotamian chronology; according to Amnon Ben-Tor the evidence of Hazor is compatible only with the *New Chronology* by Gasche *et al.* 1998a; 1998b).

However, the *New Chronology* can be ruled out, since, among other arguments, nine generations of Hittite rulers between Mursilis I and Suppiluliuma I would put pressure on the raising of the Mesopotamian chronology. The time-span of nine generations could be calculated using 30 years, 28 or 25 years per generation, resulting in sum-totals of 270, 252 or 225 years. This would take us from the Dahamunzu affair at *c.* 1317 BC[8] at the latest after the death of Tutankhamun (on the assumption Dahamunzu had been Ankhesenamun (see Breyer 2010), back to *c.* 1587 or to *c.* 1567 or to *c.* 1542 BC for the start of the reign of Mursilis I. If we calculate, starting with the death of Akhenaten in *c.* 1328 BC (Dahamunzu being equated with Nefertiti) backwards we come to a date impossibly high for the end of the Old Babylonian Period. But even our calculation from Tutankhamun's death backwards puts a stress in favour of a chronology higher than the *New Chronology*.[9]

Applying the High or Middle Mesopotamian Chronology does not square with the chronological position of Hazor Phase 3/XVI or even Phase 4/XVII, as dated by synchronization with Tell el-Dabʻa (Bietak *et al.* 2008) or by the seal impressions of the 12th and 13th Dynasty from the oldest moat of Ashkelon[10] belonging to a late phase of the Middle Bronze IIA Culture. Only the Low Mesopotamian Chronology (Hammurabi 1728–1686 BC) or the recent and 8 years' shorter chronology of Jörg Mebert (Mebert 2010) provide the time frames for meeting the narrow corridor able to harmonize the Mari correspondence with Hazor 4/XVII. Even Hazor 3/XVI is compatible only in a very limited time-span with the Mari correspondence before the conquest of the town in the 32nd year of Hammurabi within the Mebert chronology (Figure 8.5). That is why, with a view to obtaining a more comfortable time-span for this link, it would seem feasible that Hazor in the Mari correspondence could by then have been a town at the transitional phase of MB IIA/B when the extension works with the towering ramparts started, and when the town already at that stage had the power to commission such works whilst, at the same time, was by then enjoying political recognition as a major power in this part of the Levant.

To sum up, the combined chronological framework for the synchronisation between Egypt and Mesopotamia is not dictated by the Mebert Chronology, but by the chronology of Hazor and its synchronisation with Tell el-Dabʻa. It is a concise chronological architecture with a very high rate of probability and confirms the Low Chronology or the Mebert Chronology which are only 8 years apart. The dendro-chronology of Açemhüyük is used to support the Middle Chronology (Kuniholm *et al.* 1996; later: Kuniholm and Newton 2004; Manning *et al.* 2001; Manning *et al.* 2003) but one should not forget that it is a floating series and, even if the cutting dates of the trees involved were assessed correctly in time, the beams could have been taken collectively from an older building.

In this connection has to be mentioned a fragment of an Akkadian letter from Tell el-Dabʻa which can be dated, according to its writing system, to the last four or five decades of the Old Babylonian Period at the earliest (Van Koppen and Radner in Bietak and Forstner-Müller 2009). It was found in the filling of a well belonging to the latest phase of the palace of the Hyksos Khayan and is associated with pottery from the middle and the late Hyksos Period.[11] This means the letter could be from the time of Khayan or afterwards. It is hoped that more of such material will turn up over the next, few years through the continuance of excavations at this palace.

The archaeological/historical chronological framework also incorporates the date of the eruption of the Thera volcano. Radiocarbon results seem to favour a date in the second half or even the end of the 17th century BC (Manning *et al.* 2006; Manning 2009; Friedrich *et al.*, 2006; Friedrich and Heinemayer 2009; but see for a *contra*ry opinion Wiener 2009). This is not compatible with the chronological framework worked out for this area, and based on Egyptian chronology. The eruption in relative terms dates to the Late Minoan IA Period (Niemeier 1980, 74–76; Manning 1988, 26; Warren and Hankey 1989, 116–8; Merrillees 2001, 94; Warren 2009). The proposition that the inscribed calcite lid of the Hyksos Khayan found in Knossos is from a MM III context has been denied by Palmer, Pomerance and many others (Palmer 1981; Pomerance 1978, 27–28; last: Phillips 2008, II, Cat. No. 163, 97–98) because of some intrusive LM III sherds. However, re-excavation of the site by Colin Macdonald has re-confirmed that the date originally published by Evans is mainly right and the context should be placed in the MM III, most likely the MB IIIB phase with the possibility of transition to LM IA (MacDonald 2002, 44f.; MacDonald 2003. See also Warren 2010, 391; Höflmayer 2010, 218–221). We have seen above that Khayan,

	Konvolut	(286) I-e-1 Kochtopf	(293) I-e-2 Schüsseln	(298) I-e-2 Kochvase	(312) II-a Schale	(339) II-c-2 Zir Typ 4	(374) I-b-2 Schale IL	(374) I-b-2 RP-Schale IL	(429) I-e-2 Schale IL
D/2	3189 / 3206	2,3							
	3193	4,5							
	3416 / 3417	2,8							
	3490 / 3894	4,5							
	10046	0,7					0,3		
	10045						1,5		
	3182 / 3183	2,9					0,4		
D/3	3449 / 3491	7,6							
	3478 / 3633	2,2							
	3429 / 3430 / 3499								
	3551 / 3567 / 3629	1,5					0,4		
	3504 / 3507 / 3512								
	3519 / 3523 / 3524	1,9					3,1		
	3492 / 3495 / 3496	2					1,6		
	3341 / 3804	0,5					2,8		
	3342 / 3837	0,9					4,1		
	3339						7,6		
	3789	1,1					10,1		
	2580	3					10,9		
E/1	3488 / 3501 / 3502								
	3508 / 3515 / 3516								
	3518	1,1					8,2	0,7	0,4
	3450 / 3482 / 3493								
	3509 / 3510 / 3644	0,4					9,1	4,4	
	1811 / 1812 / 2103 / 2302	0,4				1,7	19,5	2,4	
	2509 / 2532	1,2				1,5	5,4	0,2	
	3350	2,9				0,5	7,9	1	
	3353	0,5				4,9	11,2	0,5	0,2
	3360 / 3371	2,4				1,3	13,2	1,5	
	3334	0,6		0,6		0,8	10,2		
	3358	1,6				0,7	10	2,3	
E/2	1611	0,5				1,7	8,1	2,5	
	3802	2,1				0,6	4,8	3,1	0,3
	2303	2,9				1,1	5,8	2,9	
	2364 / 2568 / 2573					0,8	4,2	1,2	
	2305	0,2		1		2,9	4,3	0,4	1,2
	1523 / 1565 / 1592								
	1906	0,2				2,7	3,4	1,5	
	1853	0,4				2,6	2,6	0,2	
	1882	0,8				3,3	4,3	0,3	
	2409					0,8	5,1	0,7	0,3
	2146			0,7		0,8	0,9	0,4	0,6
	2733	0,4		0,7	0,2	3	0,7	0,7	
E/3	2579			0,4		3,1	4,2		
	2470	1,2		1,5		2,6	5,4	1,1	0,3
	2588	0,6		3,1		4,6	5,7	0,3	0,6
	2836					2,1	0,2		0,2
	2300 / 2306					0,3	1	0,3	0,5
	4039 / 4182			1		5,3	3	1	0,3
	2745			0,3		8,7	0,9		
	2663			1,3		0,2	4	0,2	
	2319					2,8	2,8	0,4	
F	4231 / 4243					3,1	5,6	2,7	
	2662 / 2664			0,7		3	0,3	0,2	
	4236 / 4256			1,1		3,7	0,5	1,3	
	4249			1,1		4			0,7
	4014 / 4024	0,3		1,3		8,7	2,6		
	2474 / 2489					1,1	2,1	1,8	0,7
	4056					5,9	1,4	0,5	
	2585 / 2594 / 2618	0,2				0,9	0,5		
	2849	0,2		0,4		3,6	0,2		
	2879	1,5		0,3		6,8		0,1	
G/1–3	3484 / 3486	0,8				6,3	2		
	4229 / 4247					5,8			
	2821 / 2844 / 2981				1,2				
	3119 / 3306		0,3		0,4	2,6			
	3076	0,5			0,5	4,4	0,3		0,5
	2587 / 2629	0,4				3,2			
	3278	0,7	0,4		0,4	5,2			
	2815					3,8	0,6		
	2771				1,9	2,5			
G/4	3483	2,6				2,3			0,6
	3639								
	3479					0,1			
	3656					0,2	0,2		
	3634		0,2						
	2995 / 3319				0,7				
	3021 / 3044 / 3056								
	2983 / 3314 / 3315								
	3316								
	2817 / 2837 / 3728	0,2	0,2		0,2	0,1	0,2	0,1	0,1
	3380						0,3		
H	4275 / 4277 / 4278								
	4280 / 4283								
	2861 / 3321 / 3325								
	3326 / 3329 / 3732								
	2484 / 2895								
	2598								
	4276 / 4281 / 4282								
	4284 / 4288 / 4297								
	4299								

Figure 8.5: Battleship graph showing the abundance of wares within the time flow, according to the stratigraphy of Tell el Dab'a (after K. Kopetzky 2010, Table 9 with an inserted ideal explanation graph).

the third Hyksos, reigned according to the high historical chronology used in SCIEM 2000 between *c*. 1600 and 1580 BC (Bietak 2002; 2007). The low chronology of Krauss and Warburton, 2009) arrives at an even different position of *c*. 26 years later – which increases the gap between radiocarbon chronology and historical chronology. We also need to factor in the unknown interval between production, export and final deposition of the calcite vessel of Khayan. This would push the start of LM IA to a time which is most likely to postdate his reign. This is incompatible with the radiocarbon dates of an eruption (late in the LM IA Period) from the middle to the end of the 17th century BC. The start-date of the LM IB from 1600 BC onwards posited by Sturt Manning (Manning 2009, 225) would bring the early part of this period right back into the reign of Khayan in whose period (Ph. E/1–early D/3) we have a boom of Middle Cypriot imports at Tell el-Dab'a.[12] The assumption of such early origins is in no way substantiated by archaeological data; not a single LM IB sherd has been reported from the Khayan context in Knossos neither during his era (Ph. E/1–D/3) at Tell el-Dab'a. However, the positioning of the Khayan lid into MM IIIB would fit very well with the date of the MM IIB phase *c*. 75–100 years earlier, in the first half of the 18th century BC by Kamares Ware finds (overviews in Merrillees 2003a; Höflmayer 2010, 93–135) in Phase G/4 at Tell el-Dab'a (Walberg 1991; Bietak 2002, 41, fig. 15; Walberg 1998; on pinpointing the date to MM IIB, see MacGillivray 1995), the Moat Deposit of Phase 14 at Ashkelon in association with Egyptian pottery and seals from the early 13th Dynasty (Bietak *et al.* 2008, 51–52), and in the Khardji tombs in Beirut where the Middle Bronze Age IIA occupation of the tomb can also be dated to the same period.[13] At Sidon an older Kamares vessel, dated to MM IIA, was also found in a slightly earlier context (MacGillivray 2003; 2004; 2008). If we, however, accept an eruption date of Thera in the middle to second half (Manning *et al.* 2006, 568) or even towards the end (Friedrich *et al.* 2006; Friedrich and Heinemeier 2009; Heinemeier *et al.* 2009) of the 17th century BC and an inception of the LM IA period in *c*. 1700 BC or even 1730 BC we have to squeeze MM IIB, MMIIIA, MM IIIB into less than a century – a very unlikely scenario, while LM IA should have lasted about 150 years (Höflmayer 2009, 194–195). In such a case, Late Cypriot pottery would be found by late 13th Dynasty contexts instead of Middle Cypriot III pottery found at that time in Egypt and the Levant (Bietak and Höflmayer 2007, 18, fig. 4; Bietak *et al.* 2008; recently, Maguire 2009). Late Cypriot Wares of LC IA, such as Bichrome Wheelmade-, Proto White Slip-, White Painted VI-Wares start as imports only from the latest phase of the Hyksos Period onwards, whilst LC IB Wares such as Base Ring I, White Slip I and Red Lustrous Wheel-made Ware can be found only from the Thutmosid Period onwards in Egypt and the Late Bronze Period in the Levant (Bietak and Hein 2001; Bietak and Höflmayer 2007, 18, fig. 4).

Archaeological-historical dating is not consistent with the date of eruption of Thera in the 17th century BC. Attempts by Sturt Manning to explain the high Aegean Chronology in archaeological terms required assumptions which many find hard to accept[14] and overlooks such evidence as contradicts high chronology.[15] This starts by identifying LB I already in phase E/1 in Tell el-Dab'a by the presence of White Painted V Ware (Manning 2007, 118), which is, however, a Middle Cypriot Ware and perfectly in line in the phases cited. This kind of reasoning would not be the natural interpretation and is only considered because it is in keeping with radiocarbon results. If the archaeological material is to be assessed as independent evidence, it is important to do so on its own terms. The debate

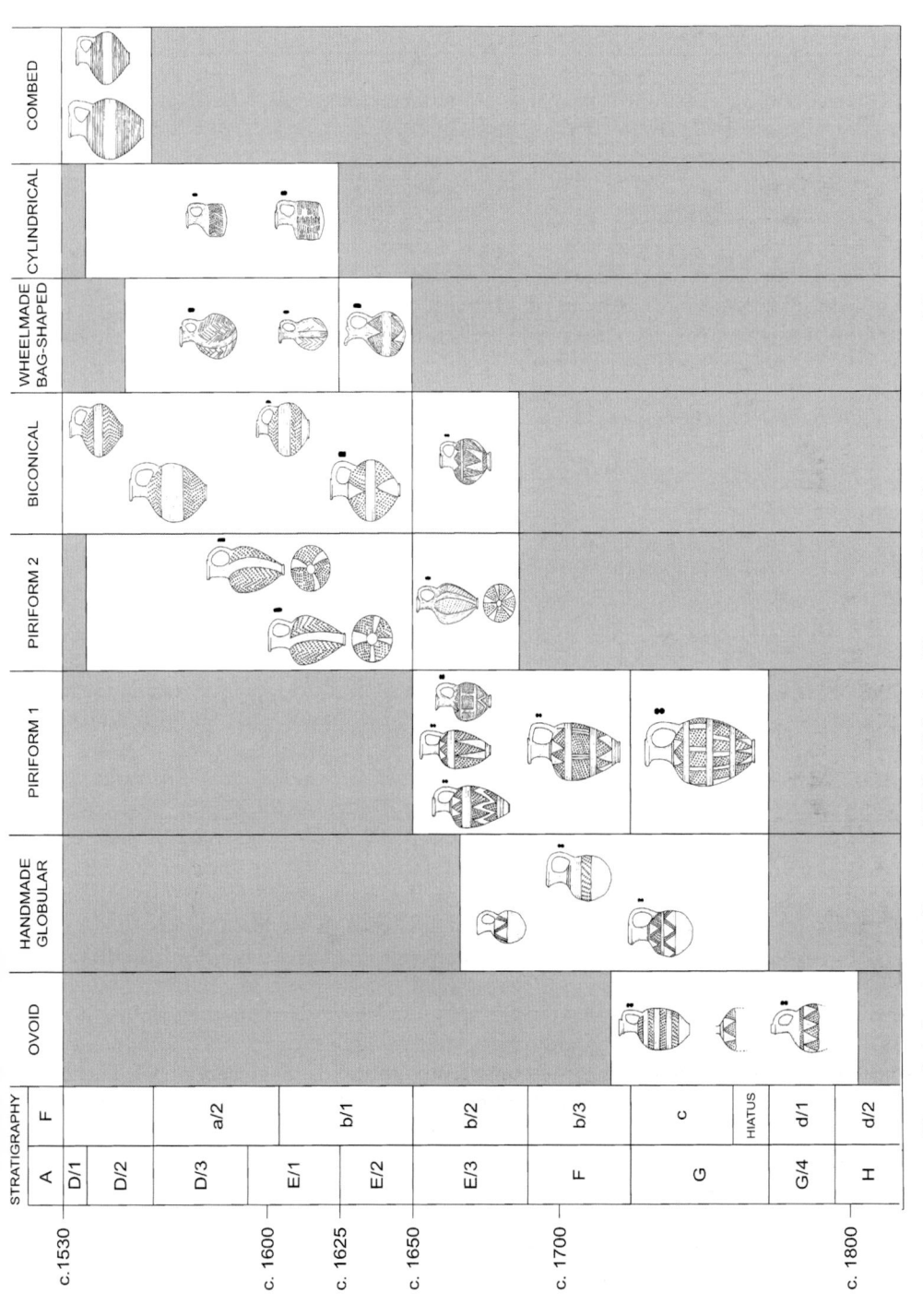

8. *Antagonisms in Historical and Radiocarbon Chronology*　　87

Figure 8.6: Stratigraphic Position of Tell el Yahudiya Ware in Tell el Dab'a (after Aston and Bietak 2012).

centres, finally, on the date of the Theran White Slip I bowl acknowledged to originate in a pre-eruption layer during the French excavations on Thera (last thorough assessment by Merrillees 2001).

There is near-consensus that the Late Minoan IA phase parallels the Late Cypriot IA phase (Merrillees 1971, 49; 2001, 94; Manning 1988, 26; Warren and Hankey 1989, 116–118). Indisputably, a French archaeological mission found a White Slip I bowl in a pre-eruption level at Thera.(Merrillees 2001). This ware neither appears in Egypt before the early Thutmosid Period (in Tell el-Dab'a Phase C/3, after 1500 BC; see Bietak 1998; Bietak and Hein 2001; Wiener 2001), nor at any site in the Levant in a safe context before the Late Bronze Age (Figure 8.4). Sturt Manning has tried to explain an earlier appearance of this ware in Thera, by claiming that the Thera bowl is from northern Cyprus and produced much earlier whereas the finds in Egypt and the Levant originate mainly from south-eastern Cyprus and produced much later (Manning 1999, 150–191), but this is not supported by detailed analysis (Manning 2007, 119–121). It is true that we have regional development in Cyprus, whilst the regions stayed intouch with each other, northern Cyprus also receiving a number of imports from Egypt during the Second Intermediate Period (Vermeule and Wolsky 1990, 386–387, Tomb V, chamber 1, intact block, MC III context) and Egypt also absorbing imports from northern Cyprus at that time (Maguire 2009, 31, fig. 10/1). Moreover, there are no scientific analyses which would have gone to show that PWS and WS I Wares were originally produced in northern Cyprus. As regards WS I, there is strong scientific evidence that this ware was produced at the foothills of the Troodos mountains around Sanidha and Kalavassos in the south of the island (Courtois 1970; Courtois and Velde 1980; Todd and Pilides 2001, 26, 40; see also for the WS II Ware Gomez *et al.* 2002, 23–36). However, other production centres also need to be factored in but, so far, there is no evidence that WS I Ware was produced in the north. Moreover, the claim that the Thera bowl belongs to an early production of this ware has the shortcoming that it does not rest on a serious analysis taking stratigraphic material or tomb groups into account. The early date of the Thera bowl is based on a purely art-historical/typological study of elements of the pattern of the Thera bowl by W. D. Niemeier (1980, 72–74), who himself relies on a study of M. Popham (1962). The problem is that there are only few reliable tomb groups which would allow a relative chronological date of the Thera bowl. Eminent specialists in Cypriot archaeology, such as Vassos Karageorghis and Robert Merrillees, acknowledge the typological assessment of Niemeier and Popham but do not date the sound parallels from Palaepaphos/ Teratsoudhia Tombs 104 before LC IB (Karageorghis 1990, 56; Merrillees 2001, 93), and at the earliest at the transition of LC IA-IB (Karageorghis 1990, 31, pl. XVIII, K. 41). Unfortunately, other good parallels from T. 19 (Swedish Expedition) from Enkomi, Hagios Iakovos and from Milea Vikla Trachonas T. 10 have no dateable contexts (Åström 1972b, 830–831). According to the parallels drawn, Karageorghis and Merrillees consider the Thera bowl as originating from southern Cyprus (finally: Merrillees 2001, 93; see also Karageorghis 1990, 27, pls. VI, XV/E11), and not from the north, as Sturt Manning suggests.[16]

The bowl also shows signs of wear and tear and was repaired during the time it was being used (Merrillees 2001, 93; see also Karageorghis 1990, 27, pls. VI, XV/E11). Good parallels are also available from the north of the island at Toumba tou Skourou but this is not proof positive that they had been produced there. It would be worthwhile conducting more scientific analyses to see whether the WS I examples cited were traded or produced locally.

Louise Maguire (2009, 84–87) maintains that the chronological appearance of Cypriot wares at sites such as Tell el-Dab'a, Tell el-'Ajjûl, Ashkelon and other Levantine sites represent export chronologies, *termini ante quos*, which cannot be verified on Cyprus itself owing to a lack of excavated stratified sites dated by imports. Conversely, it is difficult to believe that Late Cypriot Wares were already being produced more than 100 years earlier on the island before they were exported, especially as exports from Cyprus increased substantially during the Hyksos Period.

Besides such reasoning, an important way of assessing first appearances of Cypriot Wares on Cyprus is to collate Egyptian and Levantine exports to Cyprus. This should enable us to assess the accuracy of the Egyptian-Levantine dating of Cypriot exports. The application of this method is indeed possible with Tell el-Yahudiya Ware produced in Egypt. A tomb context (Tomb 1 A) in Arpera-Mosphilos (Merrillees 1974, 43–77, figs 31/14–16, 38–40) contained three such jugs which, according to NNA analysis (Kaplan 1980, 229 below), were produced in Egypt. One is a Piriform 1b type (Merrillees 1974, figs 31/14, 38; new terminology: Levanto-Egyptian Type I.2, Aston and Bietak, 2012 fig. 89) which occurs in contexts of the transition of MB IIA/B, in Tell el-Dab'a it was found in Phase F; the second is a Piriform 1c jug (new terminology: Levanto-Egyptian Type I.3; Bietak 1989, figs 2, 10; Aston and Bietak 2012, fig. 102); because of its rolled rim it dates already to early MB IIB, in Tell el-Dab'a in Phase E/3; the third is Piriform 1d (Levanto Egyptian Type I.4, 1A) and dates to the same period; it only occurs in Ph. E/3 in Tell el-Dab'a which is shortly before the start of the Hyksos rule (Aston and Bietak 2012, fig. 111). The tomb contexts are defined by P. Åström as middle of Middle Cypriot III (Åström 1972a, 197, no. 6), by R. Merrillees (1974, 75) as late Middle Cypriot III. Nor, however, was any Late Cypriot vessel found among the rich contents of the tomb. The first mentioned Tell el-Yahudiya jug imported from Arpera was according to Egyptian Chronology produced around 1700± 20 y BC, the two later jugs in the first half of the 17th century (see Figures 8.3 and 8.7), which would be the time shortly before the high eruption date when, according to the high Aegean chronology, Late Cypriot pottery was already being produced, a claim for which we are lacking in any evidence. We also have to take into consideration a certain time-span between the production, export and interment of the jugs, probably amounting to several decades. This evidence shows that the Middle Cypriot Period must have lasted until mid-17th century BC. We would go as far as to speculate, because of the interval between production in Egypt and burial in Cyprus, that it could have lasted well into the second half, if not to the end, of the 17th century for which we have more firm evidence with later Tell el Yahudiya jugs found in terminal MC III contexts (see below).

The following evidence is contrary to Sturt Manning's suggestion that Late Cypriot pottery was produced earlier in the north of the island than in the east, so that the new pottery has not yet reached e.g. the Arpera Mosphilos tomb collection: two examples of Piriform 1c and a fragment of the same type (Levanto-Egyptian Type I.3) of Tell el-Yahudiya jugs, one of them very late version with a globular body and candlestick rim (Vermeule and Wolsky 1990, 386–387, fig. 181, upper row right and lower row left), and a jug with lotus and bird design, bipartite handle and rolled rim (Type J.1.3), again typical of early MB IIB (found repeatedly in Phase E/3 in Tell el-Dab'a), appeared in Tomb V in a

MC III context in Toumba tou Skourou in northern Cyprus (Vermeule and Wolsky 1990, figs 182–183). The pieces have not been scientifically analysed for their origins, but the figural style moves all Tell el-Yahudiya jugs of this site in northern Cyprus into the same period as the Arpera jugs: early MB IIB (Tell el-Dabʿa, Ph. E/3). From the same context also originates a Piriform 1 juglet with zig-zag design (Vermeule and Wolsky 1990, fig. 181, 2nd row, no. 2. The jug and its pattern look to the author to be of Syrian origin), a biconical black burnished juglet with rolled rim and bipartite handle which can be dated to the same period (Vermeule and Wolsky 1990 fig. 181, 1st row no. 3). Everything looks like a context which moulds together in its combination of artefacts.

Proof that MC III definitely lasted into the second half, possibly to the end of the 17th century and even beyond, is provided by Kalopsidha, Tomb 11 where biconical Tell el-Yahudiya Ware (Types L.5, L.8; Aston and Bietak 2012 figs 167, 176, 179, 180, 182) with incised designs, produced in Egypt and most likely at Tell el-Dabʿa, from the Phases E/2 late, E/1, D/3 to D/2 were found in an undisputed MC III context (Kaplan 1980, 78, 162, figs 87b, 102b 103b; Åström 1972a, 196). The production of those types did not start before the onset of the 15th Dynasty, the Hyksos Period in Egypt (c. 1640–1530). More controversial are the contexts of these types of Tell el Yahudiya Ware in Enkomi, Swedish Expedition tomb 20/4 (Sjöquist 1940, 101; Åström 1972a, 194–5; Kaplan 1980, 78, fig. 89b, Good parallels with this jug have been found in Ph. E/1-D/3 at Tell el-Dabʿa) and French excavations Tomb 11 (Kaplan 1980, 78, figs 99a, 103d and a cylindrical juglet fig. 5f which.is assignable to Ph. E/1 at Tell el Dabʿa), assigned by E. Sjöquist (1940) to LC IA, but by P. Åström to the end of MC III (Åström 1972a, 194–195, the latest object was a WP IV–VI jug).

Taking all of this evidence together, the Egyptian Group of Tell el-Yahudiya Ware, produced during the Hyksos Period in Egypt (second half of 17th and the 16th century BC) appears in terminal MC III and LC IA contexts (Åström 1972a, 130–132, 197, no. 6, 199, 233; Merrillees 2007, 91). The latest of the Egyptian Tell el-Yahudiya Ware (with horizontally combed pattern, Type Group L13; Kaplan 1980, figs 117d–121) found at Tell el-Dabʿa (Aston and Bietak 2012: Egyptian Group L. 13, figs 202–206, 253) and at Tell el-Yahudiya (Kaplan 1980, fig. 121a) was also found on Cyprus. Unfortunately nearly all examples of this kind from the island are without records which would allow a date. The only safe context is from Enkomi, British excavation, tomb 88, but without published find circumstances (Kaplan 1980, 78). It is likeliest to date to LC IA, which would coincide with the LC IA imports such as White Painted VI-, Proto White Slip- and Bichrome Wares with linear pattern in Phase D/2 at Tell el-Dabʿa. It is the time which preceded the introduction of Black Lustrous Wheel-made-, Bichrome with figural patterns and still later Red Lustrous Wheel-made-, White Slip I-, Base Ring I-Wares (Figure 8.3). This information shows that the first appearance of Late Cypriot wares on Cyprus can, on the present evidence, be assessed at or after 1600 BC; their first appearance in Egypt about 30–40 years later in Ph. D/2.

The offset in dating between the archaeological-historical and the carbon chronology is therefore not a unique phenomenon in the Delta, created by a misperception of the dating of the stratigraphy of Tell el-Dabʿa (as claimed by Manning and Warburton; see, however, Bader 2009; Kopetzky 2004; 2010; Müller 2008). One should in this context also point out the results of the investigations of the scientists Max Bichler and his team on the first appearance of pumice from the Minoan eruption at Thera produced as a result that from

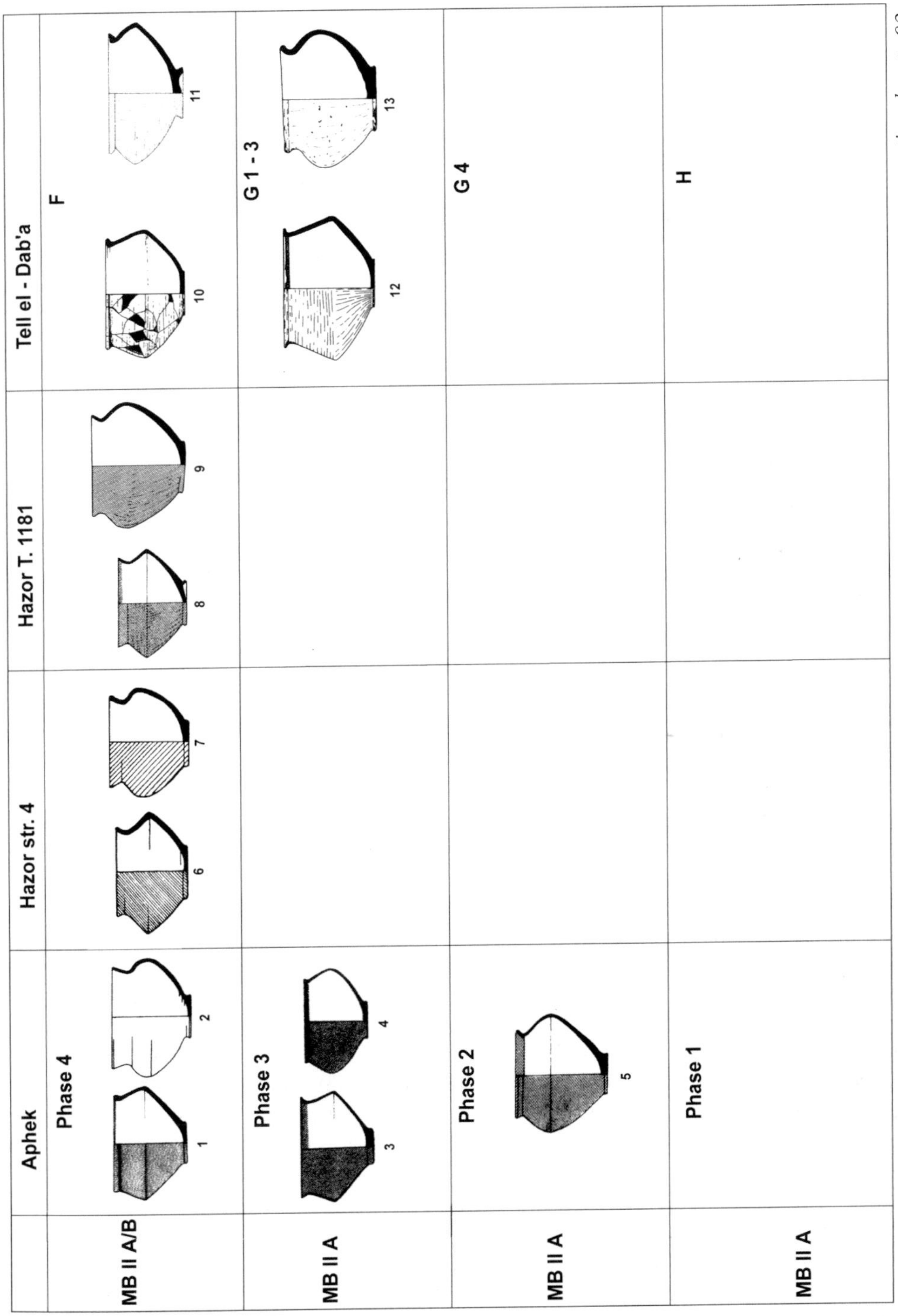

8. Antagonisms in Historical and Radiocarbon Chronology

Figure 8.7: The connection between Tell el-Dab'a and Hazor (after Ben-Tor 2004, figs. 2 and fig. 7).

continued on p. 92.

92   *M. Bietak*

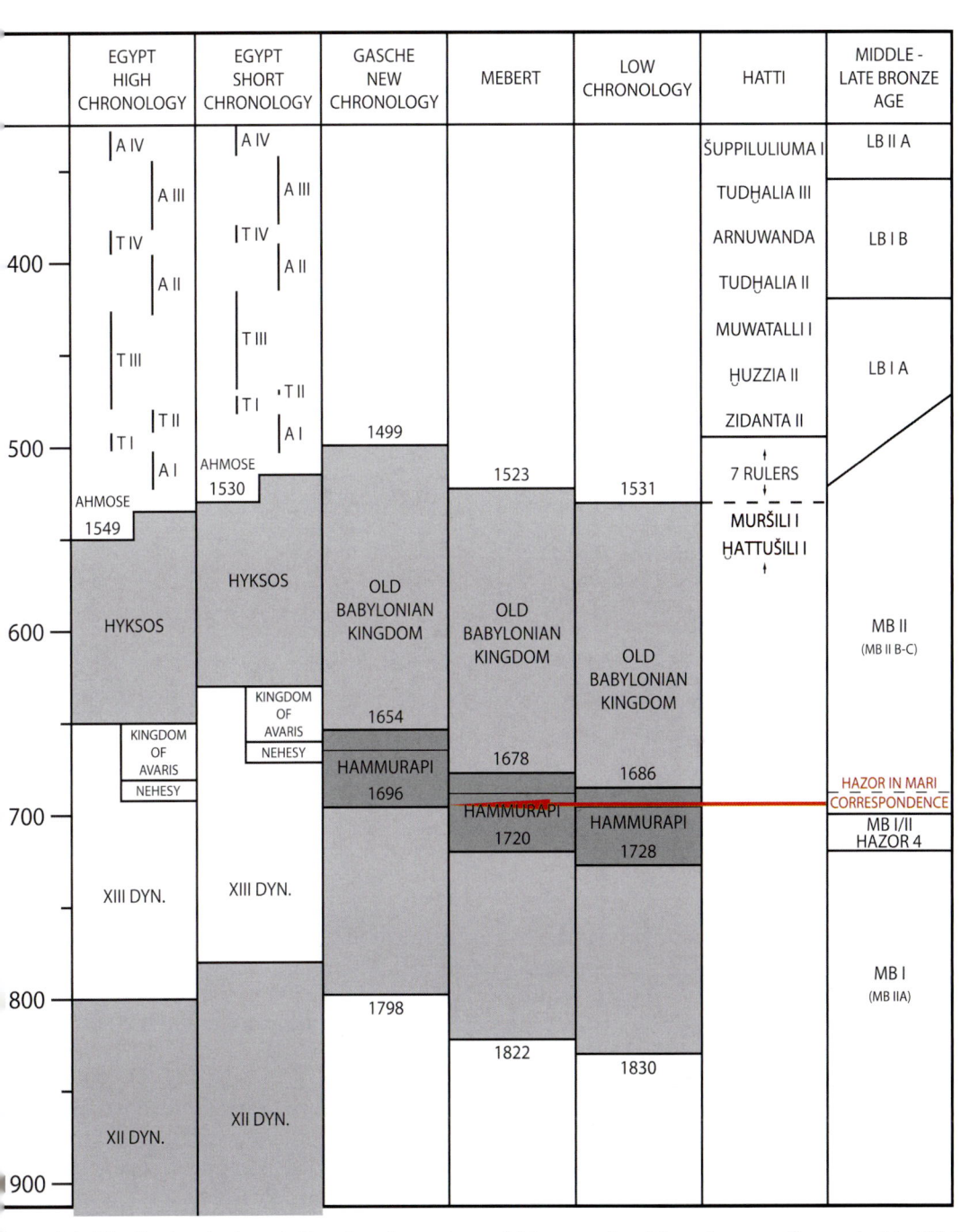

8. *Antagonisms in Historical and Radiocarbon Chronology* 93

Figure 8.8: *The Synchronisation of Egyptian, Levantine and Mesopotamian Chronology according to the Mari-Tell el-Dab'a Synchronisation (© M. Bietak 2012).*

c. 400 samples collected from archaeological excavations in Egypt and the Levant (last: Sterba *et al.* 2009). Thera pumice appeared in Egypt for the first time in the Thutmoside Period and in the Levant in the Late Bronze Age, starting to surface there only some time after the start of the 18th Dynasty (*c.* after 1500 BC; see Dever 1992; Bietak 2002; 2007). Pumice from contexts of the Middle Bronze Age in the Levant and in Egypt is all from different volcanoes such as Kos, Nisyros and others. The evidence accumulates as more samples from the Middle Bronze Age have been examined in the meantime and the evidence for a late appearance of Thera pumice is mounting. Sturt Manning rejects this evidence as proof of a low chronology, claiming that pumice was used in workshops as an abrasive and could have been collected long after it was transported by sea to distant beaches or traded long after the eruption.[17] This is not a convincing line of argument given the fact that 1st Thera pumice is of superior quality and 2nd that its first appearance is an abundant one as shown in the stratigraphy at Tell el-Dab'a (Ph. C/2), Tell Hebwa (New Kingdom), and Tell el-'Ajjûl in Horizon H5 within the same combination of pottery as in Tell el-Dab'a with Egyptian Thutmoside pottery, with Bichrome I-, WS I- and RLWM Ware (see Figure 8.2). This can hardly be a coincidence and points strongly in the same direction, namely that the Theran eruption happened in the early 18th Dynasty, shortly before the first appearance of its pumice.

When speaking of the offset between the radiocarbon and the archaeological/historical chronology and the good fit of both with the results of the Oxford Laboratory, we should not forget that the biggest radiocarbon project of Ancient Egypt before the Oxford programme, the Bonani *et al.*, 2001 – study showed for the Old and Middle Kingdoms without the application of Bayesian statistics distinct higher offsets which are 200–300 years older than the historically produced estimates (Bonani *et al.* 2001). Oxford showed that the differences could be reduced by Bayesian statistics (Dee *et al.* 2009). It is only the statistical mix of radiocarbon dates and historical data which helps to forge a chronology in harmony with historical data. Without this detailed historical knowledge, there should not be such overconfidence shown over radiocarbon accuracy. Otherwise one would date, for example, Phase C/2 at Tell el-Dab'a with a series of royal scarabs from Ahmose to Thutmose III and Amenhotep II (Bietak *et al.* 2001, 37–38) to the Hyksos Period as Manning suggests (Manning 1999, 92–95) and likewise Warburton (Warburton 2011). The offset seems to be a wider eastern Mediterranean phenomenon which can be recognized by a network of imports and exports all over the area.

For the region of the Aegean, the historical chronology has been established long ago, wholly independently from the Tell el-Dab'a excavations, by Peter Warren (1987; 1996; 2006; 2010), Vronwy Hankey (Warren and Hankey 1989), Hartmut Matthäus (1980; 1995) and others and meets in LM IA an offset of the radiocarbon chronology of over 100 years[18] as in the Tell el-Dab'a series. There are, however, regional differences and probably regional complicating factors. In Tell el-Dab'a the offset seems to be continuous from the Middle Kingdom, throughout the Second Intermediate Period. For the Aegean Felix Höflmayer, M. Wiener, B. Hänsel et al. have identified the time of the offset between archaeological-historical dating and radiometric dating as follows (Bietak and Höflmayer 2007, 20; Höflmayer 2009; Wiener 2009, 286–7; Höflmayer 2010, 317–318, 335–343; Hänsel *et al.* 2010, previous note, 362–367; see also Manning 2007, 111–112). The differences between the two dating methods seem to start with MM III, especially around the transition between

MM III and LM IA, with a hundred years or even more. The culmination of the offset is during LM IA with a difference in dating the Minoan eruption of the Thera volcano of more than 100–120 years at the end of LM IA, whereas the offset seems to diminish to about 50–70 years in LM IB. In LM III the two dating methods do not contradict each other (Warren 2010, 384). It is, from a logical point of view, inconceivable that, in the 14th century BC during the era of Amenhotep III and Akhenaten, both systems were more or less in accord and, only one and two centuries before, we have as much as a difference of 100 years in northern Egypt and in the Aegean (Bietak and Höflmayer 2007, 20). As regards, the well-researched 18th Dynasty and its regnal succession, this mistake cannot be found in archaeological-historical chronology. One can only conclude that the radiocarbon chronology asserted does not, for this region, produce results which are distributed in chronometrically proper fashion.

It is, in this context, important to notice that offsets in this period cannot be verified everywhere in the Aegean. For example, the calibrated dates for LH I at Tsoungiza/Nemea (Peloponese), albeit from charcoal, fall, according to the archaeological-historical time estimate, into the 16th and 15th century and are not in accordance with the other dates from the early Late Bronze Age in the Aegean (OxA-11312, 11313, 11314) whereas the LH I/II transitional samples of the same site provided much older results, perhaps explainable by the old-wood effect [OxA 11309 (16th century), and OxA-11310, 11311 (19th and 18th century BC)].

One should also study the radiocarbon results from Hagios Mamas/Olynth in Macedonia which represent a stratified series of 18 layers from EH to LH IIIC covering a millennium (Hänsel *et al.* 2010, no. 81). The authors of this study have modelled all dates from this site on the flow of raw data for the INTCAL 04 calibration curve by imposing a stratigraphy of equally long time-spans of strata (50 years each, Figure 8.9; Hänsel *et al.* 2010, fig. 15a). In general, the dates of strata 18-7 (no carbon dates for strata 11 and 10) can be accommodated well within the calibration curve and so do the dates of the strata 3-1. The dates of strata 6-4 (LHIIIA1 – LH IIIB early to midst) are a succession of outliers, leaving distinct wiggles of the spread of INTCAL 04 raw data and seem to be acceptable according to the analysts within the historical chronology, as established by Mycenaean pottery. In a second attempt of adapting the length of strata to the indications of the archaeological records, the fit of strata 6-4 improves but, instead, the results of the strata 3-1 become outliers (Hänsel *et al.* 2010, fig. 15b). The results teach us that we have to contend with dates which are obviously inconsistent within a chronometric time-span.

The early Late Bronze Age, and in the case of Hagios Mamas, the advanced Late Bronze Age, are not the only periods with problems in radiocarbon dating. We have heard recently in a presentation by J. Regev, P. de Miroschedji and E. Boaretto at the Radiocarbon Conference held in April 2011 in Paphos[19] and in September 2011 in Berlin that the dates of the Early Bronze Age III in Israel/Palestine, tied by exports to the Egyptian Old Kingdom, reach according to radiometric dating back to 2,900 BC and ending already at 2,400 BC (contrary to Syria and Lebanon with imports of the 6th Dynasty), covering a period of 500 years, whereas the Early Bronze II Period, equivalent to the 1st and 2nd Dynasties, would cover only 200 years, which is definitely too short. Similar results have been in the meantime produced from the excavations at Jericho and Khirbet Batrawy, Tell Abu-el-kharaz and other sites.[20]

96 M. Bietak

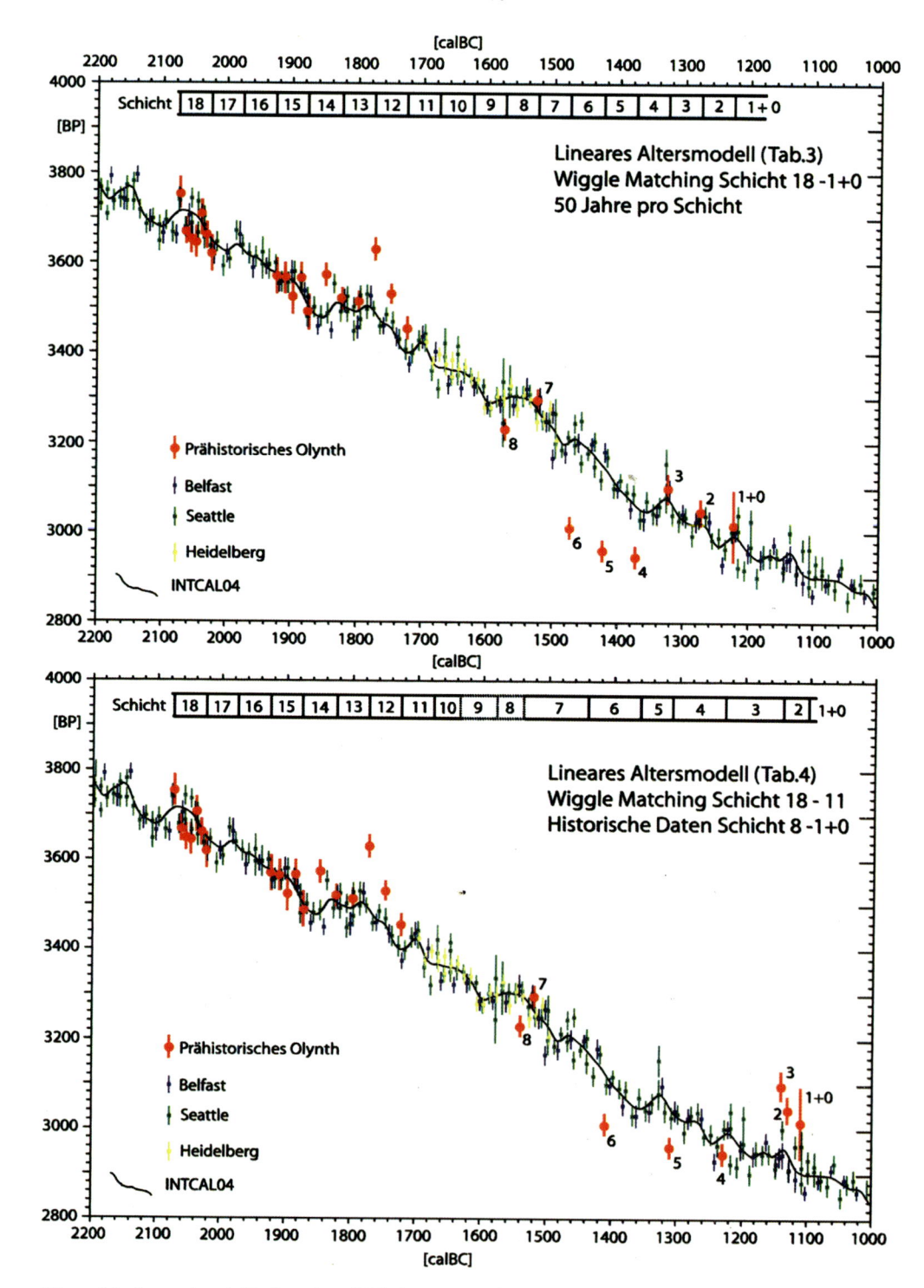

Figure 8.9: Sequencing of Early to Late Helladic series at Hagios Mamas (After Hänsel et al. 2011, fig. 15).

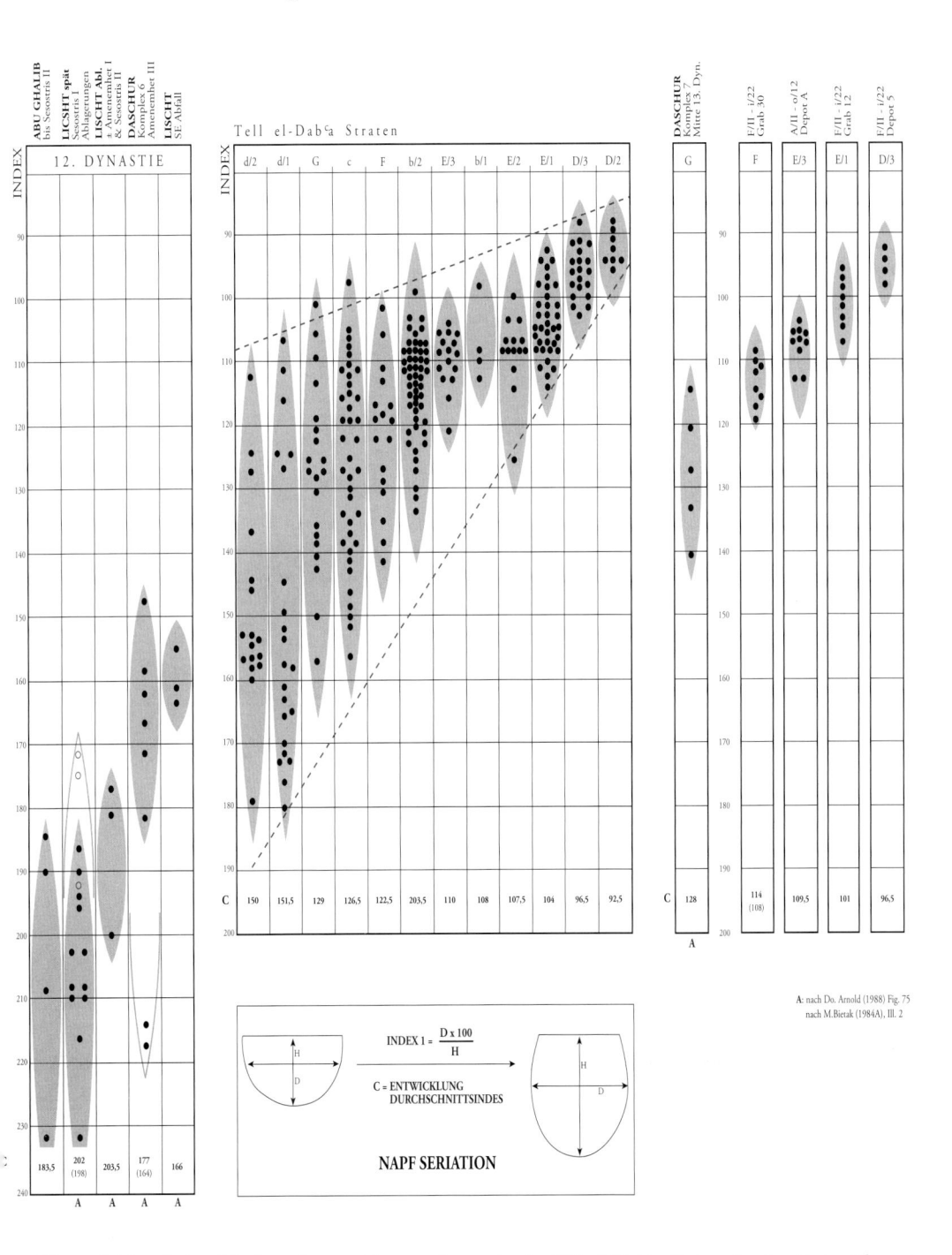

8. *Antagonisms in Historical and Radiocarbon Chronology*

Figure 8.10a: Seriated indices of round bottomed cups in the Tell el-Dab'a Series, showing that settlement collections have a wider variability than collections from tombs or closed contexts, due to the effect of redundant material (after Bietak, E & L 2, fig. 2).

98 M. Bietak

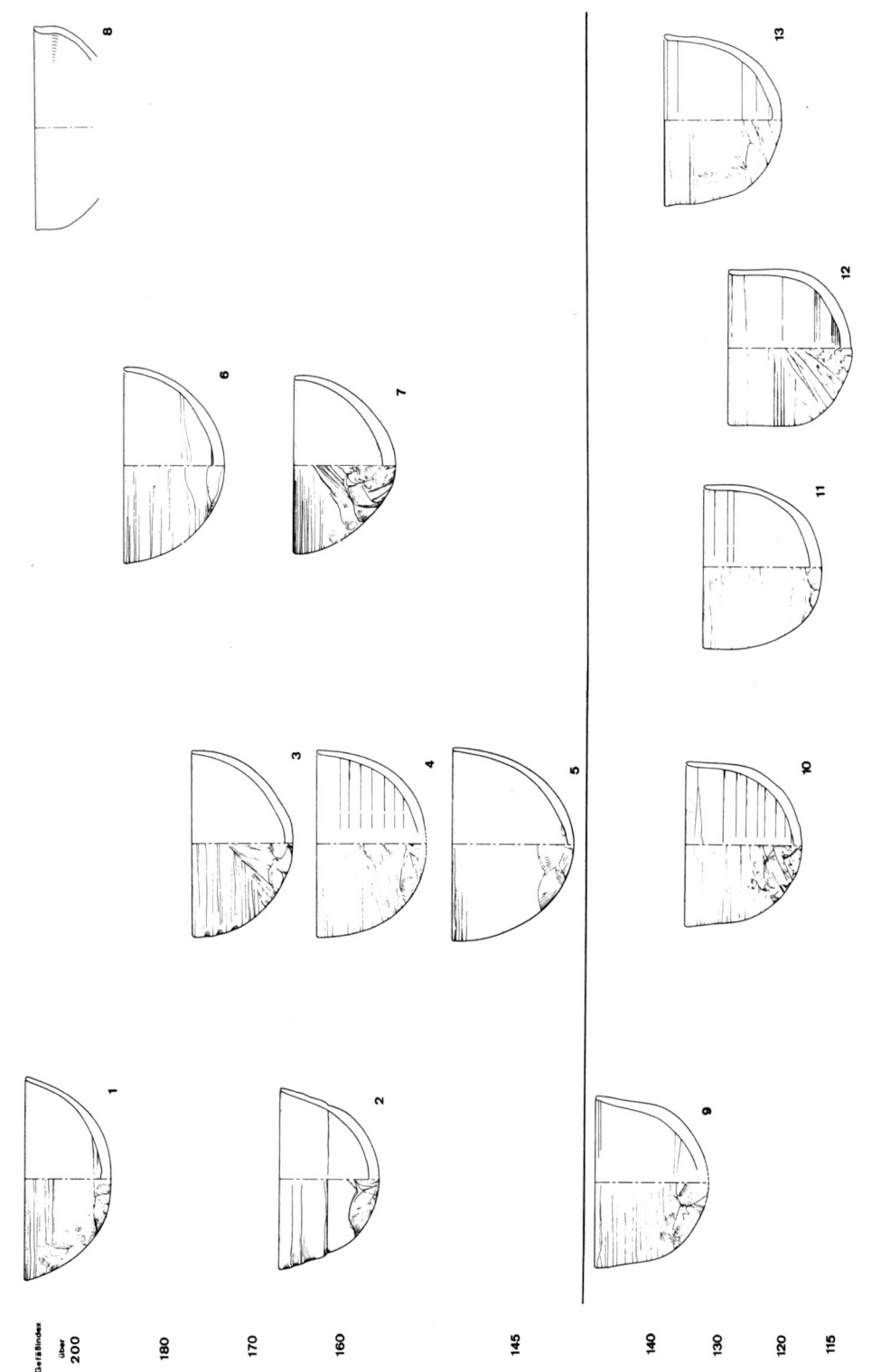

Figure 8.10b: Differences in the proportions of round bottomed cups according to the German excavations at Dahshur (after Dorothea Arnold 1982: figs 17+18)

The difficulties with the consistencies of radiocarbon data, especially the wide range of data from the same or similar contexts and the various problems which complicate dates, such as upwelling of gases with the release of old carbon, were highlighted in a series of articles by Malcolm Wiener, 2003; 2006; 2007; 2009; 2010). Needless to say, the lack of precision of radiocarbon dates can be improved by the sequencing of data and by Bayesian statistics. It is, however, debatable whether this would help reveal systemic complications. It is high time to assess the geographical position of the offset dates in the Eastern Mediterranean. The problems are complex and should be considered when identified all together, such as the seasonal offset of 19.5 years of seeds in Egypt. Yet there are other complicating factors, which have hardly been studied systematically. The offsets which bother us come from sites near the sea, that is, not only the Aegean but also the Nile Delta and, to some extent, around the coastal Levant where samples far from the sea in Middle and Upper Egypt – the backbone of the Oxford radiocarbon series – seem to produce dates which are reasonable, whilst samples from the same time horizons – but from regions near the sea or even the Dead Sea – show offsets.

This would mean that region and time could play a role in explaining the offsets. The hypothesis proposed here is that the sea and its activity could play a role in producing offsets, for example by upwelling and by the estuary effect when seawater reaches inland, which has always been the case in Tell el-Dabʿa in antiquity every spring, the drought season in Ancient Egypt. During spring, before the construction of the barrages, the Nile shrank to one-fifth of its volume and river navigation used to be difficult (Le Père 1822, 140–141). Around this time, seawater used to penetrate the nearly empty Nile channels up to about 30 km from the coast. Tell el-Dabʿa – ancient Avaris, ancient Perunefer and the southern part of ancient Piramesse – was a port city and came within the range of the seawater penetration (Bietak 2010a; 2010b, 167–169). This could have had an effect on the absorption of carbon. But this may be, surely, only one complicating factor out of several. In the Aegean the marine offset far from riverine activity is to be considered modest.[21] The effects of volcanic activity are considered by some as trivial but the literature shows the extensive scale of CO_2 venting in Italy.[22] Future research should be directed specifically to addressing different complicating factors. Such a measure would contribute to the understanding of regional and temporal offset factors which would make radiocarbon dating a more accurate tool for archaeology. Accepting only the asserted but often challenged radiocarbon dates per se and rejecting the accuracy of archaeological-historical chronology, especially of Egypt, can produce only repetition of systemic inconsistencies and will without doubt prolong the present deadlock between the two systems of dating.

Another matter that would be deserving of some consideration is the difference in the statistics between radiometric and archaeological dating. In archaeology, contexts are dated according to the latest objects. A sizeable collection of potsherds in a continuous stratigraphic settlement context normally features redundant ceramic fragments from previous layers, pushed upwards by the excavation of pits, of foundation trenches or by the decay of fabricated mud bricks from older settlement remains. Material from previous strata can be recognized quickly if the time difference is big. Redundant material in continuous settlement collections is harder to assess, but shows up, for example, in much wider variances of ceramic indices in comparison to closed context-material (Figure 8.10a). They are apt to signal more advanced age than the time-span of the stratum. The date is obtained from the latest array of the collection. Late outliers are normally met with suspicion.

Dates in radiocarbon chronology are in most cases obtained by combining the results of samples, even if spread over a considerable time. Outliers are usually omitted although the decision of what is an outlier or not is sometimes strangely biased. Redundant material can also be expected among organic matter, especially among seeds. Such matter cannot be identified by typology but may also originate from older strata or from decaying building material, or may even have been carried by the wind. Secure plant materials comprise only seeds found *in situ* in storage jars. In most cases, we are lacking in such documentation. We should therefore wonder whether more realistic results could not be obtained by putting more emphasis on the samples with the youngest dates, especially if they form a coherent series. Felix Höflmayer has shown that such considerations could lead to results which are no different from the dates obtained by archaeological-historical dating (last: Höflmayer 2010, 304–316).

Acknowledgements

The author would like to thank David A. Aston, Felix Höflmayer and Malcolm H. Wiener for reading the manuscript and giving critical advice. All mistakes remain, however, mine.

Notes

1 Preliminary results: Schneider 2008; Schneider 2010. To clarify, we use the term **a** high chronology, not **the** High Chronology, as we still stick to the beginning of Thutmose's reign at 1479 BC but raising Ramses II to 1290 BC. Nevertheless, we advocate a start of the New Kingdom at around 1550 – which is considered nowadays as a high chronology, versus a low chronology, the New Kingdom starting at 1524 BC (Krauss and Warburton 2009). There is mounting evidence that Thutmose II must have reigned more than 1 or 3 years. A minimalist calculation of chronology runs the risk of a widening inaccuracy of years.

2 In his critique of the Tell el-Dab'a-chronology, Warburton (2009 144) seems to conflate typology with seriation as a basis for dating. The former is the study of the development of shapes over time based on morphological observations and conclusions. The latter is based on a combination and quantification of artefact types and the statistically evaluated changes of such combinations/quantities over time. Needless to say, seriation may also incorporate, together with the study of combinations, the typology of shapes, but is based on context and stratigraphy. Seriation is an acknowledged and refined method used to assess relative chronology. It is a method which has developed far beyond its 19th century origins. For some key-literature, see Brainerd 1951; Baxter 2003; Robinson 1951; Kendall 1969; 1971; Michels 1973; Doran and Hodson 1975; Ihm 1978; Orton 1980; Shennan 1997; Van de Velden *et al.* 2007 and others.

3 The author rejects the claim by David Warburton 2009 that the material originates partly from foundation ditches or is mixed, and in addition any such residual material would make the dating of the phases too old, not too young.

4 The reign of Khayan started *c.* 65–72 years before the conquest of Avaris (11 years for Khamudi, 40 + x years for Apophis, 16–20 years for Khayan with a possible short reign of Yanassi (the Manethonian Iannas) in between. As we can date the conquest of Avaris to between the 18th and the 20th year of King Ahmose, the conquest of Avaris happened around ±1532–1530 BC

(for the low chronology of Krauss and Warburton which is not used here, the dates have to be lowered 26 years). This would put the start of Khayan's reign at about 1602–1595 BC which would fit.in perfectly with the date of the late phase E/1 and beginning of phase D/3 (soon after 1600 BC) at Tell el-Dab'a obtained by seriation of ceramics.

5 Stager 2002; Bietak *et al.* 2008. Also the scarabs in the transitional MB IIA/B and early MB IIB tombs of Rishon Lezion, with their scarabs dating back to the 13th and 14th Dynasty, show that only a low chronology applies to the Middle Bronze Age in the Levant (Ben-Tor 1997, 162–163; 1998; 2003, 244–46; 2007, 119–121).

6 Dever 1992; Ward and Dever 1994; see, however, amongst others Bietak 1991; 2002; 2007; Weinstein 1992; 1996; D. Ben-Tor 2003, 2007; that is why Warburton is not in touch any more with the research results in this part of the world. Even Dever himself has retracted his high chronology (verbal statements made to Daphna Ben-Tor and to myself).

7 Phase F at Tell el-Dab'a is in the middle of the two datum lines of the Tell el-Dab'a stratigraphy. It follows, however, Phases G/4 and G/1-3 with their crosslinks to Ashkelon Phase 14 and the 13th Dynasty. Its position in time is therefore assured by a terminus post quem. Moreover, within the temple precinct of Phase F and E/3, two door jambs with the cartouche of King Nehesy of the 14th Dynasty have been found. Even those stones have not been retrieved from safe contexts but from pits. The fact that two stones with cartouches of the same king are involved and that the temple was the only monumental building in this area makes a link highly likely (S. Bietak 1984).

8 The dates are calculated on the assumption that Seti reigned 9 years on the basis that the wine dockets of his tomb do not postdate his 8th year. If we assume, for Seti, at least 11 years (this date from the Gebel Barkal stela has recently, however, been put into doubt by van Dijk 2011) then all dates mentioned in this passage have to be raised 2 years.

9 This conclusion was reached by a colloquium on Mesopotamian chronology January 2009 organised by SCIEM 2000 at the Austrian Academy in Vienna with the participation of A. Ben-Tor, H. Hunger, J. Klinger, F. van Koppen, P. Matthiae, J. Meberg, R. Pruzsinszky, K. Radner, and K. R. Veenhof.

10 Stager 2002. Daphna Ben Tor 2007 dates the seals to the 12th and 13th Dynasty, whilst Christa Mlinar dates most of them to the 13th Dynasty. This dating discrepancy is irrelevant as the most recent seals are what date the context.

11 Currently being studied by D. A. Aston.

12 Middle Cypriot Pottery such as WP III–IV, WP V and RoB Wares (but not a sherd of Late Cypriot pottery) has also been retrieved from the middle Hyksos Palace with numerous seals of Khayan.

13 Saidah 1993-1994. R. Schiestl 2009, 166–168, fig. 103, No. 7345, found a perfect match of the amphora with a potmark in Tell el-Dab'a, tomb F/I- p/17-no. 14, Phase G/4 (early 13th Dynasty).

14 For example that the early Thutmoside wall paintings of Keftiu delegations depicting LMIA/LHI objects represent heirlooms (Manning 1999, 209–220); that the early 18th Dynasty calcite jar found in Shaft Grave IV (Warren 2006) could have been produced as early as the 2nd Intermediate Period without offering pertinent contexts; that the first appearance of Thera pumice in the Thutmoside Period in Egypt and the Late Bronze Age in the Levant has no significance as to the eruption date because its use is confined to workshops only, although Thera pumice is of superior quality; that LM IB and LC IB started as early as 1600 BC although we have in Egypt at that time still Middle Cypriot pottery which continued till the first third of the 16th century; that the phases and contexts at Tell el-Dab'a should be dated by radiocarbon rather than the archaeological dates, even if royal seals and inscriptions provide much later termini post quos; alongside other highly questionable and unproven assumptions mentioned in the main text.

15 For detailed criticism on assessments leading to the high Aegean chronology see Bietak (2004).
16 Manning claims to have answered my criticism with serial citations. Looking at this claim, we do not find a chronological assessment of the Theran bowl, except his citation of the old Niemeier article which deals with the bowl only on a typological basis of its ornamentation. No contexts are offered.
17 Manning 2007, 120 writes: "…These data would instead offer termini ante quos – with the length of the ante being unknown, but quite plausibly of several decades duration on any understanding (and potentially more)". – To some decades I would agree, but not to a century. This is not a convincing argument given the superior quality of the Thera pumice over the pumices from Nisyros and Kos, used in the Middle Kingdom and the Second Intermediate Period (personal communication by Max Bichler from the Atom Institute ofthe University of Technology of Vienna).
18 See the critical discussion of the offset phenomenon in the Olynth series (Hagios Mamas) by B. Hänsel *et al.* 2010, 361–367.
19 Regev, Boaretto and Miroschedji (submitted for 2011). I would like to thank the three authors for permission to use their results before the publication comes out in press.
20 Lorenzo Nigro lecture on the 14th December 2010 at the Conference on the Archaeology of Jordan in Vienna and personal communication by Felix Höflmayer for which I would like to thank him.
21 *Pers. comm.* Graham Hagens (17th of September 2011)
22 *Pers. comm.* Malcolm H. Wiener with reference to: Chiodini *et al.* 1999; Rogie 1996; Rogie *et al.* 2000.

Bibliography

Allen, J. P. 2009, The Amarna Succession, In *Causing His Name to Live: Studies in Egyptian Epigraphy and History in Memory of William J. Murnane* (eds P. J. Brand and L. Cooper), 9–20, Leiden.

Arnold, D. 1977, Zur Keramik aus dem Taltempelbereich der Pyramide Amenemhets III in Dahschur, *MDAIK*, **33**, 21–26.

Arnold, D. 1982, Keramikbearbeitung in Dahschur 1976–1981, *MDAIK*, **38**, 25–65.

Aston, D. A. 2004, in collaboration with M. Bietak, with assistance of B. Bader, I. Forstner-Müller and R. Schiestl, *Tell el-Dab'a XII, A Corpus of Late Middle Kingdom and Second Intermediate Period Pottery* (Vol. I: Text, vol. II: Plates), UZK XXIII, Vienna.

Aston, D. A., in press, Radiocarbon and the Reigns of Tuthmosis III and Ramesses II, *E & L*, **21**.

Aston, D. A. and Bietak, M. 2012, *Tell el-Dab'a VIII, The Classification and Chronology of Tell el-Yahudiya Ware*, with contributions by Hanan Charraf, Aren Maeir, Robert Mullins, Lawrence E. Stager, Ross Voss and Karin Kopetzky, UZK XII, Vienna.

Åström, P. 1972a, *The Middle Cypriote Bronze Age*, The Swedish Cyprus Expedition, vol. IV, Part 1B, Lund.

Åström, P. 1972b, *The Late Cypriote Bronze Age*, The Swedish Cyprus Expedition, vol. IV, Parts 1C and 1D, Lund.

Bader, B. 2009, *Tell el-Dab'a XIX, Auaris und Memphis in der Hyksoszeit, Vergleichsanalyse der materiellen Kultur*, UZK XXXI, Vienna.

Bagnall, R. S. and Frier, B. W. 1994, *The Demography of Roman Egypt*, Cambridge.

Baxter, M., 2003, *Statistics in Archaeology*. London.

Ben-Tor, A. 2004, Hazor and Chronology, *E & L*, **14**, 45–67.

Ben-Tor, D. 1997, The Relations between Egypt and Palestine in the Middle Kingdom as reflected by Contemporary Canaanite Scarabs, *Israel Exploration Journal*, **47**, 162–189.

Ben-Tor, D. 1998, The Relations between Egypt and Palestine during the Middle Kingdom as reflected by Contemporary Canaanite Scarabs, In *Proceedings of the Seventh International Congress of Egyptologists, Cambridge, 3–9 September 1995*, 149–163, Louvain (ed. C. J. Eyre).

Ben-Tor, D. 2003, Egyptian-Levantine Relations and Chronology in the Middle Bronze Age: Scarab Research, In *The Synchronisation of Civilizations in the Eastern Mediterranean in the Second Millennium B.C. II* (ed. M. Bietak), 239–248, CChEM IV, Vienna.

Ben-Tor, D. 2007, *Scarabs, Chronology, and Interconnections: Egypt and Palestine in the Second Intermediate Period*, OBO, Series Archaeologica, **27**, Freiburg and Göttingen.

Bietak, M. 1975, *Tell el-Dab'a II. Der Fundort im Rahmen einer archäologisch-geographischen Untersuchung über das ägyptische Ostdelta*, UZK II, Vienna.

Bietak, M. 1981, *Avaris and Piramesse, Archaeological Exploration in the Eastern Nile Delta*. Ninth Mortimer Wheeler Archaeological Lecture, The British Academy, Oxford.

Bietak, M. 1984, Zum Königreich des '3-ẕḥ-R' Nehesi, In *Festschrift für Wolfgang Helck, Studien Altägyptischer Kultur*, **11**, 59–78.

Bietak, M. 1989, Archäologischer Befund und historische Interpretation am Beispiel der Tell el-Yahudiya Ware, In *Akten des 4. Internationalen Ägyptologenkongresses. München 1985* (ed. S. Schoske), 7–34, SAK-Beihefte, Bd. 2, München.

Bietak, M. 1996, Avaris, The Capital of the Hyksos – Recent Excavations at Tell el-Dab'a. The First Raymond and Beverly Sackler Foundation Distinguished Lecture in Egyptology, British Museum Publications, London.

Bietak, M., 1996, The Late Cypriot White Slip I-Ware as an Obstacle to the High Aegean Chronology – An Abstract, In *Sardinian and Aegean Chronology: Towards the Resolution of Relative and Absolute Dating in the Mediterranean*. Studies in Sardinian Archaeology V (eds M. S. Balmuth and R. H. Tykot), 321–322, Oxbow Books, Oxford.

Bietak, M. 2001, 'Dab'a, Tell ed-', In *The Oxford Encyclopedia of Ancient Egypt* (ed. D. B. Redford), 351–354, vol. I., New York and Oxford.

Bietak, M. 2002, Relative and Absolute Chronology of the Middle Bronze Age: Comments on the Present Stage of Research, *The Middle Bronze Age in the Levant, Proceedings of an International Conference on MB II A Ceramic Materials in Vienna 24th – 26th of January 2001* (ed. M. Bietak), 30–42, CChEM III, Vienna.

Bietak, M. 2004, Review of Sturt W. Manning, *A Test of Time*. In *Bibliotheca Orientalis*, LXI N° 1–2, 199–222, Oxbow Books, Oxford.

Bietak, M. 2005, The Tuthmoside Stronghold Peru-nefer, *Egyptian Archaeology*, **26**, 13–17.

Bietak, M. 2007, Towards a Middle Bronze Age Chronology, In *Proceedings of the International Colloquium From Relative Chronology to Absolute Chronology: The Second Millennium BC in Syria Palestine, Rome 29th November – 1st December 2001* (eds P. Matthiae, L. Nigro, L. Peyronel and F. Pinnock). 121–146, Accademia Nazionale dei Lincei, Rome.

Bietak, M., 2009a, Peru-nefer; The Principal New Kingdom Naval Base, *Egyptian Archaeology*, **34**, 15–17.

Bietak, M. 2009b, Peru-nefer: An Update, *Egyptian Archaeology*, **35**, 16–17.

Bietak, M. 2010a, Minoan Presence in the Pharaonic Naval Base of Peru-nefer I, In *Cretan Offerings: Studies in Honour of Peter Warren* (ed. O. Krzyszkowska), 11–24, BSA Studies, **18**, London.

Bietak, M. 2010b, From where came the Hyksos and where did they go, In *The Second Intermediate Period Thirteenth – Seventeenth Dynasties, Current Research, Future Prospects* (ed. M. Marée), 139–181, OLA 192, Leuven.

Bietak, M., Dorner, J. and Janosi, P., 2001, Ausgrabungen in dem Palastbezirk von Avaris, Vorbericht Tell el-Dab'a/'Ezbet Helmi 1993–2000, mit einem Beitrag von A. von den Driesch. *E & L*, **11**, 27–129.

Bietak, M., Eigner, D. and Müller, M. (in preparation), *Tell el-Dab'a XIV, Siedlungsschichten und Herrenhäuser der 12.–15. Dynastie,* 3 vols. Vienna.

Bietak, M., Forstner-Müller, I. 2009, with a contribution by F. van Koppen and K. Radner, Der Hyksospalast bei Tell el-Dab'a. Zweite und dritte Grabungskampagne (Frühling 2008 und Frühling 2009), *E & L,* **19,** 91–119.

Bietak, M. and Hein I. 2001, The Context of White Slip Wares in the Stratigraphy of Tell el-Dab'a and some Conclusions on Aegean Chronology, In *The White Slip Ware of Late Bronze Age Cyprus, Proceedings of an International Conference organized by the A. L. Leventis Foundation, Nicosia, in Honour of Malcolm Wiener, Nicosia 29th–30th October 1998* (ed. V. Karageorghis), 171–194, CChEM II, Vienna.

Bietak, M. and Höflmayer, F. 2007, Introduction: High Chronology and Low Chronology, In *The Synchronisation of Civilizations in the Eastern Mediterranean in the Second Millennium B.C. III* (ed. M. Bietak and E. Czerny), 13–23, CChEM IX, Vienna.

Bietak, M., Kopetzky, K., Stager, L. E. and Voss, R. 2008, Synchronisation of Stratigraphies: Ashkelon and *Tell el-Dab'a, E & L,* **18,** 49–60.

Bietak, M. and Pusch, E. B. in press, 'Piramesse/Qantir', *Encyclopedia of Ancient History* (ed. R. Bagnell *et al.*), New York and Oxford.

Ben-Tor, A., 2004, Hazor and Chronology, *E & L,* **14,** 45–67.

Bonani, G., Hass, H., Hawass, Z., Lehner M., Nakhla, S., Nolan, J., Wenke, R. and Wölfli, W. 2001, Radiocarbon dates of Old and Middle Kingdom Monuments in Egypt, *Radiocarbon,* **43**(3), 1297–1320.

Boraik, M. 2007, Stela of Bakenkhonsu, High Priest of Amun-Re, *Memnonia,* **18,** 119–226.

Boraik, M. 2008/09, Re-writing Egypt's History: The Stela of Bakenkhonsu, *Ancient Egypt* 9.3, 24–27.

Brainerd, G. W. 1951, The place of chronological ordering in archaeological analysis, *American Antiquity,* **16,** 301–313.

Breyer, F. 2010, Egyptological Remarks Concerning Dahamunzu, *E & L,* 20, 445–451.

Bronk Ramsey, C. 2005, Improving the Resolution of Radiocarbon Dating by Statistical Analysis, In *The Bible and Radiocarbon Dating* (eds T. E Levy and T. F. G. Higham), 57–92, *Archaeology, Text and Science*, London and Oakville.

Bronk Ramsey, C., Dee, M. W., Rowland, J. M., Higham, T. F. G., Harris, S. A., Brock, F., Quiles, A., Wild, E. M., Marcus, E. S. and Shortland, A. J. 2010, Radiocarbon Based Chronology for Dynastic Egypt, *Science,* **328,** 1554–1557.

Bronk Ramsey, C., Manning, S.W. and Galimberti, M. 2004, Dating the Volcanic Eruption at Thera, *Radiocarbon,* **46,** 325–344.

Chiodini, G., Frondini, F., Kerrick, D. M., Rogie, J., Parello, F., Peruzzi, L. and Zanzari, A. R. 1999, Quantification of Deep CO_2 Fluxes from Central Italy: Examples of Carbon Balance for Regional Aquifers and of Soil Diffuse Degassing, *Chemical Geology,* **159,** 205–222.

Courtois, L. 1970, Note préliminaire sur l'origine des differentes fabriques de la poterie du Chypriote Récent, *Report of the Department of Antiquities, Cyprus* 1970, 81–85.

Courtois, L. and Velde B. 1980, Petrographic and Electron Microprobe Studies of Cypriot White Slip Ware (Late Bronze Age), *Revue d'Archéometrie: Actes du XX Symposium International d'Archéometrie,* vol. III, Supplement, 37–43.

Czerny, E. 1999, *Tell el-Dab'a IX, Eine Plansiedlung des frühen Mittleren Reiches* UZK XV, Vienna.

Czerny, E. in press, *Tell el-Dab'a XXII: Siedlung und Tempel von 'Ezbet Rushdi,* UZK, Vienna.

Dee M. W., Bronk Ramsey, C., Shortland, A. J., Higham, T. F. G. and Rowland, J. M. 2009, Reanalysis of the Chronological Discrepancies obtained by the Old and Middle Kingdom Monument Project, *Radiocarbon,* **51**(3), 1061–1070.

Dever, W. B. 1992, The Chronology of Syria-Palestine in the Second Millenium B.C.E.: A Review of Current Issues, *BASOR,* **288,** 1–25.

Doran, J. E. and Hodson, F. R. 1975, *Mathematics and Computers in Archaeology*, Edinburgh.

Eriksson, K. 2001, Cypriot Proto White Slip and White Slip I: Chronological Beacons on Relations Between Late Cypriot I Cyprus with Contemporary Societies of the Eastern Mediterranean, In *Papers of the White Slip Conference held in honour of Malcolm H. Wiener, Leventis Foundation, Cyprus 29–30th October 1998*, (ed. V. Karageorghis), 51–64, CChEM II, Vienna.

Eriksson, K. 2007, *The Creative Independance of Late Bronze Age Cyprus. An Account of the Archaeological Importance of White Slip Ware in assessing the Relative Chronology of Late Bronze Age Cyprus and the Island's Historical Links with the Societies in the Eastern Mediterranean*, CChEM X, Vienna.

Forstner-Müller, I. 2008, *Tell el-Dab'a XVI, Die Gräber des Areals A/II von Tell el-Dab'a*, UZK XXVIII, Vienna.

Friedrich, W. L., Kromer, B., Friedrich, M., Heinemeier, J., Pfeiffer, T. and Talamo, S. 2006, Santorini Eruption Radiocarbon Dated to 1627–1600 B.C., *Science*, **312**, 548.

Friedrich, W. L. and Heinemeier, J. 2009, The Minoan Eruption of Santorini Radiocarbon Dated to 1613 ± 13 BC – Geological and Stratigraphic Considerations, In *Time's Up! Dating the Minoan eruption of Santorini. Acts of the Minoan Eruption Chronology Workshop, Sandbjerg November 2007 initiated by Jan Heinemeier and Walter L. Friedrich* (ed. D. A. Warburton), 56–63, Monographs of the Danish Institute at Athens 10.

Gasche, H., Armstrong, J. A., Cole, S. W. and Gurzadyan, V. G. 1998a, *Dating the Fall of Babylon, A Reappraisal of Second Millennium Chronology (A Joint Ghent-Chicago-Harvard Project)*, Mesopotamian History and Environment, Ser. II, Mem. IV, Chicago and Ghent.

Gasche, H., Armstrong, J. A., Cole, S. W. and Gurzadyan, V. G. 1998b, A Correction to Dating the Fall of Babylon, A Reppraisal of Second Millennium Chronology, *Akkadica*, **108**, 1–4.

Gomez, G., Neff, H., Rautman, M. L., Vaughan, S. J. and Glascock, M. D. 2002, The Source Provenance of Bronze Age and Roman Pottery from Cyprus, *Archaeometry*, **44** (1), 23–36.

van de Velden, M., Groenen, P. J. F. and Poblome, J. 2007, *Seriation by constrained correspondence analysis: a simulation study*, Econometric Institute Report EI 2007–40.

Habachi, L. 1954, Khata'na-Qantir: Importance, *ASAE*, **52**, 443–559.

Habachi, L. 2001, (ed. E-M. Engel, P. Jánosi and C. Mlinar), *Tell el-Dab'a I: Tell el-Dab'a and Qantir: The Site and its Connection with Avaris and Piramesse*. UZK II, Vienna.

Hagens, G., in press, Radiocarbon Chronology for Dynastic Egypt: A Critique, and Contribution to the Tell el Dab'a Debate, *Radiocarbon*.

Hänsel, B., Horejs, B., Jung, R. and Weninger, B. 2010, Die absolute Chronologie der Schichten des prähistorischen Olynth, in: Hänsel, B., Aslanis, I., *Das Prähistorische Olynth, Ausgrabungen in der Toumba Agios Mamas 1994–1996, Die Grabung und der Baubefund*, 301–381, Prähistorische Archäologie in Südosteuropa vol. 23, Rahden/Westf.

Heinemeier, J., Friedrich, W. L., Kromer, B. and Bronk Ramsey, C. 2009, The Minoan Eruption of Santorini Radiocarbon Dated by an Olive Tree Buried by the Eruption, In *Time's Up! Dating the Minoan eruption of Santorini. Acts of the Minoan Eruption Chronology Workshop, Sandbjerg November 2007 initiated by Jan Heinemeier and Walter L. Friedrich* (ed. D. A. Warburton), 285–293, Monographs of the Danish Institute at Athens 10.

Höflmayer, F. 2009, Aegean-Egyptian Synchronisms and the Radiocarbon Chronology, In *Time's Up! Dating the Minoan eruption of Santorini. Acts of the Minoan Eruption Chronology Workshop, Sandbjerg November 2007 initiated by Jan Heinemeier and Walter L. Friedrich* (ed. D. A. Warburton), 187–195, Monographs of the Danish Institute at Athens 10.

Höflmayer, F. 2010, *Die Synchronisierung der minoischen Alt- und Neupalastzeit mit der ägyptischen Chronologie*, CChEM 32, Vienna.

Hornung, E., Krauss R., Warburton, D. A. (eds.) 2006, *Ancient Egyptian Chronology: Handbook of Oriental Studies, Section One, The Near and Middle East 83*, Leiden.

Ihm, P., 1978, *Statistik in der Archäologie* Archaeophysica **9**, Bonn.

Kaplan, M. 1980, *The Origin and Distribution of Tell el Yahudiyeh Ware*, SIMA, **63**, Gothenburg.

Karageorghis, V. 1990, Tombs at Palaepaphos I. Teratsoudhia, 2. Eliomylia, Nicosia.

Kendall, D. G. 1969, Incidence Matrices, Interval Graphs and Seriation in Archaeology, *Pacific Journal of Mathematics*, **28**(3), 565–570.

Kendall, D. G. 1971, Seriation from Abundance Matrices, In *Mathematics in the Archaeological and Historical Sciences*, (eds F. R. Hodson, D. G. Kendall and P. Tautu), 215–252, Edinburgh,.

Kopetzky, K. 1993, *Datierung der Gräber der Grabungsfläche F/I von Tell el-Dab'a anhand der Keramik*, unpublished Master script of the University of Vienna, publication in preparation.

Kopetzky, K. 2004, Typologische Bemerkungen zur Siedlungskeramik von A/V-p/19, in: I. Hein and P. Janosi, *Tell el-Dab'a XI, Areal A/V, Siedlungsrelikte der späten 2. Zwischenzeit*, UZK XXI, Vienna, 237–335.

Kopetzky, K. 2010, *Tell el-Dab'a XX: Die Chronologie der Siedlungskeramik der Zweiten Zwischenzeit aus Tell el-Dab'a*, part I–II, UZK XXXII, Vienna.

Krauss, R. and Warburton, D. A. 2009, The Basis for Egyptian Dates, In *Time's Up! Dating the Minoan eruption of Santorini. Acts of the Minoan Eruption Chronology Workshop, Sandbjerg November 2007 initiated by Jan Heinemeier and Walter L. Friedrich* (ed. D. A. Warburton), 125–144, Monographs of the Danish Institute at Athens 10.

Kuniholm, P. I., Kromer, B., Manning, S. W., Newton, M. W, Latini, C. M. and Bruce, M. J. 1996, Anatolian Tree Rings and the Absolute Chronology of the Eastern Mediterranean 2220–718 BC, *Nature*, **381**, 780–782.

Kuniholm, P. I. and Newton, M. W. 2004, A Dendrochronological Framework for the Assyrian Colony Period in Asia Minor, In *Türkiye Bilimer Akademisi Arkeoloji Dergisi : Türkish Academy of Sciences Journal of Archaeology* VII, 165–176.

Kutschera, W., Bietak, M., Wild, E. M., Ramsey, C. B., Dee, M., Golser, R. and Weninger, F. 2012, The Chronology of Tell el-Daba: A Crucial Meeting Point of 14C Dating, Archaeology, and Egyptology in the 2nd Millennium BC.Radiocarbon, **54**(3–4), 407–422.

Le Père, J. M. 1822, Mémoire sur la communication de la mer des Indes à la Méditerranée, par la mer Rouge et l'isthme de Soueys, in: *Description de l'Égypte ou recueil des observations et des recherches qui ont été faites en Égypte pendant l'expédition de l'armée française*, vol. 11, second edition, 37–370, Paris.

MacDonald, C. C. F. 2002, The Neopalatial Palaces of Knossos, In Monuments of Minos: Rethinking the Minoan Palaces, *Proceedings of the International Workshop 'Crete of the Hundred Palaces?' Université Catholique de Louvain, Louvain–la–Neuve, 14–15 December 2001* (eds. J. M. Drissen, I. Schoep and R. Laffineur), 35–54, Aegeum **23**, Liège.

MacDonald, C. C. F. 2003, The Palace of Minos at Knossos, Athena Review 3, 36–43.

MacGillivray, J. A. 1995, A Minoan Cup at Tell el-Dab'a, *E & L*, **5**, 81–84.

MacGillivray, J. A. 2003, A Middle Minoan Cup from Sidon, *The Archaeology and History in the Lebanon*, **18**, 20–24.

MacGillivray, J. A. 2004, A Middle Minoan Cup from Sidon, In *A Decade of Archaeology and History in the Lebanon* (eds. C. Doumet-Serhal in collaboration with A. Rabate and A. Resek), 124–131, Beirut.

MacGillivray, J. A. 2008, The Minoan Sidon Cup, In *The Bronze Age in the Lebanon, Studies on the Archaeology and Chronology of Lebanon, Syria and Egypt*, (eds. M. Bietak and E. Czerny), 45–49, CChEM XVIII, Vienna.

Maguire, L. C. 2009, *Tell el-Dab'a XXI: The Cypriot Pottery and its Circulation in the Levant*, UZK, XXXIII, Vienna.

Manning, S. W. 1988, The Bronze Age Eruption of Thera: Absolute Dating, Aegean Chronology and Mediterranean Cultural Interrelations, *Journal of Mediterranean Archaeology*, **1**(1), 17–82.

Manning, S. W. 1999, *A Test of Time: The Volcano of Thera and the Chronology and History of the Aegean and East Mediterranean in the Mid Second Millennium BC*, Oxford.

Manning, S. W. 2007, Clarifying the 'High' v. 'Low' Aegean/Cypriot Chronology for the Mid Second Millennium BC: Assessing the Evidence, interpretive Frameworks, and current State of the Debate, In *The Synchronisation of Civilizations in the Eastern Mediterranean in the Second Millennium B.C. III*, (eds M. Bietak and E. Czerny), 101–137, CChEM IX, Vienna.

Manning, S. W. 2009, Beyond the Santorini Eruption, In *Time's Up! Dating the Minoan eruption of Santorini. Acts of the Minoan Eruption Chronology Workshop, Sandbjerg November 2007 initiated by Jan Heinemeier and Walter L. Friedrich* (ed. D. A. Warburton), 207–226, Monographs of the Danish Institute at Athens 10.

Manning, S. W., Bronk Ramsey, C., Doumas, C., Marketou, T., Cadogan G. and Pearson, C. L. 2002b, New Evidence for an early Date for the Aegean Late Bronze Age and Thera Eruption, *Antiquity*, **76**, 733–744.

Manning, S. W., Bronk Ramsey, C., Kutschera, W., Higham, T. F. G., Kromer, B., Steier, P., Wild, E. M., 2006, Chronology for the Late Bronze Age 1700–1400 B-C., *Science*, **294**, 2532–2535.

Manning, S. W., Kromer, B., Kuniholm, P. I. and Newton, M. W. 2001, Anatolian Tree Rings and A New Chronology for East Mediterranean Bronze-Iron Ages, *Science*, **294**, 2532–2535.

Manning, S. W., Kromer, B., Kuniholm, P. I. and Newton, M. W. 2003, Confirmation of near-absolute dating of east Mediterranean Bronze-Iron Dendrochronology, *Antiquity*, **77**, 295. http://antiquity.ac.uk/ProjGall/Manning/man- ning.html.

Matthäus, H. 1980, *Die Bronzegefässe der kretisch mykenischen Kultur*, Prähistorische Bronzefunde, Abt. II, 1, Munich.

Matthäus, H. 1995, Representations of Keftiu in Egyptian Tombs and the Absolute Chronology of the Aegean late Bronze Age, *Bulletin of the Institute of Classical Studies*, **40**, 177–194.

Mebert, J. 2010, *Die Venustafel des Ammi-Saduqa und ihre Bedeutung für die astronomische Datierung der altbabylonischen Zeit*, Archiv für Orientforschung, Beiheft 31, Vienna.

Merrillees, R. S., 1971, The Early History of Late Cypriote I, *Levant*, **3**, 56–79.

Merrillees, R. S., 1974, *Trade and Transcendence in The Bronze Age Levant*, SIMA, **39**, Gothenburg.

Merrillees, R. S. 2001, Some Cypriote White Slip Pottery from the Aegean, In *The White Slip Ware of Late Bronze Age Cyprus, Proceedings of an International Conference organized by the Anastasios G. Leventis Foundation, Nicosia in Honor of Malcolm Wiener, Nicosia 29th–30th October 1998* (ed. V. Karageorghis), 195–202, CChEM II, Vienna.

Merrillees, R. S. 2003a, The First Appearances of Kamares in the Levant, *E & L*, **13**, 127–142.

Michels, J. W. 1973, *Dating Methods in Archaeology*, New York.

Müller, V. 2008, *Tell el-Dab'a XVII. Opferdeponierungen in der Hyksoshauptstadt Auaris (Tell el-Dab'a) vom späten Mittleren Reich bis zum frühen Neuen Reich*, 2 Vols., UZK XXIX, Vienna.

Niemeier, W. D. 1980, Die Katastrophe von Thera und die spätminoische Chronologie, *Jahrbuch des Deutschen Archäologischen Institutes* 95, 1–76.

Orton, C. 1980, *Mathematics in Archaeology*, Cambridge.

Phillips, J. 2008, *Aegyptiaca on the Island of Crete in their Chronological Context: A Critical Review*, vols I–II, CChEM 18, Vienna.

Palmer, I. R. 1981, The Khyan Lid Deposit at Knossos, *Kadmos*, **20**, 108–128.

Pomerance, L. 1984, A Note on the Carved Stone Ewers from the Khyan Lid Deposit, In *Studies in the Aegean Chronology*, Studies in Mediterranean Archaeology and Literature Pocket-Book (eds. P. Åström, L. R. Palmer and L. Pomerance), Gothenburg.

Popham, M. R. 1962, The Proto White Slip Pottery of Cyprus, Appendix I in P. Åström and G.R.H. Wright, Two Bronze Age Tombs at Dhenia in Cyprus, *Opuscula Atheniensia* 4, 277–297.

Regev, J., de Miroschedji, P. and Boaretto E. 2012, Early Bronze Age Chronology in the Southern Levant: Modeling of 14C Dates Based on Archaeological Data, *Radiocarbon* **54**, 525–566.

Robinson, W. R. 1951, A Method for Chronologically Ordering Archaeological Deposits, *American Antiquity*, **16**, 293–301.

Rogie, J. D. 1996, Lethal Italian Carbon Dioxide Springs Key to Atmospheric CO_2 Levels, *Penn State Earth and Environmental Systems Institute, News and Events: News Archives.* http://www.eesi.psu.edu/news_events/archives/Lethal.shtml.

Rogie, J. D., Kerrick, D. M., Chiodini, G. and Frondini F. 2000, Flux Measurements of Nonvolcanic CO_2 Emission from Some Vents in Central Italy, *Journal of Geophysical Research*, **105**(B4), 8435–45.

Saidah, R., 1993–1994, Beirut in the Bronze Age: The Kharji Tombs, *Berytus*, **41**, 137–222.

Schiestl, R. 2010, *Tell el-Dab'a XVIII, Die Palastnekropole von Tell el-Dab'a, Die Gräber des Areals.F/I der Straten d/2 und d/1,* UZK XXX, Vienna 2009.

Schneider, T. 2003, Siptah und Beja, *ZÄS*, **130**, 134–146.

Schneider, T. 2008, Das Ende der kurzen Chronologie: eine kritische Bilanz der Debatte zur absoluten Datierung des Mittleren Reiches und der zweiten Zwischenzeit, *E & L*, **18**, 275–313.

Schneider, T., 2010, Contributions to the Chronology of the New Kingdom and the Third Intermediate Period, *E & L*, **20**, 373–403.

Shennan, St. 1997, *Quantifying Archaeology,* Edinburgh.

Sjöquist, E. 1940, Problems of the Late Cypriote Bronze Age, Stockholm.

Stager, L. E. 2002, The MBIIA Ceramic Sequence at Tel Ashkelon and its Implications for the "Port Power" Model of Trade, In *The Middle Bronze Age in the Levant, Proceedings of an International Conference on MB IIA Ceramic Materials in Vienna 24th–26th of January 2001,* (eds M. Bietak, and H. Hunger), 353–363, CChEM III, Vienna.

Sterba, Johannes H., Foster, K. P., Steinhauser, G. and Bichler, M. 2009, New Light on Old Pumice: the Origins of Mediterranean Volcanic Material from Ancient Egypt, *Journal of Archaeological Science*, **36**, 1738–44.

Todd, I. A. and Pilides, D. 2001, The Archaeology of the White Slip Production, In *The White Slip Ware of Late Bronze Age Cyprus* (ed. V. Karageorghis), 26–43, CCEM.II, Vienna.

van de Velden, M., Groenen, P. J. F., Poblome, J. 2007, *Seriation by constrained correspondence analysis: a simulation study.* Econometric Institute Report EI 2007–40.

Van Dijk, J. 2008, New Evidence on the Length of the Reign of Haremhab, *Journal of the American Research Center in Egypt*, **44**, 193–200.

Van Dijk, J., 2011, The Date of the Gebel Barkal Stela of Seti I, In *Under the Potter's Tree, Studies Presented to Janine Bourriau on the Occasion of her 70th Birthday,* (eds D. Aston, B. Bader, C. Gallorini, P. Nicholson and S. Buckingham), 325–332, OLA 204, Leuven.

Van Seters, J. 1966, *The Hyksos, A New Investigation*, New Haven and London.

Vermeule, E. D. T. and Wolsky, F. 1990, *Toumba tou Skourou, A Bronze Age Potters' Quarter on Morphou Bay in Cyprus,* Cambridge.

Walberg, G. 1991, Finds at Tell el-Dab'a and the Middle Minoan Chronology, *E & L* **2**, 115–120.

Walberg, G. 1998, The Date and Origin of the Kamares Cup from Tell el-Dab'a, *E & L*, **8**, 107–108.

Warburton, D. A. 2009, Chronology, Stratigraphy, Typology and Tell el-Dab'a, In *Time's Up! Dating the Minoan eruption of Santorini. Acts of the Minoan Eruption Chronology Workshop, Sandbjerg November 2007 initiated by Jan Heinemeier and Walter L. Friedrich* (ed. D. A. Warburton), 139–144, Monographs of the Danish Institute at Athens 10.

Warburton, D.A., 2011, The Fall of Babylon in 1499: Another Update, *Akkadica*, **132**, 1–22.

Ward, W. A. and Dever, W. B., 1994, *Scarab Typology and Archaeological Context: An Essay on Middle Bronze Age Chronology*, Studies on Scarab seals 3, San Antonio.

Warren, P., 1987, Absolute Dating of the Aegean Late Bronze Age, *Archaeometry*, **29**, 205–211.

Warren, P. 1988, Further Arguments against an Early Date, *Archaeometry*, **29**, 176–179.

Warren, P. 1996, The Aegean and the Limits of Radiocarbon Dating, In *Absolute Chronology, Archaeological Europe 2500–500 BC* (ed. K. Randsborg), 283–290, Acta Archaeologica 67 and Acta Archaeologica Suppementa I, Copenhagen.

Warren, P. 2006, The Date of the Thera Eruption in Relation to Aegean-Egyptian Interconnections. and the Egyptian Historical Chronology, In *Timelines, Studies in Honour of Manfred Bietak* (ed. E. Czerny, *et al.*), 305–321, vol. II, OLA 149, Leuven-Paris-Dudley, MA.

Warren, P. 2009, The Date of the Late Bronze Age Eruption of Santorini, In *Time's Up! Dating the Minoan eruption of Santorini. Acts of the Minoan Eruption Chronology Workshop, Sandbjerg November 2007 initiated by Jan Heinemeier and Walter L. Friedrich* (ed. D. A. Warburton), 181–186, Monographs of the Danish Institute at Athens 10.

Warren, P. 2010, The Absolute Chronology of the Aegean ca. 2000 B.C.–1400 B.C. A Summary, In *Die Bedeutung der minoischen und mykenischen Glyptik*, (ed. W. Müller), 383–394, Corpus der Minoischen und Mykenischen Siegel Beiheft 8, Mainz.

Warren, P. and Hankey, V. 1989, *Aegean Bronze Age Chronology*, Bristol.

Weinstein, J. 1992, The Chronology of Palestine in the Early Second Millennium B.C.E., *BASOR*, **288**, 27–46.

Weinstein, J., 1996, A Wolf in Sheep's Clothing: How the High Chronology became the Middle Chronology, *BASOR*, **304**, 1996, 55–63.

Wiener, M. H. 2001, The White Slip I of Tell el-Dab'a: Critical Challenge for the Aegean Chronology, In *The White Slip Ware of Late Bronze Age Cyprus. Proceedings of an International Conference organized by the Anastasios G. Leventis Foundation, Nicosia in Honor of Malcolm Wiener, Nicosia 29th–30th October 1998* (ed. V. Karageorghis), 195–202. CCEM II, Vienna.

Wiener, M. H. 2003, Time out: The Current Impasse in Bronze Age Archaeological Dating, In *Metron: Measuring the Aegean Bronze Age*, Aegeum **24**, (eds K. Pollinger Foster and R. Laffineur), 363–399, Liège and Austin.

Wiener, M. H. 2006, Egypt and Time, *E & L*, **16**, 325–339.

Wiener, M. H. 2007, Times Change: The Current State of the Debate in Old World Archaeology, In *The Synchronisation of Civilizations in the Eastern Mediterranean in the Second Millennium B.C. III*, (eds M. Bietak and E. Czerny), 25–47, Austrian Academy of Sciences Press, Vienna.

Wiener, M. H. 2009, Cold Fusion: The Uneasy Alliance of History and Science, In *Tree-Rings, Kings, and Old World Archaeology and Environment: Papers Presented in Honor of Peter Ian Kuniholm* (eds S. W. Manning and M. J. Bruce), 277–292, Oxford.

Wiener, M. H., 2010, A Point in Time, In *Cretan Offerings: Studies in Honour of Peter Warren* (ed. O. Krzyszkowska), 367–94, British School at Athens Studies 18, London.

CHAPTER 9

Radiocarbon Data for Aegean Pottery in Egypt: New Evidence from Saqqara (Lepsius) Tomb 16 and its Importance for LM IB/LH IIA

F. Höflmayer, A. Hassler, W. Kutschera and E. M. Wild

While radiocarbon dates for dynastic Egypt are generally in accordance with historical estimations based on textual data, absolute calendar dates for the Aegean early Late Bronze Age are still under discussion. Estimations based on archaeological synchronisms with Egypt are up to 120 years younger than radiocarbon data for the Late Minoan IA and IB periods. In this respect, further radiocarbon data from Egyptian contexts containing Aegean imports are of considerable interest for the ongoing chronological debate. In this contribution, we present new scientific dating evidence for Saqqara (Lepsius) tomb 16, containing an imported Late Helladic IIA alabastron and discuss its importance for absolute calendar dates for Late Minoan IB and Late Helladic IIA.

Introduction

Synchronising the Aegean Late Bronze Age with Egypt

Absolute calendar dates for the Aegean early Late Bronze Age, especially for the Late Minoan (LM) IA–B phases and their Greek mainland equivalents, Late Helladic (LH) I–IIA, are still under discussion. The so-called 'high' chronology is based on a substantial number of mostly short-lived radiocarbon dates from Crete, the Greek mainland, the island of Santorini (Thera) and the Anatolian coast, covering Middle Minoan (MM) III up to LM II. These dates place the eruption of Santorini (Thera) which occurred during the late LM IA period in the second half of the 17th century BC. Based on dates from Chania, Myrtos-Pyrgos and Mochlos, proponents of the 'high' chronology originally argued for a date around 1500 BC for the end of the LM IB period, but afterwards lowered it to around 1450 BC (Housley *et al.* 1999; Manning 1999; Manning *et al.* 2002; Bronk Ramsey *et al.* 2004; Friedrich *et al.* 2006; Manning *et al.* 2006; Bruins *et al.* 2008; Bruins *et al.* 2009; Wild *et al.* 2010). The so-called 'conventional' or 'low' chronology, based on archaeological synchronisms with

---

Authors' Addresses: **F. Höflmayer**, German Archaeological Institute (Orient-Department); **A. Hassler**, SCIEM 2000, Austrian Academy of Sciences, Vienna 1010, Austria; **W. Kutschera** and **E. M. Wild**, Vienna Environmental Research Accelerator (VERA), Faculty of Physics, University of Vienna, Vienna 1090, Austria

Egypt and the Egyptian historical chronology, placed the date of the Minoan eruption of Santorini between 1550 and 1500 BC, after the start of the New Kingdom, while placing the end of the LM IB period late during the reign of Thutmose III, around 1450 or 1430 BC (Warren and Hankey 1989; Warren 2006; Bietak and Höflmayer 2007; Höflmayer 2008; Warren 2009; Höflmayer 2009).

The fundamental research on radiocarbon dating the Egyptian historical chronology carried out by the University of Oxford under the direction of Christopher Bronk Ramsey for the past years has shown that dates for the Middle and New Kingdom as proposed by Kenneth Kitchen are in general agreement with radiocarbon data (Bronk Ramsey *et al.* 2010; Dee *et al.* 2010; Shaw 2000; Kitchen 2000; Kitchen 2002; Kitchen 2007; cf. also: Beckerath 1997). A systematic error in the Egyptian historical chronology as an explanation for higher Aegean dates is thus unlikely. As the 'conventional' or 'low' chronology is based on Egyptian artefacts found in Aegean contexts (like Egyptian stone vessels in Mycenae) and Aegean artefacts in Egyptian contexts (like Minoan and Mycenaean pottery in tombs), new radiocarbon dates from these key synchronisms would be most important to compare archaeological and scientific estimations.

Recently Astrid Hassler was able to re-discover an almost forgotten Mycenaean straight-sided alabastron in the Egyptian Museum Berlin, which was first published by Carl Richard Lepsius in his accounts of the expedition to Egypt and Nubia sent out by the Prussian king Friedrich Wilhelm IV in the mid-19th century (Hassler in print). Coming from a closed context (Saqqara tomb 16, after Lepsius' counting), this vessel is of considerable interest for archaeological synchronisation, as most other diagnostic objects from this burial are still preserved in the magazines of the Egyptian Museum Berlin. Furthermore, thanks to the courtesy of the Egyptian Museum, it was possible to obtain samples from pomegranates, which were found together with this burial. These samples have been submitted to the *Vienna Environmental Research Accelerator* (VERA) for radiocarbon dating. In the following, the date of the Mycenaean vessel in terms of Greek mainland relative chronological phases, the date of the burial based on associated Egyptian objects, the scientific date for the samples of the pomegranate and their implications for Aegean-Egyptian synchronisms will be discussed.

Discussion

New evidence from old tombs: Saqqara (Lepsius) tomb 16

Saqqara tomb 16, located north of the Djoser precinct, was a mastaba of the 5th Dynasty, belonging to a certain *špss-R^c*. Layout and part of its decoration were published in the accounts of the Prussian expedition to Egypt and Nubia by Carl Richard Lepsius (Lepsius 1849–1859, Textband I, 165–170). In one of the chambers (the so-called 'serdab', where originally a statue of the deceased was placed), the excavators found two secondary burials in wooden coffins, which at first were thought to be servants of the tomb owner. Subsequently it was realized that these two burials took place much later, most probably in the (early) 18th Dynasty. Both coffins were found undisturbed and all their belongings were sent to the Egyptian Museum Berlin. Although some of the objects were lost and/or destroyed during WW II, the most important pieces are still housed in the magazines of the Egyptian Museum.

One of the coffins (a) contained two bodies, a female and an infant, equipped with some personal adornments and tools, but more importantly also a kohl-pot, a black-burnished pottery juglet, which can probably be identified as a Cypriot Black Lustrous Wheel-Made (BLWM) juglet based on the published sketch, and two other vessels made of alabaster and faience were found together with the deceased. Based on the occurrence of BLWM ware and the shape of the kohl-pot, a burial-date during the early 18th Dynasty seems likely (Aston 1994, 148 form 164; Hein 2007, 97).

The second coffin (b) also contained a female body, equipped with two plaited baskets made of palm-fibres. One of them contained not only the imported Mycenaean straight-sided alabastron, but also local Egyptian pottery (a red-polished vase and a buff plate), a pair of wooden kohl-tubes, a wooden comb and needle, a small amulet and four pomegranates.

The Mycenaean straight-sided alabastron (Figure 9.1) is decorated with a hatched loop (Furumark motif (FM) 63) on the shoulder and a zig-zag pattern (FM 61) on the body. The base of this vessel is decorated with a spoked wheel. No sketch of this well-preserved vase was included in the description by Carl Richard Lepsius, but already Furtwängler and Löschke included an illustration in their work on Mycenaean pottery, which was published in 1886 (Furtwängler and Loeschcke 1886, pl. 22.159). Although the existence of this vessel

Figure 9.1: Mycenaean straight-sided alabastron from Saqqara (Lepsius) tomb 16. Egyptian Museum Berlin No. 1244. Decorated with hatched loop on shoulder and zig-zag band on body. Date: LH IIA. Photo: courtesy of Egyptian Museum Berlin.

9. *Radiocarbon Data for Aegean Pottery in Egypt*

Figure 9.2: Egyptian red polished jar (Egyptian Museum Berlin No. 1253) Photo: Astrid Hassler.

Figure 9.3: Kohl-tubes (Egyptian Museum Berlin No. 1324) Photo: courtesy of Egyptian Museum Berlin.

was known to some scholars, like Fimmen, Pendlebury, Wace, Kantor, Furumark and Buchholz (Fimmen 1924, 98, 167; Pendlebury 1930, 113; Wace and Blegen 1939, 145 no. A10; Kantor 1947, pl. 7g; Furumark 1950, 205, fig. 15g; Buchholz 1974, 443), surprisingly, this context was never used as a chronological synchronism between Aegean and Egyptian chronologies.

The Mycenaean alabastron can be dated to LH IIA. The shape of this vessel is known from LH IIA onwards and is still found in LH IIIC, the hatched loop is common in the LH IIA and IIB periods, especially on alabastra and small juglets and the spiked wheel is found on bases from the LH IIA period onwards. The zig-zag pattern on the other hand is rarely found on alabastra, where multiple stripes or rock pattern (FM 32) are more common. Parallels for shape and decoration come from the island of Kea, Aghios Ioannis in Laconia and Pylos in Messenia and all date to LH IIA (Mountjoy 1999, 871 fig. 355.22; 255 fig. 83.21; 319 fig. 106.15).

To establish a date in terms of Egyptian chronology is more difficult. Important are the red-polished pottery vase, the pair of kohl-tubes and the occurrence of pomegranates. Small carinated vases (Figure 9.2) are common during the early 18th Dynasty and similar vessels from Thutmoside contexts are known for instance from ᶜEzbet Helmi near Tell el-Dabᶜa in the Eastern Nile Delta or from Tel Dan in the northern Huleh-valley in Israel (Hein 1994, 43 fig. 12a; Martin and Ben-Dov 2007, 198–199 and fig. 6 for further parallels). Kohl-tubes (Figure 9.3) are usually dated to the times of Thutmose III and onwards, since it is assumed that these receptacles replace the earlier kohl-pots during this time (Aston 1994, 149 form 168; Pulak in: Aruz 2008, 338). This assumption, however, is based on a statement by Flinders Petrie more than 70 years ago (Petrie 1927, 28; Petrie 1937, 10). Today there are no up-to-date studies on kohl-receptacles, therefore one should not place too much emphasis on the existence of this pair of kohl-tubes in coffin (b). More important are the pomegranates found in this tomb. Pomegranates seem to be known in Egypt from the times of Thutmose I onwards, first mentioned in the tomb of an official named *Jnnj* (Theban Tomb 81) (Dziobek 1992, 61–2). The first depictions of pomegranates can be found in the so-called 'botanical garden' of Thutmose III in Karnak (Beaux 1990). Based on this evidence, a date for the burial of coffin (b) containing the imported Mycenaean vessel somewhere during the Thutmoside period, seems to be most likely somewhere in the reign of Thutmose III: accession date based on Kenneth Kitchen's chronology: 1479 (Kitchen 2000); based on radiocarbon model: 1494–1483 (68.2% probability), 1498–1474 (95.4% probability) (Bronk Ramsey *et al.* 2010: Supporting Online Material Table S8)).

Figure 9.4: Remains of a pomegranate used for radiocarbon dating (Egyptian Museum Berlin No. 1315) Photo: Felix Höflmayer.

In July 2008, thanks to the courtesy of the Egyptian Museum Berlin, samples were taken by Felix Höflmayer from pomegranate EMB 1315 (ten seeds and two pieces of paring) and submitted to the *Vienna Environmental Research Accelerator* for radiocarbon dating (Figure 9.4). Calibration was done using the OxCal 4.1 software (Bronk Ramsey 2009) and the IntCal09 calibration curve (Reimer *et al.* 2009). The calibrated age range for the pomegranate is 1496 to 1436 BC (68.2% probability) and 1527 to 1410 BC at (95.4% probability) and thus supports a date during the Thutmoside period for the burial of coffin (b) and the LH IIA straight-sided alabastron, with a most likely date during the reign of Thutmose III (Figure 9.5), proving for the first time that LH IIA-pottery was circulating in Egypt during these times.

Radiocarbon Data of LM IB-Contexts on Crete and their Relation to the LH IIA-B Transition

In order to compare this new radiocarbon date for the burial of coffin (b) in Saqqara (Lepsius) tomb 16, we will summarize archaeological and scientific dating evidence for the LM IB and LH IIA/B periods. As outlined by Peter Warren and others, LH IIA should end before LM IB (Warren 2009, 182). Whereas only some highly dubious radiocarbon dates for LH II have been published from Tsoungiza (near Nemea, north-eastern Peloponnesus) so far (see Manning *et al.* 2006 with discussion), there are reliable scientific dates for LM IB contexts from Chania, Myrtos-Pyrgos and Mochlos on Crete (Manning *et al.* 2006, Supporting Online Material; Soles 2004, Figure 9.6).

Combined results (using the *R_Combine* function of OxCal 4.1) for short-lived dates from Chania, western Crete, coming from the LM IB-destruction, originally four samples, each of them measured twice (OxA-2517, OxA-10322, OxA-2518, OxA-10320, OxA-2646, OxA-10321, OxA-2647, OxA-10323), come down to 1526 to 1496 BC at 1σ and 1605–1587 BC (4.7% probability) or 1536–1452 BC (90.7% probability) at 2σ, after excluding the oldest sample 15/TR10 from room E (OxA-2517, OxA-10322), as the full set of dates does not pass the χ^2-test (df=7 T=20.8 (5% 14.1); for details and discussion see Manning *et al.* 2006, Supporting Online Material).

Another four short-lived samples from Myrtos-Pyrgos on the southern coast of central Crete, again each measured twice (OxA-3187, OxA-10324, OxA-3188, OxA-10411, OxA-3189, OxA-10325, OxA-3225, OxA-10326), all coming from the local LM IB destruction, can be combined and date to 1515–1493 BC (42.3%) or 1476–1460 BC (25.9%) at 1σ and 1523–1452 BC at 2σ, passing the χ^2-test (df=7 T=7.6 (5% 14.1)) (for details and discussion see Manning *et al.* 2006, Supporting Online Material).

Five short-lived samples (olive pits) come from the end of the LM IB-phase at Mochlos, a small island on the north coast of eastern Crete. Using the *R_Combine* function they date to 1505–1453 BC at 1σ and 1522–1438 BC at 2σ, passing the χ^2-test (df=4 T=3.4 (5% 9.5); Soles 2004; see discussion in: Manning 2009).

Based on these dates (especially Chania and Myrtos-Pyrgos), it was originally argued that LM IB ended around 1500 or 1490 BC (Housley *et al.* 1999; Manning *et al.* 2002; Bronk Ramsey et al. 2004), whereas this date was later lowered to *c.* 1450 BC (Manning *et al.* 2006) and recently raised again to 1470/60 BC (Manning 2009, 225).

The date of the burial of coffin (b) in Saqqara (Lepsius) tomb 16 fits well to the dates from Myrtos-Pyrgos and Mochlos but seems to be slightly younger than the date for the destruction of Chania. But as LH IIA should end *before* the transition from LM IB to LM II, it could be argued that the date of Saqqara 16 is not representative for a point in time of LH IIA and the Mycenaean vessel was kept as an heirloom for several decades.

However, archaeological evidence for the transition from LH IIA to LH IIB provides us with supporting evidence. LH IIA must have ended *after* the beginning of Thutmose III (accession date based on Kenneth Kitchen's chronology: 1479 BC (Kitchen 2000); based on radiocarbon model: 1494–1483 BC (1σ), 1498–1474 BC (2σ) (Bronk Ramsey et al. 2010, Supporting Online Material Table S8)), as an Egyptian stone vessel imitating Cypriote Base Ring (BR) ware was found in chamber tomb 102 at Mycenae. This tomb can be dated to LH IIA and so far no Egyptian BR ware imitation is known from times earlier than Thutmose III or Hatshepsut (Höflmayer 2009, 189–90 with references). On the other hand LH IIB was already underway during the late reign of Thutmose III, as is evidenced by the occurrence of a LH IIB juglet in the so-called tomb of Maket in Kahun (Höflmayer 2009, 189 with references).

A calendar date for the end of LM IB around 1500 BC is not in accordance with archaeological evidence as outlined above, considering the fact that LH IIA should end *before* the transition from LM IB to LM II. Furthermore, an end-date for LM IB around 1500 BC would make the Mycenaean vessel from Saqqara 16 an heirloom of several decades. A date for the transition from LM IB to LM II around 1470/60 BC is also difficult to accept, since it would leave only little time for the Egyptian BR imitation from chamber tomb 102 at Mycenae to be produced, shipped to the Aegean, used for an unknown

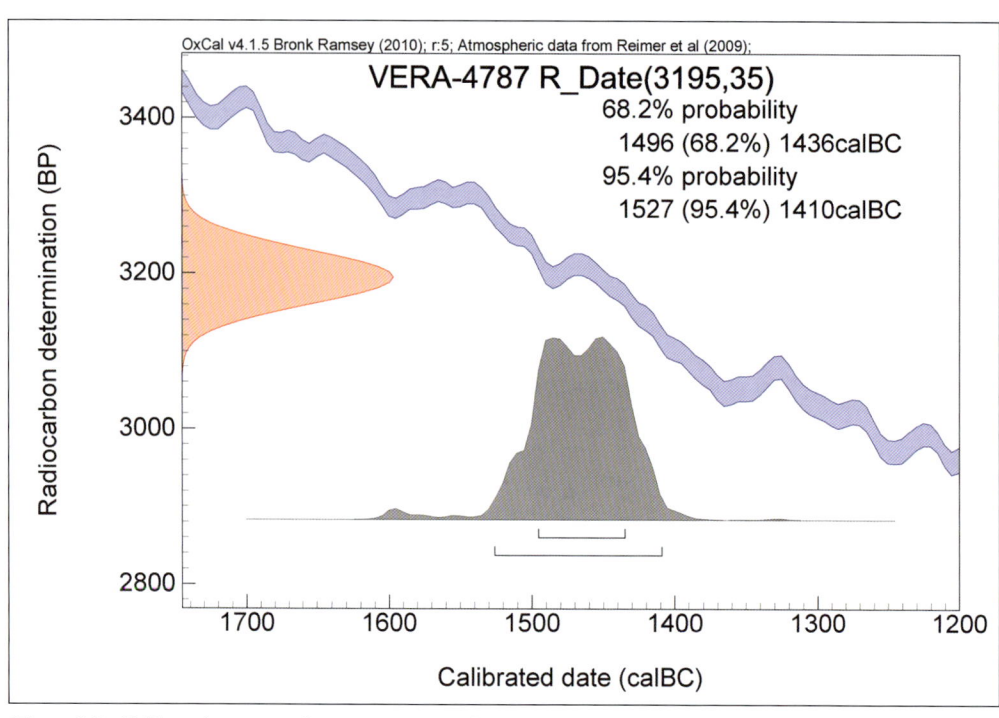

Figure 9.5: Calibrated age range for pomegranate seeds from tomb 16 using OxCal 4.1 and IntCal 2009 (Bronk Ramsey 2009; Reimer et al. 2009).

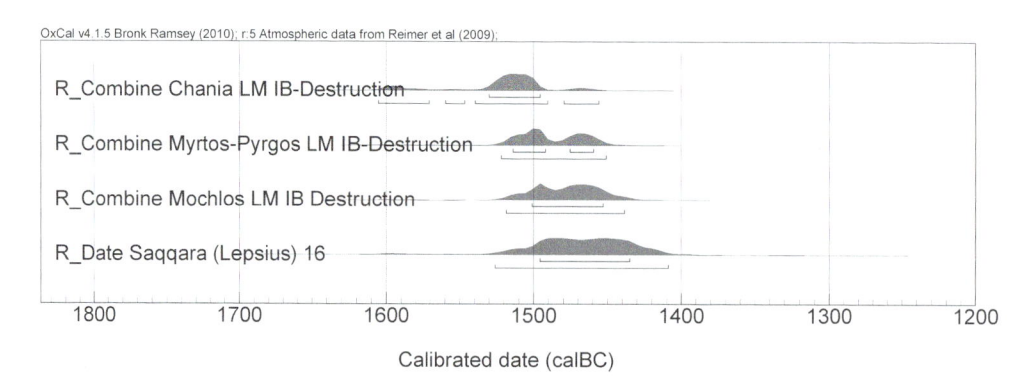

Figure 9.6: Calibrated age range for LM IB destruction layers from Chania, Myrtos-Pyrgos and Mochlos and for Saqqara tomb 16. Samples for LM IB destruction layers were combined using the R_Combine function of OxCal 4.1. The following dates have been used (for details see lists in Soles 2004 and Manning et al. 2006, Supporting Online Material): Chania: OxA-2647, OxA-10323, OxA-2646, OxA-10321, OxA-2518, OxA-10320 (two dates had to be excluded as the original set did not pass the χ^2-test); Myrtos-Pyrgos: OxA-3187, OxA-10324, OxA-3225, OxA-10326, OxA-3189, OxA-10325, OxA-3188, OxA-10411; Mochlos: #85991, #85992, #115890, #129764, #129765, #151768; Saqqara: VERA-4787.

period of time and finally deposited in the tomb. However, a transition date around 1450 BC or slightly afterwards as already suggested by Manning *et al.* a few years ago (Manning *et al.* 2006) and advocated for a long time by different archaeologists (Warren and Hankey 1989; Warren 2006; Bietak and Höflmayer 2007; Höflmayer 2008; Warren 2009; Höflmayer 2009), seems to be the best fit for radiocarbon data from Crete and Egypt as well as for the archaeological evidence. Such a scenario leaves the LM IB-dates from Chania, Myrtos-Pyrgos and Mochlos in the first half of the 15th century BC, but regards them not as representative for the *end* of this *historical* period, rather reflecting destructions *during* the phase LM IB, as is also evidenced by new research on LM IB pottery (see Manning 2009 for discussion and references).

Conclusions

The archaeological and scientific evidence places the recently re-discovered context of coffin (b) in Saqqara (Lepsius) tomb 16 in the Thutmosid period, most likely in the times of Thutmose III. This date is in accordance with the long-held synchronism of LM IB and LH IIA with the earlier part of the reign of Thutmose III. Radiocarbon data from destruction horizons from LM IB-Crete, which were thought to represent the *end* of this period should be regarded as representing several stages *during* the phase LM IB, as is also suggested by recent research on pottery of this period.

Although different opinions between archaeologists and scientists about the absolute date for the Santorini eruption and the late LM IA period seem to prevail, careful analysis of available data (both archaeological and scientific) for the subsequent LM IB and LH IIA periods shows, that there is no difference between radiocarbon dating and archaeological estimations based on synchronisms and the now science-backed Egyptian historical chronology. Complementary scientific data from Egyptian contexts can contribute to the ongoing chronological debate and refine our understanding of this crucial period in the mid-second millennium BC.

Acknowledgements

Felix Höflmayer and Astrid Hassler want to thank Manfred Bietak and Walter Kutschera (first and second speaker of the SCIEM 2000 Special Research Programme) for providing funding for travel expenses and analysis carried out at the VERA-laboratory in Vienna. We would also like to thank the Egyptian Museum Berlin, especially Klaus Finneiser for invaluable help during our visits. Further thanks are due to Ricardo Eichmann (director of the Oriental Department of the German Archaeological Institute) for providing travel expenses to the 'Egyptian chronology symposium' for Felix Höflmayer.

References

Aruz, J. (ed.) 2008, *Beyond Babylon: Art, Trade, and Diplomacy in the Second Millennium B.C.*, Yale University Press, New Haven.

Aston, B. G. 1994, Ancient Egyptian stone vessels: materials and forms, *Studien zur Archäologie und Geschichte Altägyptens*, **5**, Heidelberger Orientverlag, Heidelberg.

Beaux, N. 1990, Le cabinet de curiosités de Thoutmosis III: Plantes et animaux du 'Jardin botanique' de Karnak, *Orientalia Lovaniensia Analecta*, **36**, Peeters, Leuven.

Beckerath, J. von 1997, Chronologie des pharaonischen Ägypten: Die Zeitbestimmung der ägyptischen Geschichte von der Vorzeit bis 332 v. Chr., *Münchener Ägyptologische Studien*, **46**, Philipp von Zabern, Mainz am Rhein.

Bietak, M. and Höflmayer, F. 2007, Introduction: high and low chronology, in *The synchronisation of civilisations in the eastern Mediterranean in the second millennium B.C. III* (eds M. Bietak and E. Czerny), 13–23, Verlag der Österreichischen Akademie der Wissenschaften, Wien.

Bronk Ramsey, C., Manning S. W. and Galimberti, M. 2004, Dating the volcanic eruption at Thera, *Radiocarbon*, **46**, 325–44.

Bronk Ramsey, C. 2009, Bayesian analysis of radiocarbon dates, *Radiocarbon*, **51**, 337–60.

Bronk Ramsey, C., Dee, M. W., Rowland, J. M., Higham, T. F. G., Harris, S. A., Brock, F. A., Quiles, A., Wild, E. M., Marcus, E. S. and Shortland, A. J. 2010, Radiocarbon-based chronology for Dynastic Egypt, *Science*, **328**, 1554–7.

Bruins, H. J., MacGillivray, J. A., Synolakis, C. E., Benjamini, C., Keller, J., Kisch, H. J., Klügel, A. and van der Plicht, J. 2008, Geoarchaeological tsunami deposits at Palaikastro (Crete) and the Late Minoan IA eruption of Santorini, *Journal of Archaeological Science*, **35**, 191–212.

Bruins, H. J., van der Plicht, J. and MacGillivray, J. A. 2009, The Minoan Santorini eruption and tsunami deposits in Palaikastro (Crete): dating by geology, archaeology, ^{14}C and Egyptian chronology, *Radiocarbon*, **51**, 397–411.

Buchholz, H.-G. 1974, Ägäische Funde und Kultureinflüsse in den Randgebieten des Mittelmeeres. Forschungsbericht über Ausgrabungen und Neufunde, 1960–1970, *Archäologischer Anzeiger*, **1974**, 325–462.

Dee, M. W., Brock, F., Harris, S. A., Bronk Ramsey, C., Shortland, A. J., Higham, T. F. G. and Rowland, J. M. 2010, Investigating the likelihood of a reservoir offset in the radiocarbon record for ancient Egypt, *Journal of Archaeological Science*, **37**, 687–93.

Dziobek, E. 1992, Das Grab des Ineni: Theben Nr. 81, *Archäologische Veröffentlichungen*, **68**, Philipp von Zabern, Mainz am Rhein.

Fimmen, D. 1924, *Die Kretisch-Mykenische Kultur*, Teubner, Leipzig.

Friedrich, W. L., Kromer, B., Friedrich, M., Heinemeier, J., Pfeiffer, T. and Talamo, S. 2006, Santorini eruption radiocarbon dated to 1627–1600 BC, *Science*, **312**, 548.

Furtwängler, A. and Loeschcke, G. 1886, *Mykenische Vasen*, Asher & Co., Berlin.

Furumark, A. 1950, The settlement at Ialysos and Aegean history *c*. 1550–1400 B.C., *Opuscula Archaeologica*, **6**, 150–271.

Hassler, A. in print, Mycenaean pottery in Egypt reconsidered: old contexts and new results, *Proceedings of the Xth International Congress of Egyptologists*.

Hein, I. 1994, Erste Beobachtungen zur Keramik aus ʿEzbet Helmi, *Ägypten & Levante*, **4**, 39–43.

Hein, I. 2007, The significance of the Lustrous Ware finds from ʿEzbet Helmi/Tell el Dabʿa (Egypt), in *The Lustrous Wares of Late Bronze Age Cyprus and the Eastern Mediterranean* (ed. I. Hein), 79–107, Verlag der Österreichischen Akademie der Wissenschaften, Wien.

Höflmayer, F. 2008, Das Ende von SM IB: Naturwissenschaftliche und archäologische Datierung, *Ägypten & Levante*, **18**, 157–71.

Höflmayer, F. 2009, Aegean–Egyptian synchronisms and radiocarbon chronology, in *Time's up! Dating the Minoan eruption of Santorini. Acts of the Minoan Eruption Chronology Workshop, Sandbjerg, November 2007, initiated by Jan Heinemeier and Walter L. Friedrich* (ed. D. A. Warburton), 187–95, Monographs of the Danish Institute at Athens Volume 10, The Danish Institute at Athens, Athens.

Housley, R. A., Manning, S. W., Cadogan, G., Jones, R. E., Hedges, R. E. M. 1999, Radiocarbon, calibration, and the chronology of the Late Minoan IB phase, *Journal of Archaeological Science*, **26**, 159–71.

Kantor, H. 1947, The Aegean and the Orient in the second millennium B.C., *American Journal of Archaeology*, **51**, 17–108.

Kitchen, K. A. 2000, Regnal and genealogical data of ancient Egypt (absolute chronology I). The historical chronology of ancient Egypt, a current assessment, in *The synchronisation of civilisations in the eastern Mediterranean in the second millennium B.C. I* (ed. M. Bietak), 39–52, Verlag der Österreichische Akademie der Wissenschaften, Wien.

Kitchen, K. A. 2002, Ancient Egyptian chronology for Aegeanists, *Mediterranean Archaeology and Archaeometry*, **2**, 5–12.

Kitchen, K. A. 2007, Egyptian and related chronologies – look, no sciences, no pots! in *The synchronisation of civilizations in the eastern Mediterranean in the second millennium B.C. – III* (eds M. Bietak and E. Czerny), 163–71, Verlag der Österreichische Akademie der Wissenschaften, Wien.

Lepsius, C. R. 1849–1859, *Denkmäler aus Ägypten und Äthiopien: Nach den Zeichnungen der von Seiner Majestät dem Könige von Preussen Friedrich Wilhelm IV nach diesen Ländern gesendeten und in den Jahren 1842–1845 ausgeführten wissenschaftlichen Expedition*, J. C. Hinrich, Leipzig.

Manning, S. W. 1999, *A Test of Time: The Volcano of Thera and the Chronology and History of the Aegean and East Mediterranean in the Mid-Second Millennium BC*, Oxbow Books, Oxford.

Manning, S. W. 2009, Beyond the Santorini eruption: some notes on dating the Late Minoan IB period on Crete, and implications for Cretan–Egyptian relations in the 15th century BC (and especially LM II), in *Time's up! Dating the Minoan eruption of Santorini. Acts of the Minoan Eruption Chronology Workshop, Sandbjerg, November 2007, initiated by Jan Heinemeier and Walter L. Friedrich* (ed. D. A.Warburton), 207–26, Monographs of the Danish Institute at Athens, vol. 10, The Danish Institute at Athens, Athens.

Manning, S. W., Bronk Ramsey, C., Doumas, C., Marketou, T., Cadogan, G. and Pearson, C. L. 2002, New evidence for an early date for the Aegean Late Bronze Age and Thera eruption, *Antiquity*, **76**, 733–44.

Manning, S. W., Bronk Ramsey, C., Kutschera,W., Higham, T., Kromer, B., Steier P., and Wild, E. M. 2006, Chronology for the Aegean Late Bronze Age 1700–1400 B.C., *Science*, **312**, 565–9.

Martin, M. and Ben-Dov, R., 2007, Egyptian and Egyptian-style pottery at Tel Dan, *Ägypten & Levante*, **17**, 191–203.

Mountjoy, P. A., 1999, *Regional Mycenaean Decorated Pottery*, Marie Leidorf, Rahden/Westf.

Pendlebury, J. D., 1930, *Aegyptiaca: A Catalogue of Egyptian Objects in the Aegean Area*, Cambridge University Press, Cambridge.

Petrie, W. M. F., 1927, *Objects of Daily Use: Illustrated by the Egyptian Collection in University College, London*, Quaritch, London.

Petrie, W. M. F. 1937, *The Funeral Furniture of Egypt with Stone and Metal Vases*, Quaritch, London.

Reimer, P. J., Baillie, M. G. L., Bard, E., Bayliss, A., Beck, J.W., Blackwell, P. G., Bronk Ramsey, C., Buck, C. E., Burr, G. S., Edwards, R. L., Friedrich, M., Grootes, P. M., Guilderson, T. P., Hajdas, I., Heaton, T. J., Hogg, A. G., Hughen, K. A., Kaiser, K. F., Kromer, B., McCormac, F. G., Manning, S. W., Reimer, R. W., Richards, D. A., Southon, J. R., Talamo, S., Turney, C. S. M., van der Plicht, J. and Weyhenmeyer, C. E. 2009, IntCal09 and Marine09 radiocarbon age calibration curves, 0–50,000 years cal bp, *Radiocarbon*, **51**(4), 1111–58.

Shaw, I. (ed.) 2000, *The Oxford History of Ancient Egypt*, Oxford University Press, Oxford.

Soles, J. S. 2004, Appendix A. Radiocarbon results, in *Mochlos IC Period III: Neopalatial settlement on the coast, the Artisans' Quarter and the farmhouse at Chalinomouri: the small finds* (eds J. Soles and C. Davaras), 145–9, Prehistory monographs, 9, INSTAP Academic Press, Philadelphia.

Wace, A. J. and Blegen, C. W 1939, Pottery as evidence for trade and colonisation in the Aegean Bronze Age, *Klio*, **32**, 131–47.

Warren, P. 2006, The date of the Thera eruption in relation to Aegean-Egyptian interconnections and the Egyptian historical chronology, in *Timelines: Studies in Honor of Manfred Bietak* (eds E. Czerny, I. Hein, H. Hunger, D. Melman and A. Schwab), 305–321, Peeters, Leuven.

Warren, P. 2009, The date of the Late Bronze Age eruption of Santorini, in *Time's up! Dating the Minoan eruption of Santorini. Acts of the Minoan Eruption Chronology Workshop, Sandbjerg, November 2007, initiated by Jan Heinemeier and Walter L. Friedrich* (ed. D. A. Warburton), 181–6, Monographs of the Danish Institute at Athens, vol. 10, The Danish Institute at Athens, Athens.

Warren, P. and Hankey, V., 1989, *Aegean Bronze Age Chronology*, Bristol Classical Press, Bristol.

Wild, E. M., Gauß, W., Forstenpointner, G., Lindblom, M., Smetana, R., Steier, P., Thanheiser, U. and Weninger, F. 2010, ^{14}C dating of the Early to Late Bronze Age stratigraphic sequence of Aegina Kolonna, Greece, *Nuclear Instruments and Methods in Physics Research B*, **268**, 1013–21.

CHAPTER 10

Radiocarbon Calibration in the Mid to Later 14th Century BC and Radiocarbon Dating Tell el-Amarna, Egypt

S. W. Manning, B. Kromer, M. W. Dee, M. Friedrich, T. F. G. Higham and C. Bronk Ramsey

Tell el-Amarna was the short-lived Egyptian capital city founded by Amenhotep IV (Akhenaten) and then abandoned about 15 years later. This brief Amarna episode in the mid-14th century BC represents one of the best known, historically attested, and historically dated periods in the ancient Near East for the whole of the second millennium BC. Preserved royal correspondence from the site provides specific links between the rulers of, and so the historical chronologies of, Egypt, Assyria and Babylonia. It is thus an obvious test case for assessing the reliability of radiocarbon dating. At the same time, it seems likely that a 'wiggle' in the radiocarbon calibration curve might be relevant to calendar dating around this time period. We report linked investigations of (i) the dating of the Tell el-Amarna site by radiocarbon, and (ii) the ^{14}C calibration record 1360–1200 BC.

Introduction

The site of Tell el-Amarna in Egypt comprises one of the best-documented, closely dated, short-term archaeological horizons from the entire second millennium BC (for the vast bibliography before the AD 1990s, see Martin 1991; since, see especially Gabolde 1998; Freed *et al.* 1999; and the listings at http://www.archaeowiki.org/Bibliography_of_the_Amarna_Period [last accessed 6 December 2010]). An archive of clay tablets from the site preserves correspondence between the kings of Egypt (Amenhotep III and IV and Tutankhamun)

Authors' Addresses: **S. W. Manning**, Department of Classics and Malcolm and Carolyn Wiener Laboratory for Aegean and Near Eastern Dendrochronology, B–48 Goldwin Smith Hall, Cornell University, Ithaca NY 14853–3201, USA; **B. Kromer**, Heidelberg Academy of Sciences, Heidelberg, and Klaus-Tschira Scientific Dating Laboratory, Curt-Engelhorn-Centre for Archaeometry, C 5 Zeughaus D-68159 Mannheim, Germany; **M. Friedrich**, Institute of Botany, University of Hohenheim, Garbenstraße 30, D-70593 Stuttgart, Germany
M. W. Dee, **T. F. G. Higham** and **C. Bronk Ramsey** RLAHA, University of Oxford, Dyson Perrins Building, South Parks Road, Oxford OX1 3QY, UK

and the rulers of the other main Near Eastern states, especially Assyria, Babylonia and the kingdom of the Hittites (Moran 1992, xxxiv–xxxix, for a brief review of the chronology from the letters; Cohen and Westbrook 2000). Thus, the short Amarna period in Egypt, and the Egyptian historical and astronomical-historical chronology, is at this time linked with the independent historical and astronomical-historical chronologies for Assyria and Babylonia. These multiple inter-locking linkages require approximate calendar dates for the Amarna period within relatively narrow margins (a decade or so), given the uncertainties generally thought to apply to each of the respective ancient Near Eastern chronologies (see Krauss and Warburton 2009, 130–131; 2006; Klinger 2006; von Beckerath 1997, 59–67; Kitchen 2000, 43; Brinkman 1976).

The analysis of organic samples recovered from the archaeological excavations at the site therefore offers us the possibility of testing the accuracy and precision of high-quality radiocarbon dating and of comparing the results with the dates provided by the Egyptian historical chronology (as also in Bronk Ramsey *et al.* 2010). In this paper we consider: (i) the analysis of some previously published data (Switsur 1984; Manning 2006, 335–338), and (ii) a new larger set of radiocarbon measurements on samples from the same excavation and sampling project at Amarna. We further consider the robustness and possible scale of variations in the latest radiocarbon calibration curve for the period on the basis of recently published and new ^{14}C data on known-age German oak samples (Kromer *et al.* 2010; and data in this paper below). We conclude with a discussion of the radiocarbon dates for Amarna, and the wider ramifications of the successful linking of a ^{14}C-based time-scale with the historical chronology in Egypt.

Tell el-Amarna

The site known as Tell el-Amarna was the short-lived capital of Egypt during the 'Amarna Age' under Amenhotep IV (Akhenaten; see e.g. Kemp 1984; 1987; Murnane 1985; Aldred 1988; Watterson 1999; Monserrat 2000; Giles 2001; and see http://www.amarnaproject.com/ – last accessed 6 December 2010). Foundation of the new capital occurred in Year 5 of the reign of Amenhotep IV (following Murnane and Van Siclen 1993; Hornung 2006, 206), and the city became the capital by Year 9. From about Year 2 of Tutankhamun's reign, it ceased to function as a capital and it was in the process of being destroyed by the time of Horemheb's rule. The epigraphic record of Amarna makes reference to 16 successive wine vintages from Years 5–17 of Amenhotep IV and for 3 years under his successors while the site was occupied. The vintage from Amenhotep IV's Year 4 occurred before the site was founded, but it was consumed at the site (and wine labels from the site thus attest it) in the period until the Year 5 vintage was available (Hornung 2006, 207–208).

In current standard Egyptian historical chronological assessments the accession of Amenhotep IV is dated late (November/December) in the year of *c.* 1355–1351 BC, and the accession of Horemheb is placed *c.* 1323–1319 BC (Kitchen 2000; 2007; von Beckerath 1994; 1997; Hornung *et al.* 2006), thus the period of 16 years of main occupation at Amarna is between about 1351/47 BC to 1335/30 BC. An alternative assessment offered recently suggests dates about 11 years later (due to a suggested reduction in the reign length of Horemheb to 14 years, instead of 26 or 27 years: see Krauss and Warburton 2009, 128–129), with the reign of Amenhotep IV placed 1342–1325 BC (Krauss and Warburton 2009, 134). On this scheme, the Amarna context likely lies between 1338–1322 BC. Thus the radiocarbon measurements on shorter or short-lived samples (likely approximately contemporary with find context) should date within the above calendar time spans (e.g. 1351/47 to 1335/30 BC on the standard chronology), and measurements on longer-lived samples should either date a little before this time range or into this range.

Samples

The samples from Amarna analysed in this paper come from the excavations of Kemp (1984). The data comprise: (i) 5 previously published radiocarbon measurements on a range of materials (bone, horn, skin, wood and charcoal) collected specifically for a high-quality programme of radiocarbon dating (Switsur 1984;182–184), and (ii) 11 new radiocarbon measurements on other sample material left over from this same exercise supplied by Kemp and AMS radiocarbon dated at the Oxford Radiocarbon Accelerator Unit (ORAU). These samples were too small for radiocarbon dating in the pre-AMS era. The material includes both shorter/short-lived samples and some longer-lived material (see Table 10.1).

The archaeological context of the samples was a midden, probably deposited early within the site's short history and 'thus during the reign of Akhenaten rather than that of Tutankhamun' (Switsur 1984;182–183). Some of the materials are likely to be annual-scale (grass, reeds, papyrus) but others probably embrace a few years of growth (bone, horn, skin, leather/tissue). Most should pre-date by about 0–10 years the date of their use. If work at Amarna starts about Year 5 of Amenhotep IV, then, on average the in-built age should be less than about 5 years since half of the short-lived samples are in the likely c. 0–1 year category. As a set, the samples should date no earlier than about the accession of Amenhotep IV and/or during his reign. The expected historical date range might be narrowed to between c. 1351/47 BC to 1338/34 BC on the standard Egyptian historical chronology, and c. 1338–1325 BC on the recent Krauss and Warburton (2009) chronology.

Methods

The samples measured at the ORAU (from Amarna, and also some decadal samples of known-age German oak – see Table 10.2) followed the laboratory's standard chemical pre-treatment, target preparation and AMS measurement procedures (Bronk Ramsey *et al.* 2004; Brock *et al.* 2010, and this volume, Chapter 5). Isotopic fractionation has been corrected for by employing the measured $\delta^{13}C$ values from the AMS. The reported $\delta^{13}C$ values in Tables 10.1 and 10.2 come from independent measurements on a stable isotope mass spectrometer (±0.2 ‰ relative to VPDB).

Table 10.1: Radiocarbon data from Tell el-Amarna employed in this study. Cambridge (Q) data are as previously published by Switsur (1984). The data from the Oxford Radiocarbon Accelerator Unit are presented here for the first time.

Lab ID	Amarna ID	Material	LL or SL or Marine	$\delta^{13}C$	^{14}C Age Years BP	SD
Q-2401		wood	LL		3035	35
Q-2402		charcoal	LL		3055	35
Q-2403		skin	SL		3050	35
Q-2404		horn	SL		3025	35
Q-2405		bone	SL		3088	35
OxA-14536	AMAR 40	Hair	SL	-19.1	2187	30
OxA-14537	AMAR 09	Plant remains (reed)	SL	-8.9	3116	31
OxA-14538	AMAR 27	Plant remains (Halfa grass root)	SL	-8.5	3134	32
OxA-14539	AMAR 42	Tissue (worked leather)	SL	-21.1	3058	31
OxA-14540	AMAR 46	Plant remains (reeds)	SL	-24.9	3109	33
OxA-14563	AMAT 10	Plant remains (papyrus, pith?)	SL	-9.0	3134	34
OxA-14564	AMAR 45	Plant remains (Halfa grass stalk)	SL	-9.7	3068	33
OxA-14565	AMAR 48	Tissue (leather)	SL	-17.7	3137	33
OxA-14611	AMAR 29	Charcoal	LL	-24.3	3066	32
OxA-14612	AMAR 47	Wood	LL	-26.7	3109	31
OxA-14809	AMAR 16	Shell (common clam)	Marine	-8.1	3560	34

Table 10.2: Oxford Radiocarbon Accelerator Unit radiocarbon measurements on known-age German Oak samples from Augsfeld.

Tree-Rings BC	Centre Date BC	Hohenheim Sample No.	OxA No.	$\delta^{13}C$	^{14}C Age Years BP	SD
1357–1351	1354	26218	15702	-25.5	3052	35
1350–1346	1348	26219	15651	-25.3	3046	30
1345–1341	1343	26220	15652	-24.4	3123	30
1340–1336	1338	26221	15653	-24.3	3052	30
1335–1331	1333	26222	15654	-24.3	3107	30
1330–1326	1328	26223	15655	-24.3	3094	30
1325–1321	1323	26224	15656	-23.5	3121	30
1320–1316	1318	26225	15657	-23.8	3067	31
1320–1316	1318	26225	15658	-23.8	3088	30
1315–1311	1313	26226	15659	-23.3	3045	31
1310–1306	1308	26227	15660	-24.4	3082	30
1305–1301	1303	26228	15661	-23.9	3054	30

Results And Analysis With Intcal09

The radiocarbon ages obtained for each of the samples from Amarna are listed in Table 10.1. We may make the following initial observations:

1. The radiocarbon age of OxA-14809 on a clam shell is clearly much older than all the other determinations. This is expected because shell determinations usually have a marine reservoir offset, in this case about 470 ± 36 ^{14}C years BP (the difference between the date of OxA-14809 and the weighted average of the shorter/short-lived terrestrial samples at ~3093 ± 11 ^{14}C years BP – see below – note: hereafter dates in ^{14}C years BP [from AD 1950] are expressed just as BP). This is within the range of marine reservoir offsets found in previous studies of known-age marine shells from the region (Reimer and McCormac 2002; Sinai *et al.* 2000). This translates to about 495–629 calendar years age difference at 68.2% probability in the dating model shown in Figure 10.1. The sample merely offers an irrelevant (much too old) *terminus post quem* for the Amarna horizon.
2. The radiocarbon age of OxA-14536, on a sample of hair, is much more recent than all the other data, indicating a calendar age range between 356–197 BC at 68.2% probability. This sample thus indicates an historical date somewhere from the late (Nectanebo II) 30th Dynasty through to Ptolemy V Epiphanes. The sample therefore indicates some much later post-Amarna period activity at the site (but before the later Roman-late Antique evidence known from the area: Kemp 1993; Pyke 2010); however, it is irrelevant to dating the Amarna period.
3. Four of the data may be characterised as long/longer-lived (LL): see Table 10.1.
4. The ten other remaining data (thus excluding OxA-14536, see above) may be characterized as shorter or short-lived (SL; i.e. the samples dated likely represent 0–1 to about 10 years likely biological age). It is possible to combine all these 10 samples to offer a weighted average consistent (at the 95% confidence level) with the hypothesis that they represent the same short real chronological horizon (Ward and Wilson 1978): 3093 ± 11 BP. We use this weighted average as the best estimate of the Amarna shorter/short-lived dating horizon in the model shown in Figure 10.1 (likely a period of about *c.* 5–12 calendar years at most following Switsur 1984; 182–183 and discussion above about scale of in-built age for the set).
5. We assume that the overall data set offers the approximate relative time sequence of: *OxA-14809 > LL ≥ SL > OxA-14536*
6. Analyses on 18th–19th century AD known-age plant material from Egypt has indicated that a small growing season offset – approximately 19±5 years – applies when radiocarbon dating samples which grew in Egypt in its pre-modern (that is pre-dam) hydrologic context (Dee *et al.* 2010; Bronk Ramsey *et al.* 2010; Chapter 6). We consider our analyses below initially without, and then *with* this offset factor. Dee *et al.* (2010) and Bronk Ramsey *et al.* (2010) conclude that this offset is real and ought to be included in the calibration of Egyptian samples.

We show the analysis of the Amarna data in light of points 1–5 employing OxCal 4.1 (Bronk Ramsey 1995; 2009a; 2009b) and IntCal09 (Reimer *et al.* 2009) in Figures 10.1 and 10.2. The 68.2% probability range for the dating of the shorter/short-lived (SL) samples

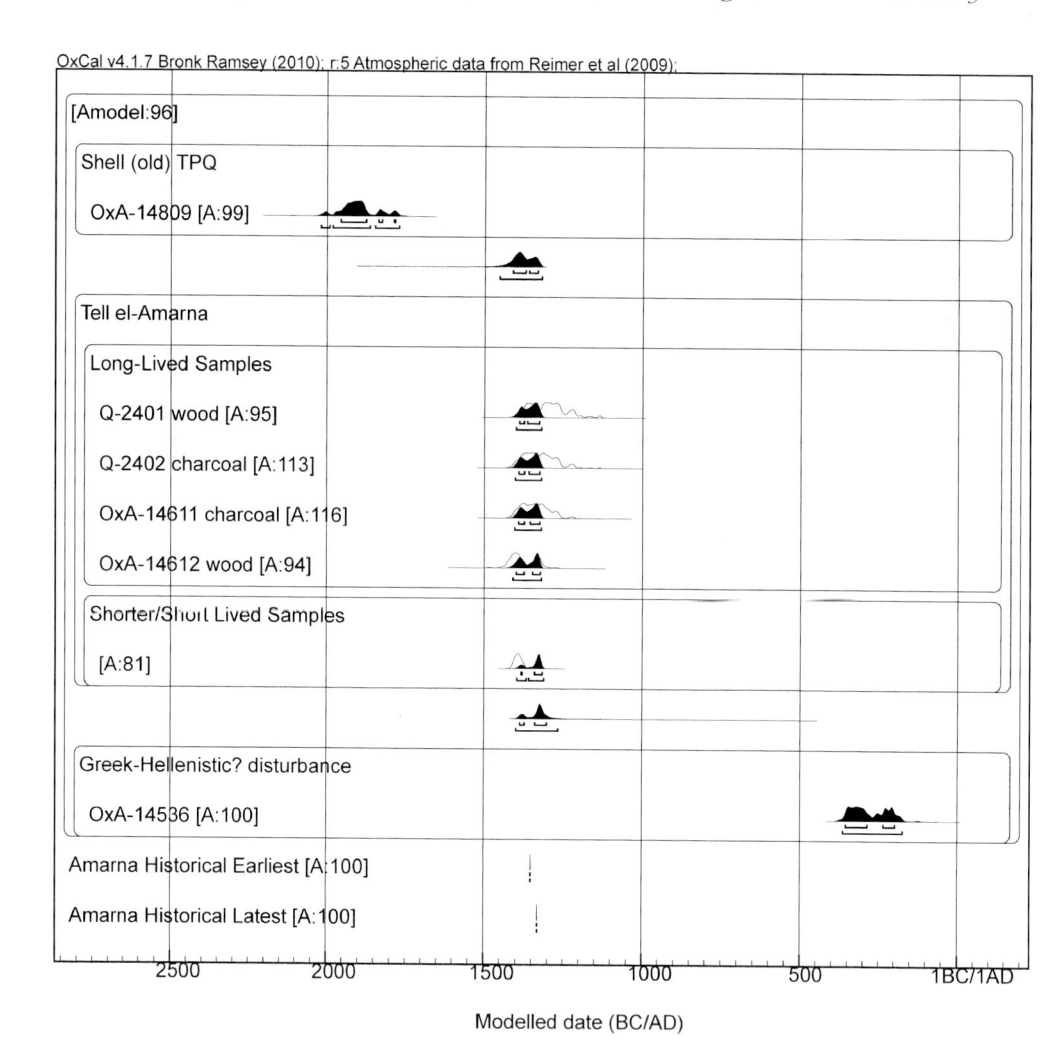

Figure 10.1: The initial Amarna dating model employed (for the outputs in Figures 10.2–10.4). The shell sample is treated as an earlier phase, and the hair from a separate later 1st millennium context. The samples from the Amarna midden are considered as first the long/longer-Lived (LL) samples and then second the weighted average of the dates on the shorter/short-lived (SL) samples. The expected historical age range for the Amarna context is indicated at the bottom. Calibration and analysis employs IntCal09 (Reimer et al. 2009) using OxCal version 4.1.7 (Bronk Ramsey 1995; 2009a; 2009b) with curve resolution set at 5. The hollow distributions show the non-modelled calibrated age probabilities and the solid distributions show the calibrated probabilities applying the dating model. The lines under each distribution indicate the 68.2% and 95.4% probability ranges for each modelled distribution. The A values in the square parentheses are the OxCal agreement values; a value ≥60 is regarded as acceptable and approximately offers a 95% agreement level. Note that any run of a Sequence analysis in OxCal will produce very slightly different outcomes, and variations of about 0–1 calendar years, or of around 0–1%, in the ranges/percentages illustrated are possible. The figures shown in this paper represent typical outcomes from several runs.

is 1384–1380 BC (3.9%) and 1342–1317 BC (64.3%), and the 95.4% probability range is 1398–1368 (20%) and 1360–1312 BC (75.4%) (Figure 10.2). Thus the most likely calibrated calendar dating range found, 1342–1317 BC (64.3% of the probability), is potentially compatible with the likely standard historical age range of 1351/47–1338/34 BC (or the recent lower historical chronology *c.* 1338–1325 BC) – *but* is tending to be a little too late (by one to two decades versus the standard chronology especially).

We then show the outcome of the same analysis but adding in point 6 above – thus including a 19±5 years offset factor to account for samples growing in Egypt (after Dee *et al.* 2010) and show the calendar age ranges achieved for the shorter/short-lived (SL) samples in Figure 10.3. The calibrated age ranges (1352–1314 at 68.2% probability) obtained become highly compatible with both the expected standard historical age range (1351/47–1338/34 BC) and the range from the revised Krauss and Warburton (2009) chronology (1338–1325 BC). Figure 10.4 shows the same analysis but employing the IntCal98 calibration curve

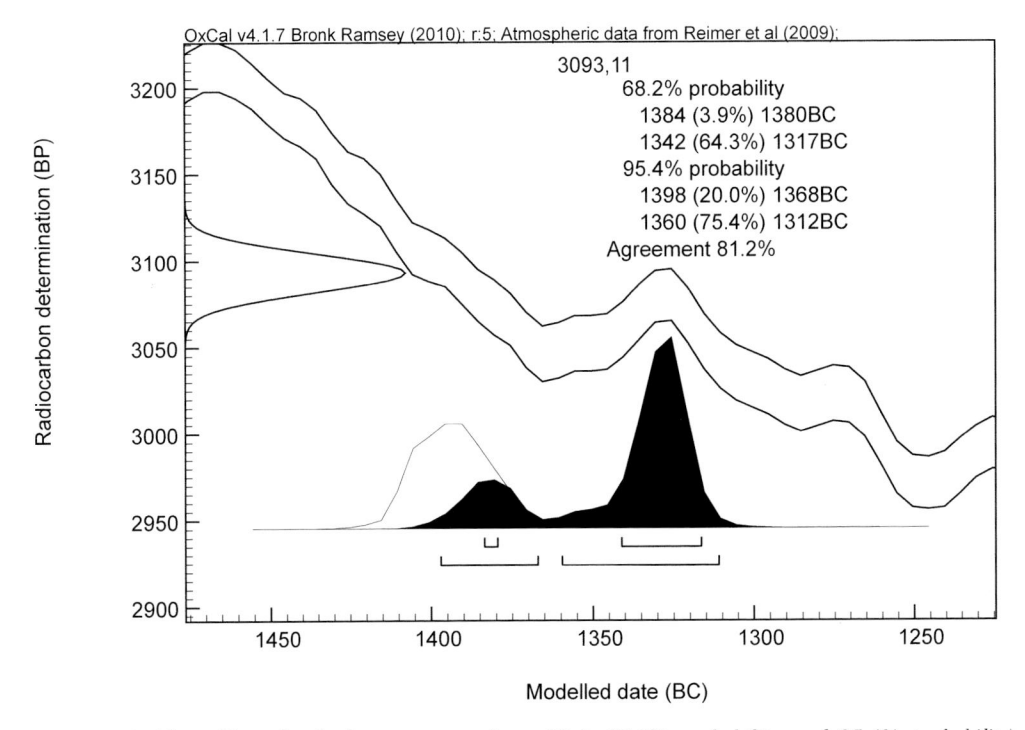

Figure 10.2: The calibrated calendar age ranges (most likely 68.2% probability, and 95.4% probability) determined for the shorter/short-lived (SL) data from Amarna in the model illustrated in Figure 10.1 run against IntCal09 (Reimer et al. 2009) using OxCal version 4.1.7 (Bronk Ramsey 1995; 2009a; 2009b) with curve resolution set at 5. The non-modelled calibrated probability distribution is shown by the hollow histogram (the right-hand-side is hidden by the solid histogram), the modelled distribution by the solid histogram. Note that any run of a Sequence analysis in OxCal will produce very slightly different outcomes, and variations of about 0–1 calendar years, or of around 0–1%, in the ranges/percentages illustrated are possible. The figures shown in this paper represent typical outcomes from several runs.

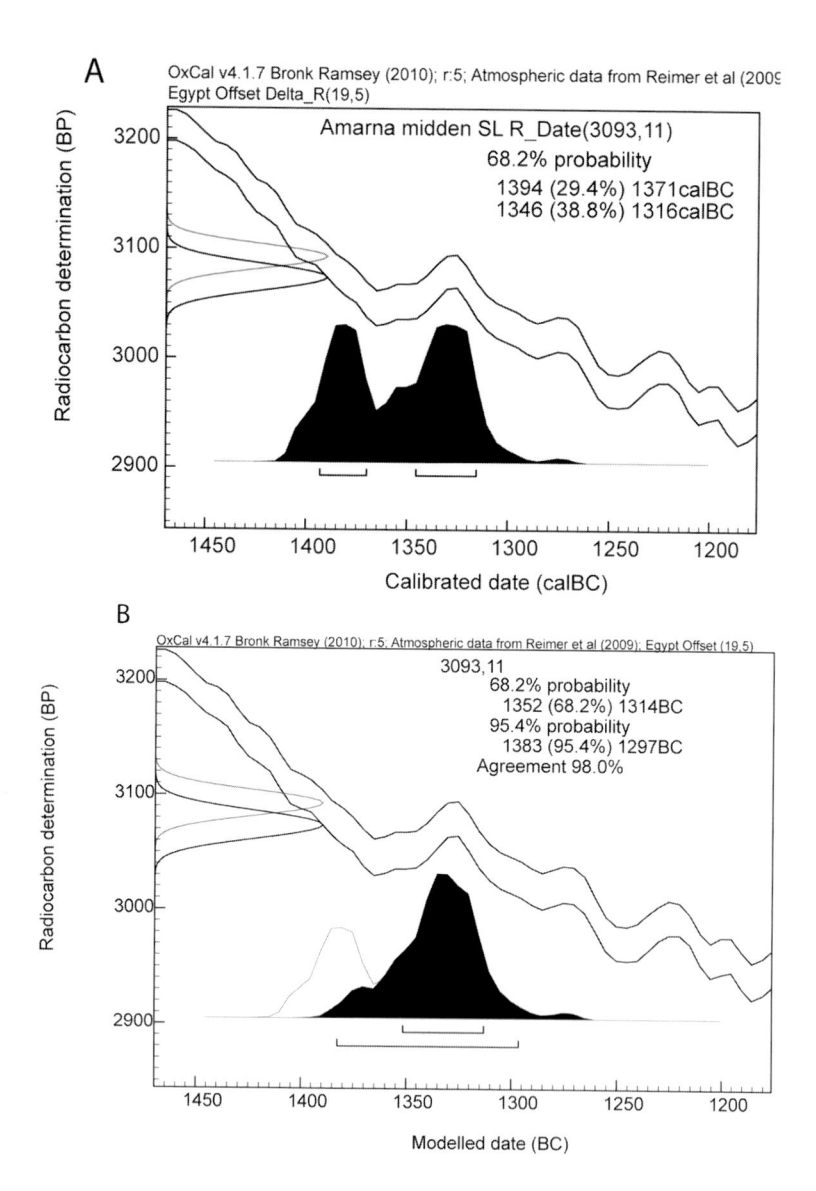

Figure 10.3: A. *The upper figure shows the non-modelled intersection of the weighted average age for the shorter/short-lived samples from the Amarna midden (Table 10.1, as used in Figures 10.1 and 10.2) adjusted by the Egyptian growing-season-related offset factor of 19 ± 5 years for samples growing/living in pre-modern, pre-dam, Egypt after Dee et al. (2010) with the IntCal09 radiocarbon calibration curve (Reimer et al. 2009), and the resultant calibrated calendar probability distribution. The most likely 68.2% probability range is shown. This shows that there are, with no other constraints, two possible dating regions for these data: (i) around 1400 BC and into the early 14th century BC on the slope in the calibration curve, and the other (ii) in the later 14th century BC on the slope leading to and around the 'wiggle' in the calibration curve. B. The lower figure shows the modelled calendar age range for the Amarna midden shorter/short-lived sample set applying the dating model in Figure 10.1 and with the Egyptian growing-season-related offset factor of 19±5 years (hence contrast with Figure 10.2). The long/longer-lived samples occupy the possible earlier dating zone ((i) above), and thus the sequence analysis resolves the ambiguity for the dating of the Amarna midden shorter/short-lived set in favour of the later ((ii) above) of the two possible initial date ranges identified in the upper figure A.*

10. *Radiocarbon Calibration in the Mid to Later 14th Century BC* 129

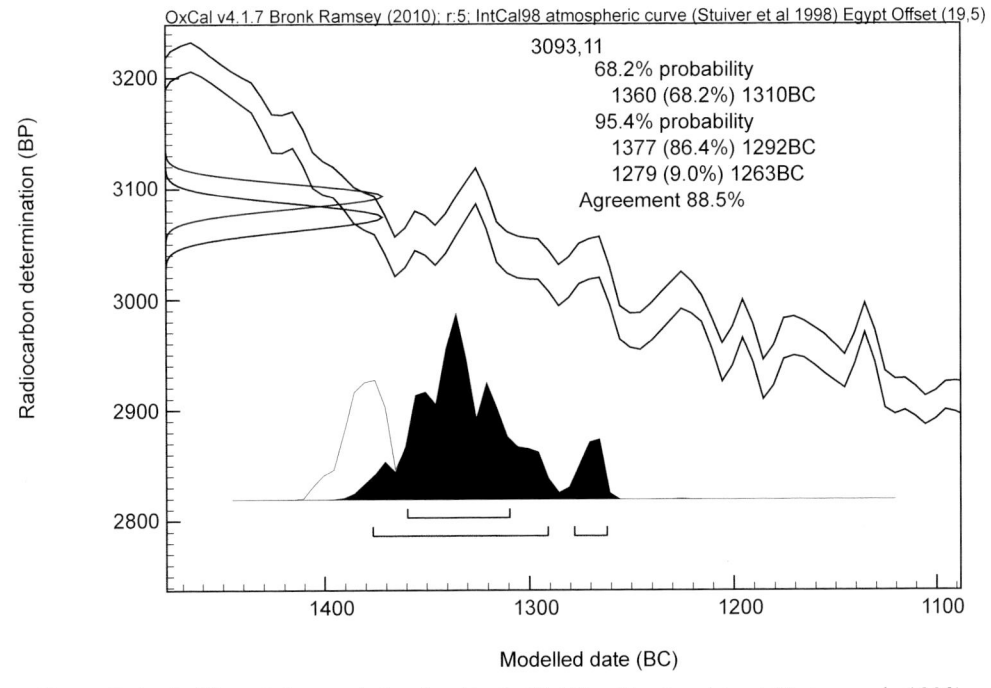

Figure 10.4: As Figure 3 but employing the older IntCal98 calibration dataset (Stuiver et al. 1998).

(Stuiver *et al.* 1998) – IntCal98 used largely the same underlying tree-ring data but has a less smoothed curve. The most likely 68.2% probability range here is 1360–1310 BC. This can also offer a good match for the standard historical chronology or the revised dates of Krauss and Warburton. The allowance for the 19±5 years growing-season-related offset factor for samples growing/living in Egypt (after Dee *et al.* 2010), however, clearly allows the Amarna samples to date in the 'expected' range during the reign of Amenhotep IV (*c.* 1351/47 BC to 1338/34 BC on the standard chronology).

Comparison With Other Data

A number of dates for short-lived material associated with contexts dating to the reign of Amenhotep IV/Akhenaten (all from Amarna), and also a set from the (shortly) subsequent reign of Tutankhamun (from Thebes) were published by Bronk Ramsey *et al.* (2010). We may compare the data on shorter/short-lived (SL) samples in the present study with these other data (Figures 10.5 and 10.6). If all of the data by their find context or constituent material groupings are considered in a sequence with only those measurements on the same sample pooled together, then, using the general outlier model of Bronk Ramsey (2009b) at the 5% level on the radiocarbon time-scale with IntCal09 and the Egyptian growing season offset included, seven data are highlighted as outliers (Figures 10.5 and 10.6). Five of these are 'certain' outliers (OxA-20482, OxA-19004, OxA-19263, VERA-4686 and VERA-4686B),

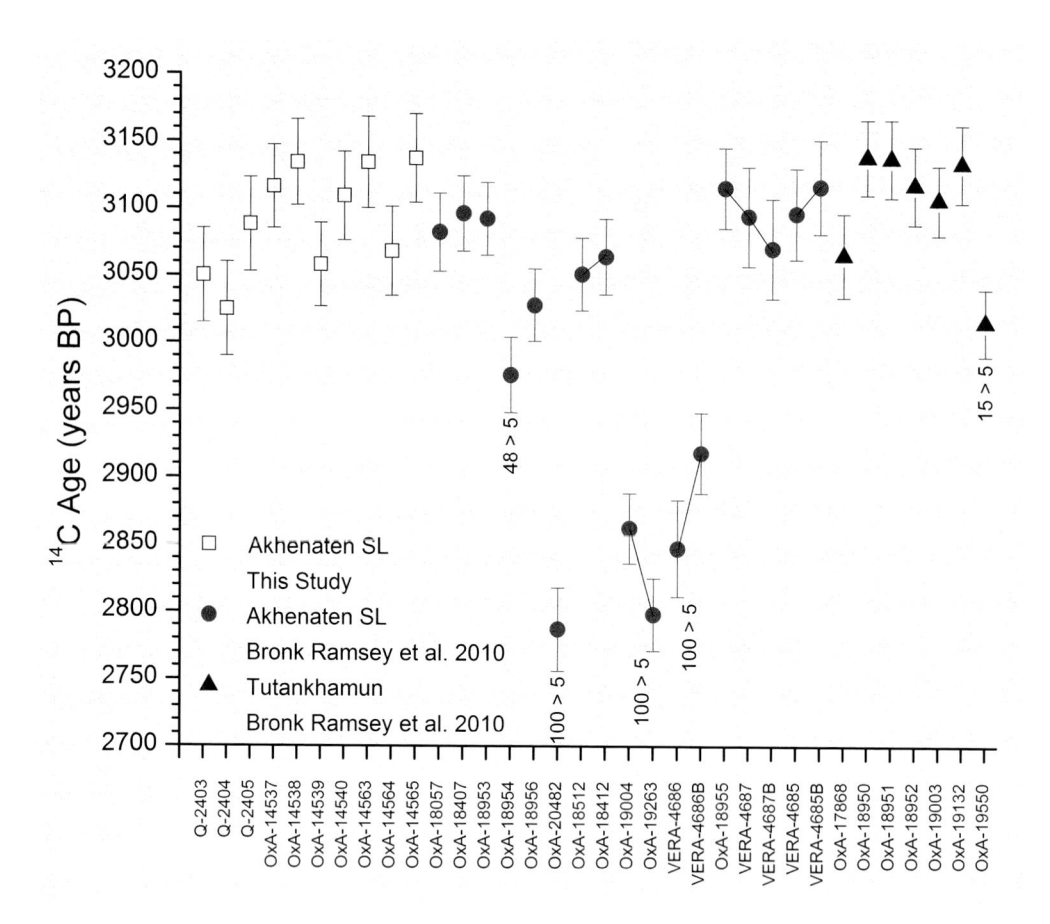

Figure 10.5: A comparison of the radiocarbon ages (1σ error bars shown) for the shorter/short-lived samples in this study (Table 10.1) from the Amenheotep IV/Akhenaten context at Amarna with other recent radiocarbon measurements on (i) short-lived samples from contexts associated with Akhenaten from Bronk Ramsey et al. (2010), and (ii) short-lived samples from the shortly subsequent reign of Tutankhamun from Bronk Ramsey et al. (2010). The following data comprise multiple measurements on the same sample: OxA-18512 + OxA-18412, OxA-19004 + OxA-19263, VERA-4686 + VERA-4686B, VERA-4685 + VERA-4685B, and OxA-18955 + VERA-4687 + VERA-4687B. Each of these groupings is indicated by the linking lines in the plot. The samples found to be outliers applying the general outlier model at the 5% level on the radiocarbon timescale in Bronk Ramsey (2009b) using IntCal09 and the Egyptian growing-season-related offset factor of 19±5 years in the sequence analysis shown in Figure 10.6 are indicated along with the calculated Posterior value when greater than the expected Prior value of 5 or less for non-outlier samples.

one is ~10 times more likely to be an outlier than the prior set (OxA-18954) and another is ~3 times more likely (OxA-19550). Since four of these exceptions relate to pairs of measurements on the same sample (thus OxA-19004 + OxA-19263, and VERA-4686 + VERA-4686B) – with both measurements clearly much more recent than the standard range for Amenhotep IV/Akhenaten contexts – it would seem likely that these data are either archaeologically mis-associated (relating to post Amenhotep IV/Akhenaten activity), or have some other unknown but consistent dating issue. Excluding these 7 data, the remaining set of 21 dates on shorter/short-lived samples from Amarna can successfully combine at the 95% confidence level (T=22.3 < 31.4 for df 20 at 0.05 level) with a weighted average of 3085 ± 7 BP.

The possible calendar ages for the Amenhotep IV/Akhenaten shorter/short-lived sample set considered in isolation are either (i) on the slope in the radiocarbon calibration curve around 1400 BC and into the early 14th century BC, or (ii) on the slope up to and around the 'wiggle' in the later 14th century BC (Figure 10.3A). The earlier 14th century BC option is ruled out, however, because this is where the long/longer-lived samples from the Amarna context have to date, and hence the shorter/short-lived set is placed in the second or later of the two possible fit positions (see Figures 10.1–10.4). This position is pretty clearly defined, whether employing the data in Table 10.1, or with the addition of the dozen comparable data from the Bronk Ramsey *et al.* (2010) study (Figure 10.5 – minus the six Amarna outliers identified in the previous paragraph). Thus the Amenhotep IV/Akhenaten shorter/short-lived data lie somewhere on the slope up to and around the 'wiggle' in the IntCal09 calibration curve *c.* 1325 BC.

Effect of Considering Additional Calibration Data

Since the Amarna short/shorter-lived data appear to lie more or less on the slope up to and around the wiggle in the IntCal09 and previous IntCal98 calibration curves *c.* 1325 BC – a situation noted also previously for the short-lived radiocarbon data from the Amarna period (or immediately post-Amarna period) Uluburun ship (Manning *et al.* 2009) – it is important to ask just how secure the calibration curve record or shape is at this time period. The East Mediterranean Radiocarbon (Inter-)Comparison Project (EMRCP) has measured additional known-age German Oak samples from the Hohenheim tree-ring chronologies (Friedrich *et al.* 2004) across this period in order to test the existing IntCal radiocarbon calibration record (n=36), and especially the reality of the 1325 BC wiggle (Kromer *et al.* 2010). In addition, as part of this project, 12 parallel samples of the same known-age German Oak were also measured at ORAU, with the same wood measured in both laboratories where applicable (see Table 10.2 for the additional Oxford data). The new data are shown against both the raw existing IntCal data, and the modelled IntCal09 calibration curve, in Figure 10.7. It is evident that the new data from both laboratories indicate a clear trend towards slightly older radiocarbon ages across the interval around and following (for several decades) 1325 BC. The average offset to older ages for the 48 new data shown versus IntCal09 (within the interval 1360–1200 BC against an extrapolated 1-year curve from IntCal09) is 27 ± 24 ^{14}C years (the offset varies: the main areas of offset are about 1327–1287 BC and 1269–1232 BC). Part of the explanation is that there were in fact relatively few data across this period

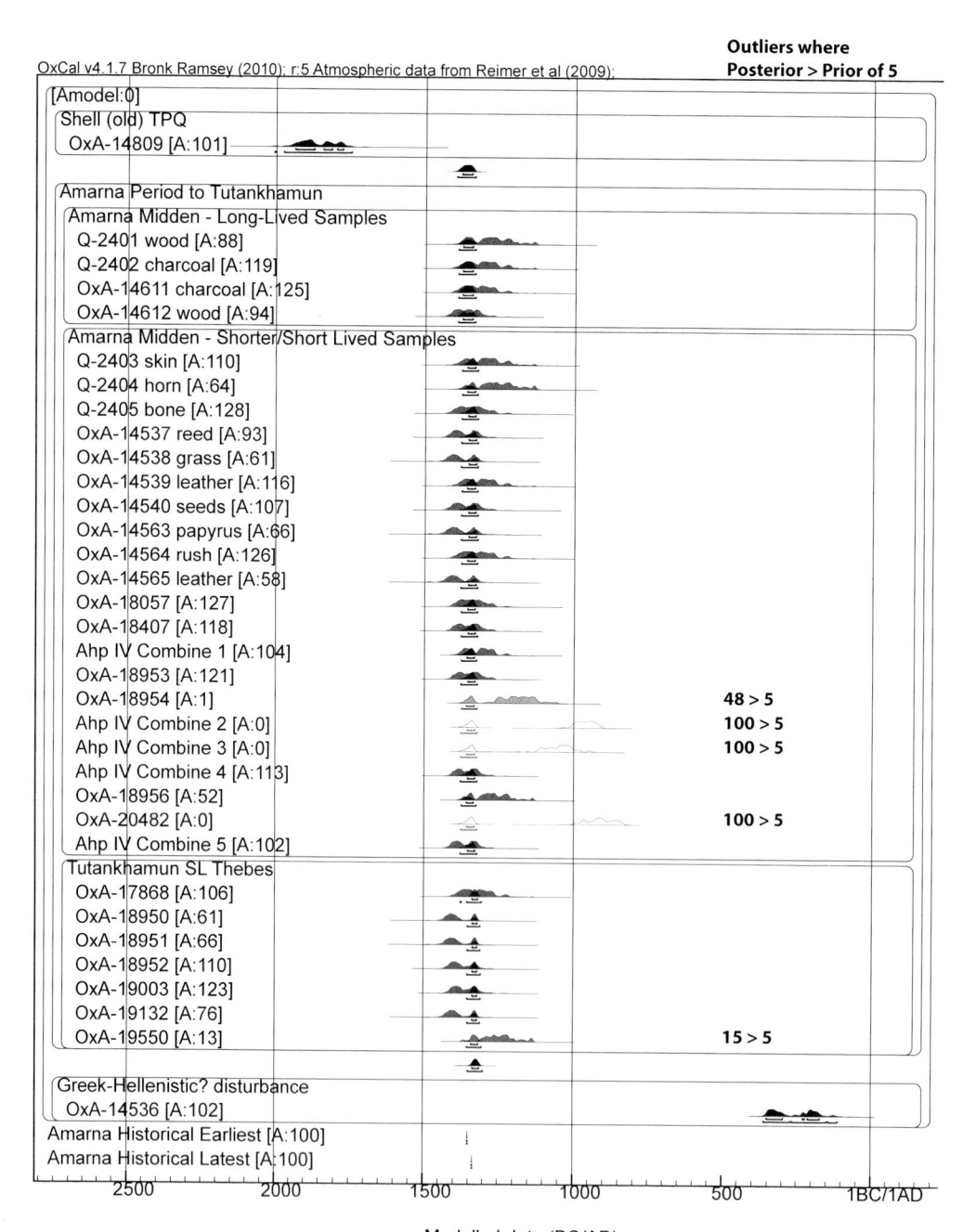

132 S. W. Manning, B. Kromer, M. W. Dee, M. Friedrich, T. F. G. Higham and C. Bronk Ramsey

OxCal v4.1.7 Bronk Ramsey (2010); r:5 Atmospheric data from Reimer et al (2009);

Outliers where Posterior > Prior of 5

[Amodel:0]
Shell (old) TPQ
  OxA-14809 [A:101]

Amarna Period to Tutankhamun
  Amarna Midden - Long-Lived Samples
    Q-2401 wood [A:88]
    Q-2402 charcoal [A:119]
    OxA-14611 charcoal [A:125]
    OxA-14612 wood [A:94]
  Amarna Midden - Shorter/Short Lived Samples
    Q-2403 skin [A:110]
    Q-2404 horn [A:64]
    Q-2405 bone [A:128]
    OxA-14537 reed [A:93]
    OxA-14538 grass [A:61]
    OxA-14539 leather [A:116]
    OxA-14540 seeds [A:107]
    OxA-14563 papyrus [A:66]
    OxA-14564 rush [A:126]
    OxA-14565 leather [A:58]
    OxA-18057 [A:127]
    OxA-18407 [A:118]
    Ahp IV Combine 1 [A:104]
    OxA-18953 [A:121]
    OxA-18954 [A:1]   48 > 5
    Ahp IV Combine 2 [A:0]   100 > 5
    Ahp IV Combine 3 [A:0]   100 > 5
    Ahp IV Combine 4 [A:113]
    OxA-18956 [A:52]
    OxA-20482 [A:0]   100 > 5
    Ahp IV Combine 5 [A:102]
  Tutankhamun SL Thebes
    OxA-17868 [A:106]
    OxA-18950 [A:61]
    OxA-18951 [A:66]
    OxA-18952 [A:110]
    OxA-19003 [A:123]
    OxA-19132 [A:76]
    OxA-19550 [A:13]   15 > 5

Greek-Hellenistic? disturbance
  OxA-14536 [A:102]
Amarna Historical Earliest [A:100]
Amarna Historical Latest [A:100]

2500   2000   1500   1000   500   1BC/1AD

Modelled date (BC/AD)

10. Radiocarbon Calibration in the Mid to Later 14th Century BC

Figure 10.6 (left): Revised and extended version of the sequence analysis in Figure 10.1 run against IntCal09 and with the Egyptian growing-season-related offset of 19±5 years (see Figure 10.1 for general explanation). The additional Amarna and Tutankhamun dates on short-lived samples from Bronk Ramsey et al. (2010) are now added. The data in the Amarna shorter/short-lived set and the Tutankhamun short-lived set are each treated independently within a phase in this analysis aimed at identifying which samples are potential (significant) outliers (and so they are not all pooled – cf. Figures 10.1 and 10.8). Only those dates on the same sample are pooled (hence Ahp IV Combine 1, etc.). The analysis was run applying the general outlier detection model of Bronk Ramsey (2009b) at the 5% level. For a sample to be an outlier its calculated Posterior value is greater than the expected Prior value of 5; just seven data in the analysis exhibited this characteristic (two sets of two dates on the same samples = 4 data, and three other individual data) – the Posterior v. Prior values for these data are shown – see also Figure 10.5. (These samples also offer poor OxCal agreement index values.)

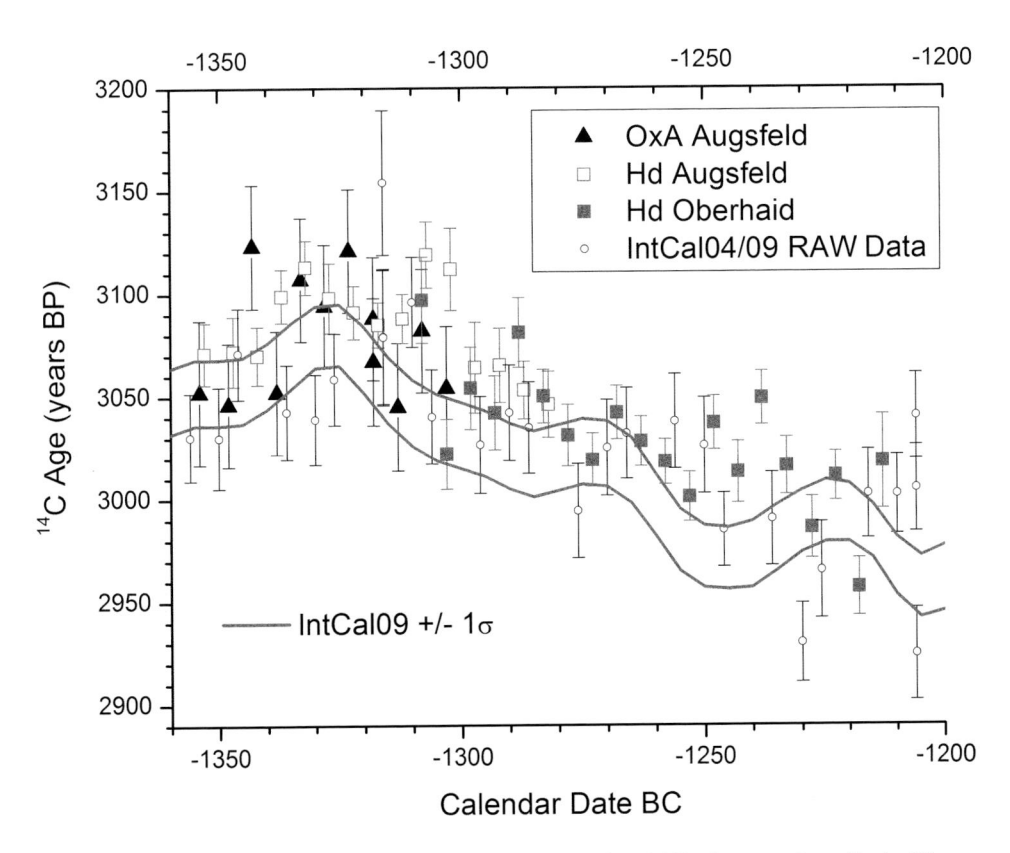

Figure 10.7: The IntCal09 1σ calibration curve (Reimer et al. 2009) shown against: (i) the 28 current IntCal04/09 raw data on which IntCal09 was based for the period 1360–1200 BC (Reimer et al. 2009) (note two data points at 1316 BC obscure each other); and (ii) the additional 48 ^{14}C calibration data now available from radiocarbon measurements on known-age German oak in the period between 1360 and 1200 BC (from Kromer et al. 2010; and from this paper, Table 10.2).

in the pre-existing IntCal dataset (n=28), but, nonetheless, between about 1330 and 1290 BC, in particular, there is a clear trend towards slightly older ages in our data (from two different radiocarbon laboratories) on known-age German Oak versus the IntCal09 values. Anatolian near-absolutely dated tree-rings in this interval appear to indicate a similar picture (Manning *et al.* 2010). We conclude that IntCal09 needs some revision for this period.

If the IntCal09 raw data, and the Heidelberg and Oxford data shown in Figure 10.7 are considered together, then modelling the data by, for example, intervals of 6 years, 8 years and 10 years shows the likely pattern of change versus the existing IntCal09 curve (Figure 10.8). There is no radical change with regard to the Amarna period, but the wiggle at about 1325 BC becomes broader and lasts through to the late 14th century BC. At the same time, however, with regard to the Amarna shorter/short-lived (SL) dataset, the apparent age trend in the overall set of now available calibration data (Figures 10.7 and 10.8) tends towards slightly higher ages from around 1340/1330 BC. The net effect, especially with allowance made also for the proposed Egyptian seasonal offset (Dee *et al.* 2010), would be to move the start of the calibrated calendar age range for the Amarna SL set a little earlier and the end a little later. Overall, then, the range for the Amarna SL set will be wider (in the absence of any additional constraining information).

The revised dataset would benefit considerably from the addition of some *terminus ante quem* constraint soon after the Amarna-Akhenaten context. This would be very useful to determine which part of a potentially wider mid-later 14th century BC section of the calibration corresponds with the Amarna period. Luckily, the study of Bronk Ramsey *et al.* (2010) included seven data on short-lived samples associated with Tutankhamun from his tomb at Thebes (see Figures 10.5 and 10.6). Tutankhamun's death was about 21–24 years after the founding of Amarna, or around 7–9 years after its abandonment; hence short-lived materials from his tomb are about 7–24 years later than the date of the samples from Amarna (give or take any small amounts of in-built age for some samples). The Tutankhamun data are similar to the range of the Amarna/Akhenaten dates, even (except one sample OxA-19550 – excluded as an outlier: see Figures 10.5 and 10.6) tending towards the higher end of this common range (Figure 10.5). The weighted average of the six coherent data (excluding OxA-19550) is 3117 ± 12 BP. Thus this set is on average some 32 ^{14}C years older than the overall Amarna-Akhenaten SL set. Allowing for the Egyptian growing-season offset of 19±5 years, this places the Tutankhamun data coeval with the *c.* 1325 BC wiggle (see Figure 10.12). This date is within a couple of years of the death of Tutankhamun according to the standard Egyptian historical chronology. This helps us to conclude that the Amarna-Akhenaten shorter/short-lived data probably lie on the slope leading up to the *c.* 1325 BC wiggle, and that the Tutankhamun data probably lie at the top of this wiggle, around 1325 BC. Such dating ranges from the radiocarbon data, and the shape of the radiocarbon calibration curve (the history of past natural atmospheric variations in radiocarbon levels), offer the potential of a close correlation with the standard Egyptian historical chronology.

In Figures 10.9–10.11 we analyse the ensemble of ^{14}C evidence collated in this paper and Bronk Ramsey *et al.* (2010), also considered in Chapter 7, from the Amenhotep IV/Akhenaten and Tutankhamun material against an expanded calibration dataset for the period that includes the data shown in Figures 10.7–10.8. We then compare these results against the date ranges available from IntCal09 (Figure 10.12). We include the set of data

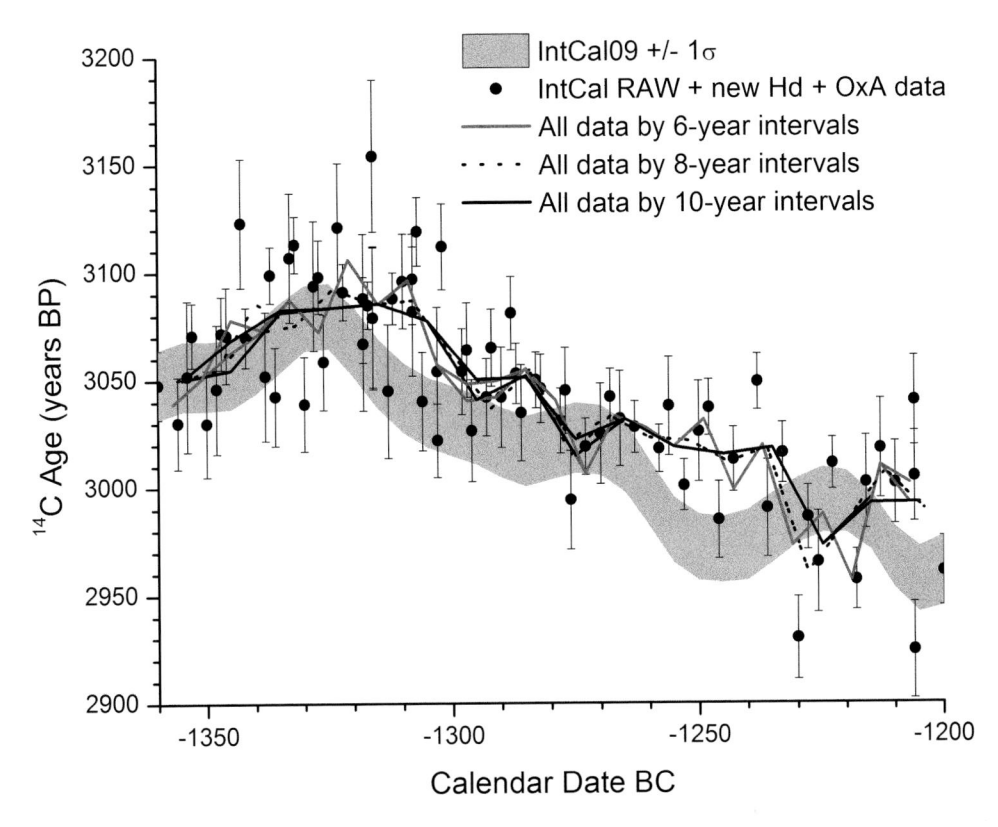

Figure 10.8. The 1σ IntCal09 calibration curve shown against the total set of raw calibration data (n=76) shown in Figure 10.6 (plus the IntCal09 data points for 1360 and 1200 BC) (1σ error bars). To highlight the differences, or trends to differences, three curves are modelled through the raw dataset on the basis of combining 6, 8 and 10 calendar year intervals.

on short-lived samples from the subsequent reign of Tutankhamun (from Bronk Ramsey *et al.* 2010; Chapter 6) as shown in Figure 10.5 as an additional age constraint (now especially relevant in view of the widening of the 1325 BC 'wiggle' as discussed above); and we insert a boundary between the Amarna shorter/short-lived set and the Tutankhamun burial data since we know there should be an interval of somewhere between 7–24 calendar years involved here. In addition, we apply the approximate 19±5 years growing season offset (as in Figures 10.3 and 10.4, after Dee *et al.* 2010; Bronk Ramsey *et al.* 2010). This exercise is of course a calibration against a much more 'noisy' data set than the modelled IntCal09 calibration curve (thus contrast the curve shape and results in Figures 10.10 and 10.11 with those in Figures 10.2 and 10.3 and 10.12). Figure 10.9 shows the dating model employed for this analysis, and Figures 10.10 and 10.11 show the calendar dating probability achieved for the shorter/short-lived (SL) sample set for Amenhotep IV/Akhenaten against the dataset in Figures 10.7 and 10.8 when (Figure 10.10) a 5-year curve resolution (smoothing) is applied and (Figure 10.11) a 10-year curve resolution (smoothing) is applied. Figure 10.12

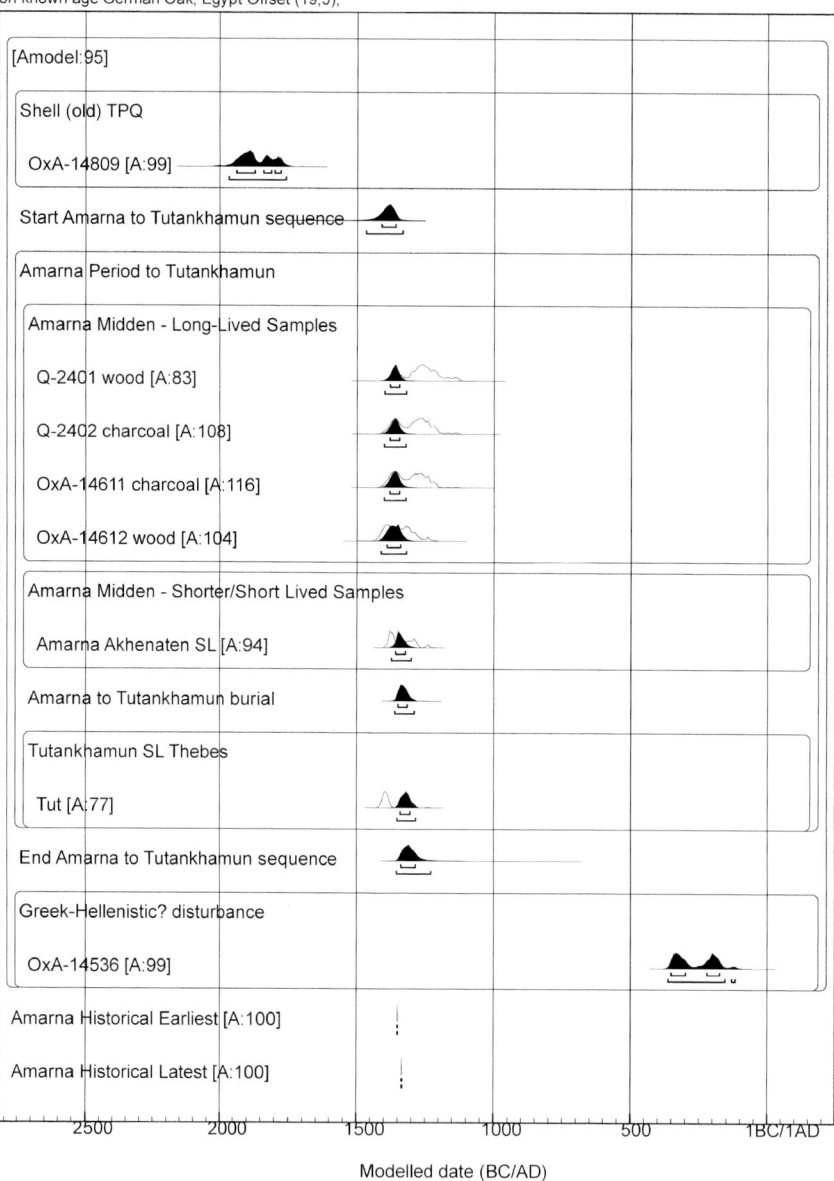

Figure 10.9: Dating model for the the Amarna or Akhenaten shorter/short-lived sample set adding the data for Amenhotep IV/Akhenaten contexts, and the (shortly) subsequent Tutankhamun contexts (the latter acting as a terminus ante quem for the former) from Bronk Ramsey et al. (2010) using the extended but coarse raw calibration dataset for 1360–1200 BC from Figures 10.7 and 10.8. We also add a boundary (Amarna to Tutankhamun burial) between the Amarna and Tutankhamun sets representing the 7–24 calendar years involved. This model is thus an extension and revision of the model in Figure 10.1.

shows the calendar dating probability achieved for the shorter/short-lived (SL) sample set for Amenhotep IV/Akhenaten with the same model but employing IntCal09. (Note: the Appendix lists the OxCal run file used for Figure 10.12 as an example.)

In each case, we find almost the same calibrated age range determined for the Amarna-Akhenaten short-lived sample grouping (at 68.2% probability 1360/1356/1352 to 1331/1325/1323 BC; and at 95.4% probability 1376/1373/1371 to 1320/1306/1301 BC). It is important to note that each run of such a sequence analysis achieves very slightly different results, typically within about 1 year. The new calibration data are important and will refine the calibration curve, but in this case their addition makes only a small difference. The calibrated ranges found provide calendar date ranges very compatible with the standard Egyptian historical chronology with each most likely 68.2% range entirely covering the expected historical range (highest to lowest standard date: from Kitchen 2000; 2007; von

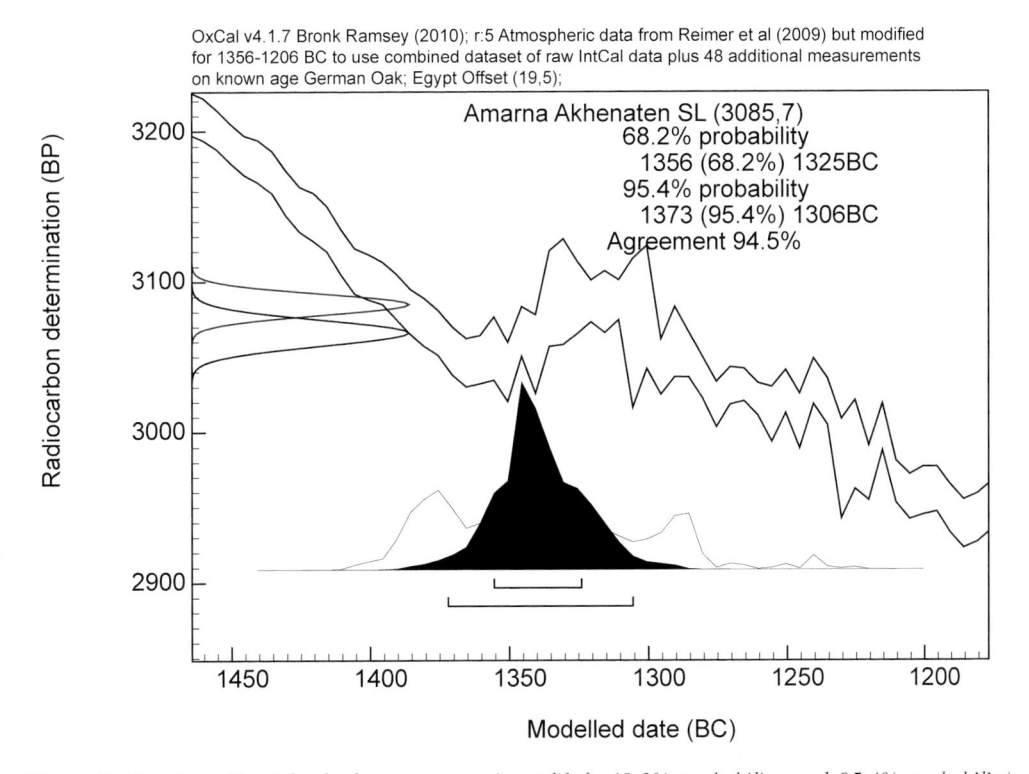

Figure 10.10: The calibrated calendar age ranges (most likely 68.2% probability, and 95.4% probability) determined for the shorter/short-lived (SL) data from Amarna from Amenhotep IV/Akhenaten contexts in the model illustrated in Figure 10.9 run against a modified version of IntCal09 (Reimer et al. 2009) employing the raw calibration data shown in Figures 10.7 and 10.8 for the period between 1360 and 1200 BC using OxCal version 4.1.7 (Bronk Ramsey 1995; 2009a; 2009b) with curve resolution set at 5. Note that any run of a Sequence analysis in OxCal will produce very slightly different outcomes, and variations of about 0–1 calendar years, or of around 0–1%, in the ranges/percentages illustrated are possible. The figures shown in this paper represent typical outcomes from several runs.

Beckerath 1994; 1997; Hornung *et al.* 2006) of 1351–1334 BC. The later part of each of the calibrated ranges could also be compatible with the lower dates (1338–1325 BC) from the recent suggestion by Krauss and Warburton (2009) of a chronology some 11 years later, but there is a less good fit. This is clear if we consider the means and medians of the calibrated probability distributions: 1343±12 and 1342 BC (Figure 10.12), 1341±17 and 1343 BC (Figure 10.11) and 1340±16 and 1341 BC respectively (Figure 10.10) – they favour a date slightly earlier than the entire Krauss and Warburton (2009) range. In contrast, they fit extremely well with the standard historical date for a point during the reign of Amenhotep IV/Akhenaten from his year 5 onwards (so from 1351/1347 BC onwards for the subsequent 12 years).

The success of the correlation with the standard Egyptian historical chronology partly depends on the use of the 19±5 years seasonal offset. If the analyses in Figures 10.10 and 10.11 are run without this offset, then the calibrated ranges for the Amarna SL set are (5 year resolution curve) 1345–1315 BC at 68.2% probability with mean 1333±17 BC and median 1331 BC, and (10 year resolution curve) 1349–1319 BC at 68.2% probability with mean 1335±15 BC and median 1334 BC. These ranges are around 6–10 years lower than those with the Egypt offset. These dates without the adjustment could still be perfectly compatible with the standard Egyptian historical chronology, but would offer a better or

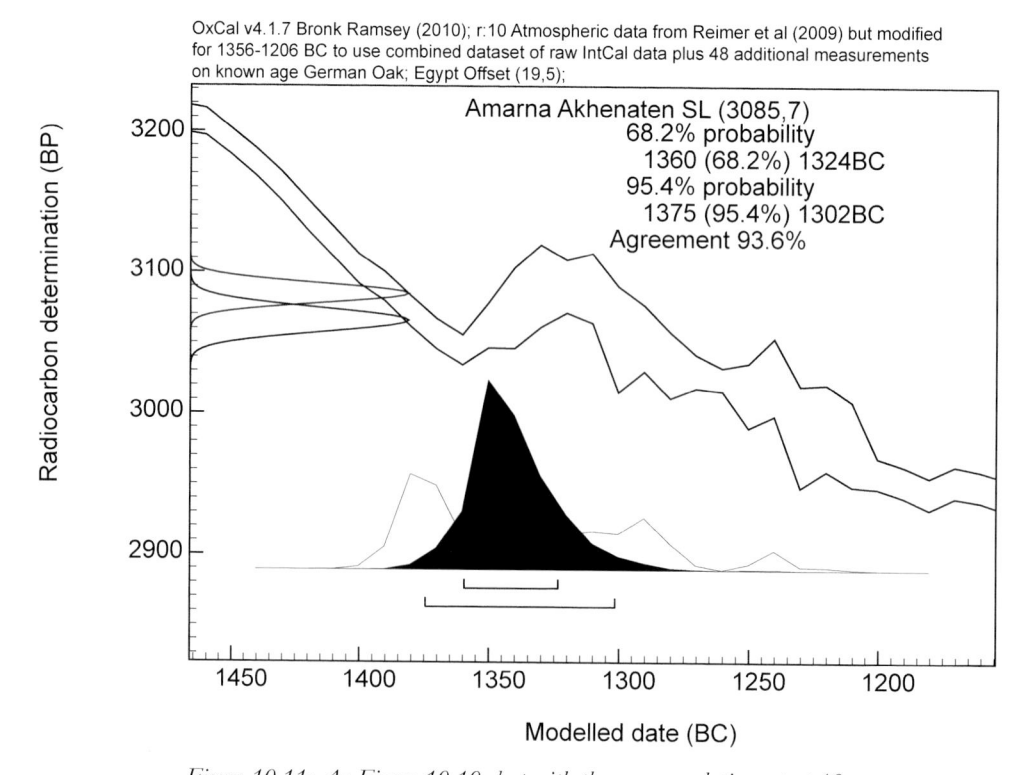

Figure 10.11: As Figure 10.10, but with the curve resolution set at 10.

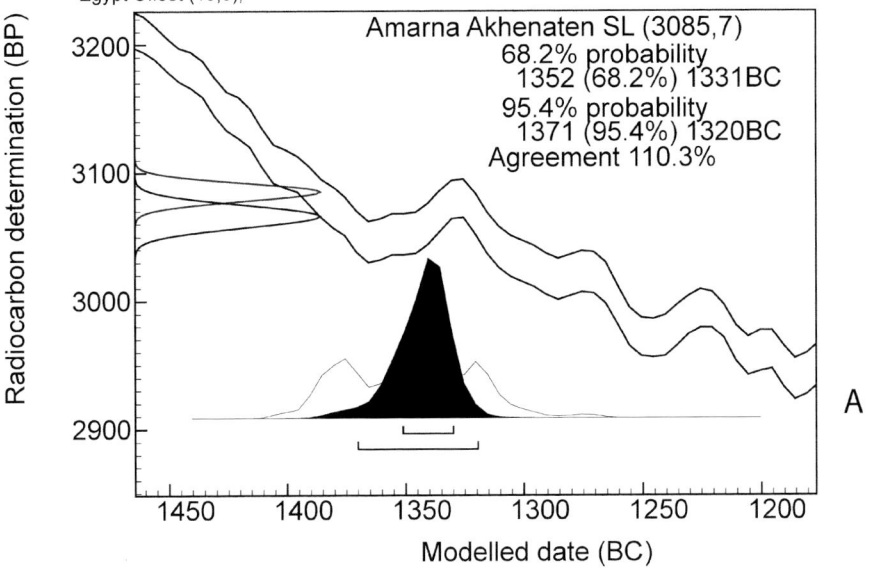

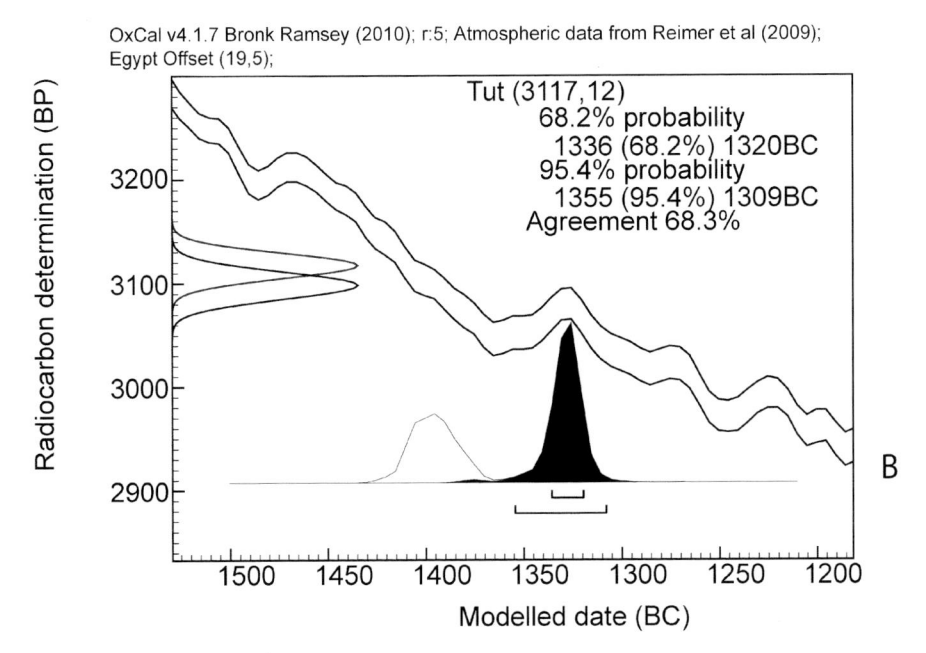

Figure 10.12: Results for the model in Figure 10.9 when run against the standard IntCal09 (Reimer et al. 2009) calibration curve (compare/contrast with Figures 10.10 and 10.11 using the expanded dataset in Figures 10.7 and 10.8 but with a much more ragged curve model). A. shows the Amarna shorter/short-lived set (compare with Figures 10.10 and 10.11). B. shows the date ranges calculated for the subsequent Tutankhamun short-lived set. Run file for this analysis listed in the Appendix.

almost equal fit with the lower chronology (contrast previous paragraph). It is interesting to observe, however, that the OxCal agreement index for the Tutankhamun set in both cases no longer offers a satisfactory value >60 (55.3 and 54.3 for the 5 and 10 year resolution cases respectively). This is because, without the seasonal offset the (good) weighted average of the Tutankhamun samples sits almost above the 1325 BC structure in the calibration curve (*even with* the additional raw data included as in Figures 10.10 and 10.11), and thus the date prefers to try to calibrate in the region 1431/1429 to 1384/1382 BC where 62.7% or 59.4% of the unmodelled calibration probability lies with no adjustment. If the standard IntCal09 calibration curve is employed (i.e. as in Figure 10.12 but without the offset) then this situation is even more apparent: the Tutankhamun set yields an agreement index value of only 21.9, well below the satisfactory level of 60 (and is an outlier at the 5% level on the general model of Bronk Ramsey 2009b with a posterior value of 7 and a prior of 5). This offers further evidence for the importance of the seasonal offset proposed by Dee *et al.* (2010). The relationship between the radiocarbon dates and the detailed structure of the calibration curve as described in this paper is a good (sensitive) example of where this type of offset is important when dating at high levels of precision.

Discussion

Bronk Ramsey *et al.* (2010) have demonstrated a good correlation between well-selected calibrated radiocarbon dates from Egyptian contexts with dates from the standard Egyptian historical chronology. Additional radiocarbon data that we have analysed in this paper from the site of Tell el-Amarna supports their conclusions.

Our work also shows that the international Northern Hemisphere radiocarbon calibration curve (IntCal09) requires slight revision in the period *c.* 1360–1200 BC. Nonetheless, even allowing for a significant amount of additional data (171% increase), we find that the likely calibrated calendar age ranges to be determined for a large set of radiocarbon dates on shorter/short-lived samples from the narrow time horizon provided by the site of Amarna remain fairly stable. If anything, the additional data appear to suggest a calibrated calendar date range even more consistent with the Egyptian historical chronology.

These findings assume great significance because they suggest that other high-quality radiocarbon chronologies in the east Mediterranean are also likely to be correct in calendar terms. In cases where good quality radiocarbon-based analyses are compared against archaeo-historic dating schemes, based on attempted material culture or stylistic linkages between contexts in the east Mediterranean and the Egyptian historical chronology, the radiocarbon-based chronology is likely to be correct since such radiocarbon chronologies work so well in the case of Egypt (see further in Manning and Kromer 2011).

One factor to consider further is the issue of the growing season offset as proposed for samples growing in Egypt (Dee *et al.* 2010). The timing of plant growth, and sowing and harvests, in pre-dam, pre-modern, Egypt almost maximizes the possible difference in the time of the year (and so the sampled part of the annual radiocarbon atmospheric record) compared with the growing season of the trees used to create the IntCal dataset. The 19±5 years offset will thus be close to a maximum possible value for the mid and south latitudes of the northern hemisphere. Even so, it makes only a small (but not unimportant) difference to calibrated outcomes. Dee *et al.* (2010, 689), for instance, found that the 'impact of this uplift is almost imperceptible'. For other east Mediterranean locations further to the north and without the strong Nile-flood hydrologic cycle of pre-modern Egypt, such an offset will inherently be smaller as the growing seasons are less offset. A study of ^{14}C data available from long time-series from the Aegean region, for example, indicates a typical growing-season-related offset perhaps of the order of 2–4 ± 2–4 years (Manning *et al.* 2010). The radiocarbon-based chronology for the mid second millennium BC Aegean (Manning *et al.* 2006; Weninger *et al.* 2010, 976–979) can therefore be regarded as secure within very small margins. This means that in order to compare Aegean archaeological contexts with Egypt, it is preferable to use the Aegean ^{14}C chronology against the standard Egyptian historical chronology (or the Egyptian ^{14}C chronology – which is the same) rather than the pre-^{14}C-Aegean archaeological dating system, which is based on interpretations, inferences and guesses. This is especially the case where there are few or no reliable cultural linkages between the Aegean and Egypt (as is the case for the 17th–16th centuries BC, for example), and/or where there is a key intermediary archaeological site like Tell el-Dab'a which has a highly suspect chronological methodology and synthesis (Warburton 2009; Manning and Kromer 2011).

The successful radiocarbon dating of Egyptian history therefore has major ramifications for the chronologies and cultural syntheses of the wider east Mediterranean and ancient Near East in the prehistoric period. It is especially relevant to the second millennium BC where there has been much scholarly debate over chronology and the correct synchronisation of the civilisations of the east Mediterranean. The direct implication of the Egyptian case is that the radiocarbon-based chronological framework proposed for the Aegean and Cyprus (e.g. Manning *et al.* 2006; Manning and Bronk Ramsey 2009; Manning 2007; 2009), and thus the so-called 'high' or 'long' Aegean chronology, and its general cultural-historical synthesis (Manning 1999), is probably correct in broad terms. It also implies that the chronology of the second millennium BC Levant and Anatolia should also be co-ordinated on the basis of an appropriate radiocarbon chronology (including via near-absolute dendrochronology where possible: Manning *et al.* 2010; 2001). A proper synchronisation of the civilisations of the east Mediterranean in the second millennium BC may now be possible.

Appendix

The OxCal runfile for the model shown in Figure 10.9 is listed below, as an example, and as used to obtain the plot shown in Figure 10.12 (thus employing IntCal09: Reimer *et al.* 2009). No outlier model is employed in this case as the outliers have already been previously identified, and are excluded from this analysis (the data with the // in front of them). Where used in other files, the general outlier model of Bronk Ramsey (2009b) was employed on the radiocarbon timescale: Outlier_Model("General",T(5),U(0,4),"r"); at the 0.05 level – thus with code {Outlier(0.05);}; This is as discussed and documented in Bronk Ramsey *et al.* (2010).

```
Options()
{
 Resolution=5;
};
Plot( )
{
 Delta_R("Egypt Offset", 19, 5);
 Sequence( )
 {
  Phase( "Shell (old) TPQ")
  {
   R_Date( "OxA-14809", 3560, 34);
  };
  Boundary("Start Amarna to Tutankhamun burial sequence");
  Sequence( "Amarna Period to Tutankhamun")
  {
   Phase( "Amarna Midden - Long-Lived Samples")
   {
    R_Date( "Q-2401 wood", 3035, 35);
    R_Date( "Q-2402 charcoal", 3055, 35);
    R_Date( "OxA-14611 charcoal", 3066, 32);
    R_Date( "OxA-14612 wood", 3109, 31);
   };
   Phase( "Amarna Midden - Shorter/Short Lived Samples")
   {
    R_Combine ("Amarna Akhenaten SL")
    {
     R_Date( "Q-2403 skin", 3050, 35);
     R_Date( "Q-2404 horn", 3025, 35);
     R_Date( "Q-2405 bone", 3088, 35);
     R_Date( "OxA-14537 reed", 3116, 31);
     R_Date( "OxA-14538 grass", 3134, 32);
     R_Date( "OxA-14539 leather", 3058, 31);
     R_Date( "OxA-14540 seeds", 3109, 33);
     R_Date( "OxA-14563 papyrus", 3134, 34);
     R_Date( "OxA-14564  rush", 3068, 33);
     R_Date( "OxA-14565 leather", 3137, 33);
     R_Date("OxA-18057", 3082, 29);
     R_Date("OxA-18407", 3096, 28);
     R_Date("OxA-18953", 3092, 27);
     //R_Date("OxA-18954", 2976, 28);
     R_Date("OxA-18956", 3028, 27);
     //R_Date("OxA-20482", 2787, 31);
     R_Date("OxA-18512", 3051, 27);
     R_Date("OxA-18412", 3064, 28);
     //R_Date("OxA-19004", 2862, 26);
     //R_Date("OxA-19263", 2798, 27);
     //R_Date("VERA-4686", 2847, 36);
     //R_Date("VERA-4686B", 2918, 30);
     R_Date("OxA-18955", 3115, 30);
     R_Date("VERA-4687", 3094, 37);
     R_Date("VERA-4687B", 3070, 37);
     R_Date("VERA-4685", 3096, 34);
     R_Date("VERA-4685B", 3116, 35);
    };
   };
   Boundary ("Amarna to Tutankhamun burial");
   Phase ("Tutankhamun SL Thebes")
   {
    R_Combine ("Tut")
    {
     R_Date("OxA-17868", 3065, 31);
     R_Date("OxA-18950", 3138, 28);
     R_Date("OxA-18951", 3137, 29);
     R_Date("OxA-18952", 3117, 29);
     R_Date("OxA-19003", 3106, 26);
     R_Date("OxA-19132", 3133, 29);
     //R_Date("OxA-19550", 3015, 25);
    };
   };
  };
  Boundary ("End Amarna to Tutankhamu Sequence" );
  Phase( "Greek-Hellenistic? disturbance")
  {
   R_Date( "OxA-14536", 2187, 30);
  };
 };
 C_Date( "Amarna Historical Earliest", -1350);
 C_Date( "Amarna Historical Latest", -1334);
};
```

Acknowledgements

Manning thanks Professor Barry Kemp for generously providing the Tell el-Amarna samples, and apologises profusely for the (very) long wait for this publication. Manning also thanks the NERC ORADS panel for funding the Oxford dating work.

References

Aldred, C. 1988, *Akhenaten: King of Egypt*, Thames and Hudson, London.
Beckerath, J. von 1994, *Chronologie des Ägyptischen Neuen Reiches,* Hildesheimer Ägyptologische Beiträge 39, Gerstenberg Verlag, Hildesheim.
Beckerath, J. von 1997, *Chronologie des Pharaonischen Ägypten, Die Zeitbestimmung der Ägyptischen Geschichte von der Vorzeit bis 332 v. Chr.*, Philipp von Zabern, Mainz.
Brinkman, J. A. 1976, *Materials and Studies for Kassite History*, Oriental Institute of the University of Chicago, Chicago.
Brock, F., Higham, T. F. G., Ditchfield, P., and Bronk Ramsey, C. 2010, Current pretreatment methods for AMS radiocarbon dating at the Oxford Radiocarbon Accelerator Unit (ORAU), *Radiocarbon*, **52**(1), 103–112.
Bronk Ramsey, C. 1995, Radiocarbon calibration and analysis of stratigraphy: the OxCal program, *Radiocarbon*, **37**(2), 425–430.
Bronk Ramsey, C. 2009a, Bayesian analysis of radiocarbon dates, *Radiocarbon*, **51**(2), 337–360.
Bronk Ramsey, C. 2009b, Dealing with outliers and offsets in radiocarbon dating, *Radiocarbon*, **51**(3), 1023–1045.
Bronk Ramsey, C., Higham, T. and Leach, P. 2004, Towards high-precision AMS: progress and limitations, *Radiocarbon*, **46**(1), 17–24.
Bronk Ramsey, C., Dee, M. W., Rowland, J. M., Higham, T. F. G., Harris, S. A., Brock, F. A., Quiles, A., Wild, E. M., Marcus, E. S. and Shortland, A. J. 2010, Radiocarbon-based chronology for dynastic Egypt, *Science*, **328**(5985), 1554–1557.
Cohen, R., and Westbrook, R. (eds) 2000, *Amarna diplomacy: the beginnings of international relations,* Johns Hopkins University Press, Baltimore.
Dee, M. W., Brock, F., Harris, S. A., Bronk Ramsey, C., Shortland, A. J., Higham, T. F. G. and Rowland, J. M. 2010, Investigating the likelihood of a reservoir offset in the radiocarbon record for ancient Egypt, *Journal of Archaeological Science*, **37**(4), 687–693.
Freed, R. E., Markowitz, Y. J. and D'Auria, S. H. (eds) 1999, *Pharaohs of the Sun: Akhenaten, Nefertiti, Tutankhamen*, Museum of Fine Arts, Boston.
Friedrich, M., Remmel, S., Kromer, B., Hofmann, J., Spurk, M., Kaiser, K. F., Orcel, C. and Küppers, M. 2004, The 12,460-year Hohenheim oak and pine tree-ring chronology from central Europe – a unique annual record for radiocarbon calibration and paleoenvironment reconstructions, *Radiocarbon*, **46**(3), 1111–1122.
Gabolde, M. 1998, *D'Akhenaton à Toutânkhamon*, Collection de l'Institut d'Archéologie et d'Histoire de l'Antiquité, Université Lumière-Lyon 2, 3, Diffusion de Boccard, Paris.
Giles, F. J. 2001, *The Amarna Age: Egypt,* Aris and Phillips, Warminster.
Hornung, E. 2006, New Kingdom, in *Ancient Egyptian Chronology* (eds E. Hornung, R. Krauss and D. A. Warburton), 197–217, Brill, Leiden and Boston
Hornung, E., Krauss, R. and Warburton, D.A. (eds) 2006, *Ancient Egyptian Chronology*, Brill, Leiden and Boston.
Kemp, B. J. 1984, *Amarna Reports I*, Occasional Publications 1, Egypt Exploration Society, London.

Kemp, B. J. 1987, The Amarna workmen's village in retrospect, *Journal of Egyptian Archaeology*, **73**, 21–50.

Kemp, B. J., 1993. Amarna's other period, *Egyptian Archaeology*, **3**, 13–14.

Kitchen, K. A. 2000, Regnal and genealogical data of ancient Egypt (absolute chronology I). The historical chronology of ancient Egypt, a current assessment, in *The Synchronisation of Civilisations in the Eastern Mediterranean in the Second Millennium BC – I* (ed. M. Bietak), 39–52, Austrian Academy of Sciences Press, Vienna.

Kitchen, K. A. 2007, Egyptian and related chronologies – look, no sciences, no pots! in *The Synchronisation of Civilizations in the Eastern Mediterranean in the Second Millennium BC – III* (eds M. Bietak and E. Czerny), 163–171, Austrian Academy of Sciences Press, Vienna.

Klinger, J. 2006, Chronological links between the cuneiform world of the ancient Near East and ancient Egypt, in *Ancient Egyptian Chronology* (eds E. Hornung, R. Krauss and D. A. Warburton), 304–324, Brill, Leiden and Boston.

Krauss, R. and Warburton, D. A. 2006, Conclusions, in *Ancient Egyptian Chronology* (eds E. Hornung, R. Krauss and D. A. Warburton), 473–498, Brill, Leiden and Boston.

Krauss, R. and Warburton, D. A. 2009, The basis for the Egyptian dates, in Time's Up! Dating the Minoan eruption of Santorini. Acts of the Minoan Eruption Chronology Workshop, Sandbjerg November 2007 initiated by Jan Heinemeier and Walter L. Friedrich (ed. D. A. Warburton), 125–139, Monographs of the Danish Institute at Athens Volume 10, The Danish Institute at Athens, Athens.

Kromer, B., Manning, S. W., Friedrich, M., Talamo, S. and Trano, N. 2010, ^{14}C calibration in the 2nd and 1st millennia BC – Eastern Mediterranean Radiocarbon Comparison Project (EMRCP), *Radiocarbon*, **52**(3), 875–886.

Manning, S. W. 1999, *A Test of Time: the Volcano of Thera and the Chronology and History of the Aegean and East Mediterranean in the Mid-Second Millennium BC*, Oxbow Books, Oxford.

Manning, S. W. 2006, Radiocarbon dating and Egyptian chronology, in *Ancient Egyptian Chronology* (eds E. Hornung, R. Krauss and D. A. Warburton), 327–355, Brill, Leiden and Boston.

Manning, S. W. 2007, Clarifying the 'high' v. 'low' Aegean/Cypriot chronology for the mid second millennium BC: assessing the evidence, interpretive frameworks, and current state of the debate, in *The Synchronisation of Civilisations in the Eastern Mediterranean in the Second Millennium B.C.–III* (eds M. Bietak and E. Czerny), 101–137, Austrian Academy of Sciences Press, Vienna.

Manning, S. W. 2009, Beyond the Santorini eruption: some notes on dating the Late Minoan IB period on Crete, and implications for Cretan-Egyptian relations in the 15th century BC (and especially LMII), in *Time's Up! Dating the Minoan eruption of Santorini. Acts of the Minoan Eruption Chronology Workshop, Sandbjerg November 2007 initiated by Jan Heinemeier and Walter L. Friedrich* (ed. D. A. Warburton), 207–226, Monographs of the Danish Institute at Athens Volume 10, The Danish Institute at Athens, Athens.

Manning, S. W. and Bronk Ramsey, C. 2009, The dating of the earlier Late Minoan IA period: a brief note, in *Time's Up! Dating the Minoan eruption of Santorini*. Acts of the Minoan Eruption Chronology Workshop, Sandbjerg November 2007 initiated by Jan Heinemeier and Walter L. Friedrich (ed. D.A. Warburton), 227–245, Monographs of the Danish Institute at Athens Volume 10, The Danish Institute at Athens, Athens.

Manning, S. W., Bronk Ramsey, C., Kutschera, W., Higham, T., Kromer, B., Steier P. and Wild, E. M. 2006, Chronology for the Aegean Late Bronze Age 1700–1400 BC, *Science* **312**(5773), 565–569.

Manning, S. W. and Kromer, B. 2011, Radiocarbon dating archaeological samples in the eastern Mediterranean 1730–1480 BC: further exploring the atmospheric radiocarbon calibration record and the archaeological implications, *Archaeometry*, **53**(2), 413–439.

Manning, S. W., Kromer, B., Bronk Ramsey, C., Pearson, C. L., Talamo, S., Trano, N. and Watkins, J. D. 2010, ^{14}C record and wiggle-match placement for the Anatolian (Gordion Area) Juniper tree-ring chronology ~1729 to 751 cal BC, *Radiocarbon*, **52**(4), 1571–1597.

Manning S. W., Kromer B., Kuniholm P. I. and Newton M. W. 2001, Anatolian tree-rings and a new chronology for the east Mediterranean Bronze-Iron Ages, *Science*, **294**(2532), 2532–2535.

Manning, S. W., Pulak, C., Kromer, B., Talamo, S., Bronk Ramsey, C. and Dee, M. 2009, Absolute age of the Uluburun shipwreck: a key Late Bronze Age time-capsule for the east Mediterranean, in *Tree-Rings, Kings and Old World Archaeology and Environment: Papers Presented in Honor of Peter Ian Kuniholm* (eds. S. W. Manning and M. J. Bruce), 163–187, Oxbow Books, Oxford.

Martin, G. T. M. 1991, *A Bibliography of the Armana Period and its Aftermath: the Reigns of Akhenaten, Smenkhkare, Tutankhamun and Ay (c. 1350–1321 BC)*. Kegan Paul, London.

Monserrat, D. 2000, *Akhenaten: History, Fantasy and Ancient Egypt*. Routledge, London.

Moran, W. 1992, *The Amarna Letters,* The Johns Hopkins University Press, Baltimore.

Murnane, W. J. 1995, *Texts from the Amarna Period in Egypt,* Scholars Press, Atlanta.

Murnane, W. J. and Van Siclen III, C. 1993, *The Boundary Stelae of Akhenaten,* Kegan Paul International, London.

Pyke, G. 2010, The Christian settlement at the Amarna north tombs. *Egyptian Archaeology* 37, 13–16.

Reimer, P. J., and McCormac, F. G., 2002, Marine radiocarbon reservoir corrections for the Mediterranean and Aegean Sea, *Radiocarbon,* **44**(1), 159–166.

Reimer, P. J., Baillie, M. G. L., Bard, E., Bayliss, A., Beck, J. W., Bertrand, C. J. H., Blackwell, P. G., Buck, C. E., Burr, G. S., Cutler, K. B., Damon, P. E., Edwards, R. L., Fairbanks, R. G., Friedrich, M., Guilderson, T. P., Hogg, A. G, Hughen, K. A, Kromer, B., McCormac, G., Manning, S., Bronk Ramsey, C., Reimer, R. W., Remmele, S., Southon, J. R., Stuiver, M., Talamo, S., Taylor, F. W., van der Plicht, J., and Weyhenmeyer, C. E. 2004, IntCal04 terrestrial radiocarbon age calibration, 0–26 cal kyr BP, *Radiocarbon,* **46**(3), 1029–1058.

Reimer, P. J., Baillie, M. G. L., Bard, E., Bayliss, A., Beck, J. W., Blackwell, P. G., Bronk Ramsey, C., Buck, C. E., Burr, G. S., Edwards, R. L., Friedrich, M., Grootes, P. M., Guilderson, T. P., Hajdas, I., Heaton, T. J., Hogg, A. G., Hughen, K. A., Kaiser, K. F., Kromer, B., McCormac, F. G., Manning, S. W., Reimer, R. W., Richards, D. A., Southon, J. R., Talamo, S., Turney, C. S. M., van der Plicht, J. and Weyhenmeyer, C. E. 2009, IntCal09 and Marine09 radiocarbon age calibration curves, 0–50,000 years cal BP, *Radiocarbon,* **59**(4), 1111–1150.

Siani, G., Paterne, M., Arnold, M., Bard, E., Metivier, B., Tisnerat, N. and Bassinot, F. 2000, Radiocarbon reservoir ages in the Mediterranean Sea and Black Sea, *Radiocarbon,* **42**(2), 271–280.

Stuiver, M., Reimer, P. J., Bard, E., Beck, J. W., Burr, G. S., Hughen, K. A., Kromer, B., McCormac, G., van der Plicht, J. and Spurk, M. 1998, IntCal98 radiocarbon age calibration, 24,000–0 cal BP, *Radiocarbon,* **40**(3), 1041–1083.

Switsur, V. R. 1984, Radiocarbon date calibration using historically dated specimens from Egypt and new radiocarbon determinations for el-Amarna, in *Amarna Reports* I, (ed. B. J. Kemp), 178–188, Occasional Publications 1, Egypt Exploration Society, London.

Ward, G. K. and Wilson, S. R. 1978, Procedures for comparing and combining radiocarbon age determinations: a critique, *Archaeometry,* **20**(1), 19–31.

Warburton, D. A. 2009, Chronology, stratigraphy, typology and Tell el-Dab'a. Postscript, in *Time's Up! Dating the Minoan eruption of Santorini*. Acts of the Minoan Eruption Chronology Workshop, Sandbjerg November 2007 initiated by Jan Heinemeier and Walter L. Friedrich (ed. D. A. Warburton), 139–144, Monographs of the Danish Institute at Athens Volume 10, The Danish Institute at Athens, Athens.

Watterson, B. 1999, *Amarna: Ancient Egypt's Age of Revolution*. Tempus, Stroud.

Weninger, F., Steier, P., Kutschera, W. and Wild, E. V. 2010, Robust ayesian analysis, an attempt to improve Bayesian sequencing, *Radiocarbon,* **52**(3), 962–983.

CHAPTER 11

The Ramesside Period: A Case of Overstretch?

Aidan Dodson

The Ramesside Period has long been regarded as something of an island of stability in the stormy seas of Egyptian chronology, built around the seemingly-solid placement of accession date of Ramesses II in 1279 BC. However, ongoing research is undermining the credibility of this date by pointing to probable reductions of one-and-a-bit decades in the span separating Ramesses' accession from next chronological 'fixed' point – the Jerusalem campaign of Shoshenq I around 925 BC. Nevertheless, there has been little appetite for lowering Ramesses II's accession year to deal with this 'overstretch', principally owing to a general scholarly confidence that the Assyrian King List (AKL) tradition provides solid dates for Ramesse's Hittite contemporaries, Muwatallish II and Hattushilish III, via their synchronisms with Adad-nirari I and Shalmaneser I of Assyria. However, while the Assyrian King List does indeed provide a sound, testable, chronological source back to time of Ashur-dan II (934–912 BC), prior to this there are periods of minimal contemporary documentation, with even the king-list and supporting limmu list in very poor condition. While broadly usable, it is not possible to verify whether the total number of years provided could be regarded with any certainty as representing a single line of kings or whether there were divisions of kingship that might mean that the total elapsed time was less than the total number of limmu-years. There are at least two points where the contemporary data may hint at a division of Assyrian kingship, which individually or cumulatively could accommodate a lowering of Ramesses II's accession date by a lunar cycle, 'soaking up' the overstretch identified above. Whether a further lowering might be desirable very much depends on the view one takes of the total duration of the 21st Dynasty whose reconstruction still leans very heavily on Manetho, given the ambiguity of the contemporary data, and is in turn tied the Jerusalem campaign 'fixed' point – itself dependent on indirect Assyrian synchronisms. However, these latter points are beyond the scope of the present paper.

The attribution of absolute dates to events in ancient Egypt has long presented difficulties prior to the accession of Taharqa in 690 BC, after which links with the other parts of the world leave little or no room for doubt. Various techniques have been used to construct a framework for preceding centuries and millennia, but although schemes have from time to time been accepted as more or less canonical, unanimity has been rare.

The problem is two-fold: on one hand there is the question of finding an appropriate 'peg' that can, with some degree of confidence, be given an absolute date. On the other, there is having sufficient information available on reign-lengths to work outwards from this 'fixed peg' to be able to attribute absolute dates to other reigns. The Ramesside Period has for a long time been regarded as the more fortunate in Egyptian history, in both having a 'fixed' point, and also having a particularly well-founded internal relative chronology. The

---

Author's Address: **A. M. Dodson**, Department of Archaeology and Anthropology, University of Bristol, 43 Woodland Road, Bristol BS8 1UU, UK

11. The Ramesside Period: A Case of Overstretch?

latter aspect relies heavily on the data derived from official documents of the Theban Necropolis, in particular the papyri and ostraca from the workmen's community at Deir el-Medina. On this basis, the sequence and length of reigns from the accession of Ramesses II down to the reign of Ramesses IX is regarded as almost certain, in some cases to the day. The only significant exception is the period between the deaths of Merenptah and Sety II, where a long-standing debate has existed over the placement of the usurper-king Amenmessu: did his period of power precede Sety II's accession, or was his reign entirely contemporary with that of the latter? The evidence is increasingly pointing towards the latter (see Dodson 2010; 31–46), with the result that four years need to be excluded from the 'conventional' year-count of the period.

The Ramesside 'fixed point' is provided by a record of a new moon in II *prt* of Ramesses II's Year 52 in Papyrus Leiden I 350, *vs.* III, 6 (Kitchen 1968–90; II, 809). Such phenomena are of course cyclical and can only be used for exact chronology when the basic target time-span has been arrived at by other means. Thus, as the overall view of New Kingdom chronology has slipped down over the past few decades, the consequent generally accepted accession year of Ramesses II has moved from 1304 BC, through 1290 BC to today's consensus of Year 52 = 1228 BC → Year 1 = 1279 BC. However, if the 'target' time-span were to be further lowered, the accession of Ramesses II could in theory to be placed one or more lunar cycles later, e.g.:

Year 52 Option (BC)	Day of New Moon[1]	Consequent Accession Year (BC)
1228	II *prt* 28	1279
1214	II *prt* 27	1265
1203	II *prt* 28	1254
1189	II *prt* 27	1240
1178	II *prt* 27	1229

In choosing the 'target' time-span, a key factor has been synchronisms with Assyrian history. This is because Assyrian chronology has long been regarded as the most secure of all ancient Near Eastern time-lines through the existence of a complete king-list tradition, built up from a series of overlapping sources (the 'Assyrian King List' – AKL: Grayson 1980–83; 101–116). On the basis of this tradition, Ashuruballit I, who corresponded with Akhenaten, is usually placed *c.* 1353–1318, while Eriba-Adad I (conventionally *c.* 1380–1353) is linked to Amenhotep III via the latter's Babylonian correspondents Kadashman-Enlil I and Burnaburiash II (cf. Giles 1997; 76–101). Ramesses II's Hittite contemporaries, Muwatallish II and Hattushilish III, corresponded with Adad-nirari I (*c.* 1295–1264 BC), while Hattushilish exchanged letters with Shalmaneser I (*c.* 1263–1234 BC). Since Hattushilish III seems to have seized the Hittite throne around Ramesses' Year 15, with Shalmaneser I becoming king soon after Hattushilish's coup, this synchronism would put Ramesses' own accession around 1279 BC, fitting neatly with the accession year based on placing the Year 52 new moon in 1228 BC.

This was for a time apparently reinforced by the dendrochronological dating of a piece of wood from the Uluburun shipwreck off Asia Minor to 1316 BC (Kuniholm *et al.* 1996).

The ship's cargo included a gold scarab of Nefertiti, with the implication that any viable chronology would have to place the queen's career prior to the last years of the fourteenth century (Weinstein 1989), thus supporting a 1279 BC accession for Ramesses II. However, there has since been a collapse in confidence in the dating of the wood (Manning *et al.* 2001; cf. Weiner 2003; 244–5; Bietak 2004; 221–22), and it now seems clear that the Uluburun evidence can no longer be called in support of any dates proposed for the general period of the 18th/19th Dynasty transition. The soundness of the dates derived from the AKL data is thus the crucial issue for considering how solid the 1279 BC chronological peg actually is (cf. the remarks of Müller 2006; 224 and van Dijk 2008; 200). There seems no question that back to the time of Ashur-dan II (934–912 BC) the combination of a complete *limmu* (eponym) list (Ungnad 1938) and contemporary material provide an unbreakable historical and chronological framework. However, prior to Ashur-dan's reign, there are periods of minimal contemporary documentation, in particular back from his accession to the death of Ashur-bel-kala, where one is almost entirely reliant on the eighth century AKL. However many reign-lengths are missing from this (Grayson 1980–83; 101–115; cf. Brinkman 1973), requiring it to be backed up by a very badly damaged section (KAV21/22) of the *limmu* list, which has lost many of its entries, although the numbers of lost lines can be estimated with some accuracy.

The key question is thus whether the total number of years provided through the latter can be regarded as representing a single line of kings – as is certainly the case from Ashur-dan II onwards, and almost certainly prior to Tukulti-Ninurta I on the basis of external data – or whether there were divisions of kingship that might mean that the total elapsed time was less than the total number of *limmu*-years. This is of course very similar to the presentation of the Intermediate Periods in the Turin and Manethonic king lists in Egypt, where parallel lines were listed as though sequential. In Assyria, the almost amuletic purpose of the AKL, purportedly demonstrating an unbroken line of succession from the earliest times to the current king, meant that such an approach was essentially *de rigeur* (cf. Henige 1996; Yamada 1994).

However, it is by no means certain that the AKL did actually contain such an unbroken line. That a division of kingship occurred at least once in Assyria is demonstrated when the 'Great King' (of Babylon) Adadshumausur wrote to the '[Smal]l Kings of Assyria', Ashur-nirari III and Ili-hadda (Poebel 1943; 56). As Ili-hadda does not appear in the king-lists as a ruler, it has been assumed that such joint-rulers did not appear in the AKL. However, there are certainly cases where rulers have been omitted from the king-lists – for example Shalmaneser II from one version of the list (cf. below) – and it is thus quite possible that Ili-hadda's omission does not mean that *no* joint-rulers are to be found within the king-lists. Indeed, the knowledge that Ashur-Nirari III shared his throne makes one suspicious of what might lie behind the complicated family relationships seen amongst those found in the AKL as successors of Tukulti-Ninurta I: Ashur-nadin-apil is listed as Tukulti-Ninurta's son, but the king-lists disagree whether the king following Ashur-nadin-apil was the offspring of Ashur-nadin-apil himself or an otherwise-unknown Ashur-nasir-apil. The next on the list, Enlil-kudurra-usur, was a son of Tukulti-Ninurta, and the next one, Ninurta-apil-Ekur, the son of Ili-hadda. It was Ninurta-apil-Ekur who was then the father of Ashur-dan I (on issues with the king-lists' genealogical data, cf. Landsberger 1954; 31–73). Against this background, Arno Poebel argued for no less than a four-fold division of Assyria after

11. The Ramesside Period: A Case of Overstretch?

Tukulti-Ninurta's death (1943; 56–57). While there is no direct evidence for this, the known duumvirate of Ashur-nirari III and Ili-hadda provides a clear possibility that the reign of Ili-hadda's son, Ninurta-apil-Ekur, and perhaps the early years of Ninurta-apil-Ekur's son, Ashur-dan I, ran in parallel with those of Ashur-nirari III and Enlil-kudurra-usur. If so, a decade could be removed from the overall Assyrian chronology of the period (the *limmu* list is of no help here, as it is hopelessly broken prior to the last years of Ashur-nasir-pal I; cf. however, just below). This would bring Ramesses II's contemporaries Adad-nirari I and Shalmaneser I down to a combined span of *c.* 1282–1222.

A further potential case of division is to be seen some two centuries later, in the case of Ashur-rabi II. The King Lists combine with the *limmu* list to give him a 41-year reign, separated from that of his father, Ashur-nasir-pal I by the reigns of his brother Shalmaneser II (12 years – and missing from one version of the AKL) and the latter's son Ashur-nirari IV (6 years: both reign-lengths are securely recorded in KAV21). However, unlike Ashur-nasir-pal, Shalmaneser and his own son, Ashur-resha-ishi II, there is no attestation of Ashur-rabi at the Assyrian capital of Ashur whatsoever: his only contemporary monument is a broken cylinder referring to public works by a vassal apparently based near the river Khabur, some 200 kilometres west of the capital city. Coupled with later kings' references to Ashur-rabi in connection with this area, one is strongly tempted to suspect that he may have been ruling in the west, while his brother Shalmaneser II and the latter's son Ashur-nirari IV ruled in Ashur. In this connection, could the exclusion of Shalmaneser II from the Nassouhi list (probably compiled under Ashur-rabi II's grandson) imply dissention as to which brother was legitimate heir on Ashurnasirpal I's death? Such a reconstruction would fit in with what we know of the Aramaean presence in central Assyria at this time. While this would of course imply a doubling-up of the *limmu* list, the existence of rival lines could quite easily lead to parallel sets of *limmu*, as one king would surely reckon time in terms of his own officials, rather than those of a potentially rival ruler. Unfortunately, any attempt at detecting such a situation within the *limmu* list is thwarted by the fact that apart from its very beginning, Ashur-rabi's list is a very poor condition, with major lacunae extending through the reigns of Ashur-resha-ishi and Tilgath-Pileser II (neither of whose eponymous years survive) and beyond. For questions as to the very historicity of the *limmu* list for this period, cf. below.

Combined with the previous possibilities concerning Tukulti-Ninurta I's successors, Ramesses II's contemporaries could be brought down as low as *c.* 1264–1204 BC. Consequent options for lowering Ramesses II's accession could thus be:

AKL Option	Shalmaneser I accession date (~Year 15/16 of Ramesses II)	Consequent Ramesses II accession date	Fit with Ramesses II lunar data
Overlapping of successors of Tukulti-Ninurta I	1251/50	1266/5	1265
Overlapping of successors of Ashur-nasir-pal I	1241/40	1256/7	1254 + 2/3
Both of above	1233	1248/9	1254 – 5/6

While none of the AKL options above can be proven at present, there seems enough circumstantial evidence to suggest that the AKL evidence is not as secure as is often insisted (e.g. in Postgate 1991), and that it could support a lowering of Ramesses II's accession date by up to two-and-a-half decades if made desirable by other factors.

That this could be the case is suggested by a number of potential reductions in the available regnal years between 1279 BC and the next 'fixed' point, with the accession of Shoshenq I around 945 BC (943 BC according to Krauss 2006; 411–2). First, as already noted, it now seems clear that Amenmessu's reign was entirely contained within that of Sety II, removing four years from the conventional year-count of the 19th Dynasty. Second, there are renewed suggestions that conventional linear succession of Ramesses IX – X – XI results in far too many anomalies within the corpus of tomb robbery papyri for it to continue to be acceptable (Thijs 1998; 1999a; 1999b; 2000a; 2000b; 2001a; 2001b; Dodson 2012; 9–38). A solution to these anomalies results in the reign of Ramesses XI overlapping with those of Ramesses IX and X, resulting in a further decade-and-a-half being lost from the year-count. Although one could try and 'soak up' some of these 'lost' years during the 21st Dynasty, where none of the reigns are of certainly-known length, the paucity of material from most of them points towards contracting them towards their minimum attested lengths, rather than extending them.

As a result, it becomes arithmetically all-but-impossible to fill up the 336 years between 1279 and 943 BC other than by gratuitously extending reigns during the 21st Dynasty – and/or rejecting the aforementioned adjustments to the 19th and 20th Dynasties on the grounds that they will not fit the macrochronological picture. Given that it has been demonstrated above that this macrochronological picture rests ultimately on an uncritical acceptance of the possibly flawed AKL, it follows that one of the lower options for Ramesses II's accession should be considered.

The most conservative – 1265 BC – accommodates the Amenmessu and Ramesses IX/X/XI compressions, while also accommodating a 21st Dynasty without any significant lengthening from the broad consensus of around 130 years. It also gives an exact day-match for the Year 52 notation, rather than the one-day error needed for 1279 BC. On the other hand, the figure of 130 years is in many ways based on Manethonic figures or manipulations thereof, and given the breakdown in the consensus as to the allocation of the various anonymous regnal years from the dynasty (i.e. Jansen-Winkeln's proposal [1992] that Herihor, Panedjem I and Menkheperre used regnal years while yet high priests – for contrary arguments see Kitchen 1996; xiv–xviii and Dodson 2012; 19, 65) it is not impossible that reductions might be possible. However, for the present, I would suggest that 1265 BC should become the 'working hypothesis' for the accession of Ramesses II, rather than 1279 BC.

This discussion assumes that the accession of Shoshenq I has been correctly 'fixed' around 945 BC, a date which ultimately rests of the synchronism between that king's Jerusalem campaign and the fifth years of king Rehoboam of Judah (cf. Kitchen 1996; 72–6), although subsequently refined via lunar data to 943 BC (Krauss 2006; 411–12). Discussion of the validity of the assumptions that underlie the calculations of the synchronism are beyond the scope of the present paper, but it should be noted that these have received a number of challenges, leaving aside those put forward by those arguing for chronological reductions far in excess of the decades considered at issue here (see James 1991; Rohl 1995).

Notes

1 The actual report is dated II *prt* 27, but the vagaries of observation allow some leeway.

References

Bietak, M. 2004, Review of S. W. Manning, A Test of Time, *Bibliotheca Orientalis* LXI (1–2), 200–222.
Brinkman, J. A. 1973, Comments on the Nassouhi Kinglist and the Assyrian king list tradition. *Orientalia,* **42**, 306–19.
Dodson, A. 2010, *Poisoned Legacy: the Decline and Fall of the Nineteenth Egyptian Dynasty*, American University in Cairo Press, Cairo.
Dodson, A., 2012, *Afterglow of Empire: Egypt from the Fall of the New Kingdom to the Saite Renaissance*, American University in Cairo Press, Cairo.
Grayson, A. K. 1975, *Assyrian and Babylonian Chronicles: Texts from Cuneiform Sources*, Augustin, New York.
Grayson, A. K. 1980–83, Königslisten und Chroniken. B. Akkadisch. *Reallexikon der Assyriologie* VI, Walter de Gruyter, Berlin and New York, 86–135.
Henige, D. 1996, Comparative chronology and the ancient Near East, *Bulletin of the American Schools of Oriental Research,* **262**, 57–68.
Jansen-Winkeln, K.1992, Das Ende des Neuen Reiches, *Zeitschrift für Ägyptische Sprache und Altertumskunde,* **119**, 22–37.
James, P. 1991, *Centuries of Darkness: A Challenge to the Conventional Chronology of Old World Archaeology*, Jonathan Cape, London.
Kitchen, K. A. 1968–90, *Ramesside Inscriptions: Historical and Biographical*, 8 volumes, Blackwell, Oxford.
Kitchen, K. A. 1996, *The Third Intermediate Period in Egypt (1100–650 BC)*, 3rd Edition, Aris and Phillips, Warminster.
Krauss, R. 2006, Lunar dates, in *Ancient Egyptian Chronology* (eds E. Hornung, R. Krauss and D. A. Warburton), 395–431, Brill, Leiden and Boston.
Kuniholm, P. I., Kromer, B., Manning, S. W., Newton, M., Latini C. E. and Bruce, M. J. 1996, Anatolian tree rings and the absolute chronology of the Eastern Mediterranean, 2220–718 BC, *Nature,* **381**, 780–3.
Landsberger, B. 1954, Assyrische Königslisten und 'Dunkles' Zeitalter, *Journal of Cuneiform Studies,* **8**, 31–73.
Manning, S. W., Kromer, B., Kuniholm, P. I. and Newton, M. W. 2001, Anatolian tree rings and a new chronology for the East Mediterranean Bronze-Iron Ages, *Science,* **294**(5551), 2532–35.
Müller, V. 2006, Wie gut fixiert ist die Chronologie des Neuen Reiches wirklich? *Ägypten und Levante,* **16**, 203–30.
Poebel, A. 1943, The Assyrian king list from Khorsabad – concluded, *Journal of Near Eastern Studies,* **2**, 56–90.
Postgate, N. 1991, The chronology of Assyria – an insurmountable obstacle, *Cambridge Archaeological Journal,* **1** (2), 22–53.
Pulak C. and Bass, G. F. 1997, Uluburun, in *Oxford Encyclopedia of Archaeology in the Near East* V (ed. E. M. Myers), 266–268, Oxford University Press, Oxford.
Rohl, D. M. 1995, *A Test of Time: I: The Bible – from Myth to History*, Century, London.
Thijs, A. 1998, Reconsidering the end of the Twentieth Dynasty, part I: The fisherman Pnekhtemope and the date of BM 10054, *Göttinger Miszellen,* **167**, 95–108.

Thijs, A. 1999a, Reconsidering the end of the Twentieth Dynasty, part II, *Göttinger Miszellen*, **170**, 83–100.

Thijs, A. 1999b, Reconsidering the end of the Twentieth Dynasty part III: some hitherto unrecognised documents from the *wḥm-mswt*, *Göttinger Miszellen*, **173**, 175–192.

Thijs, A. 2000a, Reconsidering the end of the Twentieth Dynasty, part IV: the Harshire-family as a test for the shorter chronology, *Göttinger Miszellen*, **175**, 99–104.

Thijs, A. 2000b, Reconsidering the end of the Twentieth Dynasty, part V: P. Ambras as an advocate of a shorter chronology, *Göttinger Miszellen*, **179**, 69–84.

Thijs, A. 2001a, Reconsidering the end of the Twentieth Dynasty part VI: some minor adjustments and observations concerning the chronology of the last Ramessides and the *wḥm-mswt*, *Göttinger Miszellen*, **181**, 95–103.

Thijs, A. 2001b, Reconsidering the end of the Twentieth Dynasty, part VII. The history of the Viziers and the politics of Menmare, *Göttinger Miszellen*, **184**, 65–73.

Ungnad, A. 1938, Eponymen, in *Reallexikon der Assyriologie* II, 412–45, Walter de Gruyter. Berlin and Leipzig.

Van Dijk, J. 2008, New evidence on the length of the reign of Horemheb, *Journal of the American Research Center in Egypt*, **44**, 193–200.

Weinstein, J. 1989, The Bronze Age shipwreck at Ulu Burun: 1986 campaign. III. The gold scarab of Nefertiti from Ulu Burun: its implications for Egyptian history and Egyptian-Aegean relations, *American Journal of Archaeology*, **93**, 17–20.

Yamada, S. 1994, The editorial history of the Assyrian king list, *Zeitschrift für Assyriologie und vorderasiatische Archäologie*, **84**, 11–37.

CHAPTER 12

Garlands from the Deir el-Bahri Cache

S. McAleely

The Oxford Egyptian Chronology Project radiocarbon dated three samples taken from garlands found associated with mummies discovered in tomb TT320, commonly known as the Deir el-Bahri royal mummy cache. This paper introduces garlands as a category of material cultural evidence, explains why the author thinks they provide a good material for radiocarbon dating, and discusses how the new dates might inform their interpretation. It then outlines the discovery and clearance of TT320, in order to discuss the radiocarbon dates and the issue of garland reuse in the context of the post-excavation biographies of the garlands.

Introduction

Garlands: their incidence, and role in archaeological interpretation

Organic remains in the form of deliberately placed plant material, prearranged to form bouquets, wreaths, garlands, pillows and pectoral collars, have been excavated from a number of archaeological sites, and provide evidence that this is a long-standing cross-cultural behavioural trait which has continued to the present day. Currently, most of the extant remains have been held in museum and herbarium collections for about 100 years, and are from ancient Egyptian contexts, mainly from 18th, 19th, and 21st Dynasty, and Roman Period sources (*c.* 3500 BP–2000 BP). Their current condition is variable depending on their post-excavation biographies, but all have been preserved by drying (desiccation) in antiquity. As such, they are rare and fragile artefacts, and Schweinfurth (1883, 111) writes that some of the garlands were 'broken and reduced to powder' due to careless handling when the coffins were first opened, prior to his examination of them. Most are now devoid of their original colour, appearing as lifeless objects faded to shades of brown. However, they were once vibrant, living plant material, and reports contemporary with their discovery in burial contexts allude to examples which retained both colour and scent until excavated (Schweinfurth 1883, 112), testament to the remarkable organic preservation in some Egyptian burials. More recent finds from ancient Egypt include the garlands and collars discovered in coffin E in KV63 in 2006 (see http://www.kv-63.com). Non-Egyptian material is extremely rare, but includes a recent find from a Scottish Bronze Age burial of flowers believed to be 4000 years old (Pitts 2010; Brophy 2009), and the contested pollen data from the Shanidar Neanderthal burial (Leroi-Gourhan 1975; Solecki 1971; Sommer 1999).

Author's Address: **S. McAleely**, Institute of Archaeology, UCL, 31–34 Gordon Square, London WC1H 0PY, UK

Where such floral offerings and tributes have been found in burial contexts, they elicit an empathetic and emotive response, and a number of scholars (Brophy 2009; Solecki 1971, xii), describe them as evidence of humanity which add 'a human touch'. They are in effect a means of non-verbal communication, acting as an interface for symbolic communication between humans and between humans and their beliefs (Goody 1993, 2; McAleely 2005). Depending on context, they either act as an expression of empathy towards a fellow human, living or deceased, or serve as links in an ideological chain in order to appease or please the deities. A bouquet might say 'happy birthday'; 'I mourn your death'; or 'I worship you and plead for intercession', and human beings have the cognitive capacity to read the context and understand the symbolically different messages. The notion of 'the human touch' and the question of what it means to be human in terms of modern human cognition are aspects of archaeological research for which the evidence is often ambiguous or elusive, and the author believes that data from analysis of the inherent symbolism in floral offerings will make a worthwhile contribution to our understanding of cognition and its development.

Deliberately arranged plant material artefacts also form part of the material culture of a society, and can therefore be analysed to aid interpretation in fields such as ideology, technological prowess, agency, botanical knowledge, and environmental reconstruction. In some cases, the seasonality of the plant material allows for further determinism and fine chronological resolution. Because context and interpretation are invariably linked, a secure Egyptian chronology and reliable dates for these artefacts play an important role when interpreting this category of archaeological material in terms of each of the above fields. Finally, data from the ancient Egyptian plant remains can be interpreted within the framework of the extensive Egyptian corpus, and can then be applied by analogy to plant remains and representations of plants found in other geographical locations and temporal contexts, thus demonstrating the importance of the radiocarbon dates from this project to areas of research other than the Egyptian chronology.

Much of the extant archaeobotanical arranged plant material is unpublished and has received little scholarly attention other than botanical identification and enumeration of the constituent species. Examples are listed, and sometimes described, in collection catalogues, for example Germer (1988), and in general literature pertaining to Egyptian plant material (see for example Tackholm and Tackholm 1941; Tackholm and Drar 1950; de Vartevan and Asensi Amorós 1997). These artefacts are usually catalogued by species and are often not indexed, making it difficult to locate examples in the literature. During the latter 19th century and the early 20th century when much of the extant material was excavated, scholars with botanical training identified the species present, described the artefacts and, together with several excavators, commented on aspects of their interpretation (see for example Loret 1887; Newberry 1889, 1890, 1927; Schweinfurth 1883). More recent scholars have discussed these artefacts in works describing specific categories of plant material, for example, Germer (1989), Hepper (1990), and Winlock (1941), discuss the plants found associated with the burial of Tutankhamun, and Manniche (1989) includes garlands when writing about material with herbal properties. The author (McAleely 2005) comments on ways in which arranged plant material might aid archaeological interpretation, and discusses two garland fragments in detail, including EBC40746. This garland fragment is constructed in the same way as EBC40739 (OxA-18960) which was sampled for the Oxford Project, and like EBC40739 is also believed to have been discovered in TT320 on the mummy of Neskhons. During an extensive multidisciplinary project aimed at examination and conservation of Ramesses II's mummy, a research team in France studied fragments of garlands attributed to the mummy of Ramesses II (Roubet and Layer-Lescot 1985). The author (McAleely, forthcoming) has identified a number of other holdings of garlands and flowers which are also documented as being discovered associated with the mummy of Ramesses II, and believes it would be an informative exercise in terms of the story of TT320, New Kingdom ideology, museum practice, and archaeological record keeping, to radiocarbon date a sample from each holding.

In terms of the arranged plant material artefacts sampled for the Oxford Project, Newberry (1900, 143) notes Schweinfurth's comments on the Neskhons garlands found in TT320, but to the author's knowledge apart from the author's own work (McAleely 2005, forthcoming), little research has been carried out on the sampled garlands other than identification and enumeration of the constituent species.

Research (McAleely, forthcoming) including analysis of how ancient Egyptian garlands were made, has strongly indicated that the plant material was freshly gathered, locally sourced, and was placed on mummified human remains shortly (hours rather than days) before contexts were sealed. Thus, their date should correspond with that of the death of the buried individual plus the time taken for the mummification process. This avoids the introduction of radiocarbon dating dilemmas such as the use of imported or recycled material, and the inclusion of artefacts which were made some time before being placed in a burial, or which were intrusive at a later date such as during tomb robberies or due to taphonomic processes. Thus the author suggests that garlands are excellent sources of organic material for radiocarbon dating, and that dates derived from garland samples can be used to support or refute textual and other dating evidence.

Another reason for considering garlands as carbon sources for radiocarbon dating relates to the common practice in late 19th and early 20th century Egyptology of dividing the excavated remains amongst the expedition sponsors, together with their practice of sending samples for further analysis to colleagues in other disciplines. This has conspired to ensure that a number of individual arranged plant material artefacts (garlands, wreaths etc.) were cut up and dispersed to, and subsequently curated in, diverse collections worldwide. In the author's opinion, this has resulted in a number of fragments from one context which should all have the same date, but which have been subjected post-excavation to different degrees of mechanical handling, different contaminants, varying geographical locations, and different environmental conditions; thus providing a means of testing and verifying radiocarbon methodology, in particular screening for contaminants and verifying the consistency of results. For example, fragments of the garlands and flowers found associated with the mummy of Ramesses II in TT320 are documented as being in Egypt, England, The Netherlands, France, Germany, and Sweden (the author has verified the current whereabouts of the fragments in Egypt, England, The Netherlands and Sweden).

The garlands were so well made that some have survived to the present day in remarkable condition. This raises the issue of whether garlands might have been reused in antiquity during reburials, as discussed by Schweinfurth (1883, 112). An issue further complicated when an individual's remains were reburied more than once, such as the mummy of Ramesses II found in the Deir el-Bahri cache. The radiocarbon dates have added valuable data regarding this question, which is discussed further below.

In terms of the author's current research, the radiocarbon dates for the sampled garlands not only provide data useful for our understanding of Egyptian chronology, but also support observations concerning issues other than dating, and thus add to our knowledge and interpretation of this fascinating category of material culture (McAleely, forthcoming).

TT320: its discovery and clearance

This section provides background to the discovery and clearance of TT320, providing insights into the post-depositional biographies of the garlands, which have bearing on the interpretation of the radiocarbon results.

TT320 (formerly known as DB 320) is a rock cut tomb at Deir el-Bahri, Egypt (25:44N 32:36E), accessed by a narrow vertical shaft approximately 11.5m deep and 2m wide (Maspero 1903, 410). This vertical shaft would have made removal of the tomb's contents difficult, with the possibility of coffins and their contents becoming separated, thus casting doubt on recorded context. Deir el-Bahri is a complex of mortuary temples and tombs on the west bank of the river Nile near modern day Luxor. Tomb TT320 was hastily excavated in 1881 by Emile Brugsch, and contained the so-called Royal Cache of mummies, many of which had been moved from their original burial places and reburied in TT320 in antiquity. The mummies had been moved and reburied for safekeeping to prevent looting and desecration (for evidence of this practice see Capart *et al.* 1936), although some say that the mummies were plundered by the officials who moved and reburied them in order to recover objects of value during periods of economic downturn and political uncertainty. Tomb TT320 was reopened several times in antiquity to deposit mummies, and was also looted. Therefore, the original contexts may have been disturbed. After Brugsch's excavation, TT320 was re-opened several times and was recently re-excavated in 1998–2006 by a German-Russian mission led by. E. Graefe (Graefe and Belova, 2010).

Unfortunately the tomb's original discovery, excavation and clearance has been described as a 'mass plundering' and was only poorly recorded in hindsight, introducing uncertainty regarding which mummies were garlanded. There are a number of inconsistencies in the available literature, and the author has reservations about the accuracy of the existing records. Maspero, the director of antiquities in Egypt, who was not even present when the tomb was first examined and cleared by Brugsch, wrote at least two published reports, *Rapport sur la Trouvaille de Deir-el-Bahri*, and *Les Momies Royales de Déir el-Baharî*. He finished the latter, in 1887 (Maspero 1889, 764), by which time he was "now weary of the subject" (Dawson 1947, 84). Maspero's letters to Amelia Edwards (Dawson 1947) show that not only was he dealing with a number of excavations and other issues including his wife's ill health at the time, but also that he probably did not have a good working relationship with Brugsch (Dawson 1947, 82–83). There are also a number of contemporary accounts concerning the find (for example, Maspero 1903, 408–413; *New York Times* 1881; Wilson 1883; Wilson 1887). Of the contemporary accounts, E. L. Wilson's report in *The Century Magazine* is of particular note because not only did Wilson interview Brugsch in person, but he also visited the cleared tomb in January 1882 with his aide Mohammed Abderrassoul, together with Brugsch and Maspero. Maspero (1889, 519–520) writes of this visit that they picked up garlands of flowers in the tomb which were left behind after Brugsch's 1881 hurried clearance, and Wilson (1887, 6) confirms this, reporting that "the rough way was scattered with ...bunches of papyrus plant, lotus flowers, and palm leaf stalks". This suggests that the garlands were not considered very important and that some had become separated from their mummies, questioning the validity of the contextual data. There is no mention of the fate of these artefacts.

The literature records that a local family chanced upon TT320 in the early 1870's and began to illegally sell artefacts taken from the tomb during three visits over a ten year period (Maspero 1889, 511–512). The authorities, led by Maspero, interrogated the sellers and eventually (allegedly after imprisonment, torture and sums of money were involved), one of the family confessed the location of the tomb. On 6th July 1881, in Maspero's absence, Brugsch, the assistant curator at the Boulac Museum, was taken to the entrance of the tomb and descended the vertical shaft to find a long narrow corridor leading to a small chamber (Maspero, 1889, 516). Brugsch spent two hours examining the tomb and its contents in near dark conditions, and found a profusion of objects in disorder. Fearing that the tomb would be robbed, Brugsch hastily assembled a team of two hundred workers (Maspero 1889, 519). To exemplify the discrepancies in the literature which make TT320 a difficult context to unravel, Wilson (1887, 7) quotes Brugsch, and gives a figure of three hundred workers, and there are varying subsequent accounts quoting numbers of from 200 to 600 workmen. The tomb was then cleared in 48 hours, and its contents carried to the banks of the Nile at Luxor, where they were left for three days in the heat of July to await the arrival of a steamship to carry them up the Nile to the museum at Boulac (Maspero 1889, 519). Maspero (1889, 519) writes that 12 to 16 men were required to carry some of the coffins, taking seven to eight hours to take them from the tomb down to the river bank. All told, the tomb's contents amounted to about 40 mummies and numerous artefacts. Reeves (1990, 183–243) discusses the tomb's discovery and contents, and tabulates the main finds (Reeves 1990, 200–203); the mummies (Reeves 1990, 206–209); and the coffins (Reeves 1990, 212–214).

TT320: garlands and flowers

Maspero (1889) describes the mummies and notes flowers and garlands associated with seven of them. This has been cross-checked by the author with Reeves (1990) in order to confirm the translation (see Table 12.1). Reeves (1990, 206–209) lists 40 mummies, and also notes that seven of them were garlanded with flowers. Apart from a typographical error in Reeves (1990, 206, MR pl. 4b should read MR pl.4a) the author's findings concur with those of Reeves. One of these seven mummies was sampled, an Aahmes I garland (Kew, EBC 40733, OxA-18959). In addition, there are extant remains of garlands and whole flowers labelled as associated with two other mummies from TT320; namely those of Ramesses II and Neskhons, both of which were sampled for the Egyptian Chronology Project (OxA-18051 and OxA-18960). Unfortunately, neither Maspero (1889) nor Reeves (1990) mention that these two mummies had garlands, but they bring the total of garlanded mummies to nine, approximately 25% of those found in TT320. Schweinfurth (1883, 109) writes that Maspero handed him several yards of garlands from the coffin of Ramesses II, and although the author has not viewed all of the extant fragments, photographic records indicate that the total length of extant garland approaches this figure, so we can speculate that perhaps by the time Maspero wrote his report there were no longer any garlands left

Table 12.1: Garlands and flowers found associated with mummies in TT320.

Sample	Mummy	Ref in Maspero	Ref in Reeves	Dyn.	*Date year BC	OxA	Uncal BC	^{14}C Cal BC (95.4% prob.)
OxA-18051 VMD165 flower stalk Nymphaea sp.	Ramesses II Pharaoh	No. 19 p.556-563 no mention of garlands	No.30 p.208 no mention of garlands	19th	1213	18051	2768 ± 27	997-837
OxA-18959 EBC40733 leaf Salix safsaf	Ahmose I Pharaoh	No. 3 p.533-534 pl. IVa	No. 9 p.206	18th	1525	18959	2987 ± 37	1381-1091
OxA-18960 EBC40739	Nsi Khonsou Wife of High Priest Pinodjem II	no mention of garlands	No. 24 p.207 no mention of garlands	21st	5th year of Siamun	18960	2805 ± 29	1045-858
	Amenhotpou I	No. 5 p.536-537 pl.IVb	No. 8 p.206	18th	1504			
	Sitkamos	No. 9 p.540-541	No. 7 p.206					
	Bakt?	No. 11 p.544	No. 18 p.207					
	Thoutmos II	No.14 p.456	No. 39 p.209	18th	1479			
	Ramses IX?	No. 20 p.566-568	No. 32 p.208					
	Ahmose-Inhapi?	?	No. 3 p.530	20th?				

Key: *Date – research indicates that garlands were made and placed at time of burial, so date given is that of accepted death.
VMD165. Victoria Museum of Egyptian Antiquities, Uppsala, Sweden.
EBC 40733 and EBC 40739. Royal Botanic Gardens, Kew, UK.

associated with the mummy of Ramesses II because they had all been mounted as herbarium specimens or experimented on by Schweinfurth.

Schweinfurth was a German botanist with a wide knowledge of Egyptian flora and an excellent reputation (Tackholm and Tackholm 1941, 7), who examined the plant material from the tomb after it arrived at the Boulac Museum. He identified the species present and prepared a number of herbarium quality specimens (Schweinfurth, 1883). Once prepared, these artefacts were transported to various locations. Some stayed in Egypt, some were sent to Kew, and evidence suggests that Schweinfurth took some back to Berlin. At each of these locations, records attest to the artefacts being moved from building to building, and within buildings, as collections were rehoused. Over time, some have been subject to reboxing and relabelling. They have also been handled by, and subjected to, the research requirements of various scholars. Every time an artefact is disturbed, there is the possibility that labels become detached and context lost. Some progress has been made by the author in cross-checking and collating information using methods such as the analysis of handwriting and typefaces on labels, and this work is ongoing.

As well as Schweinfurth's report, there are a number of contemporary descriptions of the plant material from TT320 (*Torrey Botanical Society* 1882, 142–143; *New York Times* 1883; Wilson 1883). Like the accounts of the discovery and clearance of TT320, these also contain inconsistencies, again exemplifying the problems associated with trying to verify the contexts of the garlands as stated on their current museum labels. One example concerns the whole *Nymphaea sp.* (waterlily) flowers found associated with several of the mummies, one of which was sampled for the Oxford Egyptian Chronology Project (OxA-18051). Schweinfurth (1883, 110) says that some of the garlands were made using petals of both *Nymphaea caerulea* (blue waterlily) and *Nymphaea lotus* (white waterlily), but that all of the whole single flowers were *Nymphaea caerulea* (blue waterlily). However, Wilson (1883, 23–25) and The Torrey Botanical Society (*Torrey Botanical Society* 1882, 142) quote Amelia Edwards' report in the 1882 September 23rd issue of *The Academy* in which she writes about Schweinfurth's work and Rhone's description of the garlands, and in which she states that "with others of the royal mummies were found fine detached specimens of both kinds of lotus, the blue and the white, with stems, blossoms and seed pods complete" (Wilson 1883, 24). According to Wilson (1883, 23), Amelia Edwards' article was published in 1882, before Schweinfurth's 1883 paper quoted above was published in *Nature*. Without access to original copies of Amelia Edwards' or Rhone's accounts, the author cannot comment where the discrepancy regarding the waterlily species first arises, and it may be a simple translation error. Schweinfurth's *Nature* paper was originally written in French (Schweinfurth 1883, 109 footnote 1), and the author has not yet been able to ascertain either when it was disseminated or who translated it for *Nature*. The archaeological evidence appears to validate Schweinfurth's version as published in *Nature*, because so far, the author has only found extant specimens of whole *Nymphaea caerulea* flowers, including from burials other than TT320. In general, we have to take Schweinfurth's work on trust: he was well used to handling and treating botanical specimens and preserving them for herbaria; his scholarship and work is respected by his contemporaries and by more recent peers (see Tackholm and Tackholm 1941, 7; Wilson 1883, 25), and the author considers his mounted specimens to be well prepared and of excellent quality, though has been unable to locate Schweinfurth's original notes. Although his specimens survived war damage to the Berlin

Botanical Museum, it is widely believed that his papers were destroyed. However, his drawing of the garlanded mummy of Ramesses II has been published (see for example, Manniche 1989, 29; Roubet and Layer-Lescot 1985, 158), and a recent paper (Nodzyńska 2007) suggests that some of his notes have survived. Based on his excellent knowledge of the layout of TT320, Graefe voiced (pers. comm. March 2010) some reservations regarding the accuracy of Schweinfurth's original drawings of Ramesses II's garland, and it is hoped that this paper will elicit further discussion.

The sampled artefacts

The forty mummies of pharaohs and other elite individuals (Reeves 1990, 206–209) recovered from TT320 (mummy count varies depending on literary source), have been attributed to five different dynasties (17th–21st), a time span in excess of 600 years. Records and artefactual evidence suggest that nine of the mummies were buried with garlands, and the Oxford Project sampled garlands and flowers found associated with three of the mummies (Table 12.1). The author was not involved in determining which garlands to sample, nor in the sampling process.

Schweinfurth (1883, 109) writes that he is sending part of the funeral garlands from Ahmose I, Amenhotep I, and Ramesses II to Hooker at Kew, and these are currently in the Economic Botany Collection, and are dated 1883. One of the samples (OxA-18959) was taken from the Ahmose I garland (EBC 40733). Like Maspero (1889) and Reeves (1990), Schweinfurth (1883) does not mention any garlands from Neskhons, but extant remains of garlands from the coffin of Neskhons (EBC 40739 and EBC 40746) are in the Economic Botany Collection at Kew. They are attributed to Schweinfurth and are dated 1884 (a year after the *Nature* paper was sent to Hooker) and EBC 40739 was sampled (OxA-18960). The third sample (OxA-18051) is attributed to Ramesses II and was taken from artefact VMD165 held in the Victoria Museum of Egyptian Antiquities, Uppsala, Sweden.

The following comments are intended to add to the debate and discussion resulting from the Oxford Project, from a botanical perspective.

1. OxA-18960

Artefact EBC 40739, Royal Botanic Gardens, Kew, UK, (Figure 12.1). This consists of garland fragments made from *Salix safsaf* (willow) leaves and *Centaurea depressa* (cornflower) flowers, found with the mummy of Neskhons. Evidence suggests that she was the 21st Dynasty wife of High Priest Pinedjem II, and that she died and was entombed in TT320 in the 5th year of Siamun (Niwiński 1988, 226). The radiocarbon date seems to concur with this.

Kew's other garland specimen from the coffin of Neskhons, EBC 40746, was made from *Salix safsaf* leaves and *Picris coronopifolia* flowers, and like EBC 40739 is dated 1884, a year later than EBC 40733 (see OxA-18959 following).

The mummy of Neskhons was partly unwrapped by Gaston Maspero on June 27th, 1886. G. E. Smith completed the unwrapping in 1906. He discovered that flowers (of an unidentified family) had been wrapped around Neskhons' big toes. Another flower on a long stem had been placed on her left foot, and another encircled her left ankle (Smith 1912, 108). The author considers that these flowers were most likely *Nymphaea sp*, and a comparison of the flowering times of the different flowers associated with Neskhons

(*Centaurea depressa*, *Picris coronopifolia* and *Nymphaea sp* might show if the garlands and flowers found associated with her were all placed in the tomb at the same time. The seasonality of the flowers is a valuable research tool, and further research concerning the species used in the various garlands should help determine which garlands (and therefore mummies) could not have been placed in the tomb on the same occasion, due to their flowers being in bloom at different times of the year. Schweinfurth (1883, 112) comments on this phenomenon, and suggests that "the presence in the same coffin of flowers belonging to different seasons of the year" can be explained by adding new garlands to the original ones when the mummies were reburied.

2. OxA-18959
Artefact EBC 40733, Royal Botanic Gardens, Kew, UK (Figure 12.2). Sample taken from a leaf from a garland fragment found with the mummy of Ahmose I, an 18th Dynasty Pharaoh, who died *c.* 1525 BC. We can be reasonably confident that this sample did come from one of the garlands associated with the mummy of Ahmose I, in particular because Schweinfurth's work is generally respected and also because a contemporary photograph depicts the garland associated with the mummy and shows that it was in reasonable condition (Maspero 1889, pl. IVa.). However, in the photograph, the garland does not drape well over the mummy, suggesting it had been removed at some stage. This could have been at the time of discovery or soon after, for example during transport from TT320, but it could also be indicative of garland reuse. One explanation for the radiocarbon date is that a new garland was made during an earlier reburial, and was then reused for the final reburial in TT320. More research is needed to assess the likelihood of this scenario.

3. OxA-18051
Artefact VMD165, Victoria Museum of Egyptian Antiquities, Uppsala, Sweden, (Figure 12.3). The sample was taken from the stalk of a whole *Nymphaea sp.* flower. A label stuck to the base of this composite artefact attributes the *Nymphaea* flower to Ramesses II, suggesting that it was one of the flowers which Schweinfurth (1883, 110) says 'were in the coffin at the side of the body, and fastened between the bands encircling the mummy'. The following details are taken from the online database of the Victoria Museum of Egyptian Antiquities, Uppsala, Sweden (http://www.gustavianum.uu.se/vm). Accession: Gift to Queen Victoria from E. Brugsch at Giza 18/4 1891 Description: fabric and flowers from the decorations of the royal mummies (now in Cairo). Lotus flowers from Ramses II. Blue flowers from Amosis. Linen from Thotmes III. Natron sample 11th Dynasty.

The radiocarbon date for this sample does not fit any simple explanation, including accepted dates for the original burial and known reburials of Ramesses II. One possibility is that the sample had become contaminated with plant material from the garland fragments from other periods mounted together with the Ramesses II flower. Another suggestion is that despite the attached labelling, the *Nymphaea* flower did not come from the mummy or coffin of Ramesses II and indeed may not even have been from TT320. For example, whole *Nymphaea caerulea* flowers were found with the mummy of Nibsoni, attributed to the 20th Dynasty (Schweinfurth 1883, 113), and there are a number of other ancient Egyptian burials which include single whole *Nymphaea caerulea* flowers that were most likely deposited in the same Egyptian museum as the Ramesses II material, and any of these could have been used in VMD165. Brugsch had a reputation for selling antiquities to raise funds for

Figure 12.1: ECB 40739, Royal Botanic Gardens, Kew, UK. Photo by Andrew McRobb, Kew, with a grant from The Institute of Archaeology, University College London.

Figure 12.2: EBC 40733, Royal Botanic Gardens, Kew, UK. Photo by Andrew McRobb, Kew, with a grant from The Institute of Archaeology, University College London.

12. *Garlands from the Deir el-Bahri Cache* 163

Figure 12.3: VMD 165, Victoria Museum of Egyptian Antiquities, Uppsala, Sweden. The author would like to thank Geoffrey Metz for photographs of VMD 165.

Figure 12.4: UC72632, The Petrie Museum of Egyptian Archaeology, University College London, UK.

the museum, and contemporary reports suggest he would not have been averse to making up a 'tourist' specimen, either to sell or to give as a gift. Possible evidence for this comes in the form of another artefact which bears a strong resemblance to VMD165, namely UC72632 (Figure 12.4) in the Petrie Museum of Egyptian Archaeology, University College London, UK. Like, VMD165, UC72632 has a label attached to its base detailing it as a gift from Brugsch. The labels are handwritten, probably by the same hand. The Petrie label mentions the *Nymphaea* flower, but unlike VMD165 does not attribute it to Ramesses II. UC72632's label states a date of 15th February 1886, whereas the label on VMD165 is clearly marked 18th April 1891, namely five and ten years after the tomb's clearance, and perhaps indicating that such composite artefacts were made up over a period of time. Further research, in particular comparing the handwritten labels on VMD165 and UC 72632 with a specimen of Brugsch's handwriting, may help clarify the origins of these composite artefacts.

Extant evidence suggests that Schweinfurth prepared herbarium quality specimens from the garlands and single *Nymphaea* flowers found associated with Ramesses II, and sampling these to give new radiocarbon dates for comparison would be very interesting. The website of the Berlin Botanical Garden (http://www.synthesys.info/de_taf_bgbm.htm, accessed on 27th February 2010, page copyright 2009) says that "flower garlands of Ramses II" from the Schweinfurth collection "have been recently C14 dated", but without any further details.

Discussion

As a direct result of the Oxford Egyptian Chronology Project, the accredited contexts for the sampled garlands have been re-evaluated, and as the discussion above indicates, it is not clear that any of the contextual data from Deir el-Bahri is secure. The radiocarbon results have indicated a possibility of garland reuse in antiquity, during the reburials, which has ideological implications. Although the issue of garland reuse could suggest that garlands are not a reliable carbon source for dating, it is still true that they provide excellent samples for dating because reburial is rare and, as in the case of TT320, usually obvious. Additionally, where the archaeological records are more precise, it should be possible to determine whether the garlands were fresh when draped over their intended resting place, because fresh plant material is pliable and naturally moulds itself to follow the contours of the shape of the underlying structure, such as a mummy or statue. As the plant material dries out, biochemical changes take place which alter the plasticity of the plant material, it becomes more rigid and cannot then be draped to fit the shape of the underlying structure. Additionally, the dried plants are more brittle than the fresh garlands and are therefore likely to be damaged when handled, and both their shape (following the contours of the underlying structure), and any damage should be evident when a garland is first excavated.

Some extant garlands are still fairly robust whereas others are extremely fragile and easily turned to dust. The difference is probably due to either the varying physiologies of the different species used in the garlands, or to the degree of desiccation. It should be noted that some herbarium samples were treated in the field, and Schweinfurth himself recommended the use of alcohol to keep the plants pliable (Anon., *Bulletin of Miscellaneous Information, Kew* 1889, 19). The author cannot comment on whether he treated the plant material from Deir el-Bahri, nor whether such treatment would affect radiocarbon results.

Conclusion

In the author's view, because of the multiple mummies, poor records, and the high probability of mixed contexts, TT320 is not a good source of garlands for the purpose of using ^{14}C to determine specific dates within the Egyptian chronology. However, garlands from other archaeological sites where reburial and poor context are not issues, should provide excellent sources of carbon for radiocarbon dating.

The results from the Oxford Egyptian Chronology Project have added valuable data to help unravel the story of TT320, and have strengthened the case that comprehensive artefact biographies are crucial wherever archaeological interpretation depends on curated material. Further radiocarbon dates for the Deir el-Bahri material would provide data towards answering some of the remaining questions about the plant material. When information is collated from the diverse research agendas of the scholars who participated in the Symposium, the radiocarbon dates will provide further insights towards understanding the Egyptian chronology and the puzzle that is Deir el-Bahri. Research into these garlands has benefited from the radiocarbon results and the author sincerely thanks the Oxford Egyptian Chronology Project's team and sponsors.

References

Brophy, K. 2009, Quoted on BBC news website on 15th Dec 2009, http://news.bbc.co.uk/1/hi/scotland/tayside_and_central/8412938.stm.

Anon., *Bulletin of Miscellaneous Information*, Kew, 1889, Schweinfurth's Method for Preserving Plants, *Bulletin of Miscellaneous Information (Royal Gardens, Kew)*, **25**, 19.

Capart, J., Gardiner, A. H. and van de Walle, B. 1936, New light on the Ramesside tomb robberies, *The Journal of Egyptian Archaeology*, **22**(2), 169–193.

Dawson, W. R. 1947, Letters from Maspero to Amelia Edwards, *Journal of Egyptian Archaeology*, **33**, 66–89.

Germer, R. 1988, *Katalog der Altägyptischen Pflanzenreste der Berliner Museen*, Wiesbaden, Harrassowitz.

Germer, R. 1989, *Die Pflanzenmaterialien aus dem Grab des Tutanchamun*, Hildesheim, Gerstenberg.

Goody, J. 1993, *The Culture of Flowers*, Cambridge University Press, Cambridge.

Graefe, E. and Belova, G. (eds), 2010, *The Royal Cache TT 320: A Re-examination*, The American University in Cairo Press, Cairo.

Hepper, F. N. 1990, *Pharaoh's Flowers: the botanical treasures of Tutankhamun*, HMSO (A Royal Botanic Gardens Kew, Publication), London.

Leroi-Gourhan, A. 1975, The Flowers Found with Shanidar IV, a Neanderthal Burial in Iraq, *Science*, **190**, 562–564.

Loret, V. 1887, *La flore pharaonique d'après les documents hiéroglyphiques et les spécimens découverts dans les tombes*, Baillière, Paris

Manniche, L. 1999, *An Ancient Egyptian Herbal*, British Museum Press, London.

Maspero, G. 1889, *Les Momies Royales de Déir el-Baharí*, E. Leroux, Paris.

Maspero, G. 1903, *Guide to the Cairo Museum* (trans. J. E. and A. A. Quibell), Institut Français d'Archéologie Orientale, Cairo.

McAleely, S. 2005, Flower Arranging in ancient Egypt? A new approach to archaeobotanical remains, In K. Piquette and S. Love (eds), *Current Research in Egyptology 2003: Proceedings of the fourth annual symposium which took place at the Institute of Archaeology, University College London, 18–19 January 2003*. Oxbow Books, Oxford.

McAleely, S. forthcoming, PhD thesis, Institute of Archaeology, University College London, UK.

Newberry, P. E. 1889, The ancient botany, In Petrie, W. M. F. 1889, *Hawara, Biahmu, and Arsinoe*, Field and Tuer, London, 46–52.

Newberry, P. E. 1890, The botany, In Petrie, W. M. F., *Kahun, Gurob and Hawara*, Kegan Paul, Trench, Trübner and Co, London, 46–50.

Newberry, P. E. 1900, Extracts from My Notebooks (III), *Proceedings of the Society of Biblical Archaeology*, **22**, 143, In P. E. Newberry, 2004 edition, *Articles Published in Proceedings of the Society of Biblical Archaeology 1899–1914*, Golden House Publications, London, 32.

Newberry, P. E. 1927, Report on the floral wreaths found in the coffins of Tut.ankh.Amen, In H. Carter, 1927, *The Tomb of Tut.Ankh.Amen, Vol 2*, London, Cassell and Company Ltd., 189–196.

New York Times 1881, Royal mummies named, *The New York Times*, 31st August.

New York Times 1883, Mummy flowers, *The New York Times*, 14th January.

Niwiński, A. 1988, The wives of Pinudjem II: a topic for discussion, *Journal of Egyptian Archaeology*, **74**, 226–230.

Nodzyńska, A. 2007, Georg Schweinfurth's nachlass in the Jagiellonian University library, *Studies in Ancient Art and Civilisation*, **10**.

Pitts, M. 2010, News: dig find proves flowers placed in Bronze Age graves, *British Archaeology*, **110**.

Reeves, C. N. 1990, *Valley of the Kings: the decline of a royal necropolis*, Kegan Paul International, London and New York.

Roubet, C., and Layer-Lescot, M. 1985, La parure florale de Ramsés II, In *La Momie de Ramsés II: Contribution Scientifique à l'Égyptologie* (eds L. Balout and C. Roubet), 158–161, Éditions Recherche sur les Civilisations, Paris.

Smith, G. E. 1912, *The Royal Mummies*, Institut Français d'Archéologie Orientale, Cairo.

Solecki, R. 1972, *Shanidar: The Humanity of Neanderthal Man*, Penguin, London.

Sommer, J. 1999, The Shanidar IV 'flower burial': a re-evaluation of Neanderthal burial ritual, *Cambridge Archaeological Journal*, **9**(1), 127–137.

Schweinfurth, G. 1883, The flora of ancient Egypt, *Nature*, **28**, 109–114.

Tackholm, G., and Tackholm, V. 1941, *Flora of Egypt: volume 1*, Cairo University Press, Cairo.

Tackholm V. and Drar, M. 1950, *Flora of Egypt, Vol II*, Fouad I University Press, Cairo.

Torrey Botanical Society 1882, Botanical notes, *Bulletin of the Torrey Botanical Club*, **9**(11), 141–143.

Vartavan, de. C. and Asensi Amorós, V. 1997, *Codex of ancient Egyptian plant remains*, Triade Exploration, London.

Wilson, E. 1883, *The Recent Archaic Discovery of Ancient Egyptian Mummies at Thebes: a Lecture Delivered to the Members of the Young Men's Christian Association, at Margate, February 15th, 1883*, Kegan Paul, Trench & Co, London.

Wilson, E. L. 1887, Finding pharaoh, *The Century Magazine*, **34**(1), 3–10.

Winlock, H. E. 1941, *Materials Used At The Embalming of King Tūt-'Ankh-Amūn*, New York, The Metropolitan Museum of Art, Papers No. 10.

Chapter 13

New Radiocarbon Dates for the 21st Dynasty

J. H. Taylor

The current 'historical' dates for the 21st Dynasty (c. 1076–944 BC according to the most recent estimate) have been calculated by dead reckoning backwards from the reign of Shoshenq I, supplemented by presumed astronomical dates. For the internal chronology of the dynasty, there is a substantial amount of textual material bearing regnal dates, although consensus has not been reached as to whether some of these refer to kings or to Theban high priests. However, the sequence of the kings in the Delta and the rulers in Upper Egypt is relatively well documented, with few areas of uncertainty. The new C14 dates relating to the 21st Dynasty come from five distinct contexts: the burial of the Chief Workman Horemkenesi from Deir el-Bahri; the mummies of kings Ahmose I and Ramesses II from the Royal Cache at Deir el-Bahri; the burial of Neskhons, wife of Pinedjem II (also from the Royal Cache); and a mud-brick without provenance, made in the time of the high priest of Amun Menkheperre, and his wife Istemkheb. Three of these contexts certainly fall within the 21st Dynasty itself (burials of Horemkenesi and Neskhons, and mud-brick of Menkheperre). The dates from the mummies of Ahmose I and Ramesses II potentially could fall within a wider time-frame, ranging from their original interments, in the 18th and 19th Dynasties respectively, through an unknown number of rewrappings and reburials, until the closure of their last resting place, the Royal Cache, in or after Year 11 of Shoshenq I. Most of the C14 dates for this period appear to show internal consistency. Seven of the eight distinct samples tested from Horemkenesi's burial fall within the same time range, which is in agreement with the expected date from historical evidence. The C14 dates from the burial of Neskhons and the Menkheperre brick also fit the historical framework. The other dates require further explanation. One sample from the Horemkenesi deposit which appears to be much older than the rest might represent older botanical material recycled by the embalmers. The sample from Ramesses II's mummy (95% probability: c. 1000–840 cal BC) could be made to 'fit' the historical picture if it is assumed to have been associated with one of the last of the several reburials which this king underwent. The sample from Ahmose I (95% probability: c. 1381–1091 BC; 68% probability: 1295–1131 BC) does not match the known history of the king's reburial, and may point to a previously undocumented intervention which took place in the Ramesside period.

Introduction

Chronology of 21st Dynasty: current state of research

The four centuries which followed the New Kingdom are now generally known as the Third Intermediate Period, and cover the 21st to 25th Dynasties. The first part of this historical phase, the 21st Dynasty, is notable for a large number of dated inscriptions, which have

---

Author's Address: **J. H. Taylor**, Dept of Ancient Egypt and Sudan, British Museum, Great Russell Street, London WC1B 3DG, UK

been used by scholars to reconstruct its internal chronology in some detail, although several questions remain. In Kenneth Kitchen's pioneering work on the Third Intermediate Period (Kitchen 1973), the 21st Dynasty was dated to *c.* 1069–945 BC on the basis of Egyptian textual sources and correlations with Near Eastern chronology. Scholarly discussion of the 21st Dynasty in the years following the appearance of Kitchen's work did not result in any substantial departure from his dates, and he himself has recently argued for *c.* 1070/1068–945 BC on the basis of inscriptional evidence alone (Kitchen 2007). In a substantial independent study of ancient Egyptian chronology, the dates for the dynasty have been given as 1076–944/943 BC, based on astronomical evidence (Hornung, Krauss and Warburton 2006, 493, cf. 412). This close agreement between the work of different scholars is indicative of the relatively small scope for variation which the currently available data allows.

The 'historical' dating of the 21st Dynasty depends on counting back from its conclusion. The only significant 'fixed point' which can link the 21st Dynasty to absolute chronology is the Palestinian campaign of Shoshenq I, founder of the following dynasty, the 22nd. The most substantial military operation attested for an Egyptian king in this period, the campaign is described in the Old Testament books of I Kings and II Chronicles. There is also a great inscription and relief which Shoshenq I had carved at the temple of Karnak to commemorate an expedition into Palestine, which is generally accepted as being the same event as that described in the Old Testament. The Biblical sources place this campaign in Year 5 of Rehoboam, king of Judah, a year which is 'fixed' at *c.* 926/925 BC from the chronology of the kings of Israel and Judah and synchronisms with Assyrian chronology (Jansen-Winkeln 2006, 232, cf. 350–1). We might note that even these dates are open to some discussion (Jansen-Winkeln 2006, 232, 474), but the degree of variation which is possible has little or no impact on the issues considered in this paper.

It is usually assumed that the Palestinian campaign took place only shortly before Shoshenq's Year 21 – when his Karnak construction and relief carving began. Thus if the campaign occurred in his Year 20, then that year was *c.* 926/925 BC, and his reign began about 945 BC – which would also mark the end of the 21st Dynasty. But the campaign might have taken place earlier in Shoshenq's reign (Jansen-Winkeln 2006, 232–3), so in theory his accession could have occurred (and the 21st Dynasty ended) several years later than is usually supposed. That possibility would not, however, affect the assessment of the new C14 datings to be discussed below, so for present purposes we will assume that the campaign took place only shortly before Year 21 of Shoshenq I, and we will retain the date of about 945 BC for the end of the 21st Dynasty.

Estimations of the duration of the 21st Dynasty have usually been based on Manetho's total of 130 years, combined with the sum of the known reign-lengths of the individual rulers, as attested by contemporary monuments. In spite of uncertainties as to whether all recorded regnal years from this period should be attributed to Tanite kings or whether some belonged to 'ruling' Theban high priests, the figures obtained by adding up the year dates have been found to agree closely with those of Manetho's excerptors. Hence Karl Jansen-Winkeln has noted that the total duration of the dynasty should lie between 124 and 130 years, his preference being for 'about 126–8 years' (Jansen-Winkeln 2006, 231). Thus if the end of the 21st Dynasty is set at about 945 BC, its beginning must have been in the date-range 1075–1069 BC. Until further evidence is forthcoming this is as far as we can go on the basis of written sources.

Discussion

The dates obtained from recent C14 measurements

New dating evidence relating to the 21st Dynasty has been obtained from radiocarbon measurements on short-lived plant remains from five distinct contexts: The burial of the Chief Workman, Horemkenesi, from Deir el-Bahri; the reburials of the kings Ahmose I and Ramesses II from the tomb known as the Royal Cache, also at Deir el-Bahri; the burial of Neskhons, wife of the high priest of Amun Pinedjem II (again from the Royal Cache); and a mud brick without provenance, made in the time of the mid-21st Dynasty high priest of Amun Menkheperre. Three of these contexts certainly fall firmly within the 21st Dynasty: the burials of Horemkenesi and Neskhons, and the making of the mud brick. The samples from the mummies of Ahmose I and Ramesses II could potentially fall within a wider timeframe, ranging from the date of their original interments, in the 18th and 19th Dynasties respectively, through an unknown number of rewrappings and reburials until the closure of their last resting place, the Royal Cache, in or after Year 11 of Shoshenq I.

Let us now look more closely at these events to establish the expected dates of their occurrence based on historical evidence, and to compare these with the actual calibrated C14 results.

Burial of Horemkenesi

Horemkenesi was the last attested holder of the title Chief Workman in the Place of Truth (Taylor 1995; Dawson *et al.* 2002). In the Ramesside period, this title was held by the head of the community of craftsmen who built the royal tombs in the Valley of the Kings, but by the 21st Dynasty, when new tombs had ceased to be built there, his main duty was probably to participate in the inspection and maintenance of the Theban necropolis. Horemkenesi's coffin and mummy were discovered in 1904–5 in an undisturbed deposit in an 11th Dynasty tomb at the mortuary complex of King Mentuhotep II at Deir el-Bahri on the Theban West Bank. The burial itself contained no textual evidence for dating, but the style of the coffin provided a clue, since the closest parallels to it date to the earlier part of the 21st Dynasty (Niwinski 1988, 112,). However, Horemkenesi is mentioned in several graffiti on the rocks of the Theban necropolis, which record some of his activities, and these contain evidence for the date at which he held office (Spencer 2002, 52–4; Taylor 1995, 16–20). One graffito is dated to a Year 20 of an unidentified ruler, who could be Ramesses XI, Smendes I, Pinedjem I or Psusennes I. On the standard chronology this indicates a date between *c.* 1086 BC and 1031 BC. This graffito also names a man called Heramunpenaef, who is known from other sources to have lived in the reign of Ramesses XI. In another graffito, Horemkenesi's name is associated with those of the well-documented necropolis scribes Thutmose and Butehamun, who were active at the end of the 20th Dynasty and in the first decades of the 21st. On this basis, the date of Horemkenesi's death has been estimated at ca 1040–1030 BC (Taylor 1995, 20). A C14 date on a sample of wood from his coffin, obtained some years ago, yielded (after calibration and revision) a possible calendar date range of 1450–1005 BC, which was considered compatible with the historical evidence (Ambers 2002, 54; Taylor 1995, 20).

There are eight new C14 dates from Horemkenesi's burial. Seven of these derive from samples of textiles and straw which were found among the wrappings of his mummy, and all fall within the same broad range (OxA-20060-20067; the dates 20061 and 20062 were based on the same sample). At 95% probability, they are dated 1259–926 cal BC, and at 68% probability 1208–941 cal BC, and are thus in agreement with the dating of Horemkenesi's career based on historical evidence. More specifically, at 68% probability four of these samples fall within the date range 1127–1012 BC, which agrees even more closely with the 'historical' date. However, the eighth sample from this burial, based on *Asteraceae* seeds (sample OxA-20201) produced a much earlier date: 1491–1316 BC at 95% probability, and 1436–1387 BC at 68% probability. These figures point to a date in the 18th Dynasty. Since the seeds were found among the packing material of the mummy's chest cavity, it is virtually impossible that they could have been intrusive from the environment of the 11th Dynasty tomb in which Horemkenesi was buried. If the C14 date were to be relied upon, it would have to be assumed that the embalmers had recycled old botanical material, perhaps taken from earlier burials. Since Horemkenesi lived at the period when the royal mummies of the New Kingdom were undergoing restoration and rewrapping in the Theban necropolis, it is theoretically possible that 18th Dynasty seeds (from old garlands or packing material?) could have been available in the embalming workshop, but this can be no more than speculation. Hence an adequate explanation for this outlying date remains to be established.

Mummies from the Royal Cache

The next three cases are from the Royal Cache at Deir el-Bahri (DB 320) – a rock-cut tomb which contained the mummies of several members of the family of the high priest of Amun Pinedjem II from the late 21st Dynasty, and also the remains of many kings, queens and other high status individuals of the 17th to 20th Dynasties (Reeves 1990, 200–203). These older mummies had been taken from their original burial places at the end of the New Kingdom and transferred from tomb to tomb as part of a lengthy process of grouping the dead pharaohs in concealed and easily guarded spots (Reeves 1990). Different degrees of intervention in the individual royal mummies took place during this process. This involved – in some cases – reconstitution and strengthening of dispersed body parts following damage by robbers, and – more frequently – rewrapping and placing of mummies in newly provided coffins, perhaps with newly fashioned floral garlands. Such restorations of the royal dead were sometimes recorded in inscriptions written on the walls of tombs, on the linen wrappings of the mummies and on their coffins. These dockets are usually dated and enable the post-interment history of some mummies to be reconstructed in detail.

First, we consider the sample from the burial of Ramesses II. His mummy was found in the cache lying in a finely carved but apparently unfinished wooden coffin which was evidently a replacement for his original casing. His primary interment in the sepulchre which was made specifically for him – tomb 7 in the Valley of the Kings – would have occurred at the conclusion of the traditional 70-day period of mourning after his death, at the end of the 13th century BC, *c.* 1213 according to the current historical chronology. Subsequently, his remains were moved on more than one occasion, before finally coming to rest in the Royal Cache (Reeves 1990, 247). Hieratic dockets on his wooden coffin and his mummy wrappings record these interventions:

- a 'renewal of (his) burial' in Year 6 of the era called the 'Renaissance' (*wehem mesut*) at the end of the 20th Dynasty – i.e. in the 1080s/70s according to the standard chronology (Reeves 1990, 94, 247);
- reburial in the tomb of his father Sety I in Year 15 of King Smendes I of the 21st Dynasty (Reeves 1990, 95, 247). Smendes reigned *c.* 1076–1052 BC;
- transfer to the *kay*-tomb of Queen Inhapi (or Tenthapi) in Year 10 of King Siamun of the 21st Dynasty (Reeves 1990, 247). Siamun reigned *c.* 986–968 BC.

The final transfer of Ramesses II to the Royal Cache (DB320) is not recorded by any docket, but appears to have occurred in or after Year 11 of Shoshenq I – i.e. *c.* 933 BC or later (Reeves 1990, 247).

Previous C14 study on Ramesses II's remains was carried out when the mummy was undergoing conservation treatment in Paris in 1976–7. Linen wrappings from two places on the body were sampled and yielded two different calibrated dates – one 3040 ± 60 BP (95% probability: 1433–1122 cal BC), the other 2840 ± 60 BP (95% probability: 1208–848 cal BC). While the first of these was too 'high' to fit the historical chronology of Ramesses' reign, the latter was interpreted as possible evidence of a restoration of the body at some time after the original burial (Delibrias 1985, 260–263).

The single new dating is based on a sample of lotus stem (OxA-18051), associated with the mummy of the king. At 95% probability, it falls in the period 1000–840 cal BC, and at 68% probability 970–850 cal BC. This date would coincide with either the reburial of Ramesses II in the reign of Siamun or the final deposition of his mummy in the Royal Cache during or after the reign of Shoshenq I.

Another sample comes from a willow wreath (OxA-18959) associated with the burial of King Ahmose I, founder of the 18th Dynasty, whose mummy was also recovered from the Royal Cache. The 'historical' chronology places Ahmose's death *c.* 1515 BC. His original tomb has not been located and the only record of the travels of his mummy before it reached the cache is a hieratic inscription on the wrappings, which stated that the king was 'Osirified' on the orders of Pinedjem I of the 21st Dynasty, in a year 8. This date has been supposed to refer to King Psusennes I of Tanis, whose reign (*c.* 1051–1006) was in part contemporary with Pinedjem I's rule at Thebes (Reeves 1990, 251). The C14 date from the wreath is 1381–1091 cal BC at 95% probability, and 1295–1131 cal BC at 68% probability. This would seem to suggest that the wreath was made at an earlier date than the 'Osirifying' of King Ahmose's mummy – a restoration which would probably have involved the rewrapping of the corpse. A possible way out of this difficulty could be to suppose that a wreath made during some earlier restoration might have been replaced on the mummy at the completion of the rewrapping in the time of Pinedjem I. There is no supporting evidence for such an earlier restoration, but it is theoretically possible that one might have occurred. Before the *wehem mesut* era the tombs of several New Kingdom rulers were entered on different occasions, usually to make good some damage which had occurred during attempts at robbery. The tombs of Amenhotep II, Tuthmosis IV, Ramesses II and Ramesses VI were all entered, and these events are known only from graffiti written on the walls of the tombs or near their entrances (Reeves 1990, 273ff and Table 10); they are not recorded on the mummy wrappings or coffins. Since the original resting place of Ahmose I has not been identified, the possibility of such a restoration of his burial having occurred during the 18th–20th Dynasties cannot be excluded.

The third sample from the Royal Cache is a specimen of plant material from the coffin of Neskhons, wife of the high priest of Amun, Pinedjem II (OxA-18960). Pinedjem was a contemporary of the 21st Dynasty kings Amenemope, Osorkon the Elder and Siamun. The Royal Cache was probably originally constructed to serve as the family tomb of this high priest (Graefe 2003, 79), and the date of Neskhons' burial there is conveniently recorded for us in a hieratic inscription which was written on the wall of the descending shaft. The event is dated to Year 5 of King Siamun (Reeves 1990, 256) – about 982 BC on the historical chronology. The new C14 date is 1045–858 BC at 95% probability, and 997–921 BC at 68% probability. This agrees very pleasingly with the historical evidence.

Brick of Menkheperre

The final sample to be considered is derived from plant remains extracted from a mud brick which bears the stamped names of the high priest of Amun Menkheperre and his wife Istemkheb (OxA-19794). Menkheperre held office in the reigns of Smendes I and Psusennes I in the second half of the 11th century BC, according to the historical sources. He was responsible for the building of numerous structures, particularly forts, at sites in Upper Egypt, using mud bricks stamped with his own name and sometimes that of his wife, Istemkheb, as well. Examples have been found at el-Hibeh, but stamped bricks of Menkheperre's buildings are also known from Shurafa, Higazeh, Gebelein, Luxor and Karnak (Kitchen 1973, 269–70; 1986, 572). The specimen from which the sample was taken is of unknown provenance and could conceivably have come from any of these sites. The new C14 date from this specimen is 1210–1007 BC at 95% probability, and 1128–1026 BC at 68% probability – dates which are compatible with those expected on the grounds of historical evidence.

Conclusions

We may conclude by noting that most of the newly obtained C14 dates agree broadly with the historical dates. Seven out of the eight samples from Horemkenesi's burial fall consistently within the same time-range; the single sample of much earlier date, however, remains to be explained and should not simply be dismissed as anomalous. The sample from the coffin of Neskhons agrees with the inscriptional evidence for the date of her burial, and that from the Menkheperre brick is consistent with the presumed dates of his building activity. The date from the reburial of Ramesses II can be made to agree with historical evidence if it is assumed that the lotus stem which was sampled was associated with one of the last stages in the mummy's travels in the Theban necropolis. The sample from the wreath of Ahmose I may point to a previously undocumented intervention in his mummy, taking place in the Ramesside period. But, like the odd 'high' date from Horemkenesi, it is the pieces that do not 'fit' the historical picture which sometimes provide clues to different interpretations of the data, and every attempt should be made to find explanations for them.

References

Ambers, J. 2002, Radiocarbon measurement of wood from the coffin, in *Horemkenesi, May he live Forever! The Bristol Mummy Project* (eds D. P. Dawson, S. Giles and M. W. Ponsford), 54, Bristol Museums and Art Gallery, Bristol.

Dawson, D. P., Giles, S. and Ponsford, M. W. (eds) 2002, *Horemkenesi, May he live Forever! The Bristol Mummy Project*, Bristol Museums and Art Gallery, Bristol.

Delibrias, G. 1985, Datation par le carbone 14 de fragments de bandelettes, in *La Momie de Ramses II: Contribution Scientifique à l'Égyptologie* (eds L. Balout and C. Roubet), 260–263, Éditions Recherche sur les Civilisations, Paris.

Graefe, E. 2003, The Royal Cache and the tomb robberies, in *The Theban Necropolis. Past, Present and Future* (eds N. Strudwick and J. H. Taylor), 74–82, British Museum Press, London.

Hornung, E., Krauss, R. and Warburton, D. A. (eds) 2006, *Ancient Egyptian Chronology*, Brill, Leiden and Boston.

Jansen-Winkeln, K. 2006, Relative chronology of Dyn. 21, in *Ancient Egyptian Chronology* (eds E. Hornung, R. Krauss and D. A. Warburton), 218–233, Brill, Leiden and Boston.

Kitchen, K. A. 1973, *The Third Intermediate Period in Egypt (1100–650 BC)*, Aris & Phillips, Warminster.

Kitchen, K. A. 1986, *The Third Intermediate Period in Egypt (1100–650 BC) Supplement*, Aris & Phillips, Warminster.

Kitchen, K. A. 2007, Egyptian and related chronologies – look, no sciences, no pots!, in *The Synchronisation of Civilisations in the Eastern Mediterranean in the Second Millennium BC III* (eds M. Bietak and E. Czerny), 163–171, Österreichische Akademie der Wissenschaften. Vienna.

Niwinski, A. 1988, *21st Dynasty Coffins from Thebes. Chronological and typological studies*. Theben 5, Philipp von Zabern, Mainz am Rhein.

Reeves, C. N., 1990, *Valley of the Kings. The Decline of a Royal Necropolis*, Kegan Paul International, London and New York.

Spencer, A. J. 2002., The decoration of the coffin and other inscriptions, in *Horemkenesi, may he live Forever! The Bristol Mummy Project* (eds D. P. Dawson, S. Giles and M. W. Ponsford), 38–54, Bristol Museums and Art Gallery, Bristol.

Taylor, J. H. 1995, *Unwrapping a mummy. The life, death and embalming of Horemkenesi*, British Museum Press in association with Bristol Museums and Art Gallery, London.

IV: The Middle Kingdom

Chapter 14

A Radiocarbon-based Chronology for the Middle Kingdom

M. W. Dee

The chronology of the Middle Kingdom is characterised by a 'high' versus 'low' debate. The division arises from ambiguities in both the absolute and relative dating evidence. The former is largely connected with the Sothic observation ascribed to the reign of Senusret III, whilst the latter centres on king-list records and the nature of royal succession during the 12th Dynasty. An added challenge to Middle Kingdom chronology arises from the fact it is bound on both sides by periods of disunity, for which the dating evidence is often only piecemeal. However, by combining king-list information with radiocarbon data, this project has made the most substantial radiometric contribution to the debate. The mathematical models presented here included 42 new radiocarbon dates made on plant materials associated with specific historical periods, in the same way as for the New Kingdom. However, in order to reflect the heightened degree of uncertainty across-the-board, the Middle Kingdom models were allowed three times more flexibility in the reign-length restriction than that employed for the New Kingdom. Variations were again run to reflect differing interpretations of the archaeological evidence. Lower levels of precision were achieved as a result of the smaller data set and relaxed constraints, but the models still generated decadal-order estimates, which preferentially selected the high chronology position.

Introduction

The chronology of the age now known as the Middle Kingdom remains unclear and incomplete. In many respects, this is because it is bound by two periods where the state was fragmented, and for which the dating evidence is incomplete. The Middle Kingdom began when the state was reunified under the reign of Mentuhotep II of the 11th Dynasty. Until recently, it was thought to have lasted until the end of the 12th Dynasty; now it is generally accepted that the period should include either some or all of the 13th Dynasty (Callender 2000).

The central objective of any radiocarbon dating study of the Middle Kingdom is to situate the long relative chronology on the absolute time-scale. At present, this task is largely accomplished by a single observation of the heliacal rising of Sothis, believed to date to the 7th year of Senusret III. However, the exact calendar year assigned to this observation remains contentious (see Parker 1976; Krauss 1985). Furthermore, the relative chronology for the period is also marred by disputes over the lengths of reigns and co-regencies (see Murnane 1977; Schneider 2006). The upshot is a schism in the academic community over the

Author's Address: **M. W. Dee**, RLAHA, University of Oxford, Dyson Perrins Building, South Parks Road, Oxford OX1 3QY, UK

dating of the Middle Kingdom, articulated once more as a 'high' versus 'low' debate. In this study, the published chronology of Shaw (2000, 479) was used to represent the former case and that of Hornung *et al.* (2006, 490), the latter. The modelling process involved combining the new set of radiocarbon data with each interpretation in turn. Once more, only the most robust historical evidence, expressed within realistic constraints, was employed. Sothic dates and all other absolute evidence were entirely excluded from the analysis.

Methodology

The Samples

A total of 35 samples were obtained for the Middle Kingdom, all comprising short-lived plant remains or items fashioned from them. The list is given in the Appendix, Table 2, and is equivalent to that published in the updated Supporting Online Material by Bronk Ramsey *et al.* (2010). The highlight of the sample set was a series of well-studied papyri from the Egyptian Museum Berlin. These documents, dating to the height of the 12th Dynasty, could all be allocated to specific reigns, and in many cases to individual regnal years. In contrast, a number of other Middle Kingdom samples could not be assigned to particular reigns. One such example was OxA-19543, a rope sling from the Tomb of Ipy, which could only be allocated to the late 11th Dynasty. The modelling of such samples was adjusted to reflect the increased degree of uncertainty.

No samples were found for the 13th Dynasty and the only reign of the 11th Dynasty for which specific samples were obtained was Mentuhotep II. Nonetheless, the latter measurements were all made on well-provenanced textiles and most of the long reigns of the 12th Dynasty were well represented in the sample set.

Absolute chronological information: the radiocarbon data

The Middle Kingdom model comprised 42 radiocarbon measurements. The data set was characterised by a lower proportion of outlying results than was the case for the New Kingdom. Two samples produced Common Era dates, and thus had to be removed (see Chapter 7). One set of duplicate dates was also excluded because the measurements (OxA-15314 and VERA-3727) were inconsistent. For the papyrus document concerned, contamination had been suspected from the outset, and the results suggested that problem had not been adequately overcome.

Rationalising why the Middle Kingdom samples were generally more reliable than the New Kingdom samples is not straightforward. The most parsimonious explanation is that the materials were supported by better quality contextual information. However, more subtle arguments may also be invoked that relate to the historical setting itself. Such factors involve the length of occupation of key sites and the liability of such locations to reworking and reuse. For example, freshly established sites, like the Middle Kingdom town of Illahun, are less likely to be characterised by the reworking of older material, which generates older-than-expected outliers.

Twelve Middle Kingdom samples were dated in duplicate. Apart from the inconsistent result for the contaminated papyrus described above, the routine duplicates made at Oxford and the inter-laboratory comparisons all showed excellent agreement (see the Appendix, Table 3).

Relative chronological information: king-list order and reign lengths

As with the New Kingdom models, king-list order and reign-length approximations were the main types of prior information included in the Middle Kingdom analysis. In fact, the historical chronology for both Kingdoms is based on many of the same primary resources; nonetheless, for a detailed account of the compilation of the Middle Kingdom chronology, see Schneider (2006).

In this study, the conventional royal succession from Mentuhotep II to the end of the 12th Dynasty was taken to be indisputable (see the Appendix, Table 1). All the Middle Kingdom samples obtained for this project related to this contiguous sequence. The Intermediate Periods immediately before and after, where the relative chronology is more equivocal, were excluded from the analysis.

The exact length of several Middle Kingdom reigns and the duration of possible co-regencies remain contentious. Advocates of co-regencies refer to particular stelae that are 'double-dated' to two kings' reigns. The quintessential example is the Amenemhat I–Senusret I 10-year co-regency implied by the stela of Antef (Murnane 1977, 2). The upshot of such debates for this study was that several scenarios had to be modelled and the reign-length restrictions relaxed across-the-board.

Model configuration and specifications

The basic coding of the Middle Kingdom models was very similar to the New Kingdom (see Chapter 7). Phases were used to represent reigns and included all the radiocarbon measurements for the given ruler. The Phases were arranged in Sequences, where they were constrained to meet king-list order. The model calculated the transition point between one Phase and the next, which was interpreted as the 'accession year' for the incoming ruler (even if their predecessor still shared power).

Reign-length information was again modelled by including an Interval command in each Phase, whether or not the Phase was populated. The standard Middle Kingdom model (MKM1) employed the Student's t-distribution with 5 degrees of freedom, as used for the New Kingdom; however, to reflect increased uncertainty across-the-board, the distribution was expanded by a factor of three. Thus, instead of requiring 95% of the reign-length selections to be within ± 2.65 calendar years of the historical estimates, the requirement was relaxed to ± 7.95 years (see Figure 14.1). Correspondingly, the iterative analysis still proceeded if the reign lengths chosen by the program were within ± 60 years of these values.

The standard Middle Kingdom model (MKM1) utilised the reign lengths published in Shaw (2000, 479). The first variation (MKM2) used the reign lengths of Hornung *et al.* (2006, 490), and for this volume a third variation (MKM3) was included based on Kitchen (2000). There are several significant differences between the data sets (see the Appendix, Table 1). The absolute positioning of Shaw and Kitchen are in closer agreement, as they

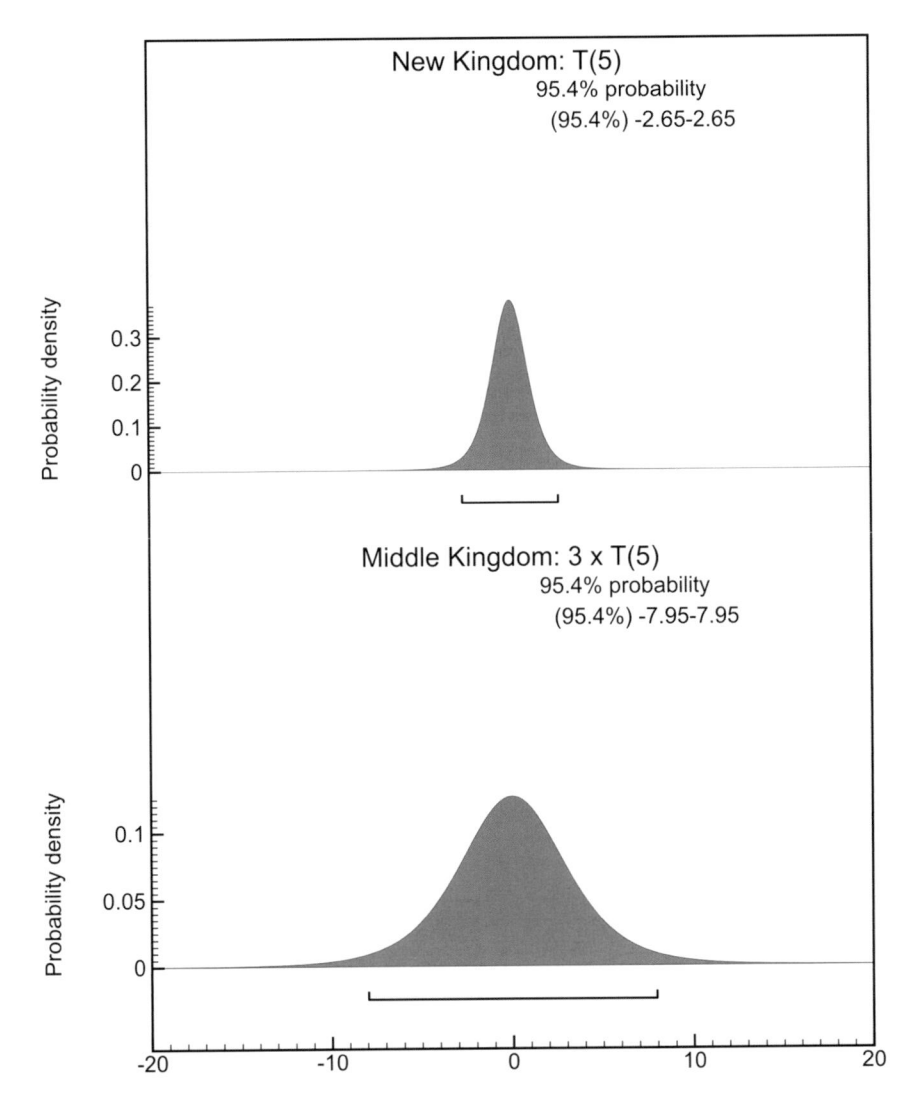

Figure 14.1: The Student's t-distribution was scaled by a factor of 3 in the standard Middle Kingdom model to reflect increased reign-length uncertainty.

both favour a higher Sothic date. However the reign lengths preferred by Kitchen are much closer to those of the low chronology of Hornung *et al*. In particular, the latter two assume much briefer reigns for Amenemhat I and Senusret III. The modelling approach adopted by this study was particularly suited to such a controversy. Specifically, the same absolute date information (radiocarbon dates) was put into each model and only the relative (reign-length) information varied; in this manner, it was possible to evaluate each scenario by considering the plausibility of the absolute dates produced for the Middle Kingdom Sothic record.

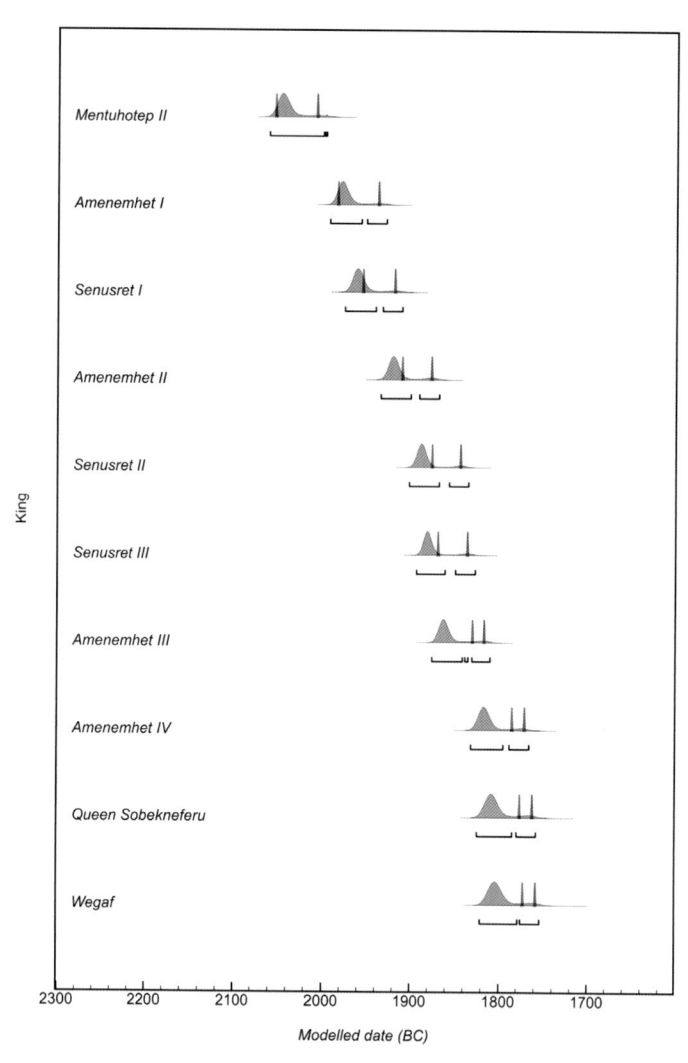

Figure 14.3: Selected accession dates from MKM2. The high chronology estimates are shown in red; low chronology in blue; modelled radiocarbon dates in grey. The calibrated ranges (95%) given by the square brackets are listed in the Appendix, Table 5.

Table 14.1: Specifications for the set of Middle Kingdom models. The outputs for each model are given in the Appendix, Table 5.

Model Name	Reign Lengths	Description
MKM1	Shaw 2000	High or standard configuration
MKM2	Hornung *et al.* 2006	Low chronology configuration
MKM3	Kitchen 2000	Alternative reign lengths
MKM4	Shaw 2000	100% outliers eliminated

14. *A Radiocarbon-based Chronology for the Middle Kingdom*

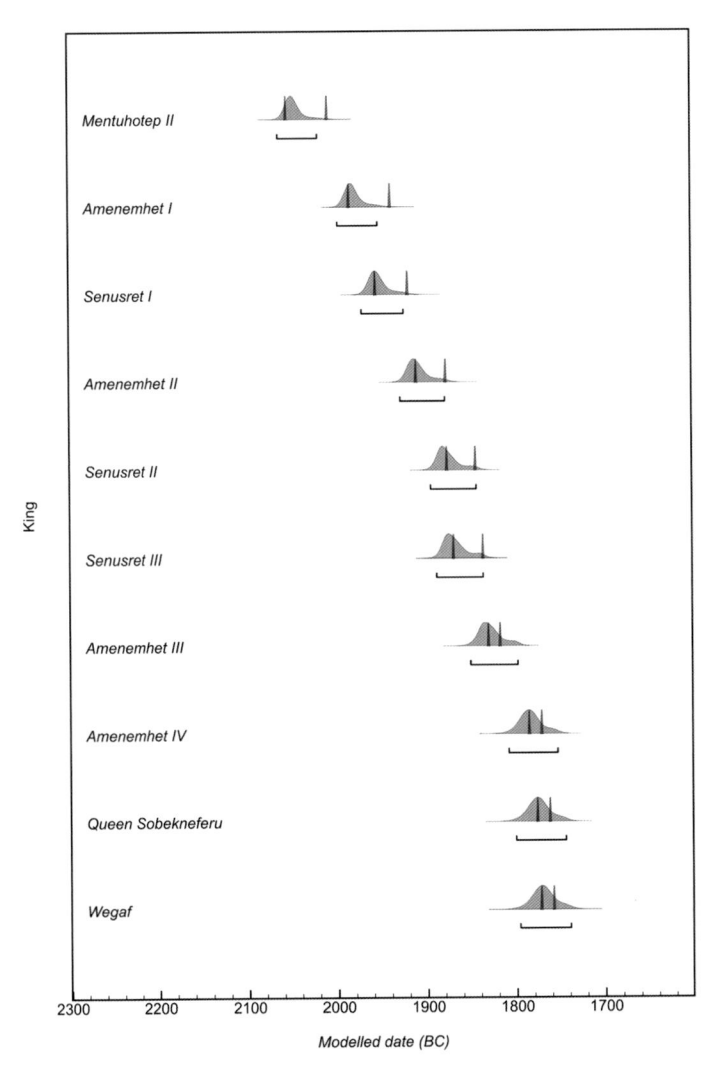

Figure 14.2: Selected accession dates from MKM1. The high chronology estimates are shown in red; low chronology in blue; modelled radiocarbon dates in grey. The calibrated ranges (95%) given by the square brackets are listed in the Appendix, Table 5.

As with the New Kingdom, a further model was included (MKM4) that excluded the samples given a 100% posterior outlier probability by MKM1. On this occasion, there was only one sample that met this criterion, although it was dated in duplicate (OxA-19553 and OxA-20019). Every other Middle Kingdom model included all 42 radiocarbon dates. A uniform outlier probability of 5% was used throughout, and the localised offset of Dee *et al.* 2010 was again built into the models. The effect of varying these parameters and doubling the reign-length uncertainty has been dealt with elsewhere (Bronk Ramsey *et al.* 2010). The Middle Kingdom models were each run for at least ten million iterations and the average convergence consistently passed 95%. The specifications for each model are summarised in Table 14.1 (see the Appendix, Table 4, for MKM1 program code).

Results and Discussion

The Radiocarbon-based Chronologies

Figure 14.2 shows the modelled calibrations obtained by MKM1 for selected accession dates between Mentuhotep II and the end of the 12th Dynasty. The full set of calendar date ranges is given in the Appendix, Table 5. The precision of MKM1 was significantly lower than NKM1, as a result of the smaller number of radiocarbon measurements, the increased reign-length uncertainty, and the plateau in the calibration curve between 1875–1750 BC. The average calendrical precision of MKM1 was 55 years (at 95% probability). The calibrations produced by MKM1 clearly favoured the high chronology. In fact, at the beginning of the sequence, the 95% probability ranges did not even overlap the low chronology.

The results of MKM2 are given in Figure 14.3. The shorter chronology caused a noticeable contraction in the sequence as a whole. Despite this, the radiocarbon data continued to direct the model toward the higher chronology position. In fact, the shorter chronology resulted in estimates that were significantly higher than even the chronology of Shaw (2000, 479). This conclusion was reiterated by MKM3, which generated posterior probabilities that were almost identical to MKM2. Finally, removing the one 100% outlier from MKM1 and then rerunning the model (MKM4) had no material impact on the date ranges produced (see the Appendix, Table 5 and Model Results, for data and figures).

The Historical Implications

The results presented here support the high chronology. The radiocarbon information clearly directs the model toward an early 19th century BC date for the accession of Senusret III, under whose rule the Sothic record was made. This does not mean, however, that the longer reign lengths were favoured. The reign-length configurations were used as prior information so only the absolute position of the whole sequence was essentially unknown prior to the calculation of the models. Moreover, at 95% probability this study cannot rule out the low chronology. Although small, some probability is allocated to a late 19th century interpretation of the Illahun papyrus. It is possible, however, that in due course radiocarbon dating may be able to resolve the dilemma. For example, if twice as many dates were available, the model might prove more conclusive. Or alternatively, the models would also be improved by new archaeological information. Great progress could be made if clarity could be gained on the co-regency issue, or the lengths of specific reigns (particularly Amenemhat I and Senusret III). If consensus could be reached on the relative sequence, then only one configuration would be required for the Middle Kingdom model, and thus it could establish the definitive position of the period in absolute time.

Conclusions

This research provides a secure and independent verification of the absolute positioning of the Middle Kingdom chronology. The key finding was that the radiocarbon-based chronology concurs best with the conventional high chronology. The low chronology was not eliminated by the analysis, but there is a significant possibility that the approach employed here may one day be able to resolve this matter conclusively.

References

Dee, M. W., Brock, F., Harris, S. A., Bronk Ramsey, C., Shortland, A. J., Higham, T. F. G. and Rowland, J. M. 2010, Investigating the Likelihood of a Reservoir Offset in the Radiocarbon Record for Ancient Egypt, *Journal of Archaeological Science*, **37**(4), 687–693.

Bronk Ramsey, C., 1995, Radiocarbon calibration and analysis of stratigraphy: the OxCal program, *Radiocarbon*, **37**(2), 425–430.

Bronk Ramsey, C., Dee, M. W., Rowland, J. M., Higham, T. F. G., Harris, S. A., Brock, F., Quiles, A., Wild, E. M., Marcus, E. S. and Shortland, A. J. 2010, Radiocarbon-based Chronology for Dynastic Egypt. *Science*, **328**(5985), 1554–1559.

Callender, G. 2000, The Middle Kingdom, In *The Oxford History of Ancient Egypt* (ed. I. Shaw), 148–183, Oxford University Press, Oxford.

Hornung, E., Krauss, R. and Warburton, D. A. (eds) 2006, *Ancient Egyptian Chronology*, Brill, Leiden and Boston.

Kitchen, K. A. 2000, Regnal and Genealogical Data of Ancient Egypt (Absolute Chronology I) The Historical Chronology of Ancient Egypt, A Current Assessment. In *The Synchronisation of Civilisations in the Eastern Mediterranean in the Second Millennium BC I* (ed. M. Bietak), 39–52, Austrian Academy of Sciences Press, Vienna.

Krauss, R. 1985, *Sothis und Mondaten*, Pelizaeus-Museum, Hildeshein.

Murnane, W. J. 1977, *Ancient Egyptian Coregencies*, Oriental Institute, University of Chicago, Chicago.

Parker, R. A. 1976, The Sothic dating of the twelfth and eighteenth dynasties, In *Studies in Honor of George R. Hughes* (eds J. F. Johnson and E. F. Wente), 177–184, Oriental Institute, University of Chicago, Chicago.

Reimer, P. J., Baillie, M. G. L., Bard, E., Bayliss, A., Beck, J. W., Blackwell, P. G., Bronk Ramsey, C., Buck, C. E., Burr, G. S., Edwards, R. L., Friedrich, M., Grootes, P. M., Guilderson, T. P., Hajdas, I., Heaton, T. J., Hogg, A. G., Hughen, K. A., Kaiser, K. F., Kromer, B., McCormac, F. G., Manning, S. W., Reimer, R. W., Richards, D. A., Southon, J. R., Talamo, S., Turney, C. S. M., van der Plicht, J. and Weyhenmeyer, C. E. 2009, IntCal09 and Marine09 radiocarbon age calibration curves, 0–50,000 years cal BP, *Radiocarbon*, **51**(4), 1111–1150.

Schneider, T. 2006, Middle Kingdom and the Second Intermediate Period, In *Ancient Egyptian Chronology* (eds E. Hornung, R. Krauss and D. A. Warburton), 168–196, Brill, Leiden and Boston.

Shaw, I. (ed.) 2000, *The Oxford History of Ancient Egypt*, Oxford University Press, Oxford.

CHAPTER 15

Correlating and Combining Egyptian Historical and Southern Levantine Radiocarbon Chronologies at Middle Bronze Age IIa Tel Ifshar, Israel

E. S. Marcus

Even before the chrono-cultural subdivision termed Middle Bronze Age IIa (MB IIa) was first defined for the southern Levant in the 1930s, the nature of its relations with Middle Kingdom (MK) Egypt was considered of crucial importance both for establishing a historical chronology and for understanding the political, economic and cultural processes that shaped the latter, as well as the former. Since then, nearly 80 years of research, both in the Levant and in Egypt, have produced data supporting a myriad of interpretations regarding many aspects of these relations. Unfortunately, chronological evidence has largely been limited to the latter part of this and the following period. Reliable archaeological evidence for synchronizing the bulk of the Middle Bronze Age IIa has been at a premium, as has been a robust absolute or calendrical chronology. In the last few decades, a focused project was initiated in order to overcome these limitations by producing a radiocarbon chronology of the southern Levant for this period. Samples of single year cultigens were selected from the stratified archaeological sequences of three principal MB IIa southern Levantine sites (Tel Ifshar, Tel Nami and Tell el-Hayyat) and faunal samples from three others (Tel Aphek, Tel Kabri and Gesher) and were submitted for AMS C14 analysis at ORAU and VERA, and in two cases for conventional analysis at the Weizmann Institute. The resulting determinations, particularly from Tel Ifshar and Tell el-Hayyat (Marcus 2003; 2010; Falconer and Berelov 2006), provided the first independent and meaningful chronology for this period and established upper and lower bounds for this cultural phase in the late 20th and mid-18th centuries BCE, respectively; an internal phasing remained largely elusive. However, based on a recent comprehensive study of the finds from Tel Ifshar (Marcus et al. 2008a) a number of relevant developments have taken place: one, a detailed stratigraphic analysis now offers more precise contextual information for the radiocarbon determinations, enabling a more robust relative phasing; two, the identification and study of a significant assemblage of MK Egyptian ceramics (Marcus et al. 2008b), including a complete vessel with a date in the first half of the 19th century BC, offers both a comparison for the radiocarbon analysis and the potential to construct a high precision chronology using Bayesian analysis. The ranges of the calibrated probability distributions for those phases containing Egyptian pottery offer a strong correspondence with Egyptian chronology. However, when combined together in a Bayesian model, the resulting internal phasing reaches a precision that one case spans only 27 years! This precision permits a correlation to be drawn between the phases at Tel Ifshar and various eastern Mediterranean processes and historical events involving Egypt. In addition, these results along with the evidence for imports and comparisons, from and with coastal and inland Syria and Lebanon respectively, offer calendrical dates for these regions and a provisional correlation with Mesopotamian chronology.

Author's Address: **E. S. Marcus**, Recanati Institute for Maritime Studies, University of Haifa, Israel

Introduction

For most historical and archaeological periods, from at least the Early Bronze Age onwards, consideration of the chronologies of Egypt and the Levant is generally inseparable, owing both to their geographical proximity and, depending on the period in question, the cultural, political and economic interaction between the two regions and their cultures. Previously, this consideration has been unidirectional, with the astrochronologically-based dynastic chronology of Egypt contributing a seemingly robust framework for the material culture-based archaeological periodization of the latter. In later historical periods, beginning in the mid-to-late Middle Bronze Age, connections between the Levant and Mesopotamia, and beyond, have offered indirect correlation with the Mesopotamian, and later the Persian and Greek chronologies, with varying degrees of reliability and success. In the last two decades, radiocarbon has contributed considerably to the discourse, but, until recently, the scientific precision and the availability of reliable dated contexts have been lacking for earlier periods, precluding any attempt to test the correlation of the Levant with Egyptian chronology. In this paper, the results of a detailed stratigraphic analysis of the Middle Bronze Age IIa (MB IIa) sequence at Tel Ifshar, Israel, the excavation of which produced the earliest Middle Kingdom (MK) Egyptian pottery found in the region and for which a suite of radiocarbon assays has been carried out, offers an unparalleled opportunity to both check the correlation with Egypt and to combine the chronological data from both regions in order to obtain unprecedented chronological precision for the southern Levant (modern Israel, Jordan and the Palestinian National Authority).

Current State of Research

For more than thirty-five years, the basis for the relative chronology of the southern Levant during the Middle Bronze Age IIa has been the well-stratified sequence at Tel Aphek (Figure 15.1; Table 15.1; Kochavi 1975; Beck 1975; 1985; 2000a; 2000b; 2000c; Yadin and Kochavi 2000; Gal and Kochavi 2000; Kochavi and Yadin 2002; Yadin 2009a; 2009b). Despite its stratigraphic reliability and the quality of the ceramic analysis, the lack of any occurrence or identification of Egyptian imports (Marcus *et al.* 2008b, 214–215), and the absence of any radiocarbon determinations, severely limited this site's utility for linking the southern Levantine sequence with that of Egypt. Moreover, at Aphek and elsewhere, little support could be obtained from scarab seal studies – a mainstay for the study of subsequent Egyptian-Levantine relations – as the adoption of these Egyptian administrative and amuletic devices only begins in the southern Levant towards the end of the period under discussion (Ben-Tor 2007). An important exception is the more than 40 clay sealings stamped with scarab seals and a handful of Egyptian *zirs* and other forms from the excavations of the MB IIa moat and earliest gate of Ashkelon (Stager 2002; Stager *et al.* 2008, 221–231, figs 14.4, 14.9, 14.27; Stager and Voss 2011: 120*–122*, pl. 1:1–3). These early 13th Dynasty style sealings provide a *terminus post quem* of *c.* 1780 BC for the beginning of Ashkelon's MB IIa sequence (Stager *et al.* 2008, fig. 14.4, but cf. Stager and Voss, 2011, 120*, n. 1). This datum and its subsequent sequence has been synchronized with that of Tell el-Dabʻa/Avaris in the eastern Egyptian Delta (Bietak *et al.* 2008), where carriers of Levantine material culture settled in the late 12th Dynasty (beginning *c.* 1830 BC during the reign of Amenemhet III), and created a hybrid Egypto-Canaanite culture that formed the basis for the later Hyksos Kingdom (Bietak 1996). This latter sequence and its Levantine synchronisms have been widely discussed and debated in the literature. However, imports to 'Ezbet Rushdi (Tell el-Dab'a) in the early 12th Dynasty (*c.* Amenemhet II), of monochrome painted wares from the northern Levant and two early storage jar rims shown, petrographically, to have come from, respectively, the Southern and Carmel Coastal Plains of Israel (Bagh 1998; 2002; Czerny 1998; 2002; Cohen-Weinberger and Goren 2004, 80–81, 92, table 1) have been largely overlooked as a potential contact between Egypt and the Levant (Marcus 2007, 160–162, 164–165). The potential of this early synchronization finds support following the publication of MK pottery in early MB IIa phases at Tel Ifshar (Marcus *et al.* 2008a; 2008b).

Despite decades of debate on the chronology of the Middle Bronze Age Levant, it was not until the early 1990s that any systematic attempt was made to apply radiocarbon to overcoming the purported lack of any Egyptian imports in the early Middle Bronze Age IIa (cf. Weinstein 1975) or any other issues. A pilot project initiated by the author in 1992 focused on two selected of sites (Tel Ifshar and Tel Nami) with well-stratified archaeobotanical remains of single year cultigens found in destruction layers (Marcus 2003, 101; Hedges *et al.* 1997, 256–257). This initial effort was followed at the end of the decade by a broader and more systematic project (Marcus 2003; Bronk Ramsey *et al.* 2002, 80–82), with a rigorous protocol for sampling from those two and from additional sites (cultigens from Tell el-Hayyat, Jordan; and animal bones from Tels Aphek and Kabri). In general, these results demonstrated a high degree of reproducibility on multiple identical samples submitted to at least two and, in some instances, three radiocarbon laboratories. However, at the time of the 2003 report, none of the sampled sites had been properly studied for final publication, and the only significant conclusions that could be drawn were that the beginning of the southern Levantine Middle Bronze Age began in the last third of the 20th century BCE, far from as early (*c.* 2000 BC) as had previously been claimed, and that the end of these calibrated ranges, in the middle of the 18th century BC, were consistent with expected results for the end of this cultural period.

Since then, there have been a number of developments. First, additional samples were submitted for radiocarbon analysis, particularly from Tel Ifshar. Second, the long-awaited final report of the excavations at Tell el-Hayyat has been published (Falconer and Fall 2006). Unfortunately, while it did not offer much in terms of stratigraphic detail for the samples' contexts (Maeir 2010, 52–53, n. 35), it did raise the issue of interpreting the radiocarbon results, which indicate that the beginning of MB IIa settlement in the Jordan Valley occurred around the turn of the 19th century BCE, i.e., it is indistinguishable chronologically from that of the coastal plain (Marcus 2010, 246–247 *contra* Falconer and Berelov 2006, 62–63). Third, in 2006, the study of the finds of MB IIa Tel Ifshar resumed (Marcus *et al.* 2008a) with the reanalysis of this sequence carried out by the author and Y. Porath, both confirming and clarifying the contexts from which the archaeobotanical finds were sampled. More importantly, the numerous imports, *inter alia*, from MK Egypt (Marcus *et al.* 2008b), the Lebanon and Syria offers a rare instance of juxtaposition between chronologically significant ceramic imports and radiocarbon dates.

Tel Ifshar

As a preliminary overview of the previous and current project, and the first two occupational phases, has already been presented (Marcus *et al.* 2008 and references), only a review of salient points is offered here, including a brief summary of those phases not previously discussed. Tel Ifshar is 4.4 ha site that is located on the presumably navigable Alexander River in the Sharon Coastal Plain of Israel (Figure 15.1). Excavations carried out between 1979 and 1992, under the direction of Yosef Porath and Samuel M. Paley, in three areas (A, B, and C) revealed a multi-period settlement, beginning in the Early Bronze I (fourth millennium BCE), followed by a long gap in occupation, and then resettled in the early Middle Bronze Age IIa. The MB IIa sequence, which is best represented and preserved in Area C, on the eastern side of the tell, is divided into eight principal phases (A–H), four of which (B, C, E and G) were destroyed by fire (Figure 15.2). Each of these destruction horizons contained numerous complete pottery vessels found *in situ* on floors along with large quantities of archaeobotanical finds, which were systematically collected and studied by Chernoff (1988; 1992; Chernoff and Paley 1998) from 1980 onwards. Following the Middle Bronze Age IIa, the site is intermittently occupied until the Byzantine period, after which it was abandoned and never reoccupied.

Phase A

This phase is a non-contiguous horizon of between two to three architectural sub-phases that have been divided stratigraphically into Phase A 'early', the founder culture and its renovations, and Phase A 'late', which represent the final accumulations and fills preceding Phase B. The former is characterized by a seemingly simple rural domestic settlement of rooms, courtyards, work areas and an oven (Figure 15.2). Despite these modest remains, evidence was found for tin-bronze casting, and among the finds were monochrome Levantine painted pottery, and clear imports from the Akkar Plain of Lebanon and from Syria. Phase A 'late' produced the first bichrome Levantine painted pottery, additional imports from the Akkar Plain of Lebanon, Syria and Upper and Lower Egypt, as well as fragments of Lebanese cedar wood (Marcus *et al.* 2008).

Radiocarbon samples

Thus far, only a single reliable context from Phase A 'early' has been identified that contained a suitable sample for radiocarbon analysis. It derives from an oven (L752) around which an ashy floor was laid on the natural hill. Although it cannot be considered a primary deposit with absolute certainty, and contained fragments of two species, its secure location within the oven in one of the earliest settlement sub-phases, which is securely sealed beneath a Phase A 'late' accumulation, as well as the subsequent Phase B floor, make it a reliable reflection of the earliest MB IIa phase of the site. This assignment to the MB IIa, rather than this sample being an earlier residual seed, is further strengthened by the long gap following the EB I period and the apparent absence of any clear evidence for a preceding Early Bronze IV/Intermediate Bronze Age settlement.

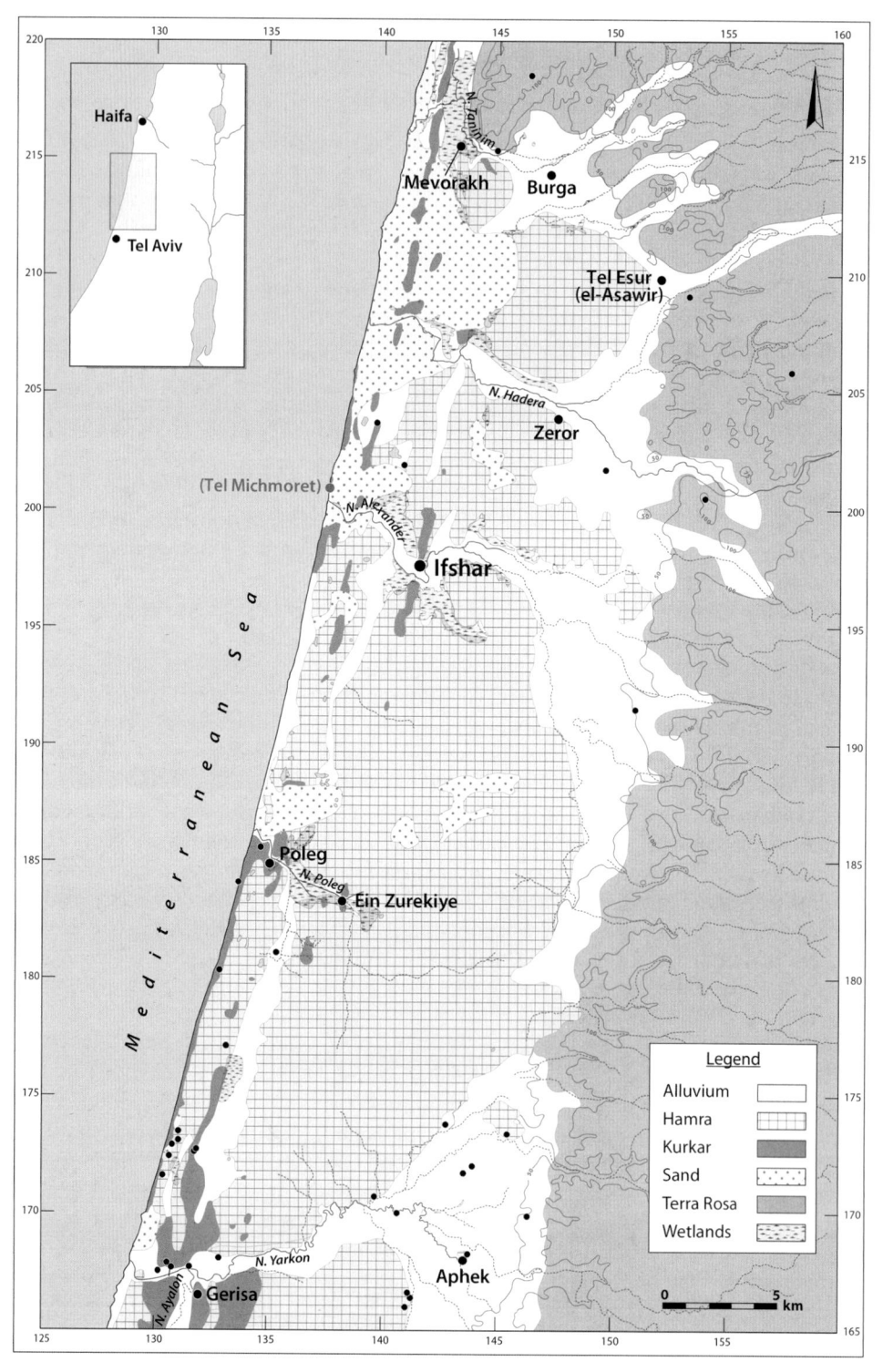

Figure 15.1: Map with location of Tel Ifshar and other MB IIa sites in their geographical setting in the Sharon Coastal Plain. Principal sites are named; smaller dots indicate rural sites (Drawn by Sapir Haad).

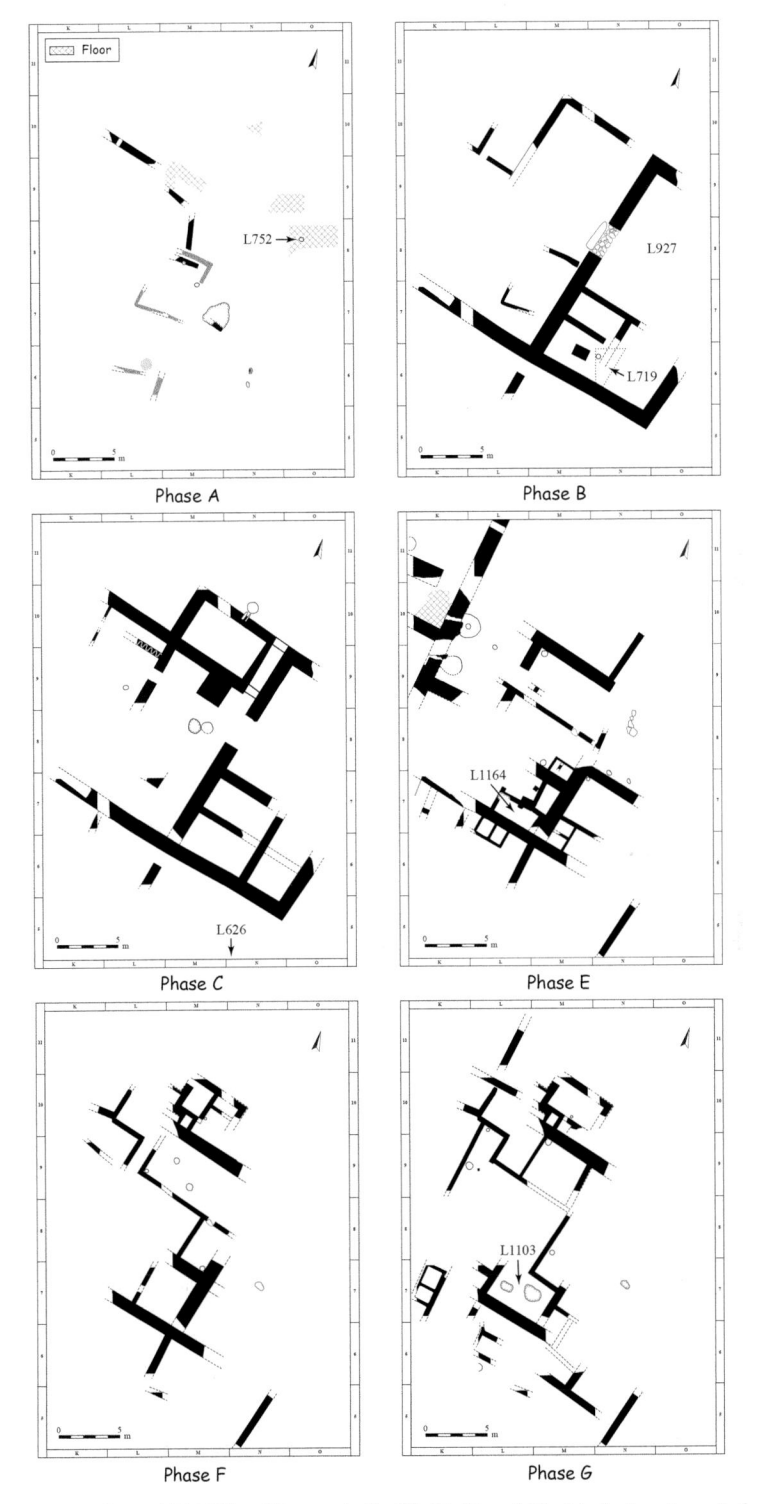

Figure 15.2: Schematic plans of Tel Ifshar Phases A, B, C2, E, F and G with the locations of the radiocarbon samples discussed in this work. (Drawn by Sapir Haad).

Phase B

This phase marks the first of two elite/public 'middle courtyard' buildings (Figure 15.2; Marcus *et al.* 2008a). This characterization is based on the presumed area of the building, *c.* 600 sqm, the width of the external load-bearing walls (1.00–1.20 m), which appear to have supported a second story, the use of cedar beams in the superstructure and *inter alia* the high status ceramic wares that were used for drinking of, presumably, alcohol (wine and beer). Apart from the cedar wood rafters, imports include fragmentary ceramics from Upper and Lower MK Egypt, and complete or restorable vessels from southern and northern Lebanon, coastal and inland Syria. Among these are numerous painted vessels, both complete and fragmentary, of Levantine Painted Ware, some of Syro-Cilician influenced styles. This building was destroyed in a fiery conflagration that sealed numerous vessels, animal remains, and archaeobotanical finds *in situ* on its floors.

Radiocarbon samples

Two contexts were sampled from Phase B, both from the eastern wing. Locus 927 comprises the northeastern room of the building, which contained numerous complete and restorable painted vessels, alongside red-slipped and burnished vessels, pithoi and large quantities of wood (including cedar). Seven measurements were carried out on samples from a quantity of 821 cc of *Vicia faba* that was concentrated along the northern wall of the room that, presumably, fell out of a broken vessel or an organic container that was burned (e.g. a sack or basket). The second sample, of which only one of three measurements survived pretreatment and produced results, is from L719, an area now considered to have been part of a basement with a stairwell that was filled with rubble, and did not contain a large concentration of cultigens. Thus, this single measurement is of a sample clearly sealed by the subsequent Phase C, but while consistent with its contemporaries and – owing partially to the lower precision – should not be considered a primary deposit.

Phase C (C1 and C2)

Following the destruction of Phase B, the building is rebuilt along the same basic plan (Phase C1), with some minor modifications (thickening of walls, changes in the division of the internal space, the construction of a drain and sump, etc.). Further renovations were carried out in subsequent sub-phase (C2) after which the building was again destroyed in an intense fire (Figure 15.2). This event also sealed quantities of complete ceramics, cedar wood, etc. on the floors of the building. A singular find is a complete MK Marl A3 jar found south of the building. The results of the recent stratigraphic analysis, which demonstrate that this vessel was deposited beneath a Phase E floor within the Phase C destruction, resolves the uncertainty that shrouded his important find since 1982 (see Marcus *et al.* 2008b, 203–205 for the research history of this vessel).

Radiocarbon samples

A large cache of over 200 *vicia faba* was found on a working surface, L626, south of the building, sealed by the same destruction debris that contained the aforementioned MK Egyptian jar. Six measurements were carried out in two laboratories on seeds from this cache.

Phases D and E

Following the destruction of the Phase C building, there appears to be a hiatus in formal settlement in this area and what appears to be squatter use characterizes the former central courtyard (Phases D1–D2). No radiocarbon samples have taken from this phase yet. When planned settlement is resumed in Phase E (Figure 15.2), the main public/elite structure appears to have shifted to the western margin of the excavation area; an additional building was also constructed to the south of the previous elite/public building (this phase also marks the beginning of occupation in Area A on the western side of the tell). The area of the former building is now an arrangement of rooms and courtyards used for grain storage (a granary, silos and bins) and food preparation (grinding and cooking). The destruction of this phase by fire preserved an enormous quantity of emmer wheat (*Triticum dioccum*), *c.* 19,000 seeds, in one of the granary's bins (Chernoff and Paley 1998).

Radiocarbon samples

Four measurements were carried out in three laboratories on samples of the emmer wheat from the granary.

Phases F and G

Following the destruction of Phase E, all of Area C in Phase F appears to undergo a gradual decline from an elite/public stature to one of relatively modest domestic character (Figure 15.2). By Phase G, the architecture is comprised of very narrow walls, delineating rooms and courtyards. This settlement experiences the final destruction of this MB IIa site by fire, which sealed, yet again, large quantities of complete or restorable pottery, fallen mud and pottery loom weights and charred cultigens. The subsequent Phase H comprises very patchy, non-contiguous features (tombs, wall stubs, an oven, etc.) that were built into the destruction of Phase G, and belongs to the transitional MB IIa–b phase, but were themselves disturbed by later activity at the site.

Radiocarbon samples

Three samples of *Vicia faba* were taken from a Phase G room, L1103, containing storage jars and pithoi and numerous cultigens on the floor.

Relative Sequence and Synchronization with Egypt

At present, the stratigraphic sequence of the northern half of Area C, whose limits are delineated by the courtyard building established in Phase B, offers the most secure relative sequence for the Middle Bronze Age IIa at Tel Ifshar. The architectural sequence south of the building, as well as that of Area A, whose analysis is still pending, only becomes prominent in Phase E. Prior to this phase, the stratigraphy of the area south of the main building sequence is only reliable along its southern wall and in discrete pockets, often on stone-paved work areas. As such, only the pottery sequence within the building and its aftermath is employed here for purposes of synchronizing Tel Ifshar with other sites. Similarly, with the exception of Phase C L626, all radiocarbon samples are from this sequence. Other samples from the area south of the building, from Phases E and G will be discussed in a future study once the overall stratigraphic phasing has been finalised.

Table 1 presents the relative synchronization between Tel Ifshar and some of the key stratigraphic sequences. This table should be considered provisional as 1) the detailed study of the pottery from Tel Ifshar is still on-going, particularly for Phases E to H; 2) only the comparable sequence of Tel Aphek has been fully published; 3) the sequences from Ashkelon and Tell el-Dab`a appear to begin late in the period, and probably correlate best with Tel Ifshar Phases E–H, which, as noted, are still being studied; and 4) some of the chronologically relevant sites, such as Sidon, are represented largely by tomb contexts, making comparison with the settlement assemblages at Ifshar somewhat difficult. Nevertheless, a fairly good correspondence can be achieved with Tel Aphek, not surprising given the close proximity between the two sites (*c.* 40 km; Figure 15.1); however, some revision of the use of the latter sequence may be necessary in light of both a review of Aphek's ceramic finds and the manner of their presentation, and the Ifshar sequence and its finds. The synchronization of Tel Ifshar with the published Levantine pottery sequence from Tell el-Dab`a is complicated by the fragmentary nature of the latter's settlement finds and its limited and selective Levantine repertoire among the better-preserved ceramics (e.g., tomb material) in the corresponding phases (H–G/1–3). Nevertheless, the earlier monochrome painted pottery and storage jars at `Ezbet Rushdi might correlate with Ifshar sometime in Phases A 'early' through Phase B. However, the bichrome Levantine Painted Ware at Tel Ifshar Phase A 'late' and, especially, Phase B, is paralleled only in fragmentary examples first in Tell el-Dab`a Phase H, which in Egyptian chronological terms is 80–100 years later (Marcus 2003, 98; 2007, 160–161).

The formal publication of the MK Egyptian pottery from Tel Ifshar, in its proper stratigraphic context, offers the earliest ceramic synchronizations between MK Egypt and the MB IIa southern Levant. In chronological terms, two of the short-lived forms from both Upper and Lower Egypt (Marcus *et al.* 2008b, 207, 209, 213, figs 2:2, 3:1), which were found in Phases A 'late' and B, respectively, established that the transition between these phases must have occurred prior to the mid-19th century (end of Senusret III's reign). Unless it is presumed to be an heirloom (see below), the complete Marl A3 jar, which has now been determined to derive from Phase C, provides a *terminus ante quem* for that destruction. The correspondence of the Egyptian and Levantine pottery is consistent with the evidence from Ashkelon, where a much later MB IIa phase is synchronized with the beginning of the 13th dynasty. Thus far, the only other early occurrence of MK pottery in the Levant, i.e., that appears with bichrome Levantine Painted Ware, is in Lebanon at Sidon tomb Phases 1–2 (Doumet-Serhal 2008, 17–22), which offers a correlation with, respectively, Ifshar Phase B and, possibly, Phase C (or later). Sidon Phase 1 has a single MK goblet with a broad chronological range (Bader 2003, 31–34), but Phase 2 has at least one example that dates no earlier that the reign of Amenemhet III (Bader *et al.* 2009).

15. Egyptian Historical and Southern Levantine Radiocarbon Chronologies

Table 15.1: *Provisional relative synchronization between Tel Ifshar and selected key sites in the southern Levant, Egypt, Lebanon and Syria. Synchronization between Ashkelon and Tell el-Dab'a is based on Bietak et al. (2008). For other sites, see Marcus, Porath and Paley (2008). S=Senusret; A=Amenemhet.*

	Ifshar	Aphek			Dab'a		Egypt	Lebanon and Syria
Period	Phase	Phase	Strata	Phase	Gen. Stratum			
MB IIa-b	H	4 'post-Palace'	AXIII–AXII	12	F		Late 12th–13th dynasties	
	G			13?	G/4–G/1–3			
	F	3 'Palace II'	AXIV	14–13?	H–G/4		A III	
	E				H			Sidon tombs, Phase 2?
	D							
MBIIa	C	2–3 'Palace I–II'	AXVI–AXIV			'Ezbet Rushdi M–L	A II–S III	Sidon tombs, Phase 1–2(?) Arqa N (Stratum 14) Mardikh IIIA2 Hama H
	B	2 'Palace I'	AXVII/BVd-c					
	A 'late'	1–2 'pre- to Palace I'	X19–17c/AXVII				S I–A II	Sidon tombs, Phase 1?
	A 'early'	1 'pre-Palace I'	X19–X18					

Radiocarbon Results

The results of the relevant Accelerator Mass Spectrometry (AMS) and conventional radiocarbon determinations are summarized in Table 15.2. Note that in some cases laboratory numbers refer to double runs carried out on the same pre-treated samples. The original results from the pilot project are also indicated in order to highlight the increase in precision since the early 1990s. In addition, in some cases, pretreatment resulted in the survival of only humic acids, while, in others, 'softer' pre-treatment preserved the reduced carbon. These are all subjects that will be discussed in separate study. Although, typically, humic acids are avoided for use in radiocarbon studies, owing to their solubility in water and possible migration in the soil, they are used here because, 1) they are consistent with their identical reduced carbon counterparts, and should be considered *in situ*; 2) they should be reported; and, 3) owing to the number of measurements and, especially, the nature of the calibration curve in this time period, their removal is largely insignificant, with the upper and lower bounds shifting typically 1–2, and no more than 5, calendar years for all models.

The initial impression of the results is the consistency among repetitive measurements of individual samples and between respective laboratories (Table 15.1; Figure 15.3). It is also quite apparent that these events, i.e., harvests, are almost indistinguishable in radiocarbon terms. Moreover, the nature of the calibration curve, with a flat wiggle between 1900 and 1750 BC results in at least a bi-, if not tri- or quadro- modal, probability distributions that span, variously, over 130 to 244 years in 2 standard deviations. Thus, a curve plot of the entire dataset would appear as an incomprehensible blur over this entire period. A modeled Bayesian sequence of this dataset with only the stratigraphic sequence as its prior provides somewhat more clarity and precision (Figures 15.4, 15.5; Table 15.3). This model incorporates boundaries between the stratigraphic phases (Bronk Ramsey 2000) and includes combined measurements of identical samples from Phases B, C, E and G, each with an additional uncertainty of 8 ^{14}C years to account for the possible discrepancy between single year samples being calibrated on a curve based on multi-year samples (Stuiver *et al.* 1998). The resulting posterior distributions are slightly shorter and the extreme limits truncated, but they all still can shift together as a sequenced set within a 120–180 year range. In particular, note how this model results in an overlap between a lone measurement from Phase B (L719; see discussion above), and combined measurements, respectively, from Phase C (L626) and Phase G (L1103). Despite this limitation, this modeled sequence provides a maximum 2 sigma range from the beginning to the end of the MBIIa at Tel Ifshar, which is largely consistent with accepted chronologies. It also confirms and refines the previous claim for the period's inception in the late, rather than the beginning of the 20th century BC (Marcus 2003). Note that, owing to the character of the calibration curve in this period, this same result is actually obtainable with less than the full suite of measurements using various combinations of identical samples from the individual events. Examination of the posterior distributions for samples from Phases A–C demonstrates a very good correspondence between the historically dated MK Egyptian pottery and the radiocarbon date ranges. The date of the Phase A–B transition prior to 1853, which was established based on MK ceramics, falls within the radiocarbon ranges for these phases. Similarly, the context in which the Marl A3 jar was found has an upper bound of 1881, again consistent with the Egyptian evidence that place this vessel in the first half of the

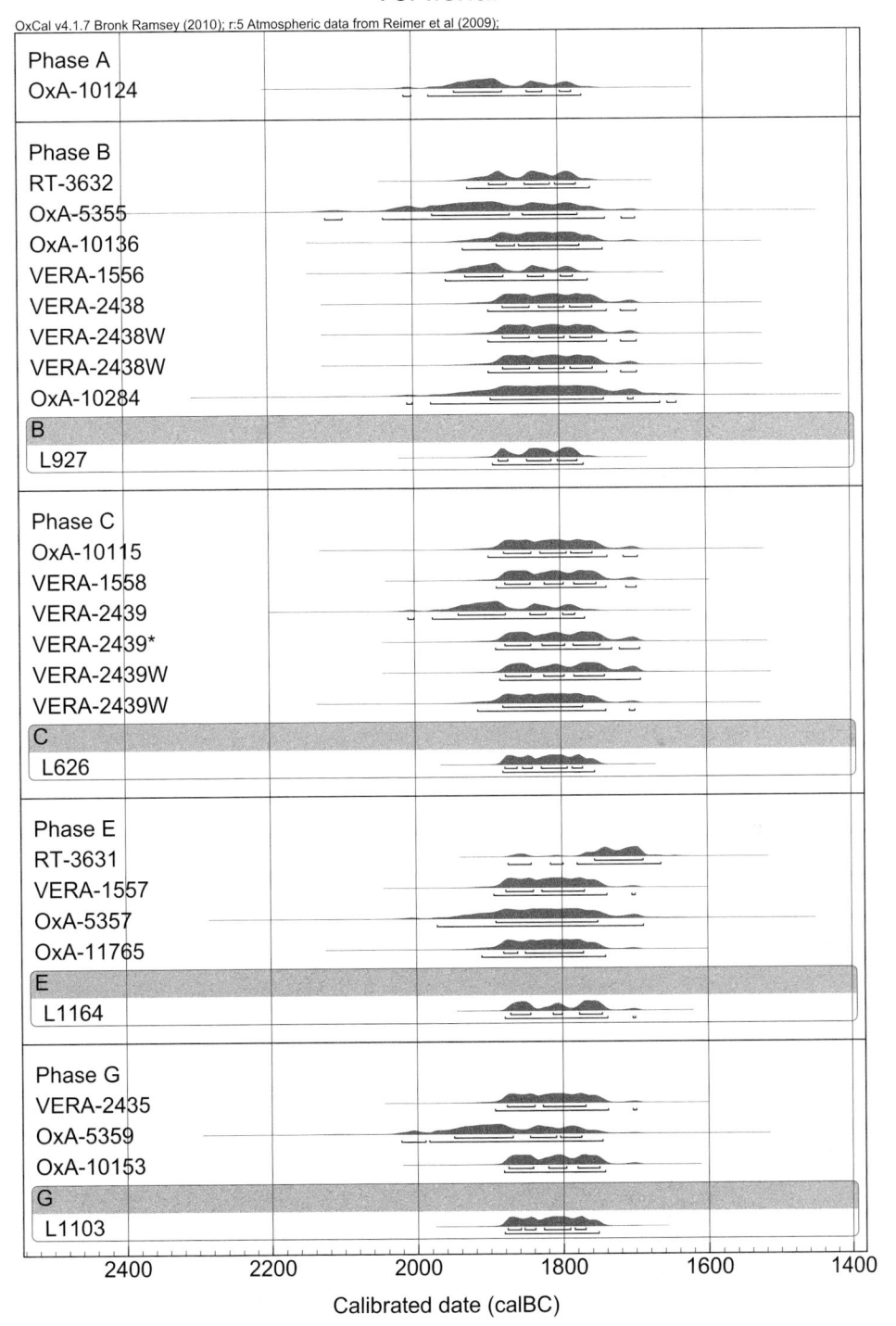

Figure 15.3: Calibrated probability distributions for individual and combined measurements radiocarbon determinations from Tel Ifshar Phases A, B, C, E and G.

Table 15.2: Results of the radiocarbon determinations from Tel Ifshar. Parenthesis refer to probability within the calibrated range; *=double runs; P=from pilot project; hu=humic acids; W=softer pretreatment; RT=Weizmann Institute, Rehovot; VERA=Viennese Environmental Accelerator; OxA=Oxford Radiocarbon Accelerator Unit; calibrated using Reimer et al. (2009), OxCal v4.17 (Bronk Ramsey 2009).

Phase	Context	Material	Lab #	BP
A early	L752	*Vicia faba* and wheat	OxA-10124*	3546±36
B	L927	*Vicia faba* horsebean	RT-3632	3522±25
			OxA-5355 P	3550±65
			OxA-10136	3504±38
			VERA-1556 hu	3540±30
			VERA-2438	3525±35
			VERA-2438W	3485±35
			VERA-2438W	3485±35
			Combined	
	L719	*Vicia faba* horsebean	OxA-10284	3490±65
C	L626	*Vicia faba* horsebean	OxA-10115*	3487±35
			VERA-1558	3480±30
			VERA-2439 hu	3545±35
			VERA-2439 hu	3475±35
			VERA-2439W	3465±35
			VERA-2439W	3495±35
			Combined	
E	L1164	*triticum dioccum* Emmer wheat	RT-3631	3430±25
			VERA-1557 hu	3490±30
			OxA-5357 P	3505±55
			OxA-11765	3498±32
			Combined	
G	L1103	*Vicia faba* horsebean	VERA-2435	3490±30
			OxA-5359 P	3545±50
			OxA-10153*	3480±23
			Combined	

Calibrated 1σ BCE	Calibrated 2σ BCE
1942 (48.1%) 1876; 1842 (11.9%) 1820; 1796 (8.2%) 1781	2011(1.5%)2000; 1977(93.9%)1767
1895 (19.0%) 1870; 1846 (27.3%) 1811; 1804 (21.9%) 1776	1925(95.4%)1756
1973 (42.0%) 1866; 1848 (26.2%) 1774	2120(1.7%)2096; 2040(92.3%)1736 1713(1.3%)1694
1885(15.3%)1860; 1854(52.9%)1771	1932(95.4%)1739
1928(43.1%)1876; 1842(14.7%)1820; 1797(10.4%)1780	1955(95.4%)1760
1878(25.3%)1840; 1827(23.0%)1792; 1784(19.8%)1754	1898(91.8%)1734; 1715(3.6%)1694
1878(25.3%)1840; 1827(23.0%)1792; 1784(19.8%)1754	1898(91.8%)1734; 1715(3.6%)1694
1884(11.8%)1871; 1845(30.9%)1812; 1803(25.5%)1776	1892(95.4%)1768
1895(66.1%)1739; 1706(2.1%)1698	2009(0.5%)2002; 1976(94.0%)1662 1652(0.9%)1640
1878(25.3%)1840; 1828(24.0%)1792; 1786(18.9%)1756	1900(92.3%)1736; 1714(3.1%)1694
1876(26.6%)1842; 1822(19.1%)1796; 1782(22.5%)1751	1888(92.8%)1737; 1710(2.6%)1696
1941(47.2%)1876; 1842(12.3%)1820; 1797(8.7%)1780	2010(1.1%)2001; 1976(94.3%)1767
1877(24.2%)1841; 1826(19.3%)1794; 1783(24.6%)1746	1890(89.0%)1730; 1720(6.4%)1692
1876(23.3%)1841; 1824(16.1%)1796; 1782(28.8%)1740	1884(95.4%)1691
1880(68.2%)1770	1915(94.4%)1738
1878(14.3%)1861; 1854(10.9%)1840; 1828(30.8%)1792 1786(12.1%)1771	1881(95.4%)1754
1756(68.2%)1689	1874(9.1%)1842; 1816(2.8%)1798 1780(83.5%)1664
1878(26.9%)1840; 1828(41.3%)1770	1894(94.9%)1738; 1704(0.5%)1700
1892(68.2%)1752	1972(95.4%)1689
1882(13.0%)1862; 1852(55.2%)1772	1912(95.4%)1741
1872(26.5%)1844; 1814(9.9%)1801; 1778(31.8%)1746	1880(94.7%)1738; 1704(0.7%)1700
1878(26.9%)1840; 1828(41.3%)1770	1894(94.9%)1738; 1704(0.5%)1700
1950(40.6%)1870; 1846(15.5%)1810; 1804(12.1%)1776	2023(5.5%)1990; 1984(89.9%)1746
1876(27.1%)1842; 1821(18.4%)1796; 1781(22.6%)1751	1882(95.4%)1743
1878(14.8%)1860; 1854(11.6%)1840; 1828(29.8%)1792 1786(12.0%)1770	1882(95.4%)1752

Tel Ifshar Stratigraphic Model

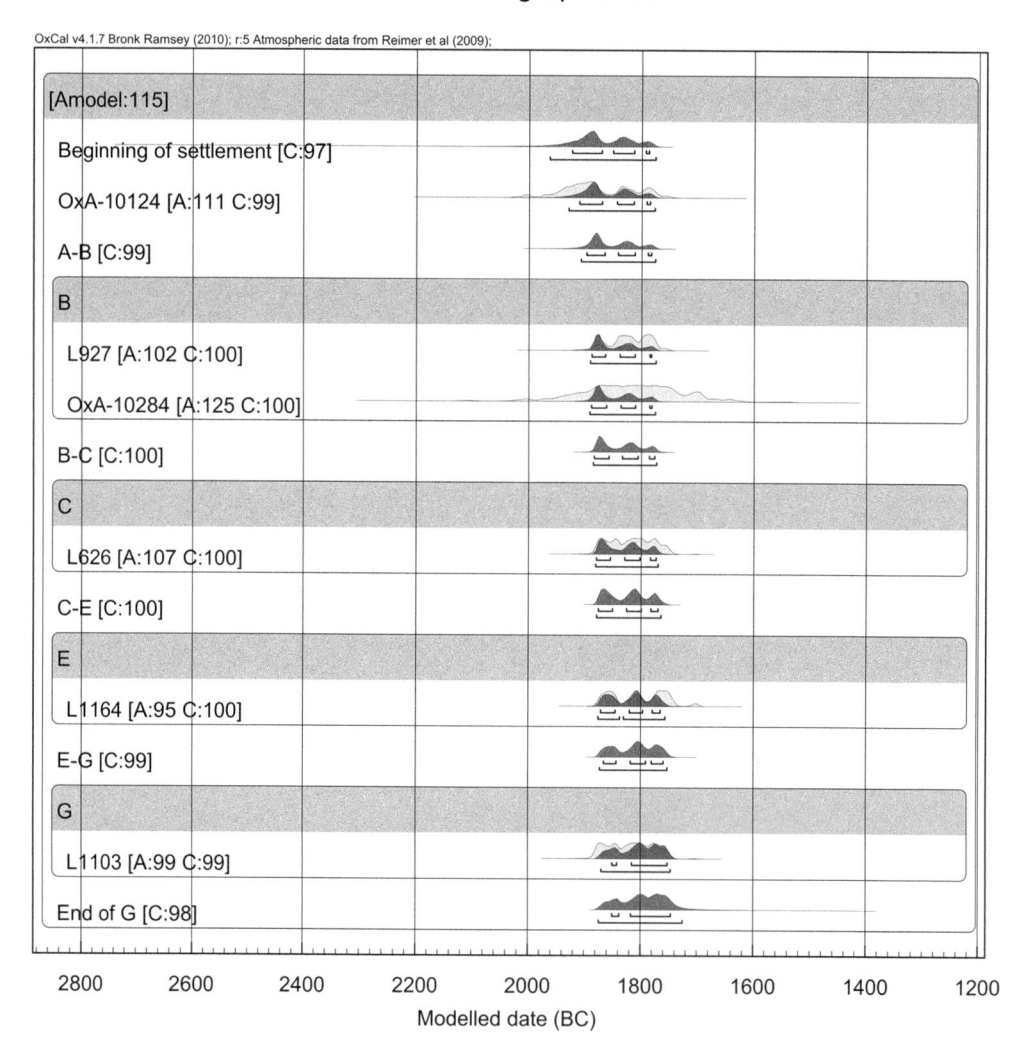

OxCal v4.1.7 Bronk Ramsey (2010); r:5 Atmospheric data from Reimer et al (2009);

[Amodel:115]
- Beginning of settlement [C:97]
- OxA-10124 [A:111 C:99]
- A-B [C:99]
- B
  - L927 [A:102 C:100]
  - OxA-10284 [A:125 C:100]
- B-C [C:100]
- C
  - L626 [A:107 C:100]
- C-E [C:100]
- E
  - L1164 [A:95 C:100]
- E-G [C:99]
- G
  - L1103 [A:99 C:99]
- End of G [C:98]

Modelled date (BC)

Figure 15.4: Multiplot of the Bayesian model of the stratified sequence Tel Ifshar Phases A to G.

19th century BCE. Unfortunately, this correspondence between radiocarbon and Egyptian historical chronology is too broad to resolve the high-low MK chronology debate.

The constraints of this relatively flat and wiggly calibration curve produce a completely different result if an additional prior of a *terminus ante quem* (TAQ) is included. In order for MK Egyptian Marl A3 jar to have been deposited within the destruction of Phase C, it would have had to arrive during the period in which it was still being produced, i.e., prior to 1853, or shortly thereafter (see further discussion below). Including this constraint within

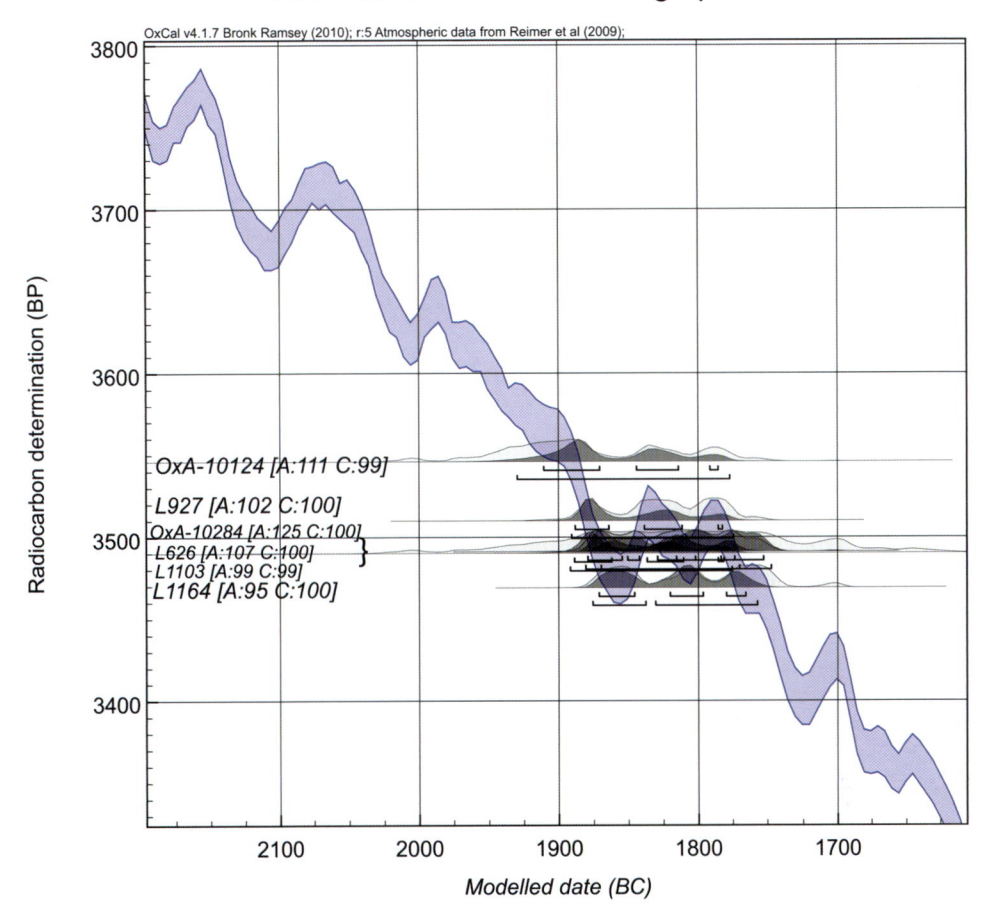

Figure 15.5: Curve plot of the Bayesian model of the stratified sequence Tel Ifshar Phases A to G.

the modeled stratigraphic sequence ostensibly bisects the posterior calibrated distributions. The determinations from Phases A, B, and C find a 'wiggle match' along the descending section of the curve between *c.* 1900 and 1860 BC (Figures 15.6–15.8; Table 15.3), as these three phases are bounded by a lower limit of 1853 BC. This sole solution for their alignment along the curve produces very high precision posterior distributions for Phases A, B, and C, respectively, of 66, 31 and 27 years in length. Phase E finds its best fit at the bottom of the first wiggle, and is followed by the solution for Phase G, which can continue into the 18th century. In this model, the aforementioned overlap between Phases C and G is resolved, as the former better fits the first mode of the probability distribution, i.e., the first descending part of the curve. The latter must follow Phase E and better matches

Table 15.3: A comparison between unmodeled and selected modeled distributions of the Tel Ifshar radiocarbon determinations.

Phase	Combined unmodeled 1σ	Combined unmodeled 2σ	Stratigraphic model 1σ
G	1878(14.8%)1860 1854(11.6%)1840 1828(29.8%)1792 1786(12.0%)1770	1882(95.4%)1752	1852(7.2%)1842 1817(61.0%)1752
E	1872(26.5%)1844 1814(9.9%)1801 1778(31.8%)1746	1880(94.7%)1738 1704(0.7%)1700	1872(25.7%)1846 1821(28.6%)1796 1780(13.9%)1766
C	1878(14.3%)1861 1854(10.9%)1840 1828(30.8%)1792 1786(12.1%)1771	1881(95.4%)1754	1880(31.4%)1854 1830(28.7%)1802 1784(8.2%)1774
B	1884(11.8%)1871 1845(30.9%)1812 1803(25.5%)1776	1892(95.4%)1768	1888(40.1%)1864 1841(28.1%)1812
A early	1942(48.1%)1876 1842(11.9%)1820 1796(8.2%)1781	2011(1.5%)2000 1977(93.9%)1767	1912(44.5%)1872 1845(23.7%)1814

the rising section of the first wiggle, but with some possibility in the first descending part of the curve. Thus, the posterior 2σ distributions of Phases E and G are actually shifted earlier and shortened with a resulting precision of 71 and 96 years. Note that the numerical values of the upper bound of Phases, C, E and G are unrealistically similar, a situation that more reflects the steep slope of the curve rather than the settlement history of the site. Obviously, the amount of time between the end of Phase C and the end of Phase E would have been much more than a single year, not the least owing to the construction time, building use, and the intervening 'squatter' Phase D; the same holds for the timespan between the destructions of Phases E and G with their intervening Phase F.

It may be argued, and probably will, that 1) this complete Egyptian vessel could be an heirloom or 2) the employment of the high Egyptian chronology is unjustified. Regarding the first argument, although this is a lone complete Egyptian object, its date is not yet contradicted by any other component of this imported assemblage. On the contrary, two of the fragmentary examples from Phases A and B are consistent with this TAQ's application. Moreover, as has already been noted, apart from the examples from Tel Ifshar and Ashkelon, MK Egyptian pottery is not documented elsewhere in the southern Levant, let alone any contemporary tradition for curating Egyptian pottery as heirlooms. Such a tradition is documented in Nubia (Bourriau 2004), but the nature of the cultural interaction between Egypt and its neighbor to the south is completely different than that which it appears to have with the southern Levant. Ironically, perhaps, the complete vessel from Tel Ifshar is

Stratigraphic model 2σ	Stratigraphic model 1σ with TAQ (1853 BCE)	Stratigraphic model 2σ with TAQ (1853 BCE)	Stratigraphic model 2σ with TAQ (1817 BCE)
1870(95.4%)1748	1874(68.2%)1836	1880(95.4%)1784	1876(95.4%)1766
1876(32.8%)1838 1831(62.6%)1758	1872(68.2%)1851	1881(92.0%)1836 1828(3.4%)1810	1879(95.4%)1797
1881(95.4%)1770	1878(68.2%)1863	1881(95.4%)1854	1881(95.4%)1818
1891(95.4%)1775	1885(68.2%)1870	1892(95.4%)1861	1892(95.4%)1819
1930(95.4%)1778	1900(68.2%)1872	1928(95.4%)1862	1930(95.4%)1822

part of a family of vessels displaying a Nubian decorative influence on Upper Egyptian pottery (Rzeuska 2006). Although the possibility of its being an heirloom exists, given the range of forms present at Tel Ifshar, from small bottles to large storage jars, such a claim seems argumentative. Nevertheless, a series of models reflecting increasingly later dates for the arrival of this vessel at Tel Ifshar were tested and do show that the length of time for each phase becomes increasingly longer and extends later, but still are shorter and earlier than the sequenced model without any TAQ prior. For example, the utilization of the low chronology with a TAQ of 1817 BC, provides 2 sigma ranges of 62–111 years depending on the phase (Table 15.3). It should be noted, however, that increasing evidence does suggest that probability favors the high chronology (Ramsey *et al.* 2010).

Interpretations and Implications

The Bayesian model presented above for the Tel Ifshar stratigraphic sequence offers a radiocarbon chronology whose precision is unprecedented in the Bronze Age Levant. This precision and its accuracy, i.e., that the results reflect the time frame of the stratigraphic phase in which the samples were found, are clearly a reflection of a number of characteristics unique to this site, so far: 1) a series of four destruction horizons in a relatively short period of time; 2) large samples of single year growth cultigens found *in situ* within these horizons;

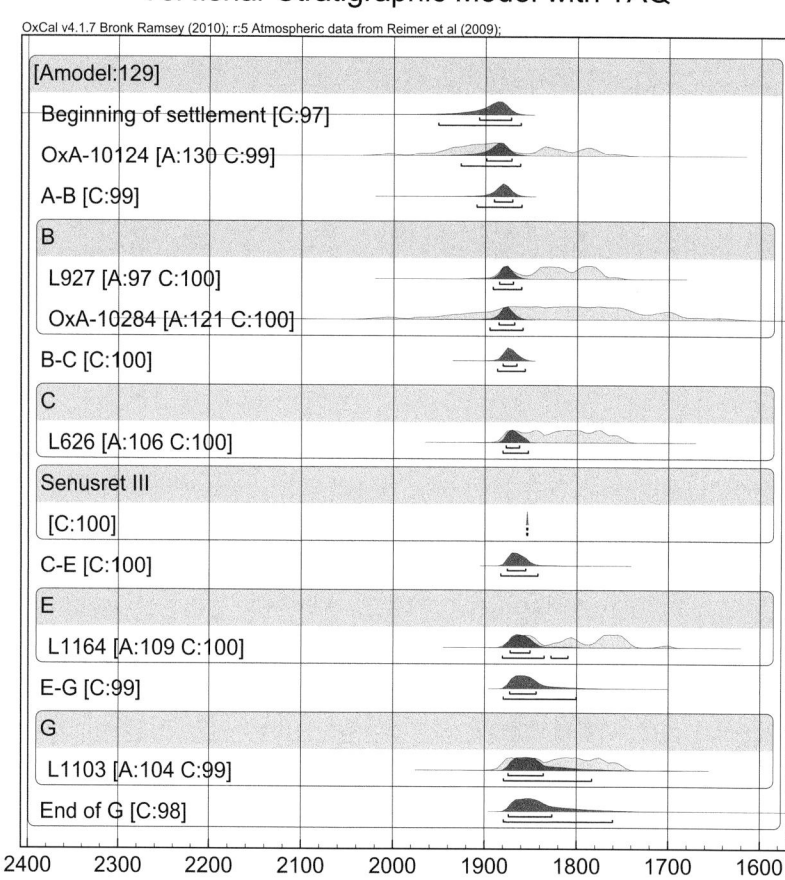

Tel Ifshar Stratigraphic Model with TAQ

OxCal v4.1.7 Bronk Ramsey (2010); r:5 Atmospheric data from Reimer et al (2009);

[Amodel:129]
- Beginning of settlement [C:97]
- OxA-10124 [A:130 C:99]
- A-B [C:99]
- B
  - L927 [A:97 C:100]
  - OxA-10284 [A:121 C:100]
- B-C [C:100]
- C
  - L626 [A:106 C:100]
- Senusret III [C:100]
- C-E [C:100]
- E
  - L1164 [A:109 C:100]
- E-G [C:99]
- G
  - L1103 [A:104 C:99]
- End of G [C:98]

Modelled date (BC)

Figure 15.6: Multiplot of the Bayesian model of the stratified sequence Tel Ifshar Phases A to G with a terminus ante quem of 1853 BCE for Phase C.

3) the presence of an archaeobotanist who systematically collected these samples with the encouragement and support of the project directors; and 4) the discovery and identification of MK Egyptian pottery, some of which can be dated to fairly short periods of time. These factors combined in a single model along with an ultimately amenable section of the calibration curve have produced results that, while representative of a single site, have much broader implications, both within the southern Levant and beyond. While many of these implications must await completion of the analysis of the stratigraphic sequence and the associated finds, others can be considered already at this stage.

First and foremost, it is critical to understand that in all instances other than Phase A, the calibrated ranges reflect the probable date of the latest harvest sampled from Tel Ifshar

Curve Plot of Stratigraphic Seq. with TAQ

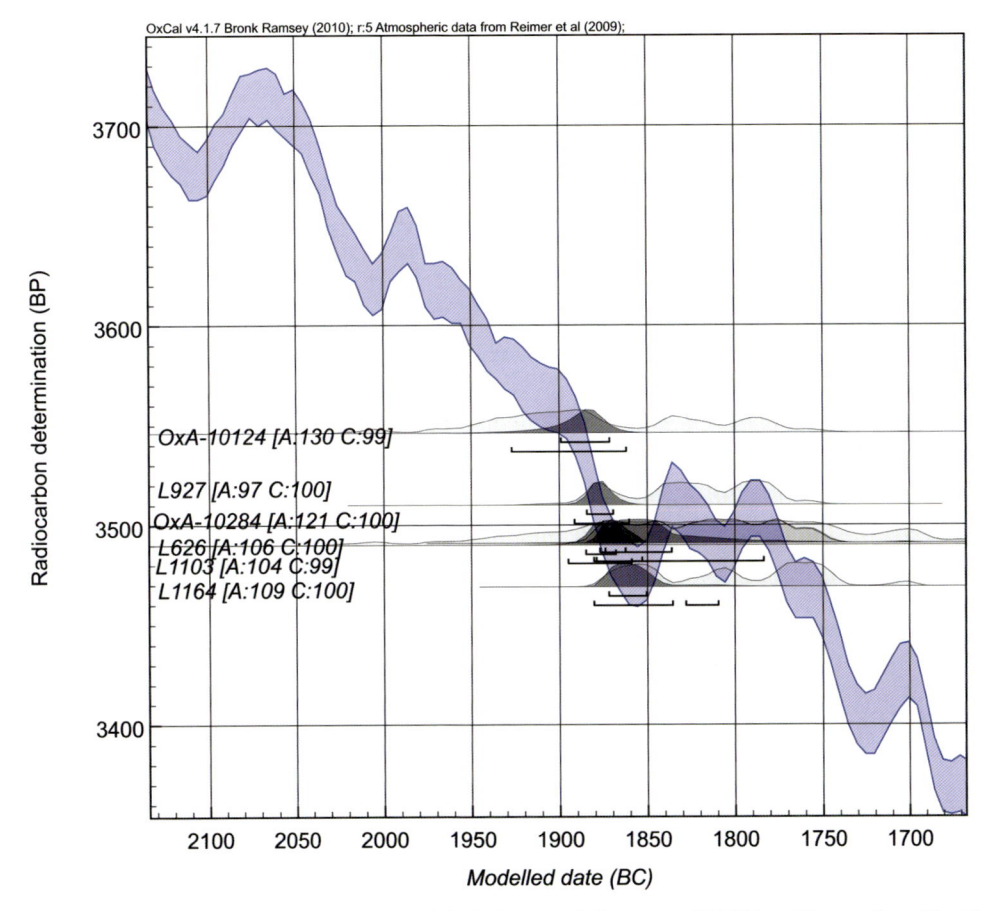

OxCal v4.1.7 Bronk Ramsey (2010); r:5 Atmospheric data from Reimer et al (2009);

OxA-10124 [A:130 C:99]
L927 [A:97 C:100]
OxA-10284 [A:121 C:100]
L626 [A:106 C:100]
L1103 [A:104 C:99]
L1164 [A:109 C:100]

Figure 15.7: Curve plot of the Bayesian model of the stratified sequence Tel Ifshar Phases A to G with a terminus ante quem of 1853 BCE for Phase C.

thus far. The upper and lower bounds of these ranges, which represent the earliest and latest date for this harvest, are proxies for the destruction of each respective phase. While clearly an incalculable amount of time could have passed between the establishment of a particular phase and its termination, given the nature of ancient food storage, it is much more probable that less than a decade could have passed between the final harvest and the destruction event. In other words, the lower bound may be seen as a more reliable datum, although the upper bound should not be ignored.

Thus, for the southern Levant, especially the Sharon Coastal Plain, this chronology offers a calendrical sequence for the process of settlement, the pace of urbanisation, and an opportunity for correlation with the archaeological, historical and palaeoenvironmental records in the Near East and Eastern Mediterranean (Table 15.4). For example, Tel Ifshar Phase A establishes, at present, the only reliable high precision datum for the beginning of resettlement of the coastal plain after a 200–300 year decline; as noted above, the timing of this coastal phenomenon correlates well with evidence from Tell el-Hayyat in the Jordan Valley. Moreover, although Tel Ifshar shows no signs, thus far, of having been fortified early in the period, if at all, Phase B, with its synchronization with Tel Aphek Phase 2/Palace I (and, eventually, with other sites), offers an upper and lower bound for the beginning of urbanization. In concert with the pottery-based relative chronological sequence, calendrical ranges for subsequent phases (C–G) can provide a temporal gauge for the changing face of the MB IIa settlement map. For example, one of the *fossile directeurs* of the earliest phase of this period, the bichrome Levantine Painted Ware, which has its appearance in Tel Ifshar Phase A 'late' and reaches its zenith in Phase B can now be dated to the late 20th/first half of the 19th century. These dates accords very well with the current evidence for a lack of any significant chronological priority among the three major painted traditions in the Ancient Near East: the Levantine Painted, the Syro-Cilician and the Khabur Wares (Oguchi 2001; 2003; Bagh 2003; Yadin 2009, 116). Regarding the seeming disparity between the dates from Tel Ifshar and its first appearance of this pottery family at Tell el-Dab`a General Stratum H, further comparative research on the ceramic assemblages from both sites is required in order to bridge this gap.

Regarding correlations with the MK Egyptian historical record, Phase A can be placed within the time frame of the earliest detailed Egyptian maritime expeditions to the Levant, as recounted in the Mit Rahina inscription from Year 3 of Amenemhet II, *c.* 1908 (Marcus 2007). Theoretically, the date ranges for Phases A through C mean that any one of them could have existed during the apparent military action taken by Egypt against Byblos during the reign of Senusret III, as recounted in the Khnumhotep III inscription (Allen 2008). A similar correlation can be made with the Khusobek stela from this king's reign (Breasted 1906, §676–§687; Delia 1980, 115–120; Baines 1987), which recounts a military raid against the district of *škmm*, which is generally identified with Shechem, the closest major highland site to Tel Ifshar. Eventually, other correlations may be possible, such as with the noted Execretion Texts, of which those written on bowls are dated typologically to the period of the mid-12th Dynasty (Dorothea Arnold as cited by Rainey 1994, 83). Among the implications of these correlations is the temporal priority between the founding of the 12th Dynasty over the beginning of MB IIa culture and resettlement along the coastal plain, which now appears to be coeval with the beginning of maritime trade (cf. Marcus 2007, 175).

The publication of future radiocarbon studies from Tel Ifshar's contemporaries will no doubt further clarify the chronology of the Levant in this period and its relationship to MK Egyptian and other chronologies. In the meantime, note that a single radiocarbon result from an animal bone deposit found under a Minoan cup in a Phase 2 context – not a tomb (Doumet-Serhal 2008, 21–22; MacGillivray 2004; Vila 2004) may be calibrated to the following 2 sigma ranges: 2031–1867 (81.1%) and 1848–1774 (14.3%). If the higher probability range is correct that would make this context coeval with Tel Ifshar Phases B or C, which accords well with the appearance of Levantine Painted Ware in Sidon Phase 2. However, only the less probable date range correlates with one of the aforementioned Egyptian vessels from this phase, which dates no earlier than Amenemhet III. Additional radiocarbon analyses on samples from this context may resolve this possible disagreement. Finally, with regards to the Mesopotamian chronology, at present, the only synchronisation is a single Syrian krater from Phase B with parallels from Hama and Tell Mardikh/Ebla (Marcus *et al.* 2008a). The calibrated radiocarbon range for Phase B accords with the admittedly broad date for the corresponding phase at the latter site (Table 15.4).

Conclusion and Future Avenues of Research

The stratified settlement sequence of MB IIa Tel Ifshar, with its unparalleled series of four destruction horizons, offers rich assemblages of local and imported pottery, archaeobotanical and other finds. Extensive sampling of single year cultigens for radiocarbon analysis from this sequence produced determinations consistent both among identical samples and between laboratories. The juxtaposition of these finds, especially the MK Egyptian pottery and radiocarbon assays, offers an opportunity to both compare radiocarbon and historical chronologies and combine the two within a Bayesian model that includes the stratigraphic sequence and the MK Egyptian chronological data. This combination has produced the first high precision calendrical chronology for a Levantine site of this period.

Further research is needed both on this site's assemblages and the Bayesian modelling in order to clarify their horizons and contribute to the development of a regional chronology. Better refinement of the site's stratigraphy, the identification of samples from already sampled and non-sampled phases (e.g., C1, D, and F) may add some increased precision to the data set and cause slight modifications in the date ranges. Naturally, developments in MK Egyptian pottery chronology may have a significant effect on the models presented here.

At present, Tel Ifshar is the most sampled site of this cultural period. It can only be hoped that the results presented here will encourage excavators of other sites to make the effort to collect archaeobotanical finds and submit suitable samples for radiocarbon analysis. Until then, with its unprecedented precision, Tel Ifshar will remain the most sampled and dated site for this cultural period, and a lone foundation stone in the ultimate construction of a local southern Levantine calendrical chronology.

Acknowledgements

Most of the radiocarbon determinations used in this study were funded by the Jubily Fund of the City of Vienna, Austrian Academy of Sciences, through a grant obtained via the SCIEM2000 project headed by Professor Manfred Bietak. My thanks to him and the SCIEM2000 project managers, Dr Angela Schwab and Dagmar Melman, for their encouragement and support. The original pilot project was funded by the ORAU committee of the Research Lab for Archaeology and Art History, University of Oxford. Research on Tel Ifshar was funded by the Israel Science Foundation Legacy Fund (grant no. 1113/06). From the beginning of this research, the field and project directors, respectively, Dr Yosef Porath and the late Professor Samuel M. Paley, kindly gave me complete access to the data and finds from the Tel Ifshar excavations carried out under the Emek Hefer Archaeological Research Project (see Marcus *et al.* 2008a, 240 for further acknowledgements). Archaeobotanical samples from Tel Ifshar were identified by Miriam

Table 15.4: Correlation between the radiocarbon chronology of Tel Ifshar and selected key sites and Egyptian chronologies. The calibrated ranges for Tel Ifshar are based on the Bayesian stratigraphic model using the 1853 terminus ante quem. The 'high' regnal chronology for MK Egypt is based on Kitchen (1996). LEC=Leverhulme Egyptian Chronology dates are based on Ramsey et al. 2010. The radiocarbon determination for Sidon calibrated to 2σ (see text) is based on Doumet-Serhal (2004). The dates for Tell Mardikh/Ebla are based on Nigro (2009, Table 2). S=Senusret; A=Amenemhet.

Phase	Ifshar	Aphek	Ashkelon	Dab'a	Egypt			Sidon	Tell Mardikh Ebla	Other Lebanese and Syrian Sites
	^{14}C w/TAQ Last harvest	Phase	Phase	Phase	King	High	LEC 2σ **accession** dates			
H		4 post-Palace	12	F	Late 12th–13th dynasties			Tombs		
G	1880–1784	3 Palace II	13?	G/4–G/1–3				?		
F	1881–1810		14–13?	H–G/4						
E				H	A III	1853–1808	1851–1798	Phase 2?		
D								2031(81.1)1867 1848(14.3)1774		
C	1881–1854	2–3 Palace I–II			S III	1872–1853	1889–1836			
B	1892–1860	2 Palace I		'Ezbet Rushdi M–L	S II	1878–1872	1895–1844	Phase 1–2(?)	IIIA2 1900–1800	Arqa N, St. 14 Hama H
A late		1–2 pre- to Palace I			A II	1911–1876	1928–1878*	Phase 1?		
A early	1928–1862	1 pre-Palace I			S I	1953–1908	1971–1924			

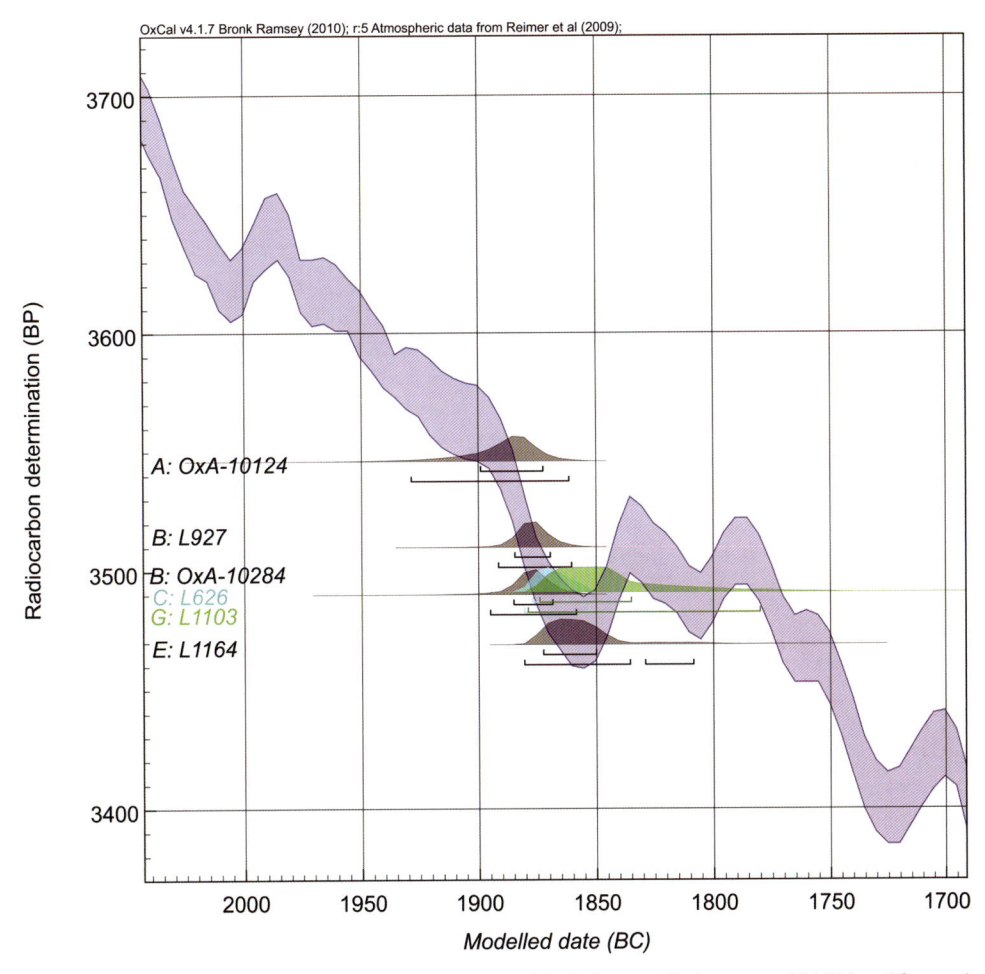

Figure 15.8: Close up of the curve plot the Bayesian model of the stratified sequence Tel Ifshar Phases A to G with a terminus ante quem of 1853 BCE for Phase C (likelihoods removed).

Chernoff, who greatly assisted in their location. Throughout, I enjoyed fruitful discussions with many colleagues too numerous to mention, but especially with members of the laboratories who carried out the radiocarbon determinations. In particular, I thank those of ORAU, who also invited me to join the LEC project and kindly invited me to the Egyptian chronology conference, where an earlier version of this paper was read. Finally, nearly 20 years ago, I first attempted to apply AMS radiocarbon to chronological issues of the MB IIa southern Levant. This attempt would never have been made without the encouragement and support of the late Professor Andrew Sherratt, whose ancient world view continues to inform and inspire my own. I am certain even he would never have imagined the precision of the results achieved in this project. This paper is dedicated to his blessed memory.

References

Allen, J. P. 2008, The historical inscription of Khnumhotep at Dahshur: preliminary report, *Bulletin of the American Schools of Oriental Research*, **352**, 29–39.

Bader, B. 2003, The Egyptian jars from Sidon in their Egyptian context, *Archaeology and History in Lebanon*, **18**, 31–37.

Bader, B., Forstner-Müller, I., Kopetzky, K., and Doumet-Serhal, C. 2009, An Egyptian Jar from Sidon in its Egyptian context. Some fresh evidence, *Archaeology & History in Lebanon*, **29**, 79–83.

Bagh, T. 1998, Ezbet Rushdi and the 12th Dynasty Levantine connection, *Egypt and the Levant*, **8**, 47–49.

Bagh, T. 2002, Painted pottery of the Middle Bronze Age: Levantine Painted Ware, In *The Middle Bronze Age in the Levant* (ed. M. Bietak), 89–101, Austrian Academy of Sciences Press, Vienna.

Bagh, T. 2003, The relationship between Levantine Painted Ware, Syro/Cilician Ware, and Khabur Ware and their chronological implications, In *The Synchronisation of Civilizations in the Eastern Mediterranean in the Second Millennium B.C. II*, (ed. M. Bietak), Austrian Academy of Sciences Press, Vienna.

Baines, J. 1987, The stela of Khusobek: private and royal military narrative and values, In *Form und Mass: Beitrage Zur Literatur, Sprache und Kunst del Alten Ägypten* (Festschrift für Gerhard Fecht, eds J. Osing and G. Dreyer), 43–61, Otto Harrasowitz, Wiesbaden.

Beck, P. 1975, The pottery of the Middle Bronze Age IIA at Tel Aphek. *Tel Aviv* **2**, 45–84.

Beck, P. 1985, The Middle Bronze Age pottery from Aphek, 1972–1984: first summary, *Tel Aviv* **12**(2), 181–203.

Beck, P. 2000a, Area A: Middle Bronze Age IIa pottery, In *Aphek-Antipatris I: Excavations of Areas A and B, the 1972–1976 Seasons* (eds M. Kochavi, P. Beck and E. Yadin), 173–238, Tel Aviv University, Tel Aviv.

Beck, P. 2000b, Area B: Pottery, In *Aphek-Antipatris I: Excavations of Areas A and B, the 1972–1976 Seasons* (eds M. Kochavi, P. Beck and E. Yadin), 93–133, Tel Aviv University, Tel Aviv.

Beck, P. 2000c, The Middle Bronze Age IIa Pottery Repertoire – a Comparative Study. In *Aphek-Antipatris I: Excavations of Areas A and B, the 1972–1976 Seasons* (eds M. Kochavi, P. Beck and E. Yadin), 239–254, Tel Aviv University, Tel Aviv.

Ben-Tor, D. 2007, Scarabs, chronology, and interconnections: Egypt and Palestine in the Second Intermediate Period, *Archaeologica*, **27**, Academic Press, Fribourg.

Bietak, M. 1996, *Avaris: The Capital of the Hyksos. Recent Excavations at Tell el-Dab'a*, British Museum Press, London.

Bietak, M., Kopetzky, K., Stager, L. E. and Voss, R. 2008, Synchronisation of stratigraphies: Ashkelon and Tell el-Dab`a, *Egypt and the Levant*, **18**, 49–60.

Bourriau, J. 1998, Classique graves at Kerma, In *Nubian Studies, Egyptian Pottery Found in Kerma Ancien, Kerma Moyen and Kerma*, (ed. T. Kendall), 3–13, Northeastern University, Boston.

Breasted, J. H. 1906, *Ancient Records of Egypt: Historical Documents from the Earliest Times to the Persian Conquest, Volume 1*, University of Chicago, Chicago.

Bronk Ramsey, C., Higham, T., Owen, D., Pike, A., and Hedges, R. 2002, Radiocarbon dates from the Oxford AMS System, *Archaeometry*, **44**(3), 1–149.

Bronk Ramsey, C. 2000, Comment on 'the use of Bayesian statistics for 14C dates of chronologically ordered samples: a critical analysis', *Radiocarbon*, **42**(2), 199–202.

Bronk Ramsey, C. 2009, Bayesian Analysis of Radiocarbon Dates, *Radiocarbon* **51**(1), 337–60.

Chernoff, M. C. 1988, *The Archaeobotanical Material from Tel el Ifshar, Israel: A Diachronic Study of Agricultural Strategies during the Third and Second Millennia, B.C.E.* (Ph.D. dissertation submitted to the Brandeis University), University Microfilms International, Ann Arbor.

Chernoff, M. C. 1992, Natural Resource Use in an Ancient Near East Farming Community. *Agricultural History*, **66**(2): 213–20.

Chernoff, M. C. and Paley, S. M. 1998, Dynamics of cereal cultivation at Tel el Ifshar, Israel during the Middle Bronze Age, *Journal of Field Archaeology*, **25**(4), 397–416.

Cohen-Weinberger, A. and Goren, Y. 2004, Levantine-Egyptian interactions during the 12th to 15th Dynasties based on the petrography of the Canaanite pottery from Tell el-Dab'a *Egypt and the Levant*, **14**, 69–100.

Czerny, E. 1998, Zur Keramik von `Ezbet Rushdi (Stand Mai 1997), *Egypt and the Levant*, **8**, 41–46.

Czerny, E. 2002, Egyptian pottery from Tell el-Dab`a as a context for Early MB IIa Painted Ware. In *The Middle Bronze Age in the Levant*, (ed. M. Bietak), 133–42, Austrian Academy of Sciences Press, Vienna.

Delia, R. D. 1980, *A Study of the Reign of Senwosret III* (Ph.D. dissertation submitted to Columbia University).

Doumet-Serhal, C. 2004, Animal bone deposit under Sidon's Minoan cup: C14 analysis. *Archaeology & History in Lebanon*, **20**, 60.

Doumet-Serhal, C. 2008, The British Museum excavation at Sidon: markers for chronology of the Early and Middle Bronze Age in Lebanon. In *The Bronze Age in the Lebanon: Studies on the Archaeology and Chronology of Lebanon, Syria and Egypt* (eds M. Bietak and E. Czerny), 11–44, Austrian Academy of Sciences Press, Vienna.

Falconer, S. E. and Berelov, I. 2006, Ceramic and radiocarbon chronology for Tell el-Hayyat. In *Bronze Age Rural Ecology and Village Life at Tell el-Hayyat, Jordan* (S. E. Falconer and P. L. Fall), 44–64, Archaeopress, Oxford.

Falconer, S. E. and Fall, P. L. 2006, *Bronze Age Rural Ecology and Village Life at Tell el-Hayyat, Jordan*, Archaeopress, Oxford.

Gal, Z. and Kochavi, M. 2000, Area B: Stratigraphy, architecture and tombs. In *Aphek-Antipatris I: Excavations of Areas A and B, the 1972–1976 Seasons* (eds M. Kochavi, P. Beck and E. Yadin), 59–92, Tel Aviv University, Tel Aviv.

Hedges, R., Pettitt, P., Ramsey, C. B. and van Klinken, G. 1997, Radiocarbon dates from the Oxford AMS system, *Archaeometry*, **39**(1), 247–62.

Kitchen, K. A. 1996, The historic chronology of ancient Egypt, a current assessment, In *Absolute Chronology: Archaeological Europe 2500–500 BC*, (ed. K. Randsborg), 1–13, Munksgaard, Copenhagen.

Kochavi, M., 1975, The first two seasons of excavations at Aphek-Antipatris, *Tel Aviv 2*, 17–42.

Kochavi, M. and Yadin, E. 2002, Typological analysis of the MB IIA pottery from Aphek According to its stratigraphic provenance, In *The Middle Bronze Age in the Levant* (ed. M. Bietak), 189–225, Austrian Academy of Sciences Press, Vienna.

MacGillivray, J. 2003, A Middle Minoan cup from Sidon, *Archaeology and History in Lebanon*, **18**, 20–24.

Maeir, A. M. 2010, *'In the Midst of the Jordan': The Jordan Valley during the Middle Bronze Age (Circa 2000–1500 BCE): Archaeological and Historical Correlates*, Austrian Academy of Sciences Press, Vienna.

Marcus, E. S. 2003, Dating the Early Middle Bronze Age in the southern Levant: a preliminary comparison of radiocarbon and archaeo-historical synchronizations, In *The Synchronisation of Civilizations in the Eastern Mediterranean in the Second Millennium B.C. II* (ed. M. Bietak), 95–110, Austrian Academy of Sciences Press, Vienna.

Marcus, E. S. 2007, Amenemhet II and the sea: maritime aspects of the Mit Rahina (Memphis) inscription, *Egypt and the Levant*, **17**, 137–90.

Marcus, E. S. 2010, Appendix B: radiocarbon determinations from the Middle Bronze Age Jordan Valley, In *'In the Midst of the Jordan': The Jordan Valley during the Middle Bronze Age (circa 2000–1500 BCE): Archaeological and Historical Correlates* (A. M. Maeir), 243–52, Austrian Academy of Sciences Press, Vienna.

Marcus, E. S., Porath, Y. and Paley, S. M. 2008a, The Early Middle Bronze Age IIa phases at Tel Ifshar and their external relations, *Egypt and the Levant*, **18**, 221–44.

Marcus, E. S., Porath, Y., Schiestl, R., Seiler, A. and Paley, S. M. 2008b, The Middle Kingdom Egyptian pottery from Middle Bronze Age IIa Tel Ifshar, *Egypt and the Levant*, **18**, 203–19.

Nigro, L. 2009, The eighteenth century BC princes of Byblos and Ebla and the chronology of the Middle Bronze Age. In *Interconnections in the Eastern Mediterranean: Lebanon in the Bronze and Iron Ages,* 159–75, BAAL, Beyrouth.

Oguchi, H. 2001, The origins of the Khabur Ware: a tentative note. *Al-Rāfidān*, **22**, 71–87.

Oguchi, H. 2003, 20th century B.C. north Mesopotamia: an archaeological dilemma. *Al-Rāfidān*, **24**, 83–100.

Rainey, A. F. 1994, Remarks on Donald Redford's Egypt, Canaan, and Israel in ancient times, *Bulletin of the American Schools of Oriental Research*, **295**, 81–85.

Ramsey, C. B., Dee, M. W., Rowland, J. M., Higham, T. F. G., Harris, S. A., Brock, F., Quiles, A., Wild, E. M., Marcus, E. S. and Shortland, A. J. 2010, Radiocarbon-Based Chronology for Dynastic Egypt, *Science*, **328**, 1554–57.

Reimer, P. J., Baillie, M. G. L., Bard, E., Bayliss, A., Beck, J. W., Blackwell, P. G., Bronk Ramsey, C., Buck, C. E., Burr, G. S., Edwards, R. L., Friedrich, M., Grootes, P. M., Guilderson, T. P., Hajdas, I., Heaton, T. J., Hogg, A. G., Hughen, K. A., Kaiser, K. F., Kromer, B., McCormac, F. G., Manning, S. W., Reimer, R. W., Richards, D. A., Southon, J. R., Talamo, S., Turney, C. S. M., van der Plicht, J. and and Weyhenmeyer, C. E. 2009, IntCal09 and Marine09 Radiocarbon Age Calibration Curves, 0–50000 Years Cal BP. *Radiocarbon*, **51**(4), 1111–50.

Rzeuska, T. I. 2010, Zigzag, triangle and fish fin. On the relations of Egypt and C-Group during the Middle Kingdom, In *Between the Cataracts* (eds W. Godlewski and A. Lajtare), 397–419, Warsaw University Press, Warsaw.

Stager, L. E. 2002, The MB IIA ceramic sequence at Tel Ashkelon and its implications for the 'port power' model of trade, In *The Middle Bronze Age in the Levant* (ed. M. Bietak), 353–62, Austrian Academy of Sciences Press, Vienna.

Stager, L. E., Schloen, J. D., Master, D. M., Press, M. D. and Aja, A. 2008, Stratigraphic overview: the north slope. In *Ashkelon 1: Introduction and Overview (1985–2006)* (eds L. E. Stager, J. D. Schloen and D. M. Master), 215–45, Harvard Semitic Museum, Boston.

Stager, L. E. and Voss, R. J. 2011, Egyptian pottery in Middle Bronze Age Ashkelon. In *Eretz Israel(Ben-Tor volume)*, 119*–126* Israel Exploration Society, Jerusalem.

Stuiver, M., Reimer, P., Bard, E., Beck, J., Burr, G., Hughen, K., Kromer, B., McCormac, G., van der Plicht, J. and Spurk, M. 1998, INTCAL98 Radiocarbon age calibration 24,000–0 cal BP, *Radiocarbon*, **40**(3), 1041–84.

Vila, E. 2003, Animal bone deposits under Sidon's Minoan cup, *Archaeology and History in Lebanon*, 18, 25.

Weinstein, J. M. 1975, Egyptian relations with Palestine in the Middle Kingdom, *Bulletin of the American Schools of Oriental Research*, **217**, 1–16.

Yadin, E. 2009a, Middle Bronze Age (Strata X19–X15), In *Aphek-Antipatris II: The Remains on the Acropolis* (eds Y. Gadot and E. Yadin), 7–40, Tel Aviv University, Tel Aviv.

Yadin, E. 2009b, The Middle Bronze Age pottery of Area X, In *Aphek-Antipatris II: The Remains on the Acropolis*, (eds Y. Gadot and E. Yadin), 111–181, Tel Aviv University, Tel Aviv.

Yadin, E. and Kochavi, M. 2000, Area A: stratigraphy, architecture and tombs. In *Aphek-Antipatris I: Excavations of Areas A and B, the 1972–1976 Seasons* (eds M. Kochavi, P. Beck and E. Yadin), 134–1725, Tel Aviv University, Tel Aviv.

V: The Old Kingdom and Early Dynastic Period

Chapter 16

A Radiocarbon-based Chronology for the Old Kingdom

M. W. Dee

High-precision radiocarbon models may make their most significant contribution to Egyptian chronology in the Old Kingdom. The absolute dating of this period is still a matter of great conjecture, and estimates commonly vary by more than a century. Fortunately, a diverse range of relative information is available that may be used to refine radiocarbon data. Indeed, although no one chronology for the Old Kingdom is universally accepted, lengthy contiguous sections are now well established. The models produced by this study included 17 new radiocarbon dates on short-lived plant materials from the Old Kingdom. Unfortunately, few samples were available for the 5th–8th Dynasties, so the analysis was heavily reliant on the dates obtained for the early reigns of the period. The models were again refined using king-list order, and adapted to match different interpretations of the archaeological evidence. The basic reign-length restriction was relaxed five-fold with respect to the New Kingdom, to reflect the increased uncertainty present. Despite these measures, the Old Kingdom model produced robust absolute dates that were precise enough to distinguish between current hypotheses. Moreover, the Old Kingdom model retains significant potential for improvement, simply by the inclusion of more radiocarbon data. Finally, by linking the outputs of the Old and Middle Kingdom models, this analysis produced the first scientific estimate for the duration of the First Intermediate Period.

Introduction

The historical age known as the Old Kingdom, epitomised by the Pyramids of Giza, has been a source of wonderment since Classical times. But no precise dates have yet been established for the period. As with the Middle and New Kingdoms, a historical chronology based on king-lists and other state-level records has been developed. This relative sequence traditionally extends from the 3rd–6th Dynasties, but sometimes the ephemeral 7th–8th Dynasties are also included.

The historical chronology for the Old Kingdom is cut off from that of Middle Kingdom by a period of parochialism that endured for an unknown length of time. In addition, the absolute tie-points for the Middle and New Kingdoms provided by the Sothic observations – albeit with limited reliability – are absent from the Old Kingdom archaeological record. Thus, the chronology of the Old Kingdom is truly a floating sequence, only tentatively positioned on the absolute time-scale. Kitchen (1991) estimated that absolute dates ascribed to the period could only be considered accurate to within 100–200 years.

Author's Address: **M. W. Dee**, *RLAHA*, University of Oxford, Dyson Perrins Building, South Parks Road, Oxford OX1 3QY, UK

Bonani *et al.* (2001) completed a major absolute dating study of Old Kingdom monuments of Giza and Saqqara. However, the radiocarbon data showed both considerable scatter and notable offsets to older-than-expected ages. Indeed, the study illustrated the complexity associated with dating monuments where short-lived samples are rare and human activity has been concentrated in the vicinity for thousands of years (see Dee *et al.* 2009). On the contrary, analysis of the celestial alignment of several monuments of the 4th and 5th Dynasties suggested much younger dates for their associated kings (see Spence 2000). The object of the current study was to improve on the dates achieved by these investigations, and to hone the absolute ages associated with each ruler.

Methodology

The Samples
The difficulty of finding good radiocarbon samples for the Old Kingdom exemplifies the challenge of studying this remote time period. Museum collections often contain pieces, which are too precious for destructive analysis, or have been too heavily conserved to justify sampling. Yet freshly excavated organic materials are currently unable to be analysed outside of Egypt. As a result, only 16 samples were successfully obtained for the Old Kingdom. The list is given in the Appendix, Table 2, and is equivalent to that published in the updated Supporting Online Material by Bronk Ramsey *et al.* (2010).

One group of 4 samples was recovered from the galleries beneath the Step Pyramid at Saqqara. They were thought to either belong to the reign of king Djoser, to whom the monument is dedicated, or his likely predecessor, Khasekhewmy, the last king of the 2nd Dynasty. A further 5 items were also sampled for the reign of Djoser, one of which was a piece of commiphora wood. This exception to the rule of only choosing short-lived plants was made on account of the paucity of available material and the fact that commiphora trees are not especially long-lived. Of the few samples that were obtained for the 5th–6th Dynasties, one exceptional piece was a papyrus document from the reign of Djedkara, sampled at the British Museum.

Absolute chronological information: the radiocarbon data
A total of 18 radiocarbon measurements were made on the Old Kingdom samples. One result (OxA-18054) was modern and hence removed (see Chapter 7). The commiphora wood sample was dated in triplicate and produced consistent results.

Relative chronological information: king-list order and reign-lengths
As with the Middle and New Kingdom models, king-list order and reign-length information were the main types of prior knowledge built into the Old Kingdom analysis. The historical record for the period relies on many of the same primary resources as the other two Kingdoms, but an important addition is the Palermo Stone. This royal annal includes the names of kings and the lengths of their reigns from the mythological period preceding

Table 16.1: Specifications for the set of Old Kingdom models. The outputs for each model are given in the Appendix, Table 5.

MODEL NAME	REIGN LENGTHS	DESCRIPTION
OKM1	Shaw 2000	High or standard configuration
OKM2	Hornung *et al.* 2006	Low chronology configuration
OKM3	Kitchen 2000	Alternative reign lengths
OKM4	Shaw 2000	100% outliers eliminated

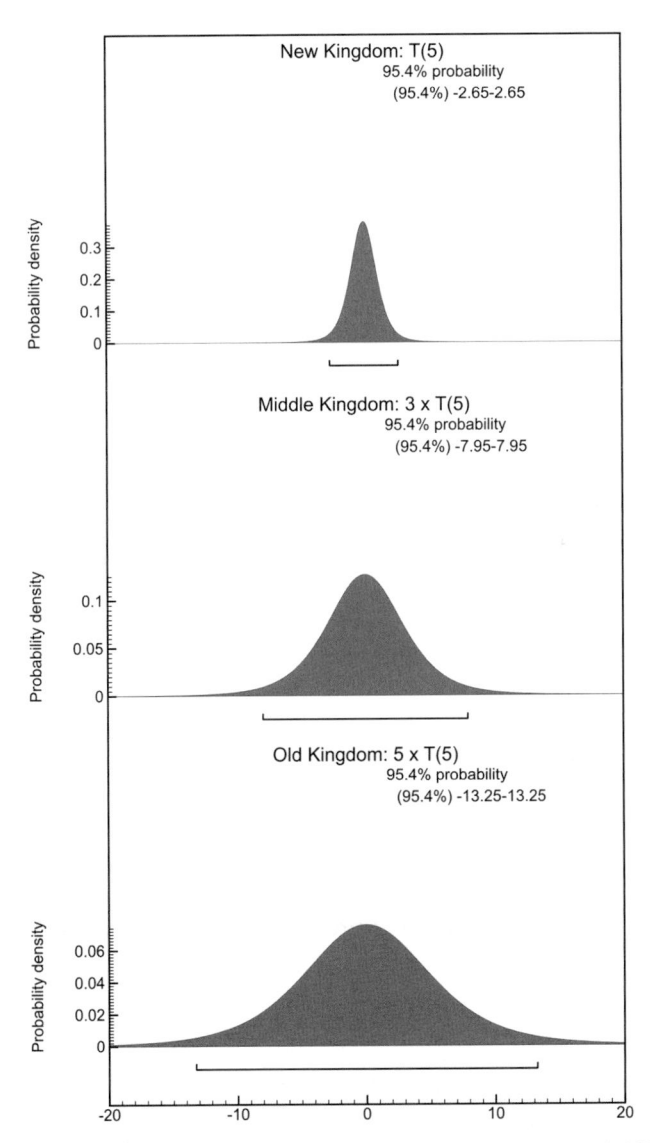

Figure 16.1: The Student's t-distribution was scaled by a factor of 5 in the standard Old Kingdom model to reflect increased reign-length uncertainty.

212   *M. W. Dee*

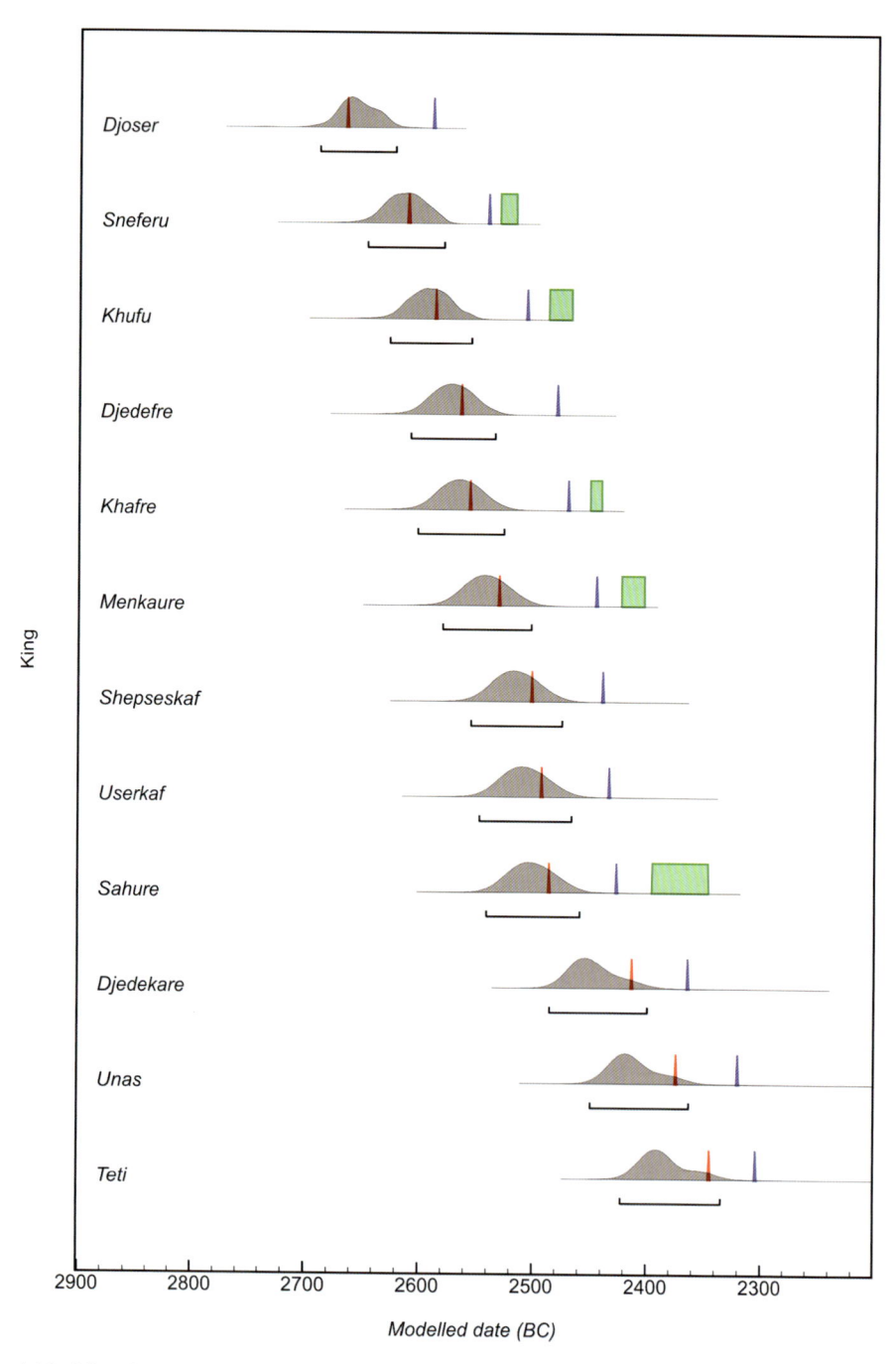

Figure 16.2: Selected accession dates from OKM1. The high chronology estimates are shown in red; low chronology in blue; modelled radiocarbon dates in grey. The green boxes relate to the astro-chronological sequence of Spence (2000). The calibrated ranges (95%) given by the square brackets are listed in the Appendix, Table 5.

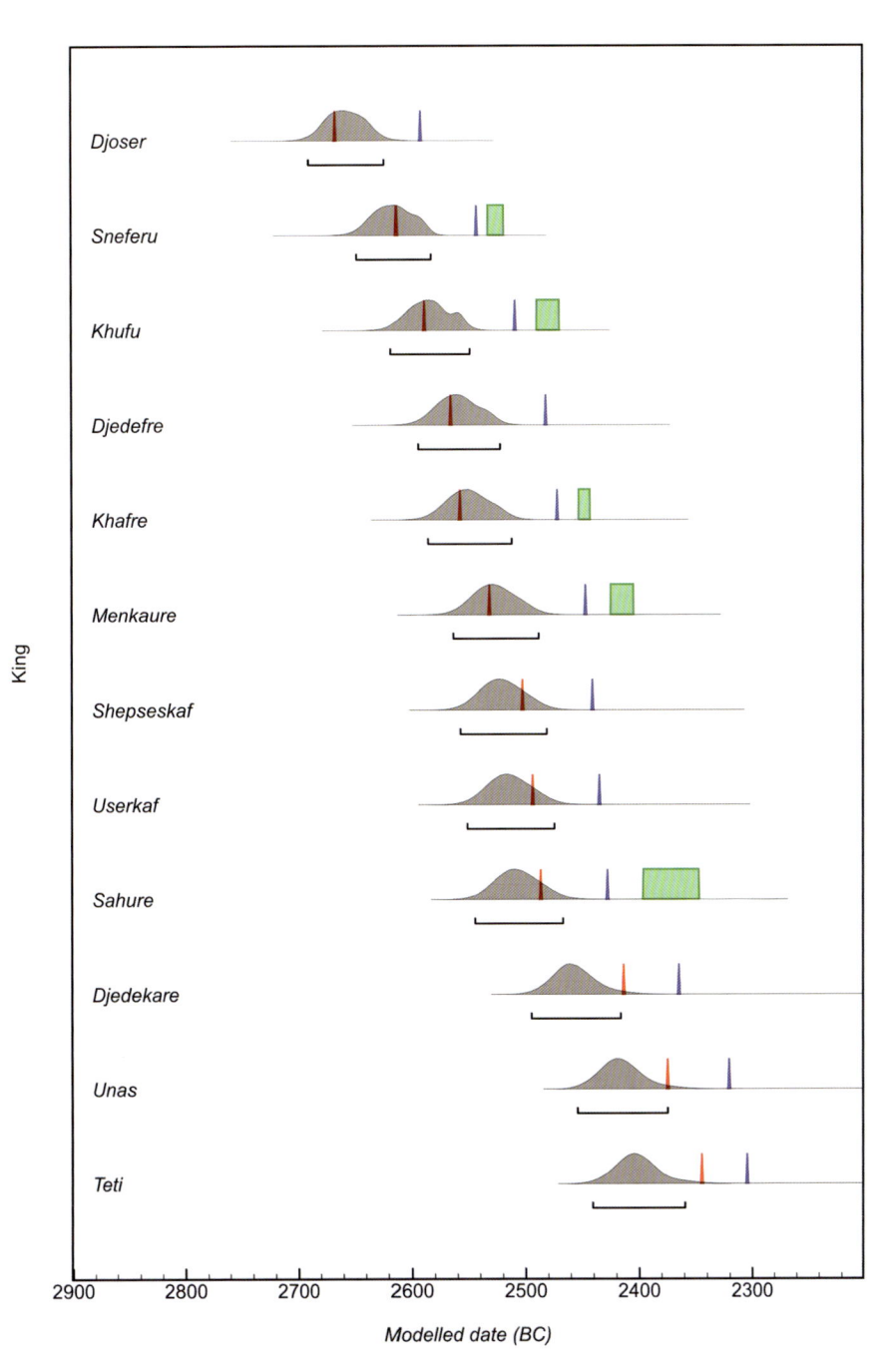

16. *A Radiocarbon-based Chronology for the Old Kingdom* 213

Figure 16.3: Selected accession dates from OKM2. The high chronology estimates are shown in red; low chronology in blue; modelled radiocarbon dates in grey. The green boxes relate to the astro-chronological sequence of Spence (2000). The calibrated ranges (95%) given by the square brackets are listed in the Appendix, Table 5.

the 1st Dynasty up to the 5th Dynasty. Detailed accounts of the establishment of the Old Kingdom historical chronology are given elsewhere (see Part II, Hornung *et al.* 2006)

Although Old Kingdom chronologies often include reign lengths, the variability of such accounts reveals their inherent uncertainty. In comparing the 'high' chronology of Shaw (2000, 479) with the 'low' chronology of Hornung *et al.* (2006, 490), for example, a number of reigns differ by more than 10 years, and a few by more than 20 (see the Appendix, Table 1). Moreover, even the identity and ordering of certain kings is not the same. As a result of these considerations, the modelling agenda for the Old Kingdom was much less prescriptive than for the later periods.

Model Configuration and Specifications

The Old Kingdom models were formatted in the same way as the New and Middle Kingdoms (see Chapter 7 for details, and the Appendix, Table 4, for OKM1 model code). Due to the shortage of measurements, on several occasions one Phase had to represent a series of reigns, to stop the model failing on account of insufficient data. For example, no new samples were found for the middle of the 5th Dynasty, so one Phase was used for the 6 reigns from Sahure to Menkauhor. Similar modifications had to be employed where hiatuses occurred between reigns and where the order of succession was different between the relative chronologies employed.

Due to the obvious variability in reign-length estimates, the Student's t-distribution was expanded by a factor of five in the standard Old Kingdom model (OKM1). Thus, the reign lengths selected were only required to be within ± 13.25 calendar years of the historical estimates (see Figure 16.1), and the iterative process still proceeded if the reign-lengths chosen by the program were within ± 100 years of these values. In cases where one Phase was used to represent several reigns, the reign-length uncertainty was further widened by a factor equal to the square root of the number of reigns included.

The standard Old Kingdom model (OKM1) used the reign lengths published in Shaw (2000, 479) to define the midpoints of the Student's t-distributions. The first variation (OKM2) used the reign lengths of Hornung *et al.* (2006, 490), and a further model (OKM3) was developed for this publication that used those of Kitchen (2000). The chronologies differ significantly (see the Appendix, Table 1). For example, Shaw allocates 505 years to the whole Old Kingdom sequence, whilst the chronology of Hornung *et al.* (2006, 490) is 31 years shorter and that of Kitchen (2000) is 50 years longer.

As with the New and Middle Kingdom models, a configuration (OKM4) was run which excluded the results from OKM1 that were determined to be 100% outliers (OxA-18052, OxA-18063 and OxA-19793). For all the Old Kingdom models, a uniform prior outlier probability of 5% was used, and the localised offset of Dee *et al.* 2010 was again included. The effect of varying these parameters and doubling the reign-length uncertainty has been dealt with elsewhere (Bronk Ramsey *et al.* 2010). The models were each run for a least ten million iterations and the average convergence consistently passed 95%. The specifications for each model are summarised in Table 16.1 (see the Appendix for OKM1 program code).

Results and Discussion

The Radiocarbon-based Chronologies

The historical dates proposed for Egypt during the 3rd millennium are inherently less precise than those already achievable by radiocarbon dating. Indeed, although the models produced here used only 17 measurements, the standard Old Kingdom model (OKM1) reached an average calendrical precision of 84 years (95% probability). Such ranges would likely halve – without the need to change the historical assumptions – if as many as 100 radiocarbon dates were available.

Figure 16.2 shows the modelled calibrations obtained by OKM1 for selected accession dates between Djoser and the start of the First Intermediate Period. It is again pertinent to note that no absolute information or restrictions were placed on OKM1, or any other Old Kingdom model; the resultant calendar dates are solely the product of the radiocarbon determinations and the relative information described above. The radiocarbon-based estimates are again in very good agreement with the historical chronologies, although on this occasion they are able to categorically distinguish between the different scenarios. OKM1 favours the high chronology given in Shaw (2000, 470), and in actual fact offers no significant probability at all to the lower estimates of both Hornung *et al.* (2006, 490) and the astro-chronology of Spence (2000). Furthermore, even when the shorter reign lengths were employed the model was essentially invariant (see Figure 16.3). The chronology contracted somewhat, but did not shift on the absolute time-scale. The stability of the model was reiterated by the results obtained by OKM3 (see the Appendix, Table 5 and Model Results, for data and figures). The significantly longer chronology of Kitchen (2000) only resulted in the Old Kingdom starting at a slightly earlier date and ending at a slightly later date. Unfortunately, as OKM4 only included 14 dates, the model failed to satisfactorily converge.

The Historical Implications

The shortage of samples obtained for the Old Kingdom means that the results generated here must be treated with some caution. Indeed, the accession date estimates for the latter half of the model, from the 5th – 8th Dynasties, are essentially just projections based on the relative chronology employed in each case. On the contrary, the fact that a number of measurements were obtained for the reign of Djoser and the accession date produced was 50–100 years earlier than most chronologies provides compelling information in itself. Moreover, due the short-lived nature of these samples and the internal consistency of the raw dates, it is unlikely that additional samples would substantially change this result. It is more probable, as mentioned above, that the precision of the chronology would just be enhanced and its absolute position would remain relatively stable. In fact, re-running the Old Kingdom model with more data remains one of the key outstanding tasks of this research.

The Old Kingdom model was run independently of, but together with, the Middle Kingdom model. This enabled a further output to be generated. By comparing the calendrical solutions for the start of the First Intermediate Period with those for the accession date of Mentuhotep II, the program was able to make the first chronometric estimate for the duration of the First Intermediate Period. This was not attempted for

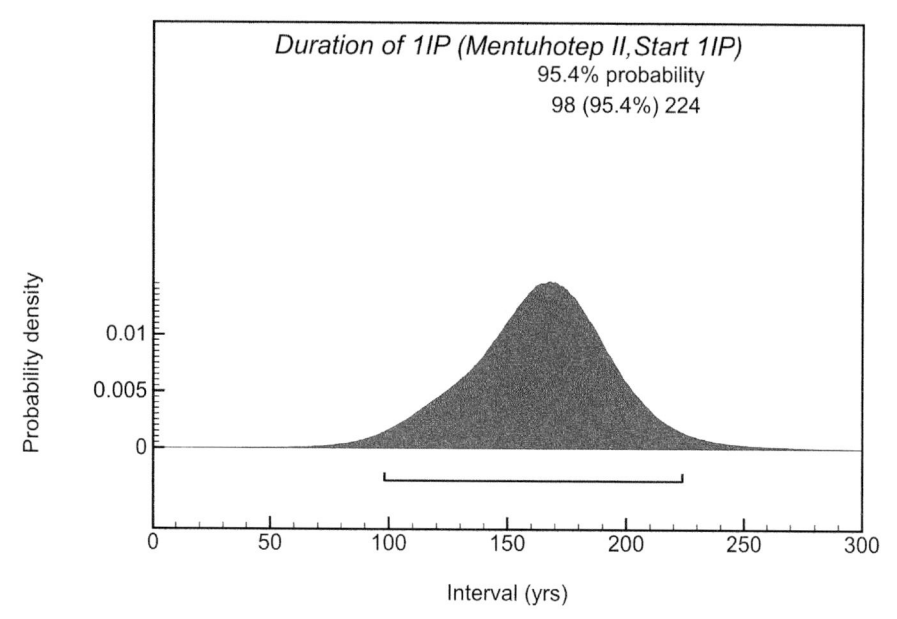

Figure 16.4: The chronometric estimate produced by OKM1 and MKM1 for the length of the First Intermediate Period

the Second Intermediate Period because of the lack of historical consensus around when exactly the Middle Kingdom ended. The estimate for the duration of the First Intermediate Period from the OKM1 and MKM1 models is given in Figure 16.4. The 95% probability range for this interval peaks around 170 years. Such a span is considerably longer than most historical estimates for the interval. For example, Shaw (2000, 479) allocates 105 years between the start of First Intermediate Period and the accession of Mentuhotep II; Hornung *et al.* (2006, 490), 109 years, and Kitchen (2000), just 93 years. The reliability of the chronometric estimate would be substantially enhanced by the acquisition of more data for the latter stages of the Old Kingdom. Nonetheless, modelling such gaps in the state-level record, where the archaeological information is less complete, is a further area where radiocarbon dating may make a significant contribution to Egyptian chronology.

Conclusions

The historical chronology for the Old Kingdom is currently disconnected from both the relative sequence of the Middle Kingdom and undisputed tie-points with absolute time. The radiocarbon-based chronology presented here represents an absolute record for the Old Kingdom that relies on only the most secure relative information. The results support a high chronology similar to that proposed by Shaw (2000, 479). Moreover, the inclusion of more data may enable radiocarbon dating to fully resolve this important period of Egyptian history.

References

Bonani, G., Hass, H., Hawass, Z., Lehner, M., Nakhla, S., Nolan, J., Wenke, R. and Wolfli, W. 2001, Radiocarbon dates of Old and Middle Kingdom monuments in Egypt, *Radiocarbon*, **43**(3), 1297–1320.

Dee, M. W., Bronk Ramsey, C., Shortland, A. J., Higham, T. F. G. and Rowland, J. M. 2009, Reanalysis of the chronological discrepancies obtained by the Old and Middle Kingdom monuments project, *Radiocarbon*, **51**(3), 1061–1070.

Dee, M. W., Brock, F., Harris, S. A., Bronk Ramsey, C., Shortland, A. J., Higham, T. F. G. and Rowland, J. M. 2010, Investigating the Likelihood of a Reservoir Offset in the Radiocarbon Record for Ancient Egypt, *Journal of Archaeological Science*, **37**(4), 687–693.

Bronk Ramsey, C. 1995, Radiocarbon calibration and analysis of stratigraphy: the OxCal program, *Radiocarbon*, **37**(2), 425–430.

Bronk Ramsey, C., Dee, M. W., Rowland, J. M., Higham, T. F. G., Harris, S. A., Brock, F., Quiles, A., Wild, E. M., Marcus, E. S. and Shortland, A. J. 2010, Radiocarbon-based Chronology for Dynastic Egypt. *Science*, **328**(5985), 1554–1559.

Hornung, E. 2006, The New Kingdom, In *Ancient Egyptian Chronology* (eds R. Krauss and D. A. Warburton), 197–217, Brill, Leiden and Boston.

Kitchen, K. A. 1991, The chronology of ancient Egypt, *World Archaeology*, **23**(2), 201–208.

Kitchen, K. A 2000, Regnal and Genealogical Data of Ancient Egypt (Absolute Chronology I) The Historical Chronology of Ancient Egypt, A Current Assessment. In *The Synchronisation of Civilisations in the Eastern Mediterranean in the Second Millennium BC I* (ed. M. Bietak), 39–52, Austrian Academy of Sciences Press, Vienna.

Reimer, P. J., Baillie, M. G. L., Bard, E., Bayliss, A., Beck, J. W., Blackwell, P. G., Bronk Ramsey, C., Buck, C. E., Burr, G. S., Edwards, R. L., Friedrich, M., Grootes, P. M., Guilderson, T. P., Hajdas, I., Heaton, T. J., Hogg, A. G., Hughen, K. A., Kaiser, K. F., Kromer, B., McCormac, F. G., Manning, S. W., Reimer, R. W., Richards, D. A., Southon, J. R., Talamo, S., Turney, C. S. M., van der Plicht, J. and Weyhenmeyer, C. E. 2009, IntCal09 and Marine09 radiocarbon age calibration curves, 0–50,000 years cal BP, *Radiocarbon*, **51**(4), 1111–1150.

Shaw, I. (ed.) 2000, *The Oxford History of Ancient Egypt*, Oxford University Press, Oxford.

Spence, K. 2000, Ancient Egyptian chronology and the astronomical orientation of pyramids, *Nature*, **408**(6810), 320–324.

CHAPTER 17

Radiocarbon Dates for the Old Kingdom and their Correspondences

M. Bárta

The principal aim of this contribution is to compare recently established radiocarbon dates for the Old Kingdom period with the traditional chronological scheme used by the Egyptologists. Two historically important periods will be discussed. The first period is middle of the 5th Dynasty when the beginning of a slow political and economic decline that led to the eventual demise of the Old Kingdom is well documented. The second period is the end of the 6th Dynasty which is traditionally seen as a point of ultimate social, political, administrative and economic collapse of the ancient Egyptian state (Malek 2000, 109–17). In this context, the '2200 BC event' in Egypt, Syria and Palestine will be reconsidered. With support of the absolute chronology we can now anchor most eligible dates for several important processes in the history of the Near East and ancient Egypt.

Reign of Nyuserre and the end of Early Bronze Age III

The reign of Nyuserre marks a profound change in the history of Old Kingdom Egypt. According to the latest relative scheme, Nyuserre reigned between 2402–2374 BC, most likely 11–31 years (Verner 2006, 139). Following the radiocarbon results provided by the current Oxford Radiocarbon project, Nyuserre probably ascended the throne around 2448 BC based on addition of his 31 regnal years. However, it was already Kitchen who, using his retrograde scheme of historical dates for ancient Egyptian kings, established that Nyuserre's reign can be dated to an interval 2470–2439 BC and thus arrived at a very similar date (Kitchen 2001, 48). His successor to the throne, Menkauhor, reigned for seven years which makes, according to radiocarbon chronology, the likeliest accession date of Djedkare around 2410 BC.[1] This is quite a neat match of both chronologies – compared to previous situation – resulting in a small difference of about 46 years.[2]

In this context, it is important to mention that the Oxford Radiocarbon project date for ascension of Djedkara (2410 BC) is almost identical with the historical date suggested by Jürgen von Beckerath in the 'high' chronology – 2405 BC (Beckerath 1997, 155). Based on relative chronology published most recently by Hornung and others (Hornung *et al.* 2006), Djedkara Isesi, took the throne around 2365 BC and died around 2322 BC. Again, the difference in both applied chronologies is relatively small, being 45 years. And Kitchen adds another small difference, suggesting slightly earlier date for Djedkara's accession – year 2431 BC (Kitchen 2000, 48). In both cases, the differences between the relative and absolute chronologies are negligible. We may also note one important feature having

---

Author's Address: **M. Bárta**, Czech Institute of Egyptology, Charles University, Prague

profound historical and archaeological implications, namely that the radiocarbon date for Djedkara's accession to the throne is very close to the date proposed for the end of the Early Bronze Age III in Syria and Palestine, which is set around 2350 BC (Ben-Tor 1992, 82). Within this chronological framework it seems accession dates from Kate Spence's recent analysis of astrochronological data less probable, as they are rather low though not extremely low. Thus, according to the method used for the purpose of Spence's study (analysis of the northern alignment of the pyramids based on simultaneous transit of two circumpolar stars), Djoser would accede to the throne extremely late, around 2526 BC ± 7 (Spence 2000, 320–324, Table 1) as contrasted with *c*. 2592 BC (Hornung, Krauss and Warburton, eds 2006, 491) and 2670 BC (Oxford project). Or Neferirkare 2359 BC ± 25 (Hornung, Krauss, and Warburton, eds, 2006, 491) and 2483/2433–2463/2413 BC (von Beckerath 1997, 188).

Historical framework

Many fundamental changes occur during the latter part of the 5th Dynasty. Specifically from the reign of Nyuserre on, one can observe the appearance and dynamic development of several important phenomena that characterise ancient Egyptian society of the day. There is a significant increase in the number of wealthy tombs of the highest officials of the state; some of these tombs even incorporate elements from royal architecture (Bárta 2005). This growth corresponds with the increasing number of non-royal officials in the elite administration. At the same time, the Osiris concept becomes accessible to non-royal persons as well. Thus every mortal can after his death become Osiris (Bárta 1995). This process is sometimes called, for lack of a more appropriate terminology, the 'democratisation of the afterlife'. It comes as no surprise that shortly thereafter, royal burial chambers are decorated with Pyramid Texts. This happens during the reign of Unas, which starts around 2365 BC by absolute chronology or 2321 BC according to relative chronology.

The relative chronology of this specific period is also characterised by the sudden lack of imported vessels from the Syro-Palestinian region. From the reign of Nyuserre, and from the tomb of his favourite official Ptahshepses, originates only one relief that shows the transportation of one of these typical Syro-Palestinian amphora with two handles. These vessels were frequently imported to Egypt as containers for luxurious liquids including wine and oils. They are characteristic of EB II and III periods and seemingly do not occur any later (Bárta 2009). The iconographic evidence for this artefact from Abusir is very likely the last of its kind, as this metallic ware disappears by the end of Early Bronze Age III, which is only very shortly after the reign of Nyuserre. For possibly the closest date to this event, we may use the date of ascension of Djedkara or even the end of Nyuserre's rule. This is around 2410 BC by absolute chronology or 2365 BC by relative chronology, which is actually the end of the Early Bronze Age III in Syria and Palestine. It has traditionally been supposed that EB III was roughly parallel with the Egyptian 4th and 5th Dynasties. Now it is possible to go even further and claim that the end of EB III was parallel to the reign of Djedkare. Parallel to troubled times in Syria and Palestine, the reign of Djedkare marks the beginning of a steady decline of the Old Kingdom (for general situation of Egypt in this period, see Wilkinson 2011, 77–98).

The Demise of the Old Kingdom and the Date for the End of the Sixth Dynasty

Around the reign of Djedkare, Syria and Palestine enter troubled times dominated by vital changes in subsistence economy, the culture of city-states disappears rather quickly and the process of urbanisation reverses. As a consequence, most of the area becomes populated with nomads. There are three alternative explanations for this development: a sudden drop in annual precipitation, external influences – a wave of Amorite warriors from the north or destruction of individual city states caused by their atrocities. This major setback was used by the Egyptians who, despite their economic decline, seem to have organised an unusually high number of military campaigns to Palestine, as witnessed by reliefs of besieged cities depicted in some late 5th Dynasty tombs at Saqqara and Deshasha and by a military account of Weni (Ben-Tor 1992, 122–25).

To counteract the increasing power of the high officials in Egypt, Djedkare started a series of reforms focusing on administration in the province that continued throughout the 6th Dynasty. This king ascended the throne around 2365 BC, or 2410 BC. according to radiocarbon chronology. It is thanks to a magisterial study of Kanawati that we can examine in detail the nature of this process. The character of these reforms indicates that their primary purpose was to curb the increasing independence of the far-away regions south of Memphis. From the late 5th Dynasty onwards these regions became places where local wealthy families extended their influence as witnessed, by the famous family of Weni from Abydos (Richards 2002). Also of some vital significance is the fact that most of these reforms were directed toward the provinces of Upper Egypt, so as to neutralize their independent tendencies. It is interesting to see that each king following Djedkare considered it important to come up with new reforms that always attempted specifically to respond to the actual development in the south (Kanawati 1980).

The formation of a large group of elite administrators from the 5th Dynasty onwards, both in the Memphite region and the provinces, started soon to paralyse the central administration. The policies of the kings regarding the remote yet economically important provinces of the country provide evidence for the generally accepted assumption that there was a gradual erosion of power and authority of the central government: for example, by the creation of the office of the Overseer of Upper Egypt by Djedkare; if not earlier, by the installation of two viziers, one in Memphis and one in Upper Egypt by Teti; or the political marriages of Pepy I to the daughters of an Abydos nomarch. These all demonstrate that the king was trying to re-establish his influence over those remote provinces. Even official texts from the given period provide some interesting details about the king's behaviour towards loyal officials who were given rich gifts such as important stone elements for their tombs.

The beginning of the 6th Dynasty is traditionally connected with the accession of Teti at 2305 BC based on historical dates (reigned until 2279 BC, see Hornung *et al.* 2006, 491) whereas according to radiocarbon dates, he acceded to the throne around 2340 BC. The 6th Dynasty ends around 2153 BC (traditional chronology) or 2197 BC based on radiocarbon dates, from the result of 2270 BC being the accession of Merenra, minus 73 years of his reign and that of Pepy II. We can thus see that there are only small differences in terms of both alternative chronologies, in this case 44 years. Yet once again, the Syria and Palestine dating is very close to the radiocarbon one.

Conclusions

I wish to emphasize one more phenomenon related to chronological issues, be it relative or an absolute one. The experience with the beginning of development after the reign of Nyuserre and the subsequent decline of the Old Kingdom shows clearly that there is no specific year that the collapse started. We have always been dealing with long-term trends that may be discernable at some point, but their effects take a relatively long time to demonstrate explicitly in the historical and archaeological sources. In the case of the Old Kingdom decline, for instance, we may be right in claiming that this phenomenon lasted for more than a century.[2]

In my opinion, the Oxford project contributes significantly to the convergence of relative and absolute chronological approaches as the discrepancies between the historical and radiocarbon chronology are no longer as much as a century (Manning 2006, 355). They are only several decades at maximum, which to me, as an archaeologist, is proof of reliability (von Beckerath 1997; Hornung *et al.* 2006). Thus, we may be able now to set up with higher precision 'anchoring' points in history that would help us to establish more precise framework for specific historical processes as well as single events, taking part in Egypt, Palestine and Syria.

Probability peaks for the accession of selected Old Kingdom rulers based on the Oxford Project:

Djoser	2670 BC
Nyuserra	2390 BC
Djedkara	2410 BC
Unas-Teti	2350 BC
Pepy II (End of reign)	2170 BC

Dates for selected Old Kingdom rulers based on a standard relative chronology (Hornung *et al.* 2006):

Djoser	2592 BC (accession)
Nyuserra	2402–2374 BC
Djedkara	2365 BC (accession)
Unas/–Teti	2321–2305 BC
Pepy II	2153 BC (End of reign)

Appendix

Only during the process of the publication was it possible to obtain report from the Radiocarbon dating laboratory of the French Archaeological Institute in Cairo which also fits in with the latest results of the Oxford Project in that it agrees with a proposed interval for the reign of Huni (last king of the Third Dynasty): 2678–2561 BC.[3] Relative chronologies also get very close to the date – around 2544 BC (Hornung *et al.* 2006, 490) and 2663–2613 and 2639–2589 respectively (in this case only the time frame for the end of the Third Dynasty involving three kings, von Beckerath 1997, 187).
Sample IFAO_412

Place of origin: Abusir South, Mastaba AS 54 (anonymous), estimated archaeological date: end of the Third Dynasty (Huni) (Bárta 2011). The sample originates from a plank of *Acacia sp.* used in the construction of the niched wall to the east of the mastaba.

Radiocarbon Dating : Conventional ^{14}C age: 4069 ± 57 BP.
δ^{13}C estimated at – 24 ‰ vs PDB.

Calibrated ^{14}C Date (1σ):
2848 BC : 2813 BC, 10.1%
2740 BC : 2730 BC, 2.0%
2693 BC : 2688 BC, 1.1%
2678 BC : 2561 BC, 41.2%
2536 BC : 2492 BC, 13.8%

(Calibration curve : IntCal 09 : Reimer PJ and al., 2009, IntCal 09 and marine 09 radiocarbon age calibration curves, 0–50,000 years cal BP. Radiocarbon 51, Nr4, 1111–1150).

Notes

1 All ^{14}C data used in the article are based on the results of the Oxford Project which were kindly provided to the participants of the conference.
2 Some authors, such as Weiss and Bradley (2001) claim the opposite, e.g. rather quick process.
3 I wish to acknowledge the help of the laboratory director, Michel Wuttmann and his assistant Mohammed Mahran. Ahmad Fahmy, University of Helwan, kindly determined the kind of wood of the sample.

Acknowledgement

This study was supported by the Charles University Scientific developement programme No. 14: Archaeology of non-European areas, sub-project: Ancient Egyptian civilisation research: cultural and political adaptations of the North African civilisations in Antiquity (5,000 BCE–1,000 AD).

References

Bárta, M. 1995, *Archaeology and Iconography: bedja and aperet bread moulds and 'Speisetischszene' development in the Old Kingdom, Sudien zur Altägyptischen Kultur* **22**, Hamburg: Busske Verlag, 21–35.
Bárta, M. 2005, *Architectural Innovations in the development of the non-royal tomb during the reign of Nyuserra. In Structure and Significance. Thoughts on acient Egyptian Architecture* (ed. P. Jánosi), Vienna: Akademie Verlag 105–130.
Bárta, M. 2009, A mistake for the afterlife? In *Studies on Old Kingdom Pottery* (eds T. I. Rzeuska and A. Wodzinska), 43–48, Neriton, Warsaw.
Bárta, M. 2011, An Abusir mastaba from the reign of Huni. In *Times, signs and Pyramids. Studies in Honour of Miroslav Verner on the Occasion of His Seventieth Birthday* (eds V. G. Callender, L.Bareš, M. Bárta, J. Janák and J. Krejčí), 41–50, Czech Institute of Egyptology, Prague.

Ben-Tor, A. 1992, *The archaeology of ancient Israel*, Yale University Press, New Haven.
Bonani, G., Haas, H., Hawass, Z., Lehner, M., Nakhla, S., Nolan, J., Wenke, R. and Wölfli. W. 2001, Radiocarbon dates of Old and Middle Kingdom monuments in Egypt, *Radiocarbon*, 43(3), 1297–1320.
Greenberg, R. and Porat, N. 1996, A third millennium Levantine pottery production center: typology, petrography, and provenance of the metallic ware of northern Israel and adjacent regions, *Bulletin of the American Schools of Oriental Research*, 301, 5–24.
Hornung, E., Krauss, R. and Warburton, D.A. (eds) 2006, *Ancient Egyptian Chronology*, Brill, Leiden and Boston.
Kanawati, N. 1980, *Governmental kingdom reforms in Old Egypt*. Warminster, England, Aris & Phillips.
Kitchen, K. 2011, Regnal and genealogical data of Ancient Egypt (Absolute chronology I). The historical chronology of ancient Egypt, a current assessment, in M. Bietak (ed.), *The synchronization of civilisations in the eastern Mediterranean in the second millennium B.C.*, Verlag der Österreichischen Akademie der Wissenschaften, Wien, 39–51.
Manning, S. W. 2006, Radiocarbon dating and Egyptian chronology, in *Ancient Egyptian Chronology* (eds E. Hornung, R. Krauss and D. A. Warburton), 327–355, Brill, Leiden and Boston.
Malek, J. 2000, The Old Kingdom, *The Oxford History of Ancient Egypt* (ed. I. Shaw), 89–117, Oxford University Press, Oxford.
Richards, J. 2002, Text and context in late Old Kingdom Egypt: the archaeology and historiography of Weni the Elder, *Journal of the American Research Center in Egypt*, **39**, 75–102.
Spence, K. 2000, Ancient Egyptian chronology and the astronomical orientation of pyramids, *Nature* **408**(6810), 16 November 2000, 320–324.
Verner, M. 2001, Archaeological remarks on the 4th and 5th Dynasty chronology, *Archiv Orientalni* 69.3, 363–418.
von Beckerath, J. 1997, *Chronologie des Pharaonischen Ägypten*, Münchner ägyptologische Studien 46.
Weiss, H. and Bradley, R. S. 2001, What drives societal collapse?, *Science*, **291**(5520), 609–10.
Wilkinson, T. 2011, *The Rise and Fall of Ancient Egypt*, Random House, New York.

Chapter 18
Early Dynastic Egyptian Chronologies

E. C. Köhler

This paper will discuss several approaches relevant to the chronology of the Early Dynastic Period in Egypt. It will first summarize the historiography and current historical evidence of the period and how they compare to other phases of Pharaonic Egyptian history. For example, while the sequence of rulers of the 1st Egyptian Dynasty is relatively well defined and generally accepted, there are still outstanding problems relating to the so-called ephemeral rulers that do not seem to fit the current sequence as, for example, supported by ancient historiographers. Also, in contrast to the 1st Dynasty, the sequence of kings of the 2nd Dynasty is even less understood and poses significant problems for the political history, and thus historical chronology, of this time, which has obvious implications for any attempts at an absolute chronology, at least as far as historical data are concerned. The paper will further discuss currently available chronological frameworks resulting from relative dating in the Early Dynastic Period. For example, it will address the existing parameters more recently proposed by Werner Kaiser and Stan Hendrickx that primarily result from the excavations in the Early Dynastic royal necropolis at Abydos. The basic principle of this chronology is the observation that certain diagnostic ceramic types either occur in certain royal tombs or carry the names of Early Dynastic rulers, which obviously helps in establishing ceramic sequences and a correlation of ceramic data with the historical chronology. On the other hand, the paper will also highlight problems in this approach that have arisen from the on-going excavations in the large private necropolis at Helwan, where this chronology has only limited applicability. In conclusion, this paper will raise a number of issues, including historiography, the lack of historical evidence as well as problems in the application of current relative and absolute chronologies of the Early Dynastic Period in order to identify areas where definite answers are yet to be found and where scholarship needs to proceed before new absolute scientific data can successfully be synchronized and integrated in an overall historical chronology of Pharaonic Egypt.

Introduction

The first 500–700 years of Pharaonic history, also known as the Archaic or Early Dynastic Period, is one of the more problematic phases whose precise chronological delineation is still much debated. When aiming at synchronizing absolute and historical chronology, as was the objective of this project, there are still vast abysses to be bridged before these two can be correlated. There are a number of reasons for this and its successful resolution depends both on various definitions, as well as the methods and sources chosen in this attempt. It is important to investigate the period from a variety of angles and at three different levels, namely historical, relative and absolute chronology, although these are not always consistent

---

Author's Address: **E. C. Köhler**, Institute for Egyptology, University of Vienna, Frankgasse 1, A-1090, Vienna, Austria

18. Early Dynastic Egyptian Chronologies

Table 18.1: Overview of early Pharaonic chronologies

		0TH DYNASTY /PROTODYNASTIC	1ST DYNASTY	2ND DYNASTY	3RD DYNASTY
HISTORICAL CHRONOLOGY					
	Min. length in years	60?	110	140	48
	Max. length in years	200?	225	225	75
RELATIVE CHRONOLOGY		Naqada IIIA1/2 – IIIB	Naqada IIIC1–3	Naqada IIID	?
ABSOLUTE CHRONOLOGY IN YEARS c. BC	Hornung et al. (2006)		2900–2730	2730–2590	2592–2544
	Shaw (2000)		3000–2890	2890–2686	2686–2625
	Grimal (1992)		3150–2925	2925–2700	2700–2625
	^{14}C	3300–3100	3100–2850	2850–2680	2680–2620

or complementary and are yet to be fully reconciled (Table 18.1, see also Rowland 2008, 10–11). In the following, we will discuss these three levels individually, i.e. historical, relative and absolute, in order to illustrate current problems and to propose possible solutions.

Historical chronology

According to traditional historiography, the Early Dynastic Period comprises the rulers of the 1st and 2nd Dynasties, from the first apparent historical king of Egypt down to those kings who directly preceded Djoser of the 3rd (von Beckerath 1997), although some scholars would also consider including the 3rd Dynasty in this earliest of historical periods (e.g. Hornung et al. 2006, 490; Wilkinson 1999). This traditional historical chronology is primarily based on Ancient Egyptian king-lists, such as the Abydos list in the temple of Sety I. of the 19th Dynasty, or Manetho's sequence of kings. However, in addition to the king-lists, there are also other categories of evidence, such as contemporary inscriptions, which seem to suggest that the dynastic sequence of rulers could be extended backwards by several generations. This is why many scholars include the so-called 0th Dynasty as part of the Early Dynastic Period, although the beginning and ordering of this group of rulers is also matter of ongoing discussion (e.g. there is the suggestion to insert a 00th Dynasty, but this has never been accepted as a serious option). While some would limit this term to two individuals directly preceding king Narmer, i.e. Iry-Hor and Ka/Sekhen, others would extend it back considerably further. The reasoning for the latter is that the royal cemetery at Abydos, where all of the kings of the 1st Dynasty and others are buried, probably began with the tomb of an early ruler (tomb U-j) which exhibits evidence for the major hallmarks of Early Dynastic culture, including complex architecture, political and social complexity as well as early hieroglyphic writing (Kaiser 1990, 295). The date of this tomb would extend the beginning of the Early Dynastic Period by around 150–200 years before the 1st Dynasty. However, what still needs to be attended to is the question as to what extent this 0th Dynasty actually applies to the political history and chronology of the Egyptian Nile Valley as a whole. This is because there is growing evidence to suggest that at the time, the country was not under unified, centralized control by one dynasty, but instead divided into several regional polities or 'proto-kingdoms'. Although royal names of some of the Abydene rulers are attested outside Abydos, it does not necessarily follow that they also governed in the location of such attestations. It may simply indicate diplomatic or trade contacts between polities. The chronological applicability of the term 0th Dynasty would therefore have to be reduced to the region of Abydos, where this dynasty presumably ruled. This is why some scholars have cautiously suggested re-introducing the term 'Protodynastic' for the period just prior to political unification (Köhler 2004, 310). Whatever the period is called, it represents a significant challenge to the historical chronology and its validity for the entire Egyptian Nile Valley prior to the 1st Dynasty. It may well be that, at least with regard to the beginning of political unity, the historical sources as represented in the Pharaonic king-lists could indeed reflect a degree of accuracy.

What the Egyptian king-lists generally have in common is that they start the sequence of human rulers (preceded by gods and spirits in Manetho's account, as well as in the Turin Canon) with a king named *Mnj*, or Menes. But before Manetho's 3rd century BC account of the history of the Pharaohs, the names of kings after Menes were not organised in dynasties as we refer to them today. For example, the Abydos list simply lists king after king without any attempt at internal subdivision. On the other hand, the Turin Canon occasionally provides sums or grand totals of regnal years counted after Menes, such as after the reign of Unas of the 5th Dynasty, and only for the later periods lists groups of kings that would roughly correspond to Manetho's dynasties.

Manetho allocates eight names to his 1st Dynasty, and depending on the Late Antique, and often edited, copy of Manetho's original text, this dynasty amounts to 253–262 years. But these figures have been questioned by historians, partly because some of the individual ruler's lengths seem unlikely, and partly because there is no reliable contemporary evidence to support this (von Beckerath 1997, 178–9; Kahl 2006, 100–101). Considering the temporal distance of about 2800 years between Manetho and the period in question, as well as the sometimes dubious quality of information provided by this ancient writer (e.g. the entry for Menes: "He led the army across the frontier and won great glory. He was killed by a hippopotamus," or for the seventh king: "In his reign there were many extraordinary events, and there was an immense disaster", transl. Verbrugghe and Wickersham 1996), it is also highly probable that Manetho's own sources were not entirely complete or dependable.

Although the number of eight kings for the 1st Dynasty, as suggested by Manetho, has recently found some corroboration in contemporary sources, the maximum length allocated to this dynasty still varies considerably between 110 (Shaw 2000, 480), 179 (von Beckerath 1997, 179) and 225 years (Grimal 1992, 389), which is due to the fact that there is very little evidence to determine the length of individual reigns. Apart from Manetho's sums mentioned above, such estimates are also based on the very fragmentary information

18. Early Dynastic Egyptian Chronologies

contained in the Palermo Stone, the Turin Canon, as well as sources that make reference to certain events, such as *hebsed* festivals, which allow for a rough determination of the length of a reign (Kahl 2006, 99–101).

Another, equally significant, historical problem surrounding the 1st Dynasty is the identification of some of its kings. There is one simple reason for this: the royal names in the 19th Dynasty Abydos king-list, for example, are inscribed in cartouches identifying these kings by their birth name. This is a common form of identification for deceased kings, but it is not much employed until the early Old Kingdom. However, because the standard royal titulary comprising five names was only just developing at that time, early Egyptian kings in contemporary sources were initially only known by their Horus name or *serekh* (Protodynastic/0th Dynasty and later). During the 1st Dynasty the throne name (from King Den onwards) and the so-called Mistresses name were added (late 1st Dynasty; von Beckerath 1999, 2–3), but birth names were possibly not recorded in the contemporary official sources. We therefore still do not know with certainty who is behind many of the early names (see Dreyer 1987) or, more importantly still, behind Menes himself (for discussion, see Baud 1999). Although at least this particular problem may now be solved: recent archaeological work in the royal cemetery at Abydos has produced evidence that could confirm Manetho's account of eight 1st Dynasty kings. This evidence comprises two mud seals, which once may have sealed the entrance to the tomb of king Den as well as of king Qa'a, respectively, and which bear impressions of cylinder seals that list the name of that particular king as well as his predecessors (Dreyer 1987, fig. 3; Dreyer *et al.* 1996, fig. 26; Kaiser 1987). The seal from the tomb of Qa'a, thought to be the last king of the 1st Dynasty, is therefore the most interesting one, as it names him as well as all the other kings of his dynasty in two parallel lines on top of one another; a historical source of exceptional value (Figure 18.1). It starts with the jackal deity Khontamenti on one side, with whom the deceased kings appear to be identified, followed by Horus Qa'a, then Semerkhet, Adjib, Den, Djet, Djer, Aha and finally probably Narmer, although one

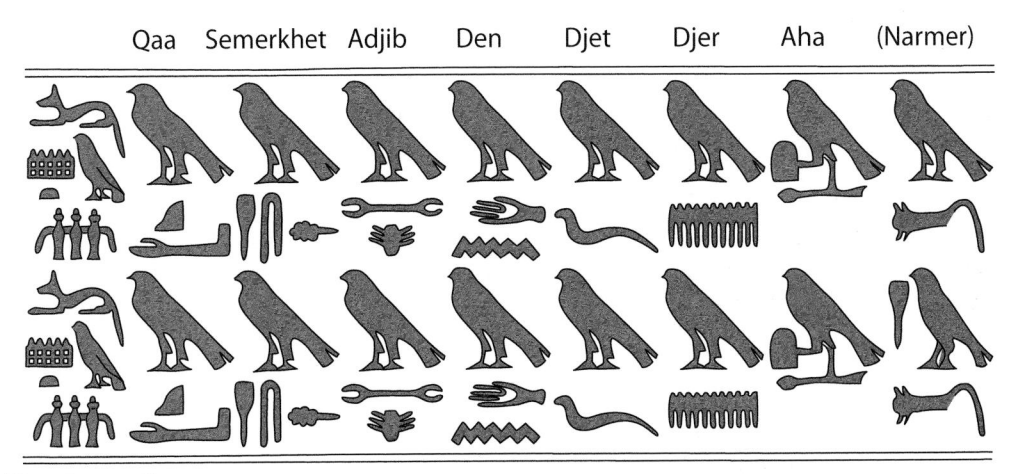

Figure 18.1: 1st Dynasty king-list from the tomb of Qa'a at Abydos (based on Dreyer et al. 1996, fig. 26).

of the signs in his name is written differently from the sources contemporary with his reign. The horizontal sign of the catfish, which is the most consistent element in his *serekhs*, is incomplete and has a long, curved animal tail, but the other part of his name, the vertical chisel sign, is inscribed before the Horus falcon in the second row, making the reading of Narmer likely. The same form of writing also occurs on the earlier seal from the tomb of king Den. What this apparent alteration of Narmer's name could illustrate is that only a few generations after this king's reign, the correct spelling of his name may already have been lost or changed. Nevertheless, synchronizing this 1st Dynasty king-list with Manetho's eight kings would therefore result in Narmer being the same ruler as Menes (but see Dreyer 1987), and thus the first historically attested king of Egypt, if we are to believe pharaonic king-lists.

However, it is possible that also this evidence is inaccurate, because there is discussion surrounding several so-called ephemeral kings, namely Horus Ba, 'Bird' and Sneferka (von Beckerath 1999, 47), whose names are recorded. For example, in the case of Sneferka, they appear on three stone vessel fragments from Saqqara in the usual form of a Horus name, in association with certain administrative institutions which are also known from the time of king Qa'a. There are currently three suggestions as to how their existence could be explained. The first proposes that the names represent alternative names for known kings (e.g. Lacau and Lauer 1959, 15; von Beckerath 1999, 46); another, that they represent separate individuals who ruled as usurpers during or after the reign of Qa'a (Emery 1958, 31; Kahl 2006, 101); and a third, that at least one of them, Sneferka, should be dated to the late 2nd Dynasty, as this name may represent a garbled spelling of king Neferkare in the Abydos king-list (Ryholt 2008). While any one of these suggestions is feasible, there is a strong possibility that these ephemeral kings did exist and represented rulers whose legitimacy was not acknowledged in later sources. This is not uncommon in ancient Egyptian historiography where, as for instance in the Abydos king-list, entire periods of up to 250 years in length have been omitted (Kemp 1989, fig. 4). If so, the discussion surrounding the historical chronology of the 1st Dynasty, which actually stands out as one of the better defined phases during this early period, is also still open.

According to the same traditional historical chronology based on pharaonic king-lists, between a minimum of 140 (Hornung *et al.* 2006, 490; von Beckerath 1997, 179) and a maximum of 225 years (Grimal 1992, 389) have been attributed to a group of seven to nine rulers of the 2nd Dynasty, but scholars are still working on their precise number and sequence. The names and sequence of the first three rulers, Hetepsekhemwy, Raneb and Nynetjer, seem to be relatively certain, but the kings subsequent to these are not (Kahl 2006, 102–108; Kahl 2007). Likewise, the 3rd Dynasty incorporates between five and seven kings and its duration is estimated at 48 (Hornung *et al.* 2006, 490), 68 (von Beckerath 1997, 179) and 75 years (Grimal 1992, 389). The 3rd Dynasty is much shorter and thus possibly better delineated than the earlier dynasties. In any case, historically and archaeologically, the 2nd Dynasty represents a greater chronological problem than the periods preceding and following it, which is largely due to the fact that many of the 2nd Dynasty royal tombs in Saqqara cannot be attributed with certainty or are yet to be found, and because there is little reliable contemporary evidence from this period.

The problems and ongoing debates surrounding the historical definition of the Early Dynastic Period clearly illustrate how the history of early Pharaonic Egypt is not a straightforward exercise of adding up names and time-lines of kings, i.e. dead reckoning, as is so often possible in later periods. One of the key sources, apart from the 1st Dynasty king-lists from Abydos, which is also relatively close in time to the Early Dynastic, is the Palermo Stone from the late Old Kingdom, but this monument is so fragmentary that it still only allows for highly speculative reconstructions (Baud 1999; Wilkinson 2000). There are no Sothic dates or any other astronomical occurrences that could be employed for the purpose of dating. The historical chronology therefore heavily relies on a variety of additional, often divergent, sources including written sources contemporary with and subsequent to the period, as well as archaeological evidence. This complementary use of such fundamentally different areas of evidence is particularly necessary in these early periods, because the written evidence is very sketchy and often inconsistent, but it also bears its own dangers, especially when trying to fill gaps in one body of evidence with the fragmentary evidence of another.

In conclusion, because of the fundamental conceptual and evidentiary shortcomings in ancient historiography, paired with the lack of comprehensive contemporary historical data, the historical sequence of the first 500–700 years of Pharaonic history alone will not be helpful as a backbone or even starting point of any synchronization.

Relative chronology

In comparison with historical sources, the Early Dynastic Period has a lot more to offer when we consider archaeological evidence. There is one simple reason for this: the very lack of comprehensive historical data forced scholars to focus on archaeological sources in order to establish temporal frameworks and sequences. In archaeological terms, the Early Dynastic can be equated with the final stage of the so-called Naqada Culture, i.e. Naqada III (cf. Table 1), which arose out of earlier, prehistoric traditions of the 5th and 4th Millennia B.C. This period was under intensive investigation during the 20th century when its internal relative chronology was established, initially by Flinders Petrie who was the first to discover the Sequence Dates and typological sequences of ceramics that are still the backbone of relative dating today (Petrie 1899). Petrie's work was refined by Werner Kaiser from the 1950s onwards (Kaiser 1957) and this work has also experienced revision by more recent scholars, in particular Stan Hendrickx, whose modifications (Hendrickx 1996; 1999) are now widely followed. However, the relative chronology, as it stands today, is still under review (Hendrickx, 2011; Köhler, 2011). The majority of studies of early relative chronology rest on the analysis of typologically diagnostic ceramic vessels deriving from mortuary contexts. But even stratified settlement remains in some regions are dated in this manner; although it may require refinement in the future. Currently, however, Naqada III is divided into 4 subphases, A–D, which have further subdivisions. For the purpose of dating in the archaeological context, it is preferable to employ these Naqada phases instead of using dynastic terms, especially in the absence of royal names or any other historical references, which applies to the vast majority of archaeological evidence of this time.

Thanks to comprehensive archaeological research in the royal cemetery at Abydos over more than 100 years, it was possible to identify diagnostic artifacts in the tomb assemblages of individual kings and thus to correlate typological sequences with the historical chronology. For example, the key type for establishing the relative chronology is Petrie's

Wavy Handled class of pottery, whose earliest stages are represented by prehistoric globular vessels with two wavy ledge handles on either side and whose further development sees a gradual straightening of the body shape, subsequent loss of function of the wavy handles in favor of a wavy decoration, followed by abandonment of the decoration and finally morphological and qualitative deterioration. There is a solid quantity of such cylindrical vessels from the early royal tombs at Abydos in various stages of development that allow for a smooth typological sequence to be established that extends well into the historical period, thus bridging prehistory and history. But importantly, there are also numerous vessels of that type that bear the names of early Egyptian rulers and it is in turn this very typological sequence that has enabled scholars to define the succession of kings from the 0th Dynasty to the early 1st Dynasty (Kaiser and Dreyer 1982). It is therefore possible to date archaeological contexts where such vessels are found, even without royal names and outside the royal necropolis, within a very narrow window of time. For example, vessels that are cylindrical in shape and have an incised line below the rim have been found bearing ink inscriptions with the Horus name of Ka/Sekhen of the 0th Dynasty. Comparing these with those of his predecessors and successors, it is possible to deduce that the typological stage with incised line, which dates Naqada IIIB in relative terms (cf. Hendrickx 1999, fig. 9), is possibly limited to a short period before the beginning of the 1st Dynasty.

What is also assisting in this chronology is the observation that many of these vessels appear to have been manufactured by either one workshop or in one region as they tend to be made of the same clay fabric, namely a fine, dense Marl clay. This further enhances their applicability for dating across Egypt, even as far as the Nile Delta and beyond as well as Nubia, where such vessels have also been found. But, this apparent advantage also poses its own limitations, because the further distant an object is found from the place of production the greater the value and use-life of such a vessel may be and the more likely it is, that it had been in circulation for longer before it ended up in its final archaeological context.

Further, it has been observed that soon after the beginning of the 1st Dynasty, these cylindrical vessels are no longer made of this particular Marl clay fabric, but instead display greater fabric heterogeneity, and indeed, there is the suggestion that they later may have been manufactured and distributed regionally. If that is the case, then there is also scope for interregional distribution variability and delay; from the point of introduction of this type, to manufacture, to distribution, usage and final deposition, depending on how the place of deposition was connected logistically and economically with the place of manufacture. This is an important point, because although these types of ceramic vessels are abundant and thus popular tools in relative dating, they also are absent in places where one would expect them and it is possible that even during a time of wide distribution, say during the 1st Dynasty, they do not necessarily occur everywhere. This problem can be illustrated with recent work at Helwan, which is the largest necropolis of the Early Dynastic Period in all of Egypt. More than 10,000 tombs have been uncovered during the 1940s and 50s, and over 200 more during the Australian (-Austrian) excavations since 1998. It was possible to record a large quantity of the ceramic material from the old excavations in on-site storage tombs (Smythe 2004; 2008). Cylindrical vessels in varying stages of typological development have been found in abundance, which allowed for a further refinement of the typological sequence. Previously, it had been suggested that this type of vessel fell out of use just before the end of the 1st Dynasty and with this, the end of Naqada IIIC was determined. Although Kaiser had included a third sub-stage in his Naqada IIIC chronology, he did not elaborate on its definition, which caused Hendrickx to condense Kaiser's three sub-stages (Naqada IIIc1–3) into two (Naqada IIIC1–2, Hendrickx 1999). The material deriving from the end of the 1st Dynasty, i.e. from the tombs of kings Semerkhet and Qa'a at Abydos, was consequently dated to the next stage, i.e. Naqada IIID, as cylindrical vessels were not attested. However, the solid quantity of vessels from Helwan provided a tight morphological sequence suggesting that Naqada IIIC again be extended by one more sub-phase, i.e. IIIC3, now including the end of the 1st Dynasty. This is because specimens of the latest typological stage, which are no longer cylindrical but slightly conical, did occur in the tombs of Semerkhet and Qa'a (Köhler 2004; Smythe 2004). On the other hand, it is currently not possible to state with certainty how long this latest stage, Naqada IIIC3, lasted because there is insufficient reliable and published evidence from early 2nd Dynasty contexts to allow for such a determination.

Furthermore, although large numbers of cylindrical vessels have been recorded from the earlier excavations at Helwan, i.e. more than 230 pieces, the recent excavations in archaeologically intact areas cannot report the same quantities, a fact which requires some attention. Although large quantities of pottery have been recovered during 14 seasons of excavations in an area known as Operation 4, sometimes more than 20,000 ceramic fragments per tomb structure, very few fragmentary specimens of cylindrical vessels have been recorded, and none of them derive from a sufficiently reliable archaeological context and therefore do not aid in our archaeological dating. There are a number of possibilities to explain this. Either, the tombs in question date outside the chronological parameters of Naqada IIIC, or the individuals buried here happened not to have used such vessels for funerary purposes. Both options are very possible and neither has been rejected yet, especially because excavations are on-going and final analysis is pending. So far, however, the tombs have largely been dated individually through examination of their architecture and assemblages as well as their parallels from other sites.

As for the possibility that the lack of cylindrical vessels could have chronological causes, it is interesting to note that there are tombs that display all the hallmarks that one would expect for Naqada IIIC funerary assemblages, i.e. architecture, ceramics and certain other artefacts, such as rectangular cosmetic palettes. However, as the current definition of this period heavily relies on this one type of ceramic vessel, the evidence is not sufficient to securely date these burials to Naqada IIIC. This is why we have labeled those tombs that belong to our earliest stage of occupation in this area Naqada IIICD to accommodate the possibility of them being later.

The other possibility, namely that the use of cylindrical vessels in funerary assemblages may have been a matter of individual preference, may have some justification, too, but is difficult to prove. From the archaeological contexts, where cylindrical vessels have previously been found, it is not possible to reduce their occurrence to any particular social, gender or even biological group of occupants. Cylindrical vessels have been found in wealthy and poor burials, as well as in animal burials (e.g. the burial of a dog with two cylindrical vessels in Saad 1969, pl. 121) and indeed actually seem very ubiquitous in the Helwan cemetery. If there were any other pre-selection factor in place, it is currently impossible to determine with certainty.

The example of the missing cylinders in Helwan obviously exposes the limitations of relative dating with the help of one index fossil alone, which should not be surprising, but it has become common practice among archaeologists dating early Egyptian contexts. It is therefore necessary to involve other dating criteria as well. For example, the close analysis of tomb assemblages from Saad's time has assisted in developing other typological sequences in order to broaden the parameters for relative dating. One such typological sequence arose out of the proportional index of so-called ceramic wine jars which are tall and well-made storage containers. It has been observed that over time, the vessels become smaller and more elongated ranging between just over double as high as wide (1:2) to over five times as high as they are wide (1:5) (Köhler and Smythe 2004; Smythe 2008). Aligning this proportional index with specimen from the royal tombs at Abydos has enabled us to establish index values for Naqada IIIB, IIIC and even beyond, and it is now possible to discover internal subdivisions of the previously ill-defined stage Naqada IIID. However, what is not clear yet is the precise correlation of Naqada IIID with the historical chronology and its relation to archaeological material from the 3rd Dynasty and the later Old Kingdom. What is clear, though, is that the material assemblages continue to develop gradually beyond Naqada IIID and that a suitable terminology for relative dating of later material is yet to be found.

Absolute chronology

Numerous absolute dates of early 3rd Millennium Egypt have been published over the years since scientific dating techniques have become more established in archaeology (e.g., Hassan 1985; Görsdorf *et al.* 1998; Savage 1998, 2001; Midant-Reynes and Sabatier 1999; Bonani *et al.* 2001; Manning 2006; Rowland 2008). A particular focus of absolute dating have been the royal tombs at Abydos and it has been concluded that some of these dates seem to be 'in good accordance with the so far established historical chronology of the dynastic period' (Görsdorf *et al.* 1998, 175), although it must be noted that some of the samples used for these date series derive from contexts of uncertain historical value, such as tomb B40. The excavator considered this tomb to belong to the 2nd king of the 1st Dynasty, Athothis I (Dreyer 1987), although the archaeological evidence is inconclusive. It must be remembered that the historical chronology itself is far from certain (see above) and that much of the analyzed material derives from either old excavations, and thus ambiguous primary contexts, or from secondary contexts (at best) resulting from repeated ancient and modern plunder as well as early excavations. A scientifically reliable correlation between scientific analysis results with historical data is therefore yet to be established. Although the 'old wood problem' does not seem to apply to Early Dynastic constructions as much as it does with Old Kingdom pyramid structures (Manning 2006, 343), the problem remains that without sufficient contextual information, any absolute dates must be considered with caution. It is obvious that a much broader quantitative and qualitative approach needs to be taken in order to solve these chronological issues. And this is precisely what is currently being attempted by teams of international scholars, whose object is to investigate the relative, historical and absolute chronologies of early Egypt[1]. It would be premature to report on results, but what seems to emerge as a possible outcome is that the chronology proposed by Hornung *et al.* (2006) is probably too low and should be corrected upwards by about 150–200 years. It is also imperative that, instead of testing and re-evaluating material from old excavations, more focused research at new excavation sites is necessary in order to determine the precise correlation first between relative and absolute chronology and second how these two could be synchronized with the historical chronology.

Note

1 As, for example, the projects currently conducted at the Oxford Radiocarbon Accelerator Unit, the group of archaeologists contributing in *Archeo-Nil* 21 (in press) as well as collaborative work under the auspices of the German Institute for Archaeology in Cairo (DAI), the French Institute for Oriental Archaeology in Cairo (IFAO) and the University of Vienna, Institute for Egyptology.

References

Baud, M. 1999, Ménès, la mémoire monarchique et la chronologie du IIIe millénaire, *Archéo-Nil*, **9**, 109–148.
Bonani, G., Hass, H., Hawass, Z., Lehner, M., Nakhla, S., Nolan, J., Wenke, R. and Wolfli, W. 2001, Radiocarbon dates of Old and Middle Kingdom monuments in Egypt, *Radiocarbon*, **43**(3), 1297–1320.
Dreyer, G. 1987, Ein Siegel der frühzeitlichen Nekropole von Abydos, *Mitteilungen des Deutschen Archäologischen Instituts Kairo*, **43**, 33–43.
Dreyer, G., Engel, E.-M., Hartung, U., Hikade, T., Köhler, E. C. and Pumpenmeier, F. 1996, Umm el-Qaab. Nachuntersuchungen im frühzeitlichen Königsfriedhof. 7./8, Vorbericht, *Mitteilungen des Deutschen Archäologischen Instituts Kairo*, **52**, 11–81.
Emery, W. B. 1958, *Great Tombs of the First Dynasty*, Vol. III, Egypt Exploration Society, London.
Görsdorf, J., Dreyer, G. and Hartung, U. 1998, ^{14}C-dating results of the archaic royal necropolis Umm el-Qaab at Abydos, *Mitteilungen des Deutschen Archäologischen Instituts Kairo*, **54**, 169–176.
Grimal, N. 1992, *A History of Ancient Egypt*, (transl. by I. Shaw), Blackwells, London.
Hassan, F. A. 1985, Radiocarbon chronology of neolithic and predynastic sites in Upper Egypt and the Delta, *The African Archaeological Review*, **3**, 95–116.
Hendrickx, S. 1996, The Relative chronology of the Naqada culture: problems and possibilities, in *Aspects of Early Egypt* (ed. J. Spencer), 36–69, Dorset Press, London.
Hendrickx, S. 1999, La chronologie de la préhistoire tardive et des débuts de l'histoire de l'Egypte, *Archéo-Nil*, **9**, 13–82.
Hendrickx, S. 2011, Naqada IIIA–B, a crucial phase in the relative chronology of the Naqada culture, *Archéo-Nil*, **21**, 65–80.
Hornung, E., Krauss, R. and Warburton, D. A. (eds.) 2006, *Ancient Egyptian Chronology*, Brill, Leiden and Boston.
Kahl, J. 2006, Dynasties 0–2, in *Ancient Egyptian Chronology* (eds E. Hornung, R. Krauss and D. A. Warburton), 94–115, Brill, Leiden and Boston.
Kahl, J. 2007, *Ra is my Lord. Searching for the Rise of the Sun God at the Dawn of Egyptian History*, Harrassowitz, Wiesbaden.
Kaiser, W. 1957, Zur inneren Chronologie der Naqadakultur, *Archaeologia Geographica*, **6**, 69–77.
Kaiser, W. 1987, Zum Siegel mit frühen Königsnamen von Umm el-Qaab, *Mitteilungen des Deutschen Archäologischen Instituts Kairo*, **43**, 115–119.
Kaiser, W. 1990, Zur Entstehung des gesamtägyptischen staates, *Mitteilungen des Deutschen Archäologischen Instituts Kairo*, **46**, 287–299.

Kaiser, W. and Dreyer, G. 1982, Umm el-Qaab. Nachuntersuchungen im frühzeitlichen Königsfriedhof. 2. Vorbericht, *Mitteilungen des Deutschen Archäologischen Instituts Kairo*, **38**, 211–269.

Kemp, B. J. 1989, *Ancient Egypt. Anatomy of a Civilisation*, Routledge, London.

Köhler, E. C. 2004, On the origins of Memphis – the new excavations in the Early Dynastic necropolis at Helwan. In *Egypt at its Origins. Studies in Memory of Barbara Adams* (eds S. Hendrickx, R. F. Friedman, C. Cialowicz, and C. Chlodnicki), 295–315, Peeters, Leuven.

Köhler, E. C. 2011, Introduction, *Archéo-Nil*, **21**, 5–11.

Köhler E. C. and Smythe, J. 2004, Early Dynastic pottery from Helwan: establishing a ceramic corpus of the Naqada III Period, *Cahiers de la Céramique Égyptienne*, **7**, 123–144.

Lacau, P. and Lauer, J.-P. 1959, *La Pyramide à Degrees, Tome IV. Inscriptions Gravées sur les Vases*, Institut français d'Archéologie orientale, Cairo.

Manning, S. W. 2006, Radiocarbon dating and Egyptian chronology, in *Ancient Egyptian Chronology* (eds E. Hornung, R. Krauss and D. A. Warburton), 327–355, Brill, Leiden and Boston.

Midant-Reynes, B. and Sabatier, P. 1999, Préhistoire et radiocarbone. *Archéo-Nil*, **9**, 83–108.

Petrie, F. W. M. 1899, Sequences in prehistoric remains, *Journal of the Anthropological Institute*, **29**, 295–301.

Rowland, J. M. 2008, Building bridges between radiocarbon, relative and historical chronologies: the case of early Egypt, in *Chronology and Archaeology in Ancient Egypt (the Third Millennium)* (eds H. Vymazalova and M. Barta), 10–22, Charles University, Prague.

Ryholt, K. 2008, King Senerferka in the king-lists and his position in the Early Dynastic period, *Journal of Egyptian History*, **1**, 159–173.

Saad, Z. Y. 1969, *The Excavations at Helwan*, Norman, Oklahoma.

Savage, S. H. 1998, AMS radiocarbon dates from the predynastic Egyptian cemetery, N7000, at Naga-ed-Dêr, *Journal of Archaeological Science*, **25**, 235–249.

Savage, S. H. 2001, Towards an AMS radiocarbon chronology of predynastic Egyptian ceramics, *Radiocarbon*, **43**, 1255–1277.

Shaw, I. (ed.) 2000, *The Oxford History of Ancient Egypt*, Oxford University Press, Oxford.

Smythe, J. 2004, The pottery from Operation 3, Tomb 1, in *Egypt at its Origins. Studies in Memory of Barbara Adams* (eds S. Hendrickx, R. F. Friedman, C. Cialowicz and C. Chlodnicki), 317–335, Peeters, Leuven.

Smythe, S. 2008, New results from a second storage tomb at Helwan. Implications for the Naqada III period in the Memphite region, in *Egypt at its Origins 2* (eds Midant-Reynes, B., Tristant, Y. and Hendrickx, S.), 151–186, Peeters, Leuven.

Verbrugghe, G. P. and Wickersham, J. M. 1996, *Berossos and Manetho, Introduced and Translated. Native Traditions in ancient Mesopotamia and Egypt*, University of Michigan Press, Ann Arbor.

Wilkinson, T. A. H. 1999, *Early Dynastic Egypt*, Routledge, London and New York.

Wilkinson, T. A. H. 2000, *Royal Annals of Ancient Egypt. The Palermo Stone and its Associated Fragments*, Kegan Paul International, London and New York.

von Beckerath, J. 1997, *Chronologie des Pharaonischen Ägypten. Die Zeitbestimmung der Ägyptischen Geschichte von der Vorzeit bis 332 v. Chr.*, Verlag Philipp von Zabern, Mainz.

von Beckerath, J. 1999, *Handbuch der Ägyptischen Königsnamen*. Verlag Philipp von Zabern, Mainz.

CHAPTER 19

Problems and Possibilities for Achieving Absolute Dates from Prehistoric and Early Historical Contexts

J. M. Rowland

The process of selecting suitable material for the absolute dating of Early Dynastic Egypt is problematic. It is not always the organic material that is in non-sustainable supply, rather the difficulty of finding suitable material from a sound archaeological provenance. As part of the Leverhulme Egyptian Chronology Project, 20 new dates were produced from organic samples dating to the 1st and 2nd Dynasties. These samples were chosen from a number of different archaeological contexts, contexts which have also provided ^{14}C measurements in the past, namely the sites of Abydos, Saqqara, Tarkhan and Maasara. A comprehensive study of the materials and contexts of such previous Early Dynastic ^{14}C measurements presented a good opportunity to examine the suitability of both context and material before proceeding to select material for the new project. It also allowed us to consider the percentage of absolute dates that we might have expected to be reliable or otherwise. For the Predynastic and early Dynastic periods, the lack of historical correlates presents a great challenge and therefore the utmost rigour is needed for sample selection if we are to look towards creating a reliable absolute chronology that will be of practical use to researchers concerned with early Egyptian archaeology. As such, the starting point for the collection of all dates on this project was that they should be short-lived plant remains, coming from objects found within secure contexts and ideally not objects which had either been subjected to conservation or objects for which the method of conservation had not been documented. This paper will therefore discuss object and material types that have proven most suitable for dating, as well as examining reliable and less reliable contexts, and it will ask how we can move forward to apply these absolute dates to current research questions in early Egyptian archaeology – in particular the mechanisms by and speed at which people and/or material culture spread at the end of the Predynastic and beginning of the Early Dynastic period.

Introduction

During the symposium, three papers diverted attention to periods outside of the main chronological focus of both the meeting, and also the Oxford chronology project. The first two of these are addressed in the contributions (this volume) by Sally McAleely and John Taylor (New Kingdom and early Third Intermediate Period) and the third here. Although the project was primarily focused upon the historical era, given its aim of synchronising historical dates with radiocarbon measurements, a small series of new dates was achieved on organic material from the first two Egyptian dynasties. The chronology of the prehistoric and early historic periods in Egypt has been shaped to a large extent by dates obtained through scientific dating since the implementation of these methods in the middle of the

Author's Address: **J. M. Rowland**, Ägyptologisches Seminar, Freie Universität Berlin, Altensteinstraße 33, 14195 Berlin, Germany

last century. Given the obvious lack of 'historical' correlates, a greater reliance has long been placed upon the Thermoluminescence (TL) and Optically Stimulated Luminescence (OSL) methods, in addition to radiocarbon measurements (^{14}C). This has resulted in a disproportionately high number of radiocarbon dates for predominantly prehistoric, but also early historic contexts.

Chronological research into the Pre- and Early Dynastic period: the emergence of relative dating systems

Chronological research into the Egyptian Pre- and Early Dynastic periods began in earnest at the turn of the last century with the realisation by J. de Morgan, working at Abydos and Naqada in 1896, that the material being excavated was in fact prehistoric (Adams 1988, 68). Although he had previously considered that the prehistoric cemeteries were to be dated to the First Intermediate Period (Petrie and Quibell 1896, 59–64; Baumgartel 1947, 25–26), Flinders Petrie was the first to systematically examine the material culture of the cemeteries of the Egyptian Nile Valley, initiating the method of ceramic seriation. At the time of the publication of *Naqada and Ballas* (Petrie and Quibell 1896), Petrie (1920, 1) noted that the subject under study was 'entirely new' and that any 'discrimination of periods' could not be attempted. Petrie initially placed the ceramics into a chronological sequence, by examining the presence and absence of certain types within burials at the cemeteries of Abadiyeh, Hu and Ballas (Petrie 1901). Once the sequence of the occurrence and co-occurrence of ceramic types was established, Petrie assigned a series of *Sequence Dates* (SD) and assigned ceramics types within this sequence. The numbering system for the Sequence Dates originally began at SD30, given that Petrie was well aware that the discovery of earlier material was inevitable and the sub SD30 dates were left available to be assigned to ceramic types as yet not found. Within his system of seriation, Petrie included non-ceramic items found within burial assemblages of the Nile Valley, including the stone vessels of various stone types, ivory objects, and cosmetic palettes. Petrie published two further volumes relating to this research, the 'Corpus of Prehistoric Pottery and Palettes' and the 'Corpus of Proto-Dynastic Pottery' (Petrie 1921, 1953).

Petrie's system of sequence dates is still actively used and referred to in the current literature; however, two further major works on the relative chronology of Predynastic and Early Dynastic contexts have emerged since the 1950s, that of Werner Kaiser (1956; 1957; 1990), and Stan Hendrickx (1996, 2006). At a time when the radiocarbon method was first being implemented on archaeological contexts within Egypt (Arnold and Libby 1949), Kaiser (1956; 1957; 1990) introduced his Naqada Stufen (I, II, III) and subdivisions thereof. This system took into account a wider geographical context than previously used, and indeed a wider corpus of material than had been available to Petrie, assigning both ceramic types and related items of the funerary assemblage within the various steps and subdivisions of the chronological system. The system assigns types to a major phase of the sequence, e.g. Naqada III, abbreviated to NIII, and then to subdivisions within this, e.g. NIId and within this, NIId2. Stan Hendrickx (1996; 2006) offered a now widely used revision of this system in the 1990s, in which he was able to take advantage of data from an even greater chronological and geographical range of cemeteries, and reconsider the divisions that Kaiser had originally implemented within his system. Hendrickx questioned the logic and objectivity of a number of major divisions within the Naqada Stufen that Kaiser had assigned, notably the break between the NII and NIII phases, the beginning of the NIIIC phase and Hendrickx's addition of NIIID from the time of Qa'a. In contrast to a number of the Stufen proposed by Kaiser (1956; 1957), Hendrickx (1996) sought to place divisions only where he considered there to be typologically clear differences between the ceramic types. Further detail as to these relative chronological systems will not be given here, but the reader should refer to Hendrickx (2006) for a very adequate review.

Before moving to consider the absolute chronology for the Early Dynastic period, a notable revision to the Naqada IIID chronology proposed by Hendrickx should be considered. Köhler and Smythe (2004) note two key factors, 1) the absence of the 'typologically latest representatives' of the cylindrical jar and, 2) the developments within the typology of small offering/beer jars. Throughout the Naqada IIID period, Köhler and Smythe (2004, 136) observe the emergence of types which are evident within a 'part of Old Kingdom material culture' and, crucially, question how late, and for how long, the Naqada cultural sequence should be extended (Rowland 2009, 12). This can be seen as constructive criticism of the way in which scholars apply chronological frameworks as a means by which to better understand developments, or rather changes, in material culture. In doing this, the fluidity of material culture over time has the potential for being overlooked and it is vital that both the positive and negative aspects of chronological frameworks are kept in mind.

Chronological research into the Pre- and Early Dynastic period: absolute dating

Having briefly introduced the relative chronological systems, it is time to turn to consider the issue of achieving absolute dates for Predynastic and Early Dynastic contexts. Estimates of the start of the Predynastic period have changed dramatically since Petrie (Petrie and Quibell 1896, 59–64; Baumgartel 1947, 25–6) proposed a date possibly as early as 8–10,000 BCE. This early date reflected the time in which he was writing and was very much affected by his belief that in the period preceding the historical era the population within Egypt must have been very much lower than subsequently. Given the high number of Predynastic burials observed at the time, and this assumption of low population, Petrie deduced that the burials must represent a large span of time, although he did admit to the possibility of the Predynastic beginning as late as 5500 BCE (Petrie and Quibell 1896, 59–64). De Morgan (1897; 1906, 47) favoured a date of *c.* 4000 BCE for the start of the 1st Dynasty (Adams 1988, 68); however, by the turn of the last century, Breasted (1906, 56) had already proposed 'an assured minimum of 3400 BCE'. The absolute dates proposed by scholars today, largely vary around the 3100/3200 BCE mark, dates which are scrutinised and revised as new archaeological data emerges and as new radiocarbon results are achieved (Rowland 2008, 10–11).

Researchers working to establish prehistoric time-scales for prehistoric contexts, either those pre-dating ceramic technology or those with no associated items of material culture to aid in the relative dating of contexts, have long been implementing radiocarbon dating to great effect. Archaeological contexts that have benefited from scientific dating include temporary encampments, where the evidence present might consist of a combination of lithic material in association with hearths, or simply hearths with remaining charcoal, or other botanical – or human – remains. Contexts with associated items of material culture often include burials, where radiocarbon measurements are run on samples of organic material originating from jar contents, from matting used to wrap burials or to line graves, for example. As described above, the resultant published dates were compiled within a project database initiated at the start of the Oxford chronology project in 2006, a database which includes radiocarbon measurements ranging from prehistory throughout the Pharaonic era, and into the post-Pharaonic periods. This database is now available for consultation online (Rowland and Bronk Ramsey 2011, https://c14.arch.ox.ac.uk/egyptdb/db.php). It includes 548 dates ranging from the Palaeolithic to the end of the 2nd Dynasty, which is undeniably a large proportion of the overall number of dates conducted on Egyptian contexts.

One of the major modern scholars concerned with the absolute chronology of early Egypt is Fekri Hassan. Hassan *et al.* (2006) have most recently provided a review of the chronology of Early Dynastic Egypt, but his other major works include the 'Radiocarbon Chronology of Neolithic and Predynastic sites in Upper Egypt and the Delta' (1985), the absolute dates presented within which still form the absolute chronological parameters cited in much current work. Hassan (1985) analysed 95 radiocarbon dates, giving basic absolute age estimates for the stages of the Fayum Neolithic, Merimdan Neolithic, Late Badarian and the early and later Naqada periods. In this paper, Hassan (1985, 103) looked at a wide range of organic materials, mostly charcoal, with other samples of grain, wood, hair, skin, shell and bone (both apatite and collagen). The dates measured on bone were rejected by him as unreliable due to their extreme difference in age when compared with other samples from the same provenience (Hassan 1985, 103). Hassan (1985, 103–104) was already concerned with two issues that have been fundamental as the Oxford chronology project progressed: 1) the issue of potential sample contamination, and 2) looking to groups of radiocarbon dates rather than samples in isolation. He explained that if single samples are used then the possibility of their being 'erroneous' or contaminated remains unchecked (Hassan 1985, 104). A higher overall number of samples also allows for dates to be statistically averaged and create greater chronological precision (Hassan 1985, 103–104). As noted, Hassan (1985) presented dates from excavated contexts for key Neolithic and Predynastic sites, for example Merimde Beni Salama, el-Omari, Ma'adi, and Fayumian sites, in addition to Upper Egyptian sites, including Hemamieh (also with TL dates) and Naqada region sites for the Middle Predynastic Naqada I period, with associated ceramics. The latter allowed for a relationship to be made with Petrie's sequence dates, including the following types associated with Naqada I, mainly Petrie's P-ware and B-ware, and also a few sherds of C-ware, W-ware and L-ware as well as rippled ceramics (Hassan 1985, 107). Other material considered included that from the Late Predynastic, Naqada II, originating from excavations in the Naqada region, including South Town, and at Hierakonpolis, from contexts which included ceramic evidence, albeit evidence which suggested the simultaneous use of ceramics associated with Naqada I and Naqada II in difference areas (Hassan 1985, 110). Finally, Hassan (1985, 110) considered material from the Terminal Predynastic, Naqada III, which came from the Naqada III cemetery at Elkab, where the ceramics suggested SD78–80. Hassan noted something essential for our better understanding of change, never more crucial than during the period prior to state formation in Egypt. He noted that if change is to be better understood, it is important that scholars consider the absolute timescale of events, particularly in reference to climatic change and changes in the river Nile (Hassan 1985, 110–111; 2002). As stated above, for scholars researching Predynastic and Early Dynastic contexts, radiocarbon is and has been an integral and accepted tool. Given that radiocarbon measurements form the very basis for our understanding of the absolute chronology of these periods, if a robust absolute chronology is sought, then increasing numbers of dates are required; these dates should preferably originate from varied geographical locations within Egypt and be measured on short-lived plant remains, as opposed to wood and wood charcoal which introduce the problem of inbuilt age (Dee *et al.* 2008, 5).

Regionalism and chronology
Although there is a solid relative ceramic chronology to work with, this can only go so far in helping to chart temporal developments both throughout Egypt and on a wider geographical scale. The issue of regionalism has been ever more present in discussions concerning prehistoric and early historic Egypt in recent years as more sites have been investigated throughout the length and breadth of Egypt (see discussion in Hassan *et al.* 2006, 693; Hassan 1988). The inclusion of Lower Egypt and especially the Delta within the debates surrounding chronology is very important and it is something that has only really become possible in recent times due to the substantial increase in archaeological investigations within the region. Christiana Köhler has been a key figure in the recent discussions concerning the importance of regionalism in Egypt and in challenging and offering up new perspectives on the processes surrounding the formation of the Egyptian state, firstly in an article in 1995 and then in a substantial review in 2008. One of the main problems is terminological. Scholars refer to material culture relating to the Naqada cultural complex, yet have largely (until recently) given insufficient thought as to how the Delta should be incorporated within the debate. From recent investigations at sites including Tell el-Farkha, Tell el-Iswid and Kom el-Khilgan (for example Ciałowicz 2008; Midant-Reynes 2007; Buchez and Midant-Reynes 2007) it is clear that there is much variability within the Delta itself, and not just in comparison with the material culture of the Nile Valley. Various terms have been used to describe the material culture of the Delta, but what is most important is that variation is recognised and that the questions of how and why the Naqada IIC/D material culture first arrives in Lower Egypt are kept central to the debate, as discussed by Köhler (2008). Increasingly, theories relating to mass migration and war have become untenable not only because of the new archaeological evidence, but also because of the lack of any substantive evidence to prove them (see Petrie 1920, 47, 48; Engelbach 1943, 197, 198; Derry 1956).

Past contexts for which radiocarbon measurements have been achieved are heavily biased towards Nile Valley sites, which represent the bias in archaeological investigation within Egypt discussed above. There are, however, a limited and growing number of radiocarbon dates from contexts within Lower Egypt. These come from important Neolithic sites, including Qasr el-Sagha (19), Kom W (5) and Kom K (24) in the Fayum (including 28 new dates published by Wendrich *et al.* 2010), from Merimde Beni Salama (18), on the western edge of the Delta, and el-Omari (7), near Helwan. From the Predynastic period, dates have come from contexts at Buto (9), Abu Ghalib (1), Minshat Abu Omar, Ma'adi (17) and Wadi Digla (2). For the Early Dynastic period Lower Egyptian dates come from

Saqqara (42) and Kafr Tarkhan (15), Minshat Abu Omar (27) and Maasara (2). South of the Fayum, radiocarbon dates have been measured from samples from the Neolithic at Siwa, Dakhleh, Kharga and Farafra oases, the Badari region, for the Predynastic at Malkata Armant, Naqada Khatara, el-Tarif, Hierakonpolis, Semaineh, Naqada, Naga ed-Dêr, Abydos and Adaïma, and for the Early Dynastic from Abydos and Elkab.

During the Neolithic–Early Dynastic period, regionalism exists both throughout and within the Nile Valley and Delta. As mentioned above, over time the material culture traditionally associated with the Upper Egyptian Nile Valley gradually enters the archaeological record in Lower Egypt, firstly in its southerly reaches at el-Gerzeh (Stevenson 2008; 2009; Petrie *et al.* 1912), then moving north into the Delta, where it is seen at the sites of Minshat Abu Omar (Kroeper and Wildung 1994; 2000), Buto (Köhler 1992; 1998) and Tell el-Farkha (Jucha 2007) for example. Prior to this an indigenous material culture exists within the Nile Delta, albeit not a homogenous culture across the Delta. These regional differences make an independent absolute chronology vital, in order that the timescale over which change occurs can be better monitored, which can help to answer the multitude of questions relating to the movement of people within Egypt, dispersal of items of material culture and the pace at which this was occurring. A robust absolute chronological framework stands to contribute to our understanding of the processes that culminate in the formation of the Egyptian state. With more and more fieldwork being conducted in the Nile Delta, the opportunity for presenting a more coherent relative and absolute chronology for this region is ever greater, but it is still difficult to talk in terms of a precise absolute chronology, particularly for the Delta. When the objects associated with the Naqada culture do become consistently apparent in sites of Lower Egypt from Naqada IIC, they do not simply replace indigenous wares, rather they slowly become integrated with indigenous wares and through time become dominant.

Oxford radiocarbon dates for early Egypt: problems and possibilities

The possibility of achieving increasing numbers of radiocarbon dates on freshly excavated material from sound archaeological contexts is improving, notably through the installation of a radiocarbon facility at the Institut Français d'Archéologie Orientale (IFAO) in Cairo. The laboratory, albeit not an AMS facility, is enabling samples to be dated within Egypt, an obvious advantage. The facility does require larger samples than those required for AMS dates (http://www.ifao.egnet.net/_c14/en/echantillons.php) and of course there is pressure upon what is currently the only working radiocarbon facility for all archaeological projects in Egypt.

Included within the Egyptian Radiocarbon Database of previously published dates, are 420 radiocarbon dates preceding Naqada III, with 223 of these ranging from the start of the Badarian to the end of the Naqada II period and 134 from Naqada III to the end of the 2nd Dynasty (Rowland 2008, 16). In an earlier article, the present author gave a brief analysis of 121 of these dates, ranging from Naqada IIA until the end of the 2nd Dynasty (Rowland 2008, 17–22), originating from Abydos, Tarkhan, Saqqara, Buhen, Helwan and Minshat Abu Omar. 53 of these dates were automatically excluded from the analysis due to failing the Waterbolk criteria (Waterbolk 1971), a check list which tests a) the security

19. Absolute Dates from Prehistoric and Early Historical Contexts

of archaeological contexts, and b) the suitability of the organic materials being used. The dates that failed the Waterbolk criteria varied by site – with Kafr Tarkhan largely having produced dates passing the criteria – including textile samples from burials, but dates from Abydos, often failing due to the type of material (for example wood, see Rowland 2008, 17–22). These issues were borne in mind when the samples were taken for the current project, with wood and charcoal avoided, in favour of short-lived plant remains. As will be seen below, the new samples came from burial contexts from the sites of Abydos, Saqqara, Tarkhan and Ma'asara. Hassan (*pers comm.*) notes that it might be expected that samples from Abydos might include re-worked material given the longevity of the site already by the Early Dynastic period, a problem that we would not expect to be so great for samples from Saqqara, for example. Before collecting new material, it was important to look at the variability in these dates – to see where real outliers appeared – and look into what might have caused these outliers, and what might be best avoided.

New Early Dynastic dates

Petrie developed the succession of the early rulers of Egypt, not only those of the 1st Dynasty, but also of the 0th Dynasty, the term referring to rulers from Abydos and Hierakonpolis prior to the 1st Dynasty (Hassan *et al.* 2006, 688). The term 00 was subsequently introduced by van den Brink (1992, vi, n. 1) to refer to those who might have been predecessors of, or overlapped with the 0th Dynasty kings, rulers buried in cemetery U at Abydos (Hassan *et al.* 2006, 688–689; Hendrickx 2006, 88). Some scholars, including Hassan, prefer to refer to these rulers as Protodynastic and avoid trying to fit them into more specific categories; these correspond to Hendrickx's Naqada IIIA1–2 and IIIB phases (Hassan *et al.* 2006, 688–689). Hassan *et al.* (2006, 706, Table 3) discuss the estimated regnal lengths for the Early Dynastic rulers from Aha to Qa'a, which vary according to the opinions of the scholars, as shown in Table 19.1. Variation within the proposed regnal lengths is as much as 16 years between modern researchers (Kaiser 1961; Helck 1974; and Barta 1981), with variations of over 20 years between the modern authors and Manetho.

Table 19.1: Estimated regnal years for 1st Dynasty kings (after Hassan et al. 2006 Table 3).

KING	KAISER (1961)	HELCK (1974)	BARTA (1981)	AVERAGE	MANETHO A/E
Narmer	–	–	–	–	62/60
Aha	33	35	34	34	57/27
Djer	41	53	52	48/52	31/39
Djet	12	13	15	13	23/42
Den	47	42	51	47	20
Anedjib	8	11	11	10	26
Semerkhet	9	9	10	9	18
Qa'a	17	33	28	26	26
TOTAL				189	253/252

The contexts from which the new samples were taken for the Oxford chronology project relate predominantly to the kings of the 1st and 2nd Dynasties.

42 new samples were collected from Egyptian contexts ranging from as early as Narmer through until the end of the 2nd Dynasty. Of these, 20 produced reliable dates. Those that were rejected can be broken down as follows: Five of these samples failed, nine samples were too small/unsuitable for dating/witheld and eight samples that were dated produced clear outliers. The remaining 20 samples produced new radiocarbon measurements for 1st and 2nd Dynasty contexts. The breakdown is as follows:

Material types

As stated above, the Oxford project focused on collecting short-lived plant remains for radiocarbon measurements in order to minimise issues of inbuilt age. The exact types of materials and species, where known, are listed below together with the successful results of the radiocarbon measurements taken from Early Dynastic contexts (see Table 19.3). A number of these contexts are contexts for which dates have also been taken in the past (see Table 19.2).

Table 19.2: Chronological breakdown of existing and new radiocarbon dates.

King/Context	Existing Dates	Samples Taken	New Dates
Narmer and/or Aha	6	7	5
Djer	7	6	2
Djet	13	3	1
Meret-Neith	–	2	1
Den	31	10	6
Anedjib	–	2	0
Semerkhet	–	1	0
Qa'a	6	2	2
General 1st Dynasty	18	0	0
Total 1st Dynasty	**81**	**33**	**17**
Peribsen	–	2	1
Khasekhemwy	–	3	0
General 2nd Dynasty (new dates: Ma'asara Grave 6)	6	4	2
Total 2nd Dynasty	**6**	**9**	**3**
General Early Dynastic	**4**	**0**	**0**
Total 1st and 2nd Dynasty	**91**	**42**	**20**

Assoc Reign	Acc. No.	Museum	Context	Site	Object Sampled	Organics	OxA No.	BP	±	Cal BC
Narmer	UC35680	Petrie Museum	Tomb B17	Abydos Umm el Qa'ab	Mud sealing fragment	organic fragments	19790	4798	32	3650–3521
Narmer	E0010	MRAH	Royal Tombs	Abydos Umm el Qa'ab	Mud sealing fragment	monocot leaves	17864	4687	34	3627–3370
Aha	MM1215C	Manchester Museum	Royal Tombs	Abydos Umm el Qa'ab	Mud sealing fragment	poaceae leaves	19136	4760	32	3640–3382
Aha	E0023	MRAH	Royal Tombs	Abydos Umm el Qa'ab	Mud sealing fragment	monocot stem fibres	17865	4562	35	3491–3104
Aha	UC35693	Petrie Museum	Tomb B19	Abydos Umm el Qa'ab	Mud sealing fragment	organic strands	19791	4764	33	3640–3383
Djer	1913.66.51	Bolton Museum	Tomb 1060	Kafr Tarkhan	Textile	cotton, flax, hemp	18060	4329	30	3019–2893
Djer	BM35555	British Museum	Tomb of Djer	Abydos Umm el Qa'ab	Seeds	*Ficus carica*	18511	4329	33	3023–2891
Djet	MM5462C	Manchester Museum	Grave 2054	Kafr Tarkhan	Matting	*Juniaceae* culm	19142	4139	29	2874–2621
Djet/Den	VM3332	Victoria Collection Uppsala	Tomb of Meret–Neith	Saqqara	Mud-brick	monocotyledous	18050	4463	31	3338–3023
Den	1913.66.30	Bolton Museum	Tomb 2038ii	Kafr Tarkhan	Textile	possibly tree bast fibres	*18061	4394	31	3097–2916
Den	1913.66.30	Bolton Museum	Tomb 2038ii	Kafr Tarkhan	Textile	possibly tree bast fibres	*18062	4315	31	3015–2888
Den	BM52887	British Museum	Mastaba 2050 intrusive burial	Kafr Tarkhan	Basketry Coffin	leaves and culms of *cyperaceae*	18555	4115	30	2866–2577
Den	MM1069B	Manchester Museum	No further information	Abydos	Mud sealing fragment	*poaceae* leaves	19114	4614	31	3514–3200
Den	MM2785	Manchester Museum	No further information	Abydos	Jar seal impression	*poaceae* leaves, palm fibres	19140	4599	30	3501–3135
Den	E0122	MRAH	Royal Tombs	Abydos Umm el Qa'ab	Mud sealing fragment	rope remains	17866	4653	35	3619–3361
Qa'a	MM2784	Manchester Museum	No further information	Abydos	Jar seal impression	*poaceae* culm and leaves	*19115	4641	33	3518–3358
Qa'a	MM2784	Manchester Museum	No further information	Abydos	Jar seal impression	*poaceae* culm and leaves	*19138	4611	30	3512–3196
Peribsen	E7296	MRAH	No further information	Abydos (?)	Jar seal impression	monocot stalks and leaf	17867	4433	36	3330–2925
2nd Dynasty	Tackholm No. 8A	Medelhavsmuseet	Grave 6, Vessel 9	Maasara	Jar contents	*hordeum hexasticbum*	19708	5762	32	4706–4536
2nd Dynasty	Tackholm No. 12	Medelhavsmuseet	Grave 6, Vessel 9	Maasara	Jar contents	*lolium temulentum*	19798	4373	28	3090–2909

* – duplicate measurements
MRAH – Royal Museums of Art and History, Brussels

Discussion: contexts, ceramics, and pre-existing dates

Eleven of the new dates achieved on Early Dynastic samples were taken from jar seal impressions, and one from a mud-brick. For the first time, two dates were achieved on jar seals associated with the time of Narmer. The dates, as can be seen in Table 19.3, were earlier than might have been expected and one possible reason is discussed below.

Six previous dates are assignable to Aha. These dates were achieved on samples taken from reed and wood/wood charcoal from Abydos and Saqqara. As Hassan *et al* (2006, 702) discuss the striking difference in the results from the two sites. The measurements from Abydos are taken on wood, 3366–3098 cal BC and 3344–3101 cal BC, with the Saqqara dates on reed; the latter have a wider range with greater margins of error: 3263–2678 cal BC, 2925–2601 cal BC, 3312–2891 cal BC and 3369–2944 cal BC. The new Oxford project dates were taken on samples of short-lived plant remains from jar seals. However, given the unexpectedly early dates resulting from two of the new samples (OxA-19136 and OxA-19791, Table 19.3) for which dates range from 3640–3382 cal BC and 3640–3383 cal BC at 95.4% confidence, it begs the question of whether the organic material dated had already been present in the mud collected to make the jar seals, rather than being introduced during the making and placement of the jar seal itself. The fact that OxA-17865 (3492–3104 cal BC) produces a younger date and that the sample was taken from what appears to be the remains of rope used during the sealing of the jar, further supports this suggestion.

Two new dates have been produced for Djer, however, in both cases the date of the tomb was assigned on the basis of the ceramic assemblage, and with no other independent textual dating criteria (Petrie 1915, 49). Given that the majority of Pre- and Early Dynastic contexts are chronologically determined through relative means, primarily through ceramics, absolute dates can also contribute to providing absolute chronological correlates for the range of ceramic types. On previous radiocarbon measurements for Djer, specifically those of reeds from Mastaba S3503 at Saqqara, Hassan *et al.* (2006, 702) give a mean estimate of 3094–3023 cal BC including one date that is much earlier than the other two, or 2942–2889 cal BC based solely on the two younger dates. The new dates produced by the Oxford project are 3019–2893 cal BC, from textile from Tarkhan, and 3023–2891 cal BC from seeds from Abydos. Notably, neither of these samples comes from jar sealings.

One new sample was taken for Meret-Neith, from her tomb at Saqqara. The sample was taken from a mud-brick and returned a date of 3338–3023 cal BC. The sampling of mud-bricks from some Pharaonic contexts during the Oxford project has produced unexpected dates, and the same issues can apply with mud-bricks as with jar seals, that the inclusion of older organic remains, not deliberately added at the time of manufacture, may explain incidences of dates much earlier than expected.

One sample was taken relating to the reign of Djet, with the relationship again based upon the ceramic sequence within tomb 2054 at Tarkhan (Petrie 1915, XX). The sample of matting produced a date of 2874–2621 cal BC. All previous radiocarbon measurements for Djet had been taken from Mastaba 3504 at Saqqara, on samples of wood and reed/twig. The calibrated pooled mean presented in Hassan *et al.* (2006, 702) is 2922–2996 cal BC, relating to just four measurements considered as consistent, out of what is a total of 12 samples.

Hassan *et al.* (2006, 703) present an average of previous radiocarbon dates for Den, giving a range of 2934–2888 cal BC derived from radiocarbon measurements on samples of reeds (all from Saqqara Mastaba 3035); the dates on linen (all from Tarkhan grave 2050) give a calibrated mean of 2906–2887 cal BC. Other samples that have been taken previously for Den include those on wood and wood charcoal from Saqqara and also Abydos. The earliest of these dates is 3517–3096 cal BC, and the youngest 3352–3035 cal BC, with the sample of charcoal returning a comparatively young date of 2888–2573 cal BC. Of the new samples measured for Den, those taken on jar seals (all from Abydos) again produce very early dates. The samples of textile and basketry (all from Kafr Tarkhan), however, returned much younger dates; the textiles from Tomb 2038ii at Kafr Tarkhan are assigned to the reign of Den based on the ceramic assemblage (Petrie 1915, XX).The textiles from Tarkhan produced 3097–2916 BC, 3015–2888 BC and the basketry coffin 2866–2577 BC.

There are two new samples relating to the reign of Qa'a, which come from Abydos, but with no clearer assignment. They are both from jar seals and, as discussed above, might in fact be providing dates for plant remains pre-existing in the mud. The dates are 3818–3358 cal BC and also 3512–3196 cal BC. Seven former dates existed for Qa'a, from Saqqara (Mastaba 3505) taken on wood charcoal and reeds, and samples of wood from Abydos (Tomb Q). Hassan *et al*. (2006, 703) gives a 'calibrated pooled mean' of 2819–2748 cal BC on the dates considered reliable.

Only five radiocarbon measurements from 2nd Dynasty contexts have been attempted prior to the project. These are two from Elkab (Tombs 12 and 60), two from Maasara (Tomb 6) and one from Saqqara Mastaba 3046. None of these have a direct link to a specific ruler, and of the new dates from the Oxford project, one sample was possible for the reign of Peribsen, which returned a date range of 3330–2925 cal BC at 95.4% confidence, coming from a seal impression from Abydos. Two new dates have been produced from samples of seeds taken from Grave 6 at the site of Maasara, in the Early Dynastic cemetery within the current Helwan concession area, which is being excavation by Köhler (Köhler 2005; Köhler and Jones 2009). The excavations from which the material was dated were directed by Larsen (1940a, b) and the description refers to samples being taken from vessel 9 within Grave 6. Ceramics from the same tomb are in the Medelhavsmuseet in Stockholm. The first sample produced a much earlier date than expected, with a range of 4706–4536 cal BC, however, the second sample gave a date in the range of 3090–2909 cal BC, in line with conventional ceramic chronology for the reign. Previous dates were achieved on samples from the same context, one sample of charcoal producing 2471–2138 cal BC and the second, on charred seeds, 2853–1892 cal BC. The latter had a wide error margin of ±150.

Future possibilities

The results show that there is potential for an absolute chronology for prehistoric and early historic Egypt. It is apparent that samples from jar seals and also mud-bricks might be better avoided, unless the organic material from the jar seals are remains of the rope used at the time of the sealing of the jar (e.g. OxA-17865). Furthermore, as we extend back into prehistory, it becomes increasingly important to synchronise absolute dates with ceramic types to investigate the absolute date range of various types – taking into account context (settlement versus cemetery) and also geographical location. The results stand to contribute towards our understanding of the processes linked with the formation of the state.

At the time of writing, a new project is well underway at Oxford to investigate previously measured radiocarbon dates in addition to acquiring new dates for the Early Dynastic period. If new material from ongoing excavations in Egypt is able to be sampled as part of this research, then these initiatives, combined, will help to contribute to a robust new series of dates. Depending upon the contexts that it is possible to sample, and the number

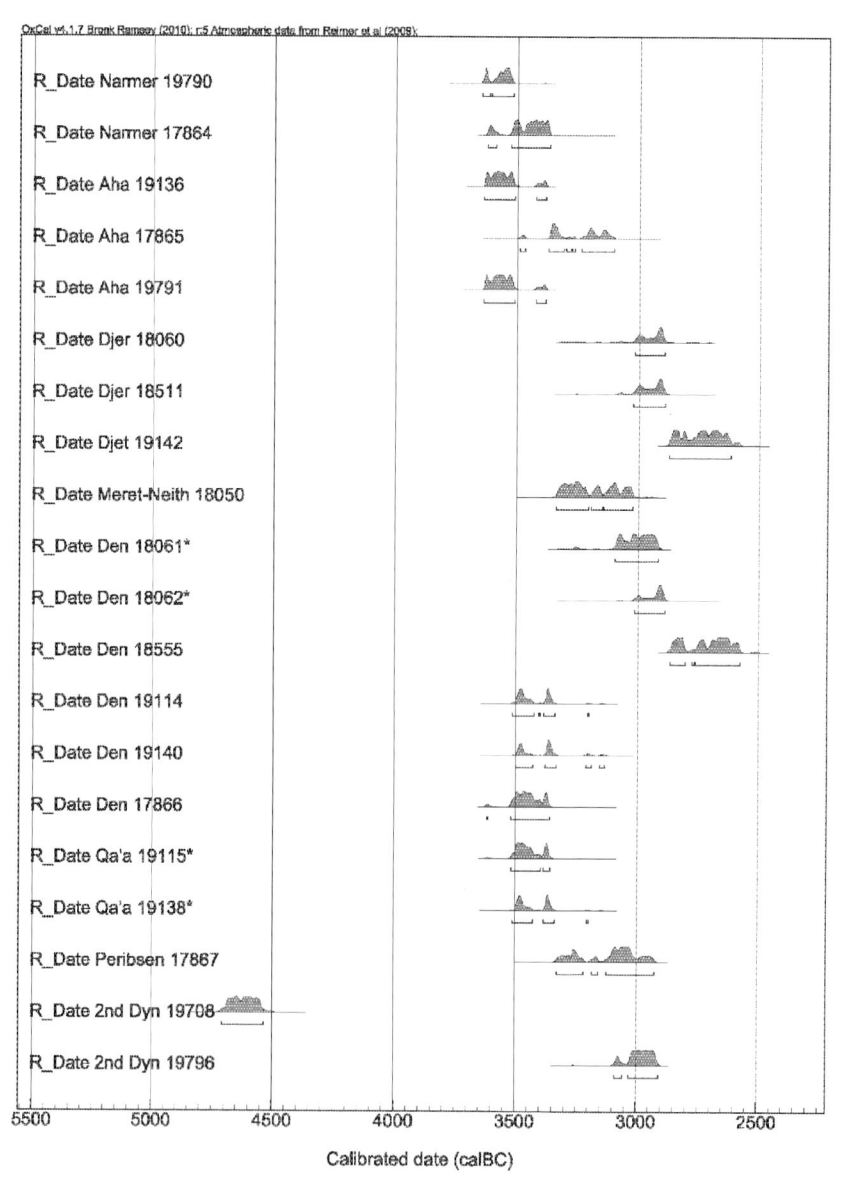

Figure 19.1: New radiocarbon dates for the 1st and 2nd Dynasties at the 95.4% confidence range.

of measurements that can be achieved, it may become possible for researchers to use this new data in order to reconsider the absolute time-scale at which events are occurring in Egypt during the Early Dynastic period – and in time this might be possible for the Predynastic period too. Possibilities exist both from ongoing excavations, e.g. Tell el-Farkha, Helwan, Buto and Sais, and also through material being located through drill coring with a continuous core, albeit not with the hand auger. The IFAO radiocarbon facility in Cairo will go a long way to assisting in the analysis of new samples, and whether the future will see the installation of a new AMS facility in Cairo remains to be seen.

References

Adams, B. 1988, *Predynastic Egypt*, Shire Publications Ltd, Princes Risborough.
Arnold, J. R. and Libby, W. F. 1949, Age determinations by radiocarbon content: checks with samples of known age, *Science*, **110** (2869), 678–680.
Barta, W. 1981, Die chronologie der 1. bis 5. Dynastie nach den Angaben des rekonstruierten Annalensteins. *Zeitschrift für Ägyptische Sprache und Altertumskunde* **108**, 11–23.
Baumgartel, E. J. 1947, *The Cultures of Prehistoric Egypt*, Oxford University Press. Oxford.
Breasted, J. H. 1906, *Ancient Records of Egypt. Volume I: The First to the Seventeenth Dynasties*, University of Chicago Press, Chicago, 56.
Buchez, N. and Midant-Reynes, B. 2007, Le site prédynastique de Kom el-Khilgan (Delta oriental). Données nouvelles sur les processus d'unification culturelle au IVe millénaire, *Bulletin de l'Institut Français d'archéologie orientale*, **107**, 43–70.
Ciałowicz, K. M. 2008, The nature of the relation between Lower and Upper Egypt in the Protodynastic Period. A view from Tell el-Farkha. In Midant-Reynes, B. and Tristant, Y. (eds), *Egypt at its Origins 2*, OLA 172, 501–513.
Dee, M., Bronk Ramsey, C. and Rowland, J. M. 2008, Evaluating the effectiveness of radiocarbon studies of the Old Kingdom, In *Chronology and Archaeology in Ancient Egypt (the Third Millennium BC)*, (eds H. Vymazalová, H and M. Bartá), 1–9, Czech Institute of Egyptology, Prague.
Derry, D. E. 1956. The Dynastic Race in Egypt, *Journal of Egyptian Archaeology*, **42**, 80–85.
Engelbach, R. 1943. An Essay on the Advent of the Dynastic Race in Egypt and its Consequences, *Annales du Service des Antiquités de l'Egypte*, **42**, 193–221.
Hassan, F. A. H. 1985, Radiocarbon chronology of Neolithic and Predynastic sites in Upper Egypt and the Delta, *African Archaeological Review*, **3**, 95–116.
Hassan, F. A. 2002, Ecological Changes and Food Security in the Later Prehistory of North Africa: Looking Forward, in F. A. Hassan (ed.), *Droughts, Food and Culture*, 321–333. New York: Kluwer Academic/Plenum Publishers.
Hassan, F. A. 1988. The Predynastic of Egypt, *Journal of World Prehistory*, **2**, 135–185.
Hassan, F. A., Jiménez Serrano, A. and Tassie, G. J. 2006, The sequence and chronology of the Protodynastic and Dynasty I rulers. In *Archaeology of Northeast Africa, Studies in Memory of Lech Krzyżaniak* (eds M. Chlodnicki, K. Kroeper and M. Kobusiewicz), Archaeological Museum, Poznan.
Helck, W. 1974, Bemerkungen zum Annalenstein, *Mitteilungen des Deutschen Archäologischen Instituts Abteilung Kairo* 30, 31–35.
Hendrickx, S. 1996, The relative chronology of the Naqada culture: problems and possibilities. In *Aspects of Early Egypt* (ed. A. J. Spencer), 36–69. British Museum Press, London.
Hendrickx, S. 2006, Predynastic-Early Dynastic chronology. In *Ancient Egyptian Chronology* (eds R. Krauss and D. A. Warburton), 55–93, Brill, Leiden and Boston.

Jucha, M. A. 2007, *Naqada IId2/IIIa1 Pottery in the Nile Delta. A View from Tell el-Farkha*, Studies in Ancient Art and Civilization 10.
Kaiser, W. 1956, Stand und probleme der Ägyptischen vorgeschichtsforschung, *Zeitschrift für Ägyptische Sprache und Altertumskunde,* **81**, 87–109.
Kaiser, W. 1957, Zur inneren chronologie der Naqadakultur, *Archaeologia Geographica,* **6**, 69–77.
Kaiser, W. 1961, Einige bemerkungen zur Ägyptischen Frühzeit II, *Zeitschrift für Ägyptische Sprache und Altertumskunde,* **86**, 39–61.
Kaiser, W., 1990, Zur Entstehunge das gesamtägyptischen Staates, *Mitteilungen des Deutschen Archäologischen Instituts Abteillung Kairo,* **46**, 287–299.
Köhler, E. C. 1992, The Pre- and Early Dynastic pottery of Tell el-Fara'in (Buto). In *The Nile Delta in Transition; 4th–3rd Millennium BC.* (ed. E. C. M. van den Brink), 11–22, Tel Aviv.
Köhler, E. C. 1995, The state of research on Late Predynastic Egypt: new evidence for the development of the Pharaonic state, *Göttinger Miszellen,* **147**, 79–92.
Köhler, E. C. 1998, *Buto III. Die Keramik von der Späten Vorgeschichte bis zum Frühen Alten Reich (Schicht III bis VI),* Philipp von Zabern, Mainz am Rhein.
Köhler, E. C. and Smythe, J. 2004, Early Dynastic pottery from Helwan: establishing a ceramic corpus of the Naqada III, *Cahiers de la Céramique Égyptienne,* **7**, 123–143.
Köhler, E. C. 2005, *Helwan I. Excavations in the Early Dynastic Cemetery. Season* 1997/98, Heidelberg.
Köhler, E. C. 2008, The interaction between and the roles of Upper and Lower Egypt in the formation of the Egyptian state. Another review, In *Egypt at Its Origins 2* (eds B. Midant-Reynes and Y. Tristant), 513–540, Orientalia Lovaniensia Analecta, Leuven.
Köhler, E. C. and Jones, J. 2009, *Helwan II. The Early Dynastic and Old Kingdom Funerary Relief Slabs,* SAGA 25, Rahden.
Kroeper, K. and Wildung, D. 1994, *Minshat Abu Omar – Ein vor- und Frühgeschichtlicher Friedhof im Nildelta I,* Philipp von Zabern, Mainz am Rhein.
Kroeper, K. and Wildung, D. 2000, *Minshat Abu Omar – Ein vor- und Frühgeschichtlicher Friedhof im Nildelta II,* Philipp von Zabern, Mainz am Rhein.
Larsen, H. 1940a, Three Shaft Tombs at Maasara, Egypt, *Acta Archaeological,* **11**, 161–206.
Larsen, H. 1940b, Tomb Six at Maasara: an Egyptian Second Dynasty tomb, *Acta Archaeologica,* **11**, 103–124.
Midant-Reynes, B. 2007, Tell al-Iswid, (in) Pantalacci, L. and Denoix, S. (eds), Travaux de l'Institut français d'archéologie oreintale en 2006–2007. *Bulletin de l'Institut Français d'archéologie orientale,* **107**, 272–275.
De Morgan, J. 1897, *Recherches sur les Origines de l'Égypte: Ethnographié Préhistorique et Tombeau Royal de Négadah.* Ernest Leroux, Paris.
De Morgan, J. 1906, Les Recherches Archéologiques Leur But el Leur Procédés 47.
Olsson, I. 1959 'Uppsala Natural Radiocarbon Measurements I', *Radiocarbon,* **1**, 87–102.
Petrie, W. M. F. and Quibell, J. E. 1896, *Naqada and Ballas,* B. Quaritch, London.
Petrie, W. M. F. 1901, *Diospolis Parva: the Cemeteries of Abadiyeh and Hu 1898–9,* Egypt Exploration Fund, London.
Petrie, W. M. F., Wainwright, G. A. and Mackay, E. 1912, *The Labyrinth, Gerzeh and Mazghuneh.* British School of Archaeology in Egypt, London.
Petrie, W. M. F. 1915, *Heliopolis, Kafr Ammar and Shurafa,* British School of Archaeology in Egypt, London.
Petrie, W. M. F. 1920, *Prehistoric Egypt,* B. Quaritch, London.
Petrie, W. M. F. 1921, *Corpus of Prehistoric Pottery and Palettes,* British School of Archaeology in Egypt, London.
Petrie, W. M. F. 1953. *Corpus of Proto-Dynastic Pottery,* British School of Archaeology in Egypt and B. Quaritch, London.

Rowland, J. M. 2008, Building bridges between radiocarbon, relative and historical chronologies: The case of early Egypt. In *Chronology and Archaeology in Ancient Egypt (the Third Millennium BC)* (eds H. Vymazalová, H and M. Bartá), 10–22, Czech Institute of Egyptology, Prague.

Rowland, J. M. and Bronk Ramsey, C. 2011, Online C14 database for Egypt, *Egyptian Archaeology*, **38**, 33–34.

Stevenson, A., 2008, Ethnicity and migration? The Predynastic cemetery of el-Gerzeh, In *Egypt at Its Origins 2* (eds B. Midant-Reynes and Y. Tristant), 543–560, Orientalia Lovaniensia Analecta, Leuven.

Stevenson, A. 2009, *The Predynastic Cemetery of el-Gerzeh: Social Identities and Mortuary Practices* (OLA 186), Peeters, Leuven.

van den Brink, E. C. M. 1992, *The Nile Delta in Transition; 4th–3rd Millennium BC. Proceedings of the Seminar held in Cairo, 21–24 October 1990, at the Netherlands Institute of Archaeology and Arabic Studies.* Tel Aviv: Edwin C. M. van den Brink.

Waterbolk, H. T. 1971, Working with radiocarbon dates, *Proceedings of the Prehistoric Society*, **37**(2), 15–33.

Wendrich, W., Taylor, R. E. and Southon, J. 2010, Dating stratified settlement sites *at* Kom K and Kom W: Fifth millennium BCE radiocarbon ages for the Fayum Neolithic, *Nuclear Instruments and Methods in Physics Research B*, **268**, 999–1002.

Appendix and Model Results

Table 1: Historical Chronologies.

	Dynasty	King	(A) Shaw (2000) Accession Date (BC)	(A) Shaw (2000) Reign Length (Years)
		Khasewhemwy	-	-
OLD KINGDOM	3rd	Nebka	2686	19
		Djoser	2667	19
		Sekhemkhet[1]	2648	8
		Khaba[2]	2640	0
		Sanakht/Nebkha[3]	-	3
		Huni	2637	24
	4th	Sneferu	2613	24
		Khufu	2589	23
		Djedefra	2566	8
		Bikheris	-	0
		Khafra	2558	26
		Menkaura	2532	29
		Shepseskaf	2503	9
	5th	Userkaf	2494	7
		Sahura	2487	12
		Neferirkara	2475	20
		Shepseskara[4]	2455	7
		Raneferef	2448	3
		Nyuserra	2445	24
		Menkauhor	2421	7
		Djedkara	2414	39
		Unas	2375	30
	6th	Teti	2345	22
		Userkara	2323	2
		Pepy I	2321	34
		Merenra	2287	9
		Pepy II	2278	94
		Nitiqret[5]	2184	3
	7th–8th	(various)	2181	21

Appendix and Model Results

(B) Hornung et al. (2006)		(C) Kitchen (2000)		Variance		
Accession Date (BC)	Reign Length (Years)	Accession Date (BC)	Reign Length (Years)	(A)–(B)	(A)–(C)	(B)–(C)
2610	18			-	-	-
-	-			-	-	-
2592	27	2691	19	-8	0	8
2565	6	2672	6	2	2	0
2559	16	2666	6	-16	-6	10
-	-	2660	19	3	-16	-19
-	-	2641	24	24	0	-24
2543	34	2617	24	-10	0	10
2509	27	2593	23	-4	0	4
2482	8	2570	8	0	0	0
2474	2	-	0	-2	0	2
2472	25	2562	25	1	1	0
2447	6	2537	18	23	11	-12
2441	6	2519	4	3	5	2
2435	7	2515	7	0	0	0
2428	13	2508	14	-1	-2	-1
2415	11	2494	10	9	10	1
2403	1	2484	7	6	0	-6
2404	1	2477	7	2	-4	-6
2402	29	2470	31	-5	-7	-2
2373	8	2439	8	-1	-1	0
2365	44	2431	39	-5	0	5
2321	16	2392	30	14	0	-14
2305	26	2362	12	-4	10	14
-	3	2350	8	-1	-6	-5
2276	49	2342	45	-15	-11	4
2227	11	2297	10	-2	-1	1
2216	64	2287	94	30	0	-30
2152	2	2193	17	1	-14	-15
2150	32	2176	40	-11	-19	-8

			(A) Shaw (2000)	
	Dynasty	King	Accession Date (BC)	Reign Length (Years)
1IP	9th–10th	(various)	2160	35
	11th	Intef I	2125	13
		Intef II	2112	49
		Intef III	2063	8
MIDDLE KINGDOM		Mentuhotep II	2055	51
		Mentuhotep III	2004	12
		Mentuhotep IV	1992	7
	12th	Amenemhat I	1985	29
		Senusret I	1956	45
		Amenemhat II	1911	34
		Senusret II	1877	7
		Senusret III	1870	39
		Amenemhat III	1831	45
		Amenemhat IV	1786	9
		Queen Sobekneferu	1777	4
	13th–14th	(various)	1773	-
2IP	15th–17th	(various)	-	-
NEW KINGDOM	18th	Ahmose	1550	25
		Amenhotep I	1525	21
		Tuthmose I	1504	12
		Tuthmose II	1492	13
		Tuthmose III (1)	1479	6
		Queen Hatshepsut	1473	15
		Tuthmose III (2)	1458	31
		Amenhotep II	1427	27
		Tuthmose IV	1400	10
		Amenhotep III	1390	38
		Amenhotep IV/Akhenaten	1352	14
		Neferneferuaten/Smenkhkare	1338	2
		Tutankhamun	1336	9
		Ay	1327	4
		Horemheb	1323	28
	19th	Rameses I	1295	1
		Sety I	1294	15
		Rameses II	1279	66
		Merenptah	1213	10
		Amenmessu	1203	3

(B) Hornung et al. (2006)		(C) Kitchen (2000)		Variance		
Accession Date (BC)	Reign Length (Years)	Accession Date (BC)	Reign Length (Years)	(A)–(B)	(A)–(C)	(B)–(C)
2118	-	2136	26	35	9	-26
-	-	2110	10	13	3	-10
2066	50	2100	49	-1	0	1
2016	7	2051	8	1	0	-1
2009	51	2043	51	0	0	0
1958	11	1992	12	1	0	-1
1947	8	1980	7	-1	0	1
1939	19	1973	20	10	9	-1
1920	42	1953	42	3	3	0
1878	33	1911	33	1	1	0
1845	8	1878	6	-1	1	2
1837	19	1872	19	20	20	0
1818	46	1853	45	-1	0	1
1772	9	1808	9	0	0	0
1763	4	1799	4	0	0	0
1759	-	1795	-	0	0	0
-	-	-	-	0	0	0
1539	25	1540	25	0	0	0
1514	21	1515	21	0	0	0
1493	11	1494	12	1	0	-1
1482	3	1482	3	10	10	0
1479	0	1479	0	6	6	0
1479	21	1479	22	-6	-7	-1
1458	33	1457	30	-2	1	3
1425	25	1427	26	2	1	-1
1400	10	1401	10	0	0	0
1390	37	1391	38	1	0	-1
1353	17	1353	15	-3	-1	2
1336	-	1338	2	2	0	-2
-	13	1336	9	-4	0	4
1323	4	1327	4	0	0	0
1319	27	1323	28	1	0	-1
1292	2	1295	1	-1	0	1
1290	11	1294	15	4	0	-4
1279	66	1279	66	0	0	0
1213	11	1213	10	-1	0	1
1202	3	1203	3	0	0	0

	Dynasty	King	(A) Shaw (2000)	
			ACCESSION DATE (BC)	REIGN LENGTH (YEARS)
NEW KINGDOM	20th	Sety II	1200	6
		Saptah	1194	6
		Queen Tausret	1188	2
		Sethnakht	1186	2
		Rameses III	1184	31
		Rameses IV	1153	6
		Rameses V	1147	4
		Rameses VI	1143	7
		Rameses VII[6]	1136	7
		Rameses VIII	1129	3
		Rameses IX	1126	18
		Rameses X	1108	9
		Rameses XI	1099	30
3IP	21st	Smendes	1069	26
		Amenemnisu[7]	1043	4
		Psusennes I	1039	46
		Amenemope	993	9
		Orsokon the Elder	984	6
		Siamun	978	19
		Psusennes II	959	14

[1] Kitchen (2000) names the second reign of the 3rd Dynasty as Djoser-Teti
[2] Hornung *et al.* (2006) add 16 years to the end of the 3rd Dynasty without subdividing it
[3] Shaw (2000) adds 3 years here that are unallocated; Hornung *et al.* (2006) and Kitchen (2000) substitute Nebka for Sanakht
[4] Hornung *et al.* (2006) reverse the order of Shepseskara and Raneferef
[5] Kitchen (2000) places three kings after Pepi II but still in 6th Dynasty: Merenre II, Neterkare and Menkare
[6] Kitchen (2000) allocates a total of 66 years to Rameses VII-XI without subdividing it
[7] Hornung *et al.* (2006) reverse the order of Amenemnisu and Psusennes I

(B) Hornung ET AL. (2006)		(C) Kitchen (2000)		Variance		
Accession Date (BC)	Reign Length (Years)	Accession Date (BC)	Reign Length (Years)	(A)–(B)	(A)–(C)	(B)–(C)
1202	5	1200	6	1	0	-1
1197	5	1194	6	1	0	-1
1192	2	1188	2	0	0	0
1190	3	1186	2	-1	0	1
1187	31	1184	31	0	0	0
1156	7	1153	6	-1	0	1
1149	4	1147	4	0	0	0
1145	7	1143	7	0	0	0
1138	8	1136	66	-1	-59	-58
1130	1	-	-	2	3	1
1129	19	-	-	-1	18	19
1110	4	-	-	5	9	4
1106	30	-	-	0	30	30
1076	25	1070	26	1	0	-1
1005	3	1044	4	1	0	-1
1051	46	1040	46	0	0	0
1002	10	994	9	-1	0	1
992	6	985	6	0	0	0
986	19	979	19	0	0	0
967	24	960	15	-10	-1	9

Table 2: Details of archaeological samples selected for AMS dating.

Sample No. (OxA-)	Duplicate Number	Collection Location	Collection Reference	Site	King
17850		Medelhavsmuseet, Stockholm	Tackholm No. 4	Saqqara	Khasekhemwy/Djoser
18500		Medelhavsmuseet, Stockholm	Tackholm No. 7	Saqqara	Khasekhemwy/Djoser
18053		Medelhavsmuseet, Stockholm	Tackholm No. 10	Saqqara	Khasekhemwy/Djoser
18406		Medelhavsmuseet, Stockholm	Tackholm No. 11	Saqqara	Khasekhemwy/Djoser
18957		Royal Botanic Gardens, Kew	EBC26775	Saqqara	Khasekhemwy/Djoser
19005		Royal Botanic Gardens, Kew	EBC40750	Saqqara	Khasekhemwy/Djoser
18052		Medelhavsmuseet, Stockholm	MM30948	Saqqara	Djoser
19793		Petrie Museum, London	UC57892	Beit Khallaf	Djoser
20767 20768 20736	1	H. Haas	261	Saqqara	Djoser
19542		Metropolitan Museum of Art, New York	12.187.54	Tarkhan	
18514		Liverpool World Museum	56.21.428	Meydum	Sneferu
19141		Manchester Museum	MM5176	Meydum	Sneferu
18054		Medelhavsmuseet	MM11389	Giza	Khafre
20212		British Museum, London	BM10735/10	Abusir	Djedkare
18553		Liverpool World Museum	56.21.427	Saqqara	Pepy I
18063		Bolton Museum	1930.33.71	Mostagedda	
18520		British Museum, London	BM41580	Beni Hasan	Early Middle Kingdom (?)
18055 18058	2	Musées Royaux d'Art et d'Histoire, Brussels	E6855	Deir el-Bahri (?)	Mentuhotep II
18056 18059	3	Musées Royaux d'Art et d'Histoire, Brussels	E6876	Deir el-Bahri (?)	Mentuhotep II
18413 18414	4	British Museum, London	BM40921	Deir el-Bahri	Mentuhotep II
18415		British Museum, London	BM47627	Deir el-Bahri	Mentuhotep II
18416		British Museum, London	BM49458	Deir el-Bahri	Mentuhotep II
18556		British Museum, London	BM49458	Deir el-Bahri	Mentuhotep II
20179		Staatliches Museum Ägyptischer Kunst, Munich	-		Mentuhotep II
20017		Metropolitan Museum of Art, New York	26.3.27	Deir el-Bahri?	Mentuhotep II
19543		Metropolitan Museum of Art, New York	22.3.312	Deir el-Bahri	Late 11th Dyn
16838 VERA-4075	5	Metropolitan Museum of Art, New York	22.3.5239	Heqanakht	Amenemhat I/Senusret I
18502		Bolton Museum	1979.211.576	Rifeh	
19551 19552	6	Metropolitan Museum of Art, New York	20.3.210	TT22 Tomb of Wah	Amenemhat I

Dynasty	Material Group		Pretreatment Code	Date	±	Outlier Probability
	Type	Identification				
2nd/3rd	Seeds	*Scorpiurus muricatus*	UV	4084	32	2
2nd/3rd	Seeds	*Vicia lutea*	UV	4177	28	1
2nd/3rd	Seeds	*Lathyus hirsutus*	UW	4108	30	1
2nd/3rd	Short-lived plant part	*Lolium temulentum*	UV	4135	30	1
3rd	Short-lived plant part	*Triticum* sp.	UW	4145	32	1
3rd	Short-lived plant part	*Triticum* sp.	UW	4168	27	1
3rd	Short-lived plant part	*Cyperus papyrus*	UV	2421	28	100
3rd	Short-lived plant part	Poaceae	UV	3313	27	100
3rd	Short-lived wood	?*Commiphora* sp.	UW	4081	29	
			UW	4172	28	1
			UW	4115	32	
3rd/4th Border	Short-lived plant part	Arecaceae	UV	3954	27	96
4th	Textile		VV	4091	29	0
4th	Short-lived plant part		UV	4140	31	1
4th	Short-lived plant part		UV	107	24	-
5th	Short-lived plant part	*Cyperus papyrus*	UV	3911	31	1
6th	Textile		UV	3979	29	5
8th	Textile	*Linum* sp.	UV*	3562	29	100
-	Textile	?*Linum* sp.	VV*	3664	28	-
11th	Textile	*Linum* sp.	UV*	3625	29	3
			UV*	3573	30	
11th	Textile	*Linum* sp.	UV*	3616	29	6
			UV*	3561	30	
11th	Textile	?*Linum* sp.	UV	3660	29	0
			UV	3668	28	
11th	Textile	?*Linum* sp.	UV	3734	30	2
11th	Textile	?*Linum* sp.	UV	1707	27	-
11th	Textile	?*Linum* sp.	UV	1697	25	-
11th	Textile		UV	3583	30	5
11th	Short-lived plant part	?*Linum* sp.	UV	3651	28	1
11th	Short-lived plant part	Poaceae	UV	3715	25	1
12th	Short-lived plant part	*Cyperus papyrus*	WW*	3620	32	1
			2	3679	29	
12th	Textile	*Linum* sp.	UV	3518	28	1
12th	Textile	Probably mixed *Linum* sp. and *Gossypium* sp.	UV	3656	27	0
			UV	3623	27	

Sample No. (OxA-)	Duplicate Number	Collection		Site	King
		Location	Reference		
19553 20019	7	Metropolitan Museum of Art, New York		Tomb of Meketre TT	Amenemhat I
20307		H. Haas	481	Lisht	Senusret I
20479		H. Haas	482	Lisht	Senusret I/Amenemhat II
20308		H. Haas	527	Lahun	Senusret II
20200		Petrie Museum, London	UC6536	Lahun	Senusret II
15313 VERA-3726	8	Berlin	10009	Lahun	Senusret III (Yr 5)
15317 VERA-3730	9	Berlin	10092	Lahun	Senusret III (Yr 5)
15318 VERA-3731	10	Berlin	10345d	Lahun	Senusret III (Yr 5)
15315 VERA-3728	11	Berlin	10041	Lahun	Senusret III (Yr 14)
15311		Berlin	10248	Lahun	Senusret III (Yr 14)
VERA-3732		Berlin	10077	Lahun	Senusret III (Yr 14)
15316 VERA-3729	12	Berlin	10053	Lahun	Amenemhat III (Yr 4)
15310		Berlin	10018Bd	Lahun	Amenemhat III (Yr 4)
VERA-3733		Berlin	10091	Lahun	Amenemhat III (Yr 4)
15314 VERA-3727	13	Berlin	10038 b+c	Lahun	Amenemhat III (Yr 37)
VERA-3734		Berlin	10038	Lahun	Amenemhat III (Yr 37)
15309		Berlin	10081c	Lahun	Amenemhat III (Yr 37)
15312		Berlin	10419a	Lahun	Amenemhat III (Yr 38)
VERA-3735		Berlin	10044	Lahun	Amenemhat III (Yr 40)
20016		Metropolitan Museum of Art, New York	12.182.130c	Meir	Amenemhat III (?)
20480		H. Haas	557	Dahshur	Amenemhat III
20014		Metropolitan Museum of Art, New York	Gallery 6a/10/4	Lisht	
18554		Liverpool World Museum	1973.1.469	Esna	
20018		Metropolitan Museum of Art, New York	19.3.10	Thebes	
20015		Metropolitan Museum of Art, New York	19.3.247	Lisht	
19788		Metropolitan Museum of Art, New York	25.3.146	Deir el-Bahri	Early 18th
19715		Metropolitan Museum of Art, New York		Deir el-Bahri	Early 18th
19716		Metropolitan Museum of Art, New York		Deir el-Bahri	Early 18th
18417		British Museum, London	BM6639 g-h/9	Thebes	Early 18th

Dynasty	Material Group Type	Material Group Identification	Pretreatment Code	Date	±	Outlier Probability
12th	Textile	?*Linum* sp.	UV	3277	26	100
			UV	3236	27	
12th	Short-lived plant part	Poaceae	UW	3652	28	1
12th	Short-lived plant part	Poaceae	UW	3498	32	1
12th	Short-lived plant part	Poaceae	UW	3557	28	1
12th	Textile	?*Linum* sp.	VV	3546	27	1
12th	Short-lived plant part	*Cyperus papyrus*	WW	3503	30	0
			2	3543	29	
12th	Short-lived plant part	*Cyperus papyrus*	WW	3532	31	1
			2	3529	29	
12th	Short-lived plant part	*Cyperus papyrus*	WW	3518	31	0
			2	3513	29	
12th	Short-lived plant part	*Cyperus papyrus*	WW	3513	31	1
			2	3565	29	
12th	Short-lived plant part	*Cyperus papyrus*	WW	3532	31	1
12th	Short-lived plant part	*Cyperus papyrus*	2	3563	29	1
12th	Short-lived plant part	*Cyperus papyrus*	WW	3542	30	1
			2	3563	29	
12th	Short-lived plant part	*Cyperus papyrus*	WW	3560	33	1
12th	Short-lived plant part	*Cyperus papyrus*	2	3568	28	1
12th	Short-lived plant part	*Cyperus papyrus*	WW*	3755	33	-
			2	3522	29	
12th	Short-lived plant part	*Cyperus papyrus*	2	3512	29	1
12th	Short-lived plant part	*Cyperus papyrus*	WW	3626	33	17
12th	Short-lived plant part	*Cyperus papyrus*	WW	3485	31	1
12th	Short-lived plant part	*Cyperus papyrus*	2	3550	29	1
12th	Textile	?*Linum* sp.	UW	3556	28	1
12th	Short-lived plant part	Poaceae	UW	3489	34	1
12th/13th Border	Textile	?*Cannabis* sp.	UW	3469	27	1
17th	Textile		UV	3232	27	26
17th/18th Border	Short-lived plant part	Poaceae	UW	3268	27	2
17th/18th Border	Textile	?*Cannabis* sp.	UV	3278	26	2
18th	Short-lived plant part	?*Acacia* sp.	UV	2984	26	100
18th	Short-lived plant part	*Nymphaea* sp.	UV	2934	26	100
18th	Short-lived plant part	*Ziziphus* sp.	UV	3288	28	1
18th	Short-lived plant part	?*Linum* sp.	WW	3336	30	2

Sample No. (OxA-)	Duplicate Number	Collection		Site	King
		Location	Reference		
18506		British Museum, London	BM6009	Thebes (?)	Thutmose I
18411		British Museum, London	BM6009	Thebes (?)	Thutmose I
16833 VERA-4070	14	Metropolitan Museum of Art, New York	25.3.51	Deir el-Bahri	Hatshepsut (CoR)-
16834 VERA-4071	15	Metropolitan Museum of Art, New York	25.3.52	Deir el-Bahri	Hatshepsut (CoR)
16835 VERA-4072	16	Metropolitan Museum of Art, New York	25.3.54	Deir el-Bahri	Hatshepsut (CoR)
16836 VERA-4073	17	Metropolitan Museum of Art, New York	27.3.416	Deir el-Bahri	Hatshepsut (CoR)
16837 VERA-4074	18	Metropolitan Museum of Art, New York	27.3.418	Deir el-Bahri	Hatshepsut (CoR)
19008		Ashmolean Museum, Oxford	1895.151	Deir el-Bahri	Hatshepsut (CoR)
19448 SacA-11129	19	Musée du Louvre, Paris	E14477	Deir el-Medina	Hatshepsut (CoR)
19449 SacA-11130	20	Musée du Louvre, Paris	E14477	Deir el-Medina	Hatshepsut (CoR)
19450 19451 SacA-11131	21	Musée du Louvre, Paris	E14477	Deir el-Medina	Hatshepsut (CoR)
19546		Metropolitan Museum of Art, New York		Deir el-Bahri	Hatshepsut (CoR)
19252		Metropolitan Museum of Art, New York	25.3.54	Deir el-Bahri	Hatshepsut (CoR)
19547		Metropolitan Museum of Art, New York	27.3.416	Deir el-Bahri	Hatshepsut (CoR)
19789		Metropolitan Museum of Art, New York	36.3.71	Tomb of	Hatshepsut (CoR)
19153 SacA-11169	22	Musée du Louvre, Paris	E14617	Deir el-Medina	Hatshepsut (CoR)
19154		Musée du Louvre, Paris	E14617	Deir el-Medina	Hatshepsut (CoR)
SacA-11170		Musée du Louvre, Paris	E14617	Deir el-Medina	Hatshepsut (CoR)
SacA-11132		Musée du Louvre, Paris	E14477	Deir el-Medina	Hatshepsut (CoR)
SacA-11168		Musée du Louvre, Paris	E14617	Deir el-Medina	Hatshepsut (CoR)
19147		Musée du Louvre, Paris	E14665	Deir el-Medina	Thutmose III (after CoR)
19148		Musée du Louvre, Paris	E14665	Deir el-Medina	Thutmose III (after CoR)
19453		Musée du Louvre, Paris	E14488	Deir el-Medina	Thutmose III (after CoR)
SacA-11148		Musée du Louvre, Paris	E14488	Deir el-Medina	Thutmose III (after CoR)
19480		Musée du Louvre, Paris	E14488	Deir el-Medina	Thutmose III (after CoR)
19149 SacA-11151	23	Musée du Louvre, Paris	E14491	Deir el-Medina	Thutmose III (after CoR)
19481 SacA-11152	24	Musée du Louvre, Paris	E14480	Deir el-Medina	Thutmose III (after CoR)

Dynasty	Material Group Type	Material Group Identification	Pretreatment Code	Date	±	Outlier Probability
18th	Short-lived plant part/ wood	Mixed Poaceae & wood fragments	WW	3244	27	1
18th	Short-lived plant part/ wood	Mixed Poaceae & wood fragments	UV	3228	29	1
18th	Seeds	*Vitis sp.*	UV 1	3179 3249	31 32	1
18th	Seeds	*Mimusops laurifolia*	UV 1	3191 3203	31 29	1
18th	Seeds	*Phoenix dactylifera*	UW 1	3245 3204	31 30	1
18th	Short-lived plant part	*Ziziphus sp.*	UV 1	3191 3240	31 31	1
18th	Seeds	*Vitis sp.*	UW 1	3193 3173	32 30	2
18th	Short-lived plant part		UV	2972	26	100
18th	Short-lived plant part	Arecaceae	UV	3245 3165	30 30	1
18th	Short-lived plant part	Arecaceae	UV	3275 3200	31 25	1
18th	Textile		UV UV	3291 3237 3230	31 30 20	1
18th	Short-lived plant part		UW	3237	26	1
18th	Short-lived plant part	Frass	UW	3210	31	1
18th	Short-lived plant part	?*Ziziphus sp.*	UW	3171	25	3
18th	Bread		UV	1341	25	-
18th	Short-lived plant part	*Cyperus papyrus*	UV	110 110	23 23	-
18th	Textile		UW	3209	28	1
18th	Textile			3285	20	9
18th	Short-lived plant part	Mixed *Cyperus papyrus* & woody		3170	25	2
18th	Short-lived plant part			3760	60	100
18th	Short-lived plant part	Poaceae [Halfa grass]	UV	3261	32	2
18th	Short-lived plant part	Arecaceae	UV	3186	28	1
18th	Short-lived plant part	Poaceae [Halfa grass]	UV	3264	29	2
18th	Short-lived plant part	Poaceae [Halfa grass]		3090	30	73
18th	Short-lived plant part	Arecaceae	UW	3251	26	1
18th	Short-lived plant part	*Cyperus papyrus*	UW	165 260	23 25	-
18th	Short-lived plant part	Poaceae [Halfa grass]	UV	3233 3180	25 25	1

Sample No. (OxA-)	Duplicate Number	Collection		Site	King
		Location	Reference		
19150		Musée du Louvre, Paris	E14480	Deir el-Medina	Thutmose III (after CoR)
SacA-11153		Musée du Louvre, Paris	E14480	Deir el-Medina	Thutmose III (after CoR)
19482 SacA-11154	25	Musée du Louvre, Paris	E14487	Deir el-Medina	Thutmose III (after CoR)
19151 SacA-11155	26	Musée du Louvre, Paris	E14487	Deir el-Medina	Thutmose III (after CoR)
19581 SacA-11156	27	Musée du Louvre, Paris	E14479	Deir el-Medina	Thutmose III (after CoR)
19483 SacA-11158	28	Musée du Louvre, Paris	E14479	Deir el-Medina	Thutmose III (after CoR)
19484 SacA-11159	29	Musée du Louvre, Paris	E14479	Deir el-Medina	Thutmose III (after CoR)
19485 SacA-11160	30	Musée du Louvre, Paris	E14483	Deir el-Medina	Thutmose III (after CoR)
19152 SacA-11161	31	Musée du Louvre, Paris	E14483	Deir el-Medina	Thutmose III (after CoR)
SacA-11150		Musée du Louvre, Paris	E14491	Deir el-Medina	Thutmose III (after CoR)
18508		British Museum, London	BM6011	? Thebes	CoR or Thutmose III
18513		British Museum, London	BM41202; 1904 10-8, 302	Deir el-Bahri	CoR or Thutmose III
19452 SacA-11139	32	Musée du Louvre, Paris	E16394	Deir el-Medina	CoR or Thutmose III
19146 SacA-11143	33	Musée du Louvre, Paris	E16397	Deir el-Medina	CoR or Thutmose III
19486 SacA-11162	34	Musée du Louvre, Paris	E16401	Deir el-Medina	CoR or Thutmose III
19556 VERA-4788A	35	Kunsthistorisches Museum, Vienna			CoR or Thutmose III
SacA-11134		Musée du Louvre, Paris	E14489	Deir el-Medina	CoR or Thutmose III
SacA-11135		Musée du Louvre, Paris	E14489	Deir el-Medina	CoR or Thutmose III
SacA-11136		Musée du Louvre, Paris	E14489	Deir el-Medina	CoR or Thutmose III
SacA-11137		Musée du Louvre, Paris	E16390	Deir el-Medina	CoR or Thutmose III
SacA-11140		Musée du Louvre, Paris	E16396	Deir el-Medina	CoR or Thutmose III
SacA-11141		Musée du Louvre, Paris	E16396	Deir el-Medina	CoR or Thutmose III
SacA-11144		Musée du Louvre, Paris	E16391	Deir el-Medina	CoR or Thutmose III
SacA-11145		Musée du Louvre, Paris	E16391	Deir el-Medina	CoR or Thutmose III
SacA-11163		Musée du Louvre, Paris	E16401	Deir el-Medina	CoR or Thutmose III
SacA-11164		Musée du Louvre, Paris	E16401	Deir el-Medina	CoR or Thutmose III
SacA-11172		Musée du Louvre, Paris	E16425	Deir el-Medina	CoR or Thutmose III

Dynasty	Material Group		Pretreatment Code	Date	±	Outlier Probability
	Type	Identification				
18th	Short-lived plant part	Arecaceae	UV	3153	27	2
18th	Short-lived plant part	Arecaceae		3260	30	2
18th	Short-lived plant part	Arecaceae	UV	3277	26	37
				3305	25	
18th	Short-lived plant part	Poaceae [Halfa grass]	UV	3107	27	100
				3040	25	
18th	Short-lived plant part	Poaceae [Halfa grass]	UW	3258	26	1
				3200	25	
18th	Textile		UV	3226	26	4
				3285	20	
18th	Short-lived plant part	Arecaceae	UV	3257	26	16
				3305	25	
18th	Short-lived plant part	Poaceae [Halfa grass]	UW	3262	25	1
				3200	20	
18th	Short-lived plant part	Arecaceae	UV	3249	28	1
				3205	30	
18th	Short-lived plant part	Poaceae [Halfa grass]		3185	30	1
18th	Short-lived plant part/ wood	Mixed Poaceae & wood fragments	UV	3482	29	100
18th	Short-lived plant part		WW	3108	28	53
18th	Short-lived plant part	Poaceae [Halfa grass]	UV	3227	30	1
				3225	25	
18th	Short-lived plant part	*Cyperus papyrus*	UW	127	24	-
				165	20	
18th	Short-lived plant part	*Cyperus papyrus*	UW	182	22	-
				180	20	
18th	Textile		UV	2589	26	100
			3a	2649	35	
18th	Short-lived plant part	Poaceae [Halfa grass]		3225	20	1
18th	Short-lived plant part	Linum sp.		3095	20	97
18th	Rat dropping			695	25	-
18th	Short-lived plant part	Arecaceae		3170	25	1
18th	Short-lived plant part	Poaceae [Halfa grass]		3250	25	1
18th	Short-lived plant part	*Cyperus papyrus*		170	25	-
18th	Short-lived plant part	Poaceae [Halfa grass]		3380	50	52
18th	Short-lived plant part	Arecaceae		3195	20	1
18th	Short-lived plant part	Arecaceae		3285	20	12
18th	Short-lived plant part	Poaceae [Halfa grass]		3160	20	3
18th	Textile			3190	25	1

Sample No. (OxA-)	Duplicate Number	Collection		Site	King
		Location	Reference		
SacA-11165		Musée du Louvre, Paris	E16393	Deir el-Medina	CoR or Thutmose III
SacA-11166		Musée du Louvre, Paris	E16393	Deir el-Medina	CoR or Thutmose III
18507		British Museum, London	BM6014	Thebes (?)	Amenhotep II
19549		Metropolitan Museum of Art, New York	90.6.35	Thebes	Thutmose IV
18510		British Museum, London	BM6017	Thebes (?)	Amenhotep III
19548		Metropolitan Museum of Art, New York		Thebes	Amenhotep III
18057		Bolton Museum	1985.162.107	Amarna	Akhenaten
18407		Bolton Museum	1985.162.102	Amarna	Akhenaten
18512	36	British Museum, London	BM55135; 1921 10-8, 60	Amarna	Akhenaten
18412			BM55135; 1921 10-8, 60		
18953		Royal Botanic Gardens, Kew	EBC26799	Amarna	Akhenaten
18954		Royal Botanic Gardens, Kew	EBC26577	Amarna	Akhenaten
19004	37	Royal Botanic Gardens, Kew	EBC26577	Amarna	Akhenaten
19263					
VERA-4686	38	Royal Botanic Gardens, Kew		Amarna	Akhenaten
VERA-4686B					
18955	39	Royal Botanic Gardens, Kew	EBC26654	Amarna	Akhenaten
VERA-4687					
VERA-4687B					
18956		Royal Botanic Gardens, Kew	EBC40695	Amarna	Akhenaten
20482		VERA 14C Laboratory		Amarna	Akhenaten
VERA-4685	40	Royal Botanic Gardens, Kew		Amarna	Akhenaten
VERA-4685B					
17868		Musées Royaux d'Art et d'Histoire, Brussels	E7900	Thebes	Tutankhamun
18950		Royal Botanic Gardens, Kew	Kew No 5 Carter 277	Thebes	Tutankhamun
18951		Royal Botanic Gardens, Kew	Kew 12 Carter 527b	Thebes	Tutankhamun
18952		Royal Botanic Gardens, Kew	Kew 15 Carter 355	Thebes	Tutankhamun
19003		Royal Botanic Gardens, Kew	Kew 21 Carter 532, 534, 504	Thebes	Tutankhamun
19132		Ashmolean Museum, Oxford	1968.454	Thebes	Tutankhamun
19550		Metropolitan Museum of Art, New York		Thebes	Tutankhamun
18509		British Museum, London	BM6023	Thebes (?)	Tutankhamun-Horemheb
20208		Staatliches Museum Ägyptischer Kunst, Munich	ÄS298		Rameses I/Sety I
20175		Staatliches Museum Ägyptischer Kunst, Munich	ÄS301		Rameses I/Sety I

Dynasty	Material Group Type	Material Group Identification	Pretreatment Code	Date	±	Outlier Probability
18th	Short-lived plant part	Poaceae [Halfa grass]		3195	30	1
18th	Short-lived plant part	Arecaceae		3155	25	3
18th	Short-lived plant part/ wood	Mixed Poaceae & wood fragments	UV	3165	32	1
18th	Wood	?*Acacia* sp.	UW	3084	26	3
18th	Short-lived plant part/ wood	Mixed Poaceae & wood fragments	WW	3040	30	3
18th	Short-lived plant part	Poaceae	UV	3118	27	1
18th	Short-lived plant part		UV	3082	29	1
18th	Short-lived plant part		UV	3096	28	1
18th	Short-lived plant part		UV*	3051	27	1
			UV*	3064	28	
18th	Short-lived plant part	*Triticum* sp.	UW	3092	27	1
18th	Seeds	*Coriandrum* sp.	UW	2976	28	43
18th	Textile	?*Linum* sp.	UV	2862	26	100
			UV	2798	27	
18th	Textile	?*Linum* sp.	3a	2847	36	100
			3b	2918	30	
18th	Short-lived plant part	*Balanites aegyptiaca*	UW	3115	30	1
			3a	3094	37	
			3c	3070	37	
18th	Seeds [charred]	*Hordeum* sp.	ZR	3028	27	3
18th	Textile	*Linum* sp.	UW	2787	31	100
18th	Short-lived plant part	*Cyperus papyrus*	3a	3096	34	1
			3b	3116	35	
18th	Textile	*Linum* sp.	UV*	3065	31	1
18th	Short-lived plant part	*Triticum* sp.	UW	3138	28	2
18th	Seeds	*Phoenix dactylifera*	UW	3137	29	2
18th	Seeds	*Hordeum* sp.	UW	3117	29	1
18th	Seeds	*Ziziphus* sp.	UW	3106	26	1
18th	Textile		WW	3133	29	2
18th	Short-lived plant part	Arecaceae	UV	3015	25	16
18th	Short-lived plant part/ wood	Mixed Poaceae & wood fragments	UV	3056	27	1
19th	Short-lived plant part	?*Phoenix dactylifera*	UV	3191	28	-
19th	Short-lived plant part	?*Phoenix dactylifera*	UV	3213	29	-

Sample No. (OxA-)	Duplicate Number	Collection Location	Collection Reference	Site	King
20176		Staatliches Museum Ägyptischer Kunst, Munich	ÄS301		Rameses I/Sety I
20209		Staatliches Museum Ägyptischer Kunst, Munich	ÄS302		Rameses I/Sety I
20210		Staatliches Museum Ägyptischer Kunst, Munich	ÄS304		Rameses I/Sety I
20177 20178	41	Staatliches Museum Ägyptischer Kunst, Munich	ÄS304		Rameses I/Sety I
18501		Musées Royaux d'Art et d'Histoire, Brussels	E2596	Ramesseum	Rameses II
18505		British Museum, London	BM6019	Thebes (?)	Rameses II
19131		Ashmolean Museum, Oxford	1950.141	Tomb of Mernep	Merneptah
19143		Manchester Museum	MM5938	Thebes	Tausret
18958		Royal Botanic Gardens, Kew	EBC26788	Tomb of Qent	
19006		Royal Botanic Gardens, Kew	EBC26788	Tomb of Qent	
19554 VERA-4790A	42	Kunsthistorisches Museum, Vienna	A1991 Reg. No. 284	Funerary Temple	Rameses IV
20189		British Museum, London	BM9999/79	Thebes	Rameses IV
20213		British Museum, London	BM10326	Thebes	Rameses IX
20214		British Museum, London	BM75018	Thebes	Rameses IX
18051		Museum Gustavianum, Uppsala	D165	Deir el-Bahri	Smendes
20060		Bristol City Museum and Art Gallery	Box 4 Ha7386/120	Deir el-Bahri	Amenemnisu
20061 20062	43	Bristol City Museum and Art Gallery	Box 4 Ha7386/110 Box 4 Ha7386/110	Deir el-Bahri	Amenemnisu
20063		Bristol City Museum and Art Gallery	Box 4 Ha7386/110	Deir el-Bahri	Amenemnisu
20064		Bristol City Museum and Art Gallery	Box 4 Ha7386/110	Deir el-Bahri	Amenemnisu
20065		Bristol City Museum and Art Gallery	Box 4 Ha7386/110	Deir el-Bahri	Amenemnisu
20066		Bristol City Museum and Art Gallery	Box 4 Ha7386/113	Deir el-Bahri	Amenemnisu
20067		Bristol City Museum and Art Gallery	Box 4 Ha7386/106	Deir el-Bahri	Amenemnisu
20201		Bristol City Museum and Art Gallery	Ha7386/780	Deir el-Bahri	Amenemnisu
18959		Royal Botanic Gardens, Kew	EBC40733	Deir el Bahri	Psusennes I
19794		Petrie Museum, London	UC69665		Amenemope
18960		Royal Botanic Gardens, Kew	EBC40739	Deir el Bahri	Siamun

Not included in models

Duplicate dates

Dynasty	Material Group Type	Material Group Identification	Pretreatment Code	Date	±	Outlier Probability
19th	Short-lived plant part	Arecaceae & Cyperaceae	UV	3209	26	-
19th	Amorphous material		UV	3215	27	-
19th	Seeds	Ficus sp.	UV	3523	29	-
19th	Seeds	Phoenix dactylifera	UW	3162	27	-
			UW	3150	27	
19th	Short-lived plant part	Poaceae	UV	3171	28	97
19th	Short-lived plant part/ wood	Mixed Poaceae & wood fragments	WW	3118	27	26
19th	Textile	?Linum sp.	WW	3113	28	75
19th	Short-lived plant part		UW	2964	30	1
20th	Short-lived plant part	Phoenix dactylifera	UW	3124	29	100
20th	Wood	Tamarix sp.	UW	3139	27	100
20th	Textile	?Linum sp.	UV	3020	26	3
			1	2995	31	
20th	Short-lived plant part	Cyperus papyrus	UV	2972	27	1
20th	Short-lived plant part	Cyperus papyrus	UV	2771	28	100
20th	Short-lived plant part	Cyperus papyrus	UV	2946	29	1
21st	Short-lived plant part	Nymphaea sp.	UV*	2768	27	99
21st	Textile	?Linum sp.	UV	2901	27	1
21st	Textile	?Linum sp.	UW	2856	27	2
			UW	2880	27	
21st	Short-lived plant part	Poaceae	UV	2900	28	1
21st	Textile	?Linum sp.	UV	2930	28	2
21st	Textile	?Linum sp.	UV	2853	27	3
21st	Textile	?Linum sp.	VV	2860	30	2
21st	Textile	?Linum sp.	UV	2887	28	1
21st	Seeds	Asteraceae	VV	3127	27	100
21st	Short-lived plant part	Salix sp.	UV	2987	37	21
21st	Short-lived plant part	Poaceae	UV	2904	27	5
21st	Short-lived plant part	?Phoenix dactylifera	UV	2805	29	1

Table 3: Interlaboratory Comparisons.

ORAU versus Saclay

Duplicate No.	Description	Oxford Sample No. (OxA-)	¹⁴C Measurement Date (BP)	Error (σ)	Saclay Sample No. (SacA-)
19	Hatshepsut (CoR)	19448	3245	30	11129
20	Hatshepsut (CoR)	19449	3275	31	11130
21	Hatshepsut (CoR)	19450 & 19451	3263	23	11131
22	Hatshepsut (CoR)	19153	110	20	11169
23	After CoR	19149	165	23	11151
24	After CoR	19481	3233	25	11152
25	After CoR	19482	3277	26	11154
26	After CoR	19151	3107	27	11155
27	After CoR	19581	3258	26	11156
28	After CoR	19483	3226	26	11158
29	After CoR	19484	3257	26	11159
30	After CoR	19485	3262	25	11160
31	After CoR	19152	3249	28	11161
32	Thutmose III or CoR	19452	3227	30	11139
33	Thutmose III or CoR	19146	127	24	11143
34	Thutmose III or CoR	19486	182	22	11162

ORAU versus VERA

Duplicate No.	Description	Oxford Sample No. (OxA-)	¹⁴C Measurement Date (BP)	Error (σ)	Vienna Sample No. (VERA-)
5	Early 12th Dynasty	16838	3620	32	4075
8	Senusret III (Yr 5)	15313	3503	30	3726
9	Senusret III (Yr 5)	15317	3532	31	3730
10	Senusret III (Yr 5)	15318	3518	31	3731
11	Senusret III (Yr 14)	15315	3513	31	3728
12	Amenemhat III (Yr 4)	15316	3542	30	3729
14	Hatshepsut (CoR)	16833	3179	31	4070
15	Hatshepsut (CoR)	16834	3191	31	4071
16	Hatshepsut (CoR)	16835	3245	31	4072
17	Hatshepsut (CoR)	16836	3191	31	4073
18	Hatshepsut (CoR)	16837	3193	32	4074
30	Thutmose III	19556	2589	26	4788A
39	Amenhotep IV	18955	3115	30	4687 & 4687B
42	Rameses IV	19554	3020	26	4790A

| Saclay ^{14}C Measurement || Variance ^{14}C Measurement || Weighted Mean ^{14}C Measurement || Test Statistic |
Date (BP)	Error (σ)	Date (BP)	Error (σ)	Date (BP)	Error (σ)	
3165	30	+80	42	3205	23	3.6
3200	25	+75	40	3230	22	3.6
3230	20	+33	30	3244	18	1.2
110	23	+0	30	110	18	0.0
260	25	-95	34	209	19	7.8
3180	25	+53	35	3207	20	2.2
3305	25	-28	36	3292	20	0.6
3040	25	+67	37	3071	21	3.3
3200	25	+58	36	3228	20	2.6
3285	20	-59	33	3263	18	3.2
3305	25	-48	36	3282	20	1.8
3200	20	+62	32	3224	18	3.8
3205	30	+44	41	3229	22	1.1
3225	25	+2	39	3226	21	0.0
165	20	-38	31	149	18	1.5
180	20	+2	30	181	17	0.0
		+9	9			

| Vienna ^{14}C Measurement || Variance ^{14}C Measurement || Weighted Mean ^{14}C Measurement || Test Statistic |
Date (BP)	Error (σ)	Date (BP)	Error (σ)	Date (BP)	Error (σ)	
3679	29	-59	43	3647	25	1.9
3543	29	-40	42	3524	23	0.9
3529	29	+3	42	3530	23	0.0
3513	29	+5	42	3515	23	0.0
3565	29	-52	42	3541	23	1.5
3563	29	-21	42	3553	23	0.3
3249	32	-70	45	3208	25	2.5
3203	29	-12	42	3196	25	0.1
3204	30	+41	43	3226	25	0.9
3240	31	-49	44	3212	25	1.2
3173	30	+20	44	3183	25	0.2
2649	35	-60	44	2610	23	1.9
3082	28	+33	41	3097	22	0.6
2995	31	+25	40	3010	22	0.4

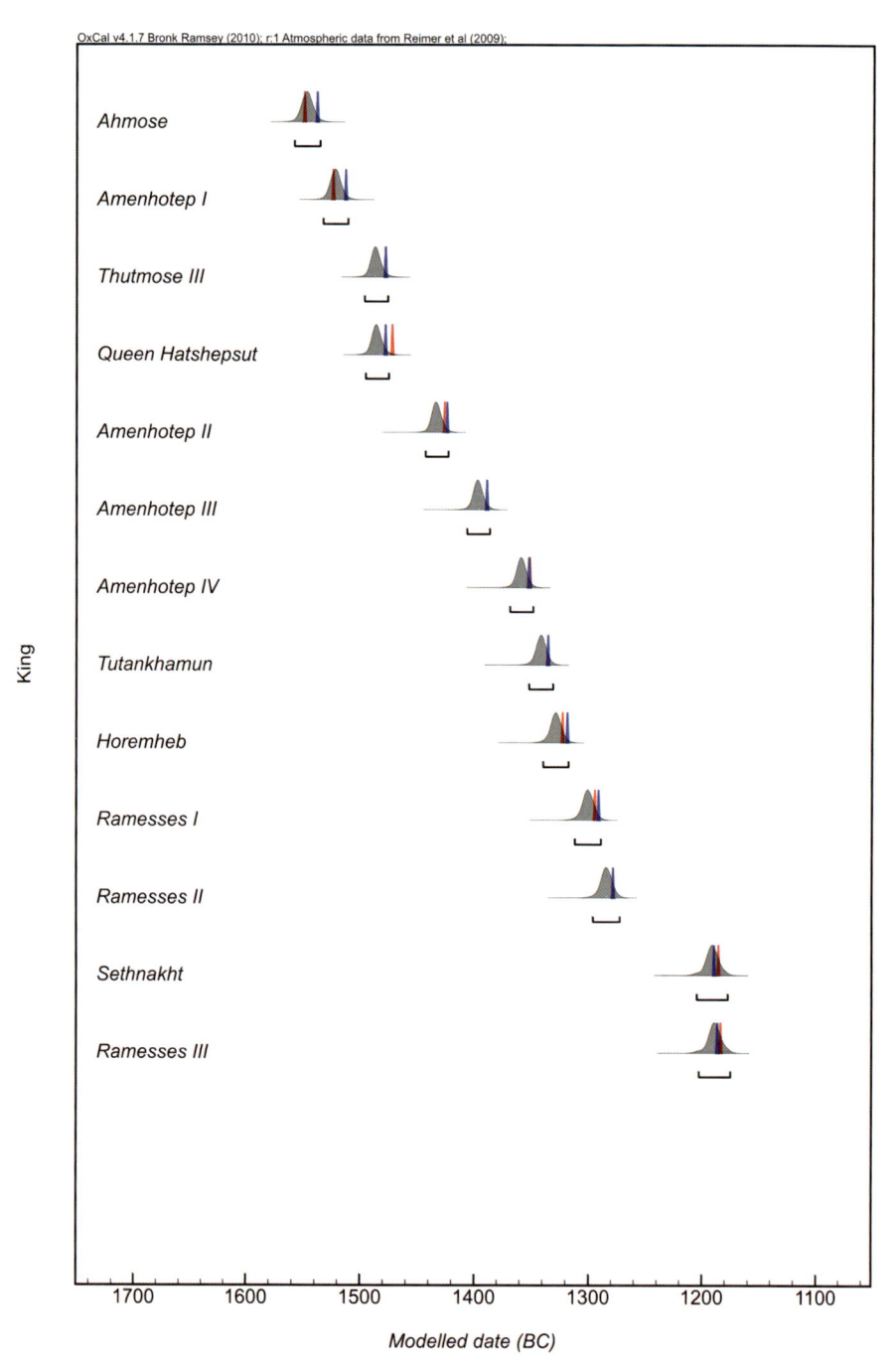

Figure 1: Selected accession dates from NKM3. The high chronology estimates are shown in red; low chronology in blue; modelled radiocarbon dates in grey. The calibrated ranges (95%) given by the square brackets are listed in Table 5, Appendix.

Appendix and Model Results 271

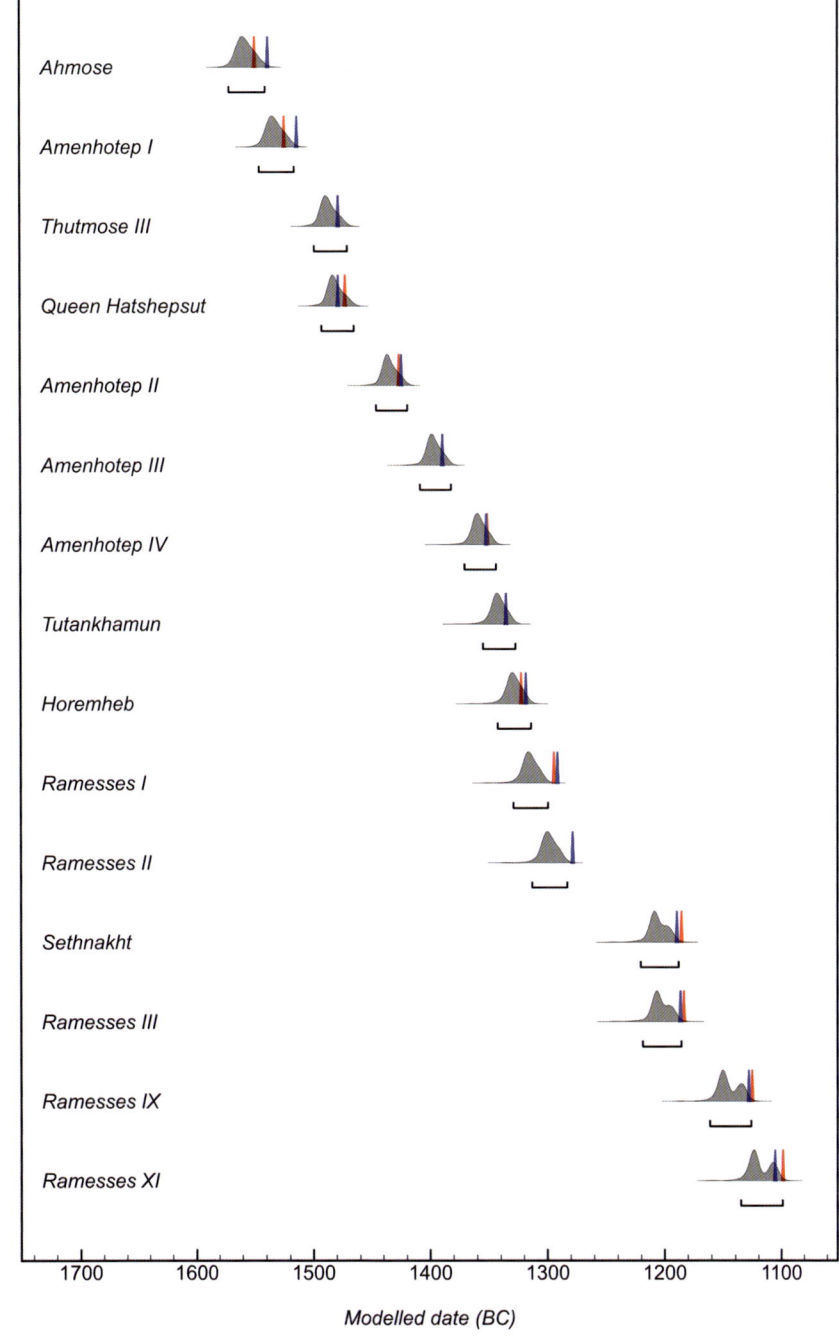

Figure 2: Selected accession dates from NKM4. The high chronology estimates are shown in red; low chronology in blue; modelled radiocarbon dates in grey. The calibrated ranges (95%) given by the square brackets are listed in Table 5, Appendix.

272 *Appendix and Model Results*

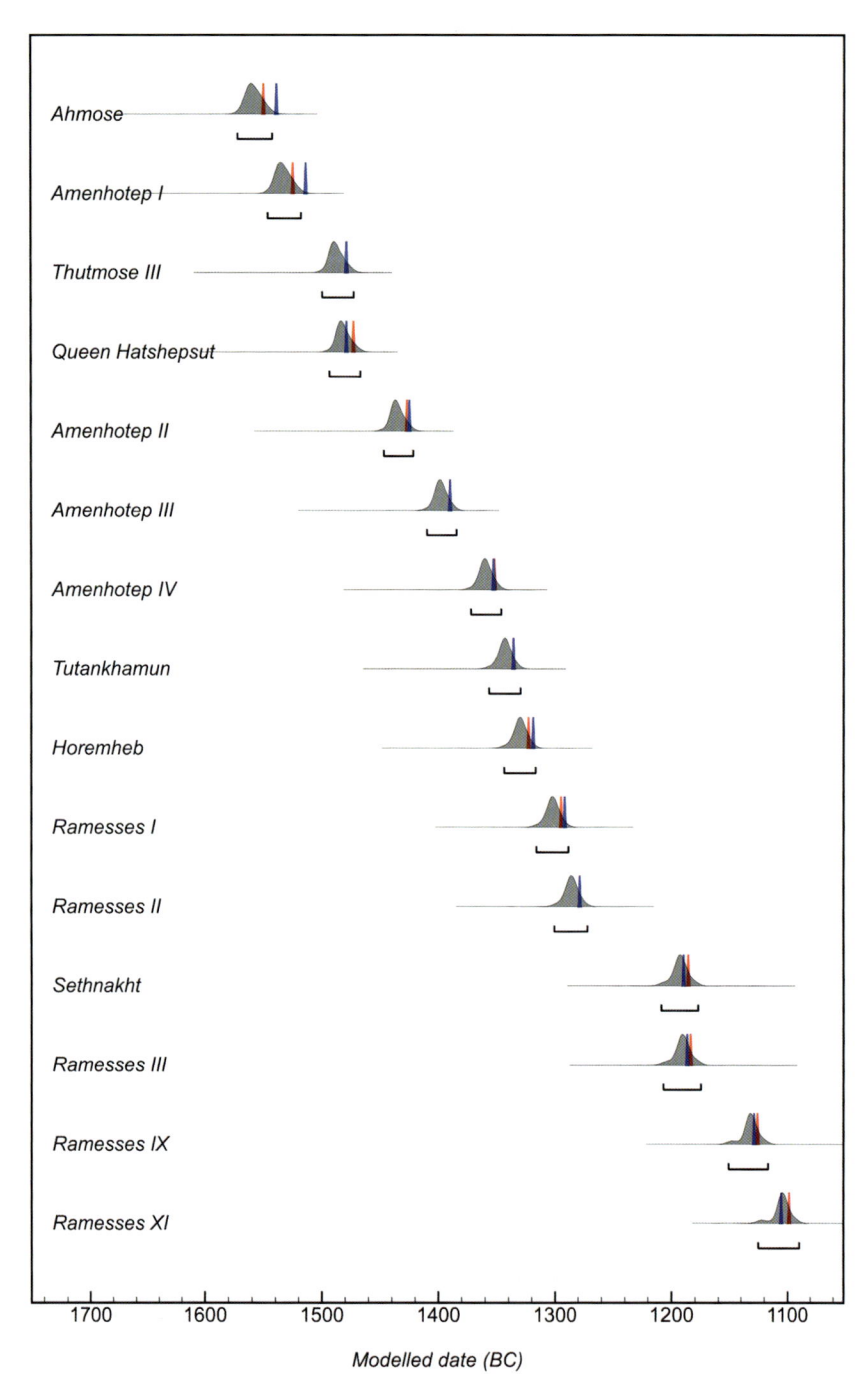

Figure 3: Selected accession dates from NKM5. The high chronology estimates are shown in red; low chronology in blue; modelled radiocarbon dates in grey. The calibrated ranges (95%) given by the square brackets are listed in Table 5, Appendix.

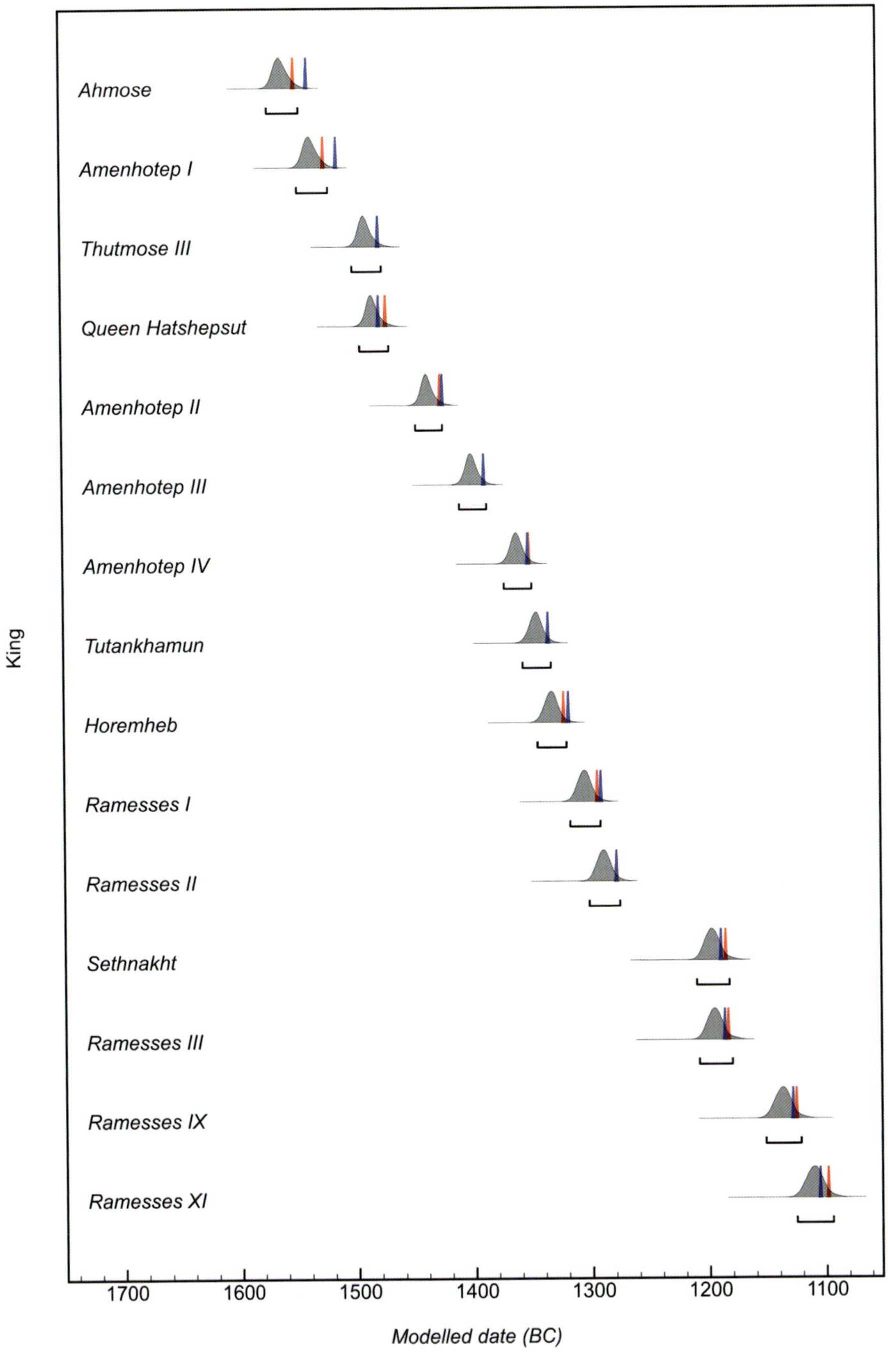

Figure 4: Selected accession dates from NKM6. The high chronology estimates are shown in red; low chronology in blue; modelled radiocarbon dates in grey. The calibrated ranges (95%) given by the square brackets are listed in Table 5, Appendix.

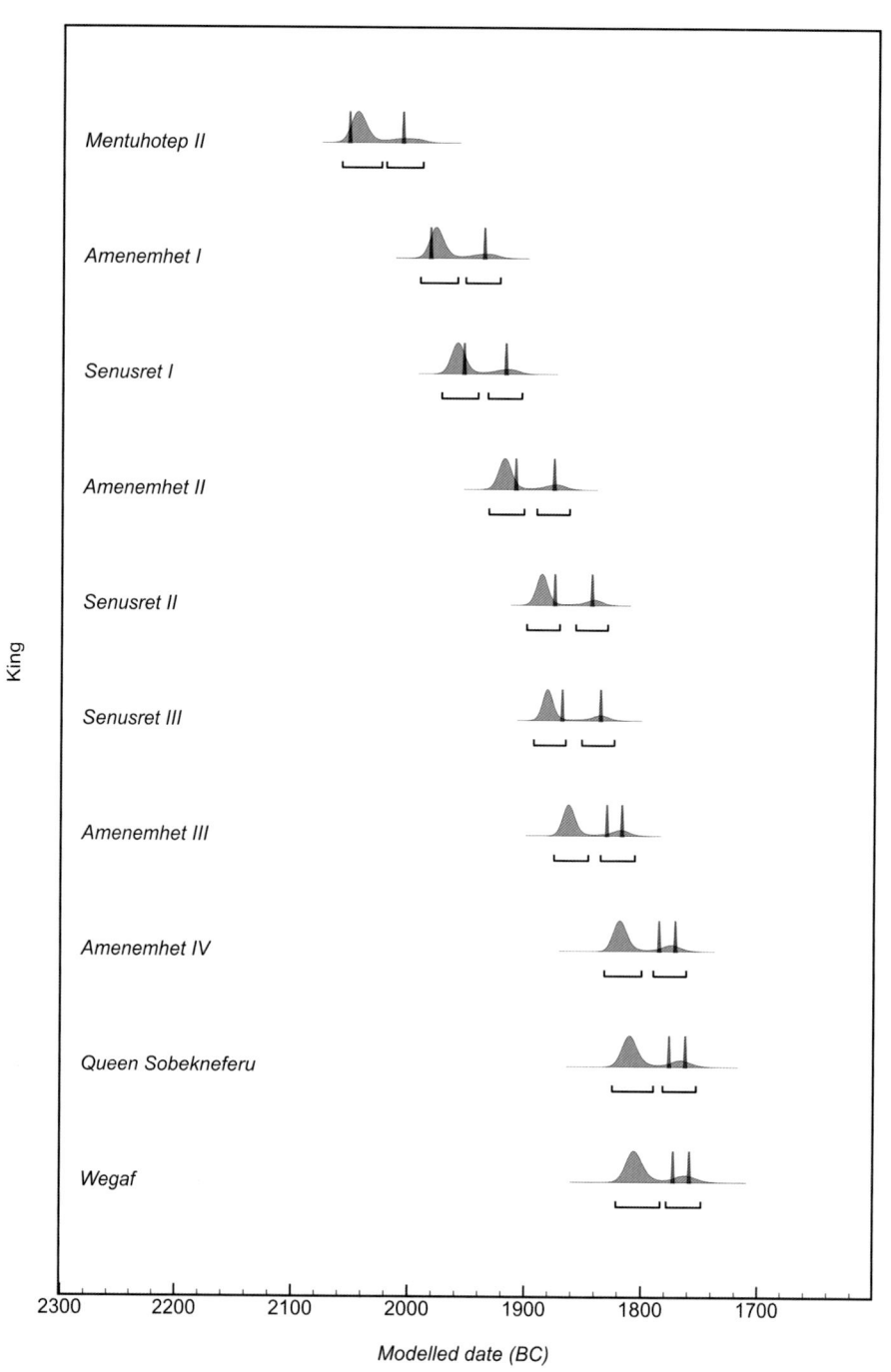

Figure 5: Selected accession dates from MKM3. The high chronology estimates are shown in red; low chronology in blue; modelled radiocarbon dates in grey. The calibrated ranges (95%) given by the square brackets are listed in Table 5, Appendix.

Appendix and Model Results 275

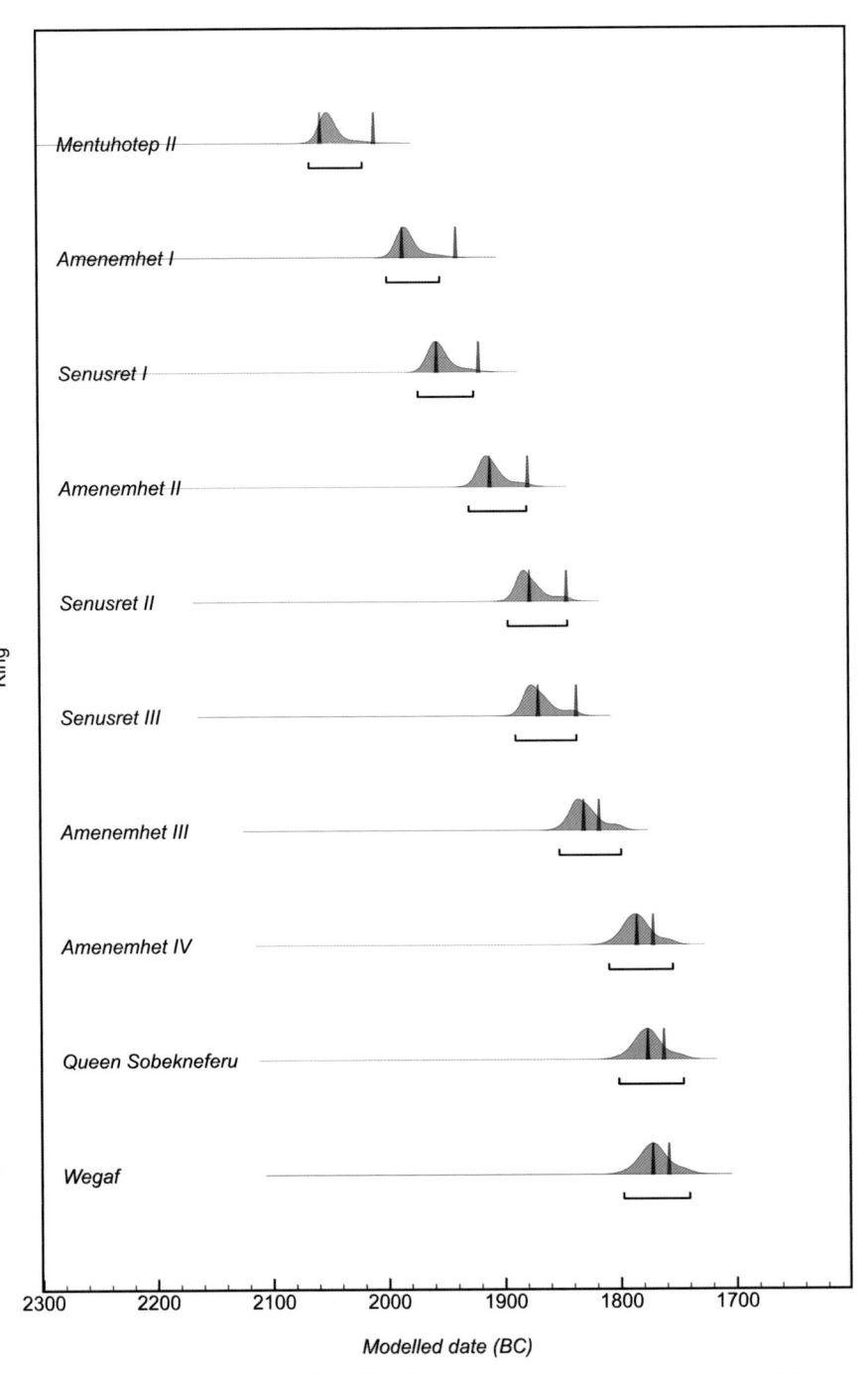

Figure 6: Selected accession dates from MKM4. The high chronology estimates are shown in red; low chronology in blue; modelled radiocarbon dates in grey. The calibrated ranges (95%) given by the square brackets are listed in Table 5, Appendix.

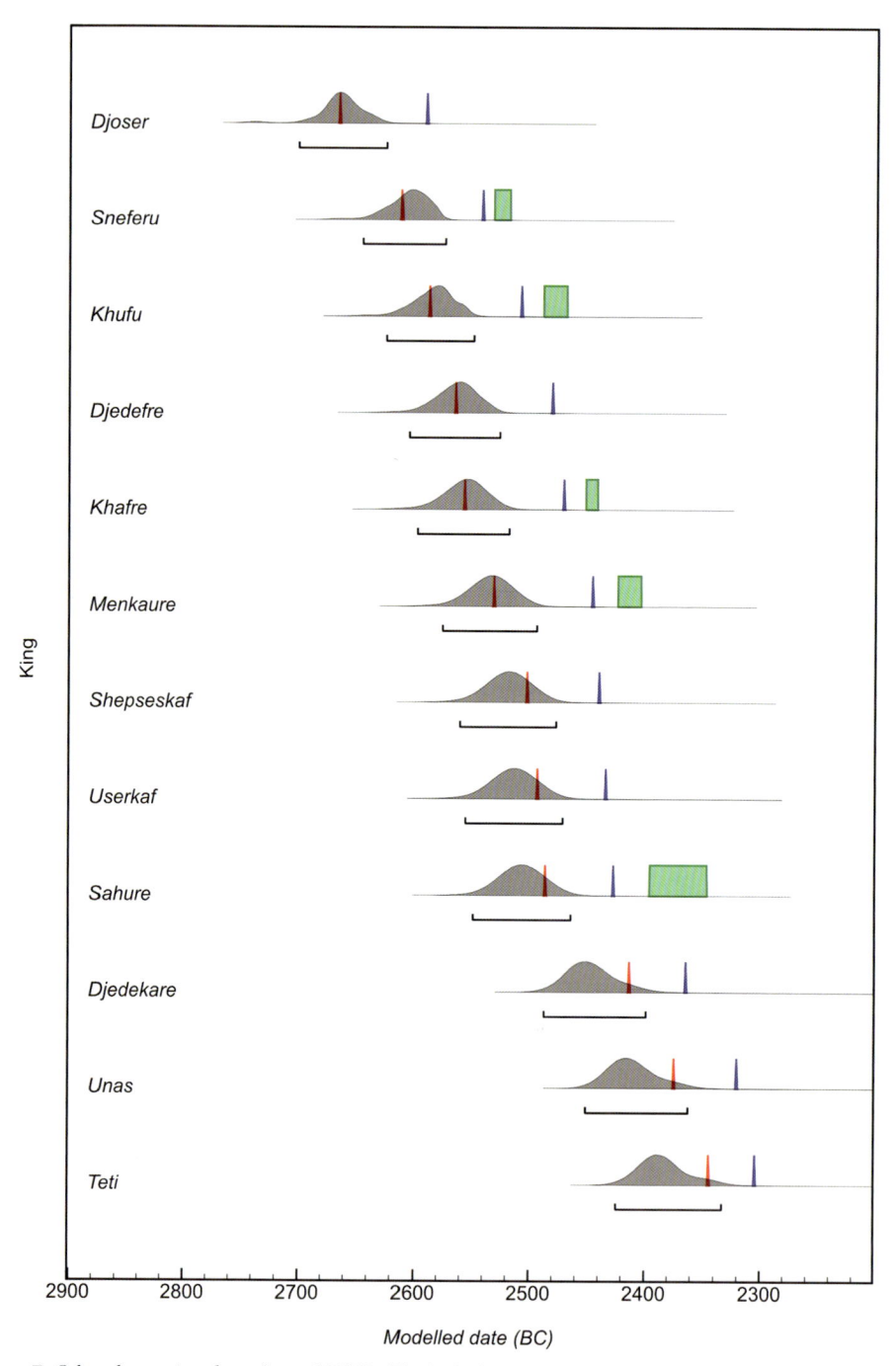

Figure 7: Selected accession dates from OKM3. The high chronology estimates are shown in red; low chronology in blue; modelled radiocarbon dates in grey. The calibrated ranges (95%) given by the square brackets are listed in Table 5, Appendix.

Table 4

NKM1 Code
```
Options()
{
 Resolution=1;
 kIterations=100;
};
Plot()
{
 Outlier_Model("General",T(5),U(0,4),"t");
 Delta_R("Seasonal Effect", 19, 5);
 Sequence("Extra Dates 1 17th/18th Dynasty Boundary")
 {
  Boundary("=Start 17th Dynasty");
  Phase("17th/18th Boundary")
  {
   R_Date("20018", 3268, 27)
   {
    Outlier(0.05);
   };
   R_Date("20015", 3278, 26)
   {
    Outlier(0.05);
   };
  };
  Boundary("=Amenhotep I");
 };
 Sequence("Extra Dates 2 Early 18th Dynasty")
 {
  Boundary("=Ahmose");
  Phase("Early 18th")
  {
   R_Date("18417", 3336, 30)
   {
    Outlier(0.05);
   };
   R_Date("19715", 2934, 26)
   {
    Outlier(0.05);
   };
   R_Date("19716", 3288, 28)
   {
    Outlier(0.05);
   };
   R_Date("19788", 2984, 26)
   {
    Outlier(0.05);
   };
  };
  Boundary("=Queen Hatshepsut");
 };
 Sequence("Extra Dates 3 Hatshepsut or Thutmose III")
 {
  Boundary("=Thutmose III");
  Phase("Hst or Thut III")
  {
   R_Date("SacA 11134", 3225, 20)
   {
    Outlier(0.05);
   };
   R_Date("SacA 11135", 3095, 20)
   {
    Outlier(0.05);
   };
   R_Date("SacA 11137", 3170, 25)
   {
    Outlier(0.05);
   };
   R_Combine("Hst or Thut III Combine 1", 8)
   {
    R_Date("19452", 3227, 30);
    R_Date("SacA-11139", 3225, 25);
    Outlier(0.05);
   };
   R_Date("SacA 11140", 3250, 25)
   {
    Outlier(0.05);
   };
   R_Date("SacA 11144", 3380, 50)
   {
    Outlier(0.05);
   };
   R_Date("SacA 11145", 3195, 20)
   {
    Outlier(0.05);
   };
   R_Date("SacA 11163", 3285, 20)
   {
    Outlier(0.05);
   };
   R_Date("SacA 11164", 3160, 20)
   {
    Outlier(0.05);
   };
   R_Date("SacA 11165", 3195, 30)
   {
    Outlier(0.05);
   };
   R_Date("SacA 11166", 3155, 25)
   {
    Outlier(0.05);
   };
   R_Date("SacA 11172", 3190, 25)
   {
    Outlier(0.05);
   };
   R_Date("18508", 3482, 29)
   {
    Outlier(0.05);
   };
   R_Date("18513", 3108, 28)
   {
    Outlier(0.05);
   };
   R_Combine("Hst or Thut III Combine 2", 8)
   {
    R_Date("19556", 2589, 26);
    R_Date("VERA-4788A", 2649, 35);
    Outlier(0.05);
   };
  };
  Boundary("=Amenhotep II");
 };
 Sequence("Extra Dates 4 Late 18th Dynasty")
 {
  Boundary("=Tutankhamun");
  Phase("Late 18th")
  {
   R_Date("18509", 3056, 27)
   {
    Outlier(0.05);
   };
  };
  Boundary("=Ramesses I");
 };
 Sequence("Extra Dates 5 20th Dynasty")
 {
  Boundary("=Sethnakht");
  Phase("20th")
  {
   R_Date("18958", 3124, 29)
   {
    Outlier(0.05);
   };
   R_Date("19006", 3139, 27)
   {
    Outlier(0.05);
   };
  };
  Boundary("=Smendes");
 };
 Sequence("New Kingdom Model")
 {
  Boundary("Start 17th Dynasty");
  Phase("17th Dynasty")
  {
   R_Date("18554", 3232, 27)
   {
    Outlier(0.05);
   };
   Interval("17th Int", 30 + T(5));
  };
  Boundary("Ahmose")
  {
```

```
z=1;
};
Phase("Ahm")
{
 Interval("Ahm Int", 25 + T(5));
};
Boundary("Amenhotep I")
{
 z=2;
};
Phase("Ahp I")
{
 Interval("Ahp I Int", 21 + T(5));
};
Boundary("Thutmose I");
Phase("Thut I")
{
 R_Date("18506", 3244, 27)
 {
  Outlier(0.05);
 };
 R_Date("18411", 3228, 29)
 {
  Outlier(0.05);
 };
 Interval("Thut I Int", 12 + T(5));
};
Boundary("Thutmose II");
Phase("Thut II")
{
 Interval("Thut II Int", 13 + T(5));
};
Boundary("Thutmose III")
{
 z=3;
};
Phase("Thut III")
{
 Interval("Thut III Int I", 6 + T(5));
};
Boundary("Queen Hatshepsut")
{
 z=4;
};
Phase("Hst")
{
 R_Combine("Hst Combine 1", 8)
 {
  R_Date("16833", 3179, 31);
    R_Date("VERA-4070", 3249, 32);
  Outlier(0.05);
 };
 R_Combine("Hst Combine 2", 8)
 {
  R_Date("16834", 3191, 31);
    R_Date("VERA-4071", 3203, 29);
  Outlier(0.05);
 };
```

```
R_Combine("Hst Combine 3", 8)
{
 R_Date("16835", 3245, 31);
   R_Date("VERA-4072", 3204, 30);
 Outlier(0.05);
};
R_Combine("Hst Combine 4", 8)
{
 R_Date("16836", 3191, 31);
   R_Date("VERA-4073", 3240, 31);
 Outlier(0.05);
};
R_Combine("Hst Combine 5", 8)
{
 R_Date("16837", 3193, 32);
   R_Date("VERA-4074", 3173, 30);
 Outlier(0.05);
};
R_Date("19008", 2972, 26)
{
 Outlier(0.05);
};
R_Combine("Hst Combine 6", 8)
{
 R_Date("19448", 3245, 30);
   R_Date("SacA-11129", 3165, 30);
 Outlier(0.05);
};
R_Combine("Hst Combine 7", 8)
{
 R_Date("19449", 3275, 31);
   R_Date("SacA-11130", 3200, 25);
 Outlier(0.05);
};
R_Combine("Hst Combine 8", 8)
{
 R_Date("19450", 3291, 31);
 R_Date("19451", 3237, 30);
   R_Date("SacA-11131", 3230, 20);
 Outlier(0.05);
};
R_Date("SacA 11132", 3170, 35)
{
 Outlier(0.05);
};
R_Date("19154", 3209, 28)
{
 Outlier(0.05);
};
R_Date("SacA 11170", 3285, 20)
{
 Outlier(0.05);
};
R_Date("19546", 3237, 26)
```

```
{
 Outlier(0.05);
};
R_Date("19252", 3210, 31)
{
 Outlier(0.05);
};
R_Date("19547", 3171, 25)
{
 Outlier(0.05);
};
R_Date("SacA 11168", 3760, 60)
{
 Outlier(0.05);
};
Interval("Hst Int", 15 + T(5));
};
Boundary("Hatshepsut End");
Phase("Thut III")
{
 R_Date("19147", 3261, 32)
 {
  Outlier(0.05);
 };
 R_Date("19148", 3186, 28)
 {
  Outlier(0.05);
 };
 R_Date("19453", 3264, 29)
 {
  Outlier(0.05);
 };
 R_Date("SacA 11148", 3090, 30)
 {
  Outlier(0.05);
 };
 R_Date("19480", 3251, 26)
 {
  Outlier(0.05);
 };
 R_Date("SacA 11150", 3185, 30)
 {
  Outlier(0.05);
 };
  R_Combine("Thut III Combine 1", 8)
 {
  R_Date("19481", 3233, 25);
    R_Date("SacA-11152", 3180, 25);
  Outlier(0.05);
 };
 R_Date("19150", 3153, 27)
 {
  Outlier(0.05);
 };
 R_Date("SacA 11153", 3260, 30)
 {
  Outlier(0.05);
 };
```

```
    R_Combine("Thut III Combine         {                                };
2", 8)                                    z=5;                            R_Date("18954", 2976, 28)
      {                                 };                                {
      R_Date("19482", 3277, 26);        Phase("Ahp II")                     Outlier(0.05);
      R_Date("SacA-11154", 3305,        {                                 };
25);                                      R_Date("18507", 3165, 32)         R_Combine("Ahp IV Combine
      Outlier(0.05);                    {                               2", 8)
      };                                  Outlier(0.05);                    {
    R_Combine("Thut III Combine         };                                  R_Date("19004", 2862, 26);
3", 8)                                  Interval("Ahp II Int ", 27 + T(5));   R_Date("19263", 2798, 27);
    {                                   };                                  Outlier(0.05);
      R_Date("19151", 3107, 27);        Boundary("Thutmose IV");            };
      R_Date("SacA-11155", 3040,        Phase("Thut IV")                  R_Combine("Ahp IV Combine
25);                                    {                               3", 8)
      Outlier(0.05);                      R_Date("19549", 3084, 26)         {
      };                                  {                                 R_Date("VERA-4686", 2847,
    R_Combine("Thut III Combine           Outlier(0.05);                36);
4", 8)                                    };                                R_Date("VERA-4686B", 2918,
    {                                   Interval("Thut IV Int", 10 + T(5));  30);
      R_Date("19581", 3258, 26);        };                                  Outlier(0.05);
      R_Date("SacA-11156", 3200,        Boundary("Amenhotep III")           };
25);                                    {                                 R_Combine("Ahp IV Combine
      Outlier(0.05);                      z=6;                          4", 8)
      };                                };                                  {
    R_Combine("Thut III Combine         Phase("Ahp III")                    R_Date("18955", 3115, 30);
5", 8)                                  {                                   R_Date("VERA-4687", 3094,
    {                                     R_Date("18510", 3040, 30)     37);
      R_Date("19483", 3226, 26);          {                                 R_Date("VERA-4687B", 3070,
      R_Date("SacA-11158", 3285,          Outlier(0.05);                37);
20);                                      };                                Outlier(0.05);
      Outlier(0.05);                      R_Date("19548", 3118, 27)         };
      };                                  {                                 R_Date("18956", 3028, 27)
    R_Combine("Thut III Combine           Outlier(0.05);                    {
6", 8)                                    };                                Outlier(0.05);
    {                                   Interval("Ahp III Int", 38 + T(5));  };
      R_Date("19484", 3257, 26);        };                                  R_Date("20482", 2787, 31)
      R_Date("SacA-11159", 3305,        Boundary("Amenhotep IV")            {
25);                                    {                                   Outlier(0.05);
      Outlier(0.05);                      z=7;                              };
      };                                };                                R_Combine("Ahp IV Combine
    R_Combine("Thut III Combine         Phase("Ahp IV")                 5", 8)
7", 8)                                  {                                   {
    {                                     R_Date("18057", 3082, 29)         R_Date("VERA-4685", 3096,
      R_Date("19485", 3262, 25);          {                             34);
      R_Date("SacA-11160", 3200,          Outlier(0.05);                    R_Date("VERA-4685B", 3116,
20);                                      };                            35);
      Outlier(0.05);                      R_Date("18407", 3096, 28)         Outlier(0.05);
      };                                  {                                 };
    R_Combine("Thut III Combine           Outlier(0.05);                  Interval("Akh Int", 14 + T(5));
8", 8)                                    };                              };
    {                                   R_Combine("Ahp IV Combine         Boundary("Neferneferuaten");
      R_Date("19152", 3249, 28);      1", 8)                              Phase("Nef")
      R_Date("SacA-11161", 3205,        {                                 {
30);                                      R_Date("18512", 3051, 27);        Interval("Nef Int", 2 + T(5));
      Outlier(0.05);                      R_Date("18412", 3064, 28);        };
      };                                  Outlier(0.05);                  Boundary("Tutankhamun")
    Interval("Thut III Int II", 31 +     };                                {
T(5));                                    R_Date("18953", 3092, 27)         z=8;
    };                                    {                                 };
    Boundary("Amenhotep II")              Outlier(0.05);                  Phase("Tut")
```

```
{
 R_Date("17868", 3065, 31)
 {
  Outlier(0.05);
 };
 R_Date("18950", 3138, 28)
 {
  Outlier(0.05);
 };
 R_Date("18951", 3137, 29)
 {
  Outlier(0.05);
 };
 R_Date("18952", 3117, 29)
 {
  Outlier(0.05);
 };
 R_Date("19003", 3106, 26)
 {
  Outlier(0.05);
 };
 R_Date("19132", 3133, 29)
 {
  Outlier(0.05);
 };
 R_Date("19550", 3015, 25)
 {
  Outlier(0.05);
 };
 Interval("Tut Int", 9 + T(5));
};
Boundary("Ay");
Phase("Ay Phase")
{
 Interval("Ay Int", 4 + T(5));
};
Boundary("Horemheb")
{
 z=9;
};
Phase("Hhb")
{
 Interval("Hhb Int", 28 + T(5));
};
Boundary("Ramesses I")
{
 z=10;
};
Phase("Ram I")
{
 Interval("Ram I Int", 1 + T(5));
};
Boundary("Sety I");
Phase("Set I")
{
 Interval("Sety I Int", 15 + T(5));
};
Boundary("Ramesses II")
{
 z=11;
```

```
};
Phase("Ram II")
{
 R_Date("18501", 3171, 28)
 {
  Outlier(0.05);
 };
 R_Date("18505", 3118, 27)
 {
  Outlier(0.05);
 };
 Interval("Ram II Int", 66 + T(5));
};
Boundary("Merenptah");
Phase("Mpt")
{
 R_Date("19131", 3113, 28)
 {
  Outlier(0.05);
 };
 Interval("Mpt Int",10 + T(5));
};
Boundary("Amenmessu");
Phase("Amu")
{
 Interval("Amu Int",3 + T(5));
};
Boundary("Sety II");
Phase("Set II")
{
 Interval("Sety II Int", 6 + T(5));
};
Boundary("Saptah");
Phase("Sap")
{
 Interval("Sap Int", 6 + T(5));
};
Boundary("Queen Tausret");
Phase("Tau")
{
 R_Date("19143", 2964, 30)
 {
  Outlier(0.05);
 };
 Interval("Tau Int",2 + T(5));
};
Boundary("Sethnakht")
{
 z=12;
};
Phase("Seth")
{
 Interval("Seth Int", 2 + T(5));
};
Boundary("Ramesses III")
{
 z=13;
};
Phase("Ram III")
{
```

```
 Interval("Ram III Int", 31 + T(5));
};
Boundary("Ramesses IV");
Phase("Ram IV")
{
 R_Combine("Ram IV Combine 1", 8)
 {
  R_Date("19554", 3020, 26);
  R_Date("VERA-4790A", 2995, 31);
  Outlier(0.05);
 };
 R_Date("20189", 2972, 27)
 {
  Outlier(0.05);
 };
 Interval("Ram IV Int", 6 + T(5));
};
Boundary("Ramesses V");
Phase("Ram V")
{
 Interval("Ram V Int", 4 + T(5));
};
Boundary("Ramesses VI");
Phase("Ram VI")
{
 Interval("Ram VI Int", 7 + T(5));
};
Boundary("Ramesses VII");
Phase("Ram VII")
{
 Interval("Ram VII Int", 7 + T(5));
};
Boundary("Ramesses VIII");
Phase("Ram VIII")
{
 Interval("Ram VIII Int", 3 + T(5));
};
Boundary("Ramesses IX")
{
 z=14;
};
Phase("Ram IX")
{
 R_Date("20213", 2771, 28)
 {
  Outlier(0.05);
 };
 R_Date("20214", 2946, 29)
 {
  Outlier(0.05);
 };
 Interval("Ram IX Int", 18 + T(5));
};
Boundary("Ramesses X");
Phase("Ram X")
{
 Interval("Ram X Int", 9 + T(5));
};
```

Appendix and Model Results

```
Boundary("Ramesses XI")
{
 z=15;
};
Phase("Ram XI")
{
 Interval("Ram XI Int", 30 + T(5));
};
Boundary("Smendes")
{
 z=16;
};
Phase("Sme")
{
 R_Date("18051", 2768, 27)
 {
  Outlier(0.05);
 };
 Interval("Sme Int", 26 + T(5));
};
Boundary("Amenemnisu");
Phase("Ame")
{
 R_Date("20060", 2901, 27)
 {
  Outlier(0.05);
 };
  R_Combine("Ame Combine 1",
8)
 {
  R_Date("20061", 2856, 27);
  R_Date("20062", 2880, 27);
  Outlier(0.05);
 };
 R_Date("20063", 2900, 28)
 {
  Outlier(0.05);
 };
 R_Date("20064", 2930, 28)
 {
  Outlier(0.05);
 };
 R_Date("20065", 2853, 27)
 {
  Outlier(0.05);
 };
 R_Date("20066", 2860, 30)
 {
  Outlier(0.05);
 };
 R_Date("20067", 2887, 28)
 {
  Outlier(0.05);
 };
 R_Date("20201", 3127, 27)
 {
  Outlier(0.05);
 };
 Interval("Ame Int", 4 + T(5));
};
```

```
Boundary("Psusennes I");
Phase("Psu")
{
 R_Date("18959", 2987, 37)
 {
  Outlier(0.05);
 };
 Interval("Psu Int", 46 + T(5));
};
Boundary("Amenemope");
Phase("Amp")
{
 R_Date("19794", 2904, 27)
 {
  Outlier(0.05);
 };
 Interval("Amp Int",9 + T(5));
};
Boundary("Osorkon the Elder");
Phase("Ors")
{
 Interval("Ors Int", 6 + T(5));
};
Boundary("Siamun");
Phase("Sia")
{
 R_Date("18960", 2805, 29)
 {
  Outlier(0.05);
 };
 Interval("Sia Int", 19 + T(5));
};
Boundary("Psusennes II");
Phase("Psu II")
{
 Interval("Psu II Int", 14 + T(5));
};
Boundary("Sheshonq I");
};
```

MKM1 & OKM1 Code

```
Options()
{
 Resolution=1;
 kIterations=100;
};

};
Plot()
{
 Outlier_Model("General",T(5),U(0,4),"t");
 Delta_R(19, 5);
 Sequence("Extra Dates 1 Kkmy or Dsr")
 {
  Boundary("=Khasekhemwy");
```

```
Phase("Kkmy or Dsr")
{
 R_Date("17850", 4084, 32)
 {
  Outlier(0.05);
 };
 R_Date("18500", 4177, 28)
 {
  Outlier(0.05);
 };
 R_Date("18053", 4108, 30)
 {
  Outlier(0.05);
 };
 R_Date("18406", 4135, 30)
 {
  Outlier(0.05);
 };
 R_Date("18957", 4145, 32)
 {
  Outlier(0.05);
 };
 R_Date("19005", 4168, 27)
 {
  Outlier(0.05);
 };
 Boundary("=Sekhemkhet");
};
Sequence("Extra Dates 2 3rd/4th Dynasty Boundary")
{
 Boundary("=Sekhemkhet");
 Phase("3rd/4th Dynasty Boundary")
 {
  R_Date("19542", 3954, 27)
  {
   Outlier(0.05);
  };
 };
 Boundary("=Khufu");
};
Sequence("Extra Dates 3 Mpt II-Sen I")
{
 Boundary("=Mentuhotep II");
 Phase("Late 11th")
 {
  R_Date("19543", 3715, 25)
  {
   Outlier(0.05);
  };
 };
 Boundary("=Amenemhet I");
 Phase("Early 12th")
 {
  R_Combine("Early 12th Combine 1", 8)
  {
```

```
    R_Date("16838", 3620, 32);
      R_Date("VERA-4075", 3679, 29);
    Outlier(0.05);
   };
  };
  Boundary("=Amenemhet II");
 };
 Sequence("Extra Dates 4 Queen of Sen I")
 {
  Boundary("=Senusret I");
  Phase("Queen of Sen I")
  {
   R_Date("20479", 3498, 32)
   {
    Outlier(0.05);
   };
  };
  Boundary("=Amenemhet III");
 };
 Sequence("Extra Dates 5 12th")
 {
  Boundary("=Amenemhet I");
  Phase("12th")
  {
   R_Date("18502", 3518, 28)
   {
    Outlier(0.05);
   };
  };
  Boundary("=Wegaf");
 };
 Sequence("Extra Dates 6 12th/13th Boundary")
 {
  Boundary("=Queen Sobekneferu");
  Phase("Sbk-Weg (13th)")
  {
   R_Date("20014", 3469, 27)
   {
    Outlier(0.05);
   };
  };
  Boundary("=Sobekhotep II");
 };
 Sequence("OK")
 {
  Boundary("Khasekhemwy");
  Boundary("Djoser");
  {
   z=1;
  };
  Phase("Dsr")
  {
   R_Date("18052", 2421, 28)
   {
    Outlier(0.05);
   };
   R_Date("19793", 3313, 27)
```

```
  {
   Outlier(0.05);
  };
   R_Combine("Djoser Combine 1", 8)
  {
   R_Date("20767", 4081, 29);
   R_Date("20768", 4172, 28);
   R_Date("20736", 4115, 32);
   Outlier(0.05);
  };
  Interval("Dsr Int", 19 + 5*T(5));
 };
 Boundary("Sekhemkhet");
 Phase("Late 3rd")
 {
   Interval("Late 3rd Int", 35 + 2*5*T(5));
 };
 Boundary("Sneferu");
 {
  z=2;
 };
 Phase("Snf")
 {
  R_Date("18514", 4091, 29)
  {
   Outlier(0.05);
  };
  R_Date("19141", 4140, 31)
  {
   Outlier(0.05);
  };
  Interval("Snf Int", 24 + 5*T(5));
 };
 Boundary("Khufu")
 {
  z=3;
 };
 Phase("Khu")
 {
  Interval("Khu Int", 23 + 5*T(5));
 };
 Boundary("Djedefre")
 {
  z=4;
 };
 Phase("Dje")
 {
  Interval("Dje Int", 8 + 5*T(5));
 };
 Boundary("Khafre")
 {
  z=5;
 };
 Phase("Kha")
 {
  Interval("Kha Int", 26 + 5*T(5));
 };
 Boundary("Menkaure")
```

```
 {
  z=6;
 };
 Phase("Men")
 {
  Interval("Men Int", 29 + 5*T(5));
 };
 Boundary("Shepseskaf")
 {
  z=7;
 };
 Phase("She")
 {
   Interval("She + Hiatus Int", 9 + 5*T(5));
 };
 Boundary("Userkaf")
 {
  z=8;
 };
 Phase("Hiatus + Use")
 {
  Interval("Use Int", 7 + 5*T(5));
 };
 Boundary("Sahure")
 {
  z=9;
 };
 Phase("Mid 5th")
 {
   Interval("Mid 5th Int", 73 + 2.45*5*T(5));
 };
 Boundary("Djedekare")
 {
  z=10;
 };
 Phase("Ddk")
 {
  R_Date("20212", 3911, 31)
  {
   Outlier(0.05);
  };
  Interval("Ddk Int", 39 + 5*T(5));
 };
 Boundary("Unas")
 {
  z=11;
 };
 Phase("Una")
 {
  Interval("Una Int", 30 + 5*T(5));
 };
 Boundary("Teti")
 {
  z=12;
 };
 Phase("Tet")
 {
  Interval("Tet Int", 22 + 5*T(5));
```

```
};
Boundary("Userkara");
Phase("Usr")
{
 Interval("Usr Int", 2 + 5*T(5));
};
Boundary("Pepy I");
Phase("Pep I")
{
 R_Date("18553", 3979, 29)
 {
  Outlier(0.05);
 };
 Interval("Pep I Int", 34 + 5*T(5));
};
Boundary("Merenra");
Phase("Late 6th Dynasty")
{
 Interval("Late 6th Dynasty Int", 106 + 1.73*5*T(5));
};
Boundary("Start 7th Dynasty");
Phase("7th-8th")
{
 R_Date("18063", 3562, 29)
 {
  Outlier(0.05);
 };
 Interval("7th-8th Int", 21 + 5*T(5));
};
Boundary("Start 1IP")
{
 z=13;
};
};
Sequence("MK")
{
Boundary("Mentuhotep II")
{
 z=14;
};
Phase("Mtp II")
{
 R_Combine("Mtp Combine 1", 8)
 {
  R_Date("18055", 3625, 29);
  R_Date("18058", 3573, 30);
  Outlier(0.05);
 };
 R_Combine("Mtp Combine 2", 8)
 {
  R_Date("18056", 3616, 29);
  R_Date("18059", 3561, 30);
  Outlier(0.05);
 };
 R_Combine("Mtp Combine 3", 8)
 {
  R_Date("18413", 3660, 29);
  R_Date("18414", 3668, 28);
```

```
  Outlier(0.05);
 };
 R_Date("18415", 3734, 30)
 {
  Outlier(0.05);
 };
 R_Date("20179", 3583, 30)
 {
  Outlier(0.05);
 };
 R_Date("20017", 3651, 28)
 {
  Outlier(0.05);
 };
 Interval("Mtp II Int", 51 + 3*T(5));
};
Boundary("Mentuhotep III");
Phase("Mtp III")
{
 Interval("Mtp III Int", 12 + 3*T(5));
};
Boundary("Mentuhotep IV");
Phase("Mtp IV")
{
 Interval("Mtp IV Int", 7 + 3*T(5));
};
Boundary("Amenemhet I")
{
 z=15;
};
Phase("Amn I")
{
 R_Combine("Amn Combine 1", 8)
 {
  R_Date("19551", 3656, 27);
  R_Date("19552", 3623, 27);
  Outlier(0.05);
 };
 R_Combine("Amn Combine 2", 8)
 {
  R_Date("19553", 3277, 26);
  R_Date("20019", 3236, 27);
  Outlier(0.05);
 };
 Interval("Amn I Int", 29 + 3*T(5));
};
Boundary("Senusret I")
{
 z=16;
};
Phase("Sen I")
{
 R_Date("20307", 3652, 28)
 {
  Outlier(0.05);
 };
```

```
 Interval("Sen I Int", 45 + 3*T(5));
};
Boundary("Amenemhet II")
{
 z=17;
};
Phase("Amn II")
{
 Interval("Amn II Int", 34 + 3*T(5));
};
Boundary("Senusret II")
{
 z=18;
};
Phase("Sen II")
{
 R_Date("20308", 3557, 28)
 {
  Outlier(0.05);
 };
 R_Date("20200", 3546, 27)
 {
  Outlier(0.05);
 };
 Interval("Sen II Int", 7 + 3*T(5));
};
Boundary("Senusret III")
{
 z=19;
};
Phase("Sen III")
{
 R_Combine("Sen III Combine 1", 8)
 {
  R_Date("15313", 3503, 30);
  R_Date("VERA-3726", 3543, 29);
  Outlier(0.05);
 };
 R_Combine("Sen III Combine 2", 8)
 {
  R_Date("15317", 3532, 31);
  R_Date("VERA-3730", 3529, 29);
  Outlier(0.05);
 };
 R_Combine("Sen III Combine 3", 8)
 {
  R_Date("15318", 3518, 31);
  R_Date("VERA-3731", 3513, 29);
  Outlier(0.05);
 };
 R_Combine("Sen III Combine 4", 8)
 {
```

```
    R_Date("15315", 3513, 31);
      R_Date("VERA-3728", 3565, 29);
    Outlier(0.05);
   };
   R_Date("15311", 3532, 31)
   {
    Outlier(0.05);
   };
   R_Date("VERA-3732", 3563, 29)
   {
    Outlier(0.05);
   };
     Interval("Sen III Int", 39 + 3*T(5));
   };
   Boundary("Amenemhet III")
   {
    z=20;
   };
   Phase("Amn III")
   {
      R_Combine("Amn III Combine 1", 8)
   {
    R_Date("15316", 3542, 30);
      R_Date("VERA-3729", 3563, 29);
    Outlier(0.05);
   };
   R_Date("15310", 3560, 33)

   {
    Outlier(0.05);
   };
   R_Date("VERA-3733", 3568, 28)
   {
    Outlier(0.05);
   };
   R_Date("VERA-3734", 3512, 29)
   {
    Outlier(0.05);
   };
   R_Date("15309", 3626, 33)
   {
    Outlier(0.05);
   };
   R_Date("15312", 3485, 31)
   {
    Outlier(0.05);
   };
   R_Date("VERA-3735", 3550, 29)
   {
    Outlier(0.05);
   };
   R_Date("20016", 3556, 28)
   {
    Outlier(0.05);
   };
   R_Date("20480", 3489, 34)
   {
    Outlier(0.05);
   };

      Interval("Amn III Int", 45 + 3*T(5));
   };
   Boundary("Amenemhet IV")
   {
    z=21;
   };
   Phase("Amn IV")
   {
      Interval("Amn IV Int", 9 + 3*T(5));
   };
   Boundary("Queen Sobekneferu")
   {
    z=22;
   };
   Phase("QSo")
   {
    Interval("Qso Int", 4 + 3*T(5));
   };
   Boundary("Wegaf")
   {
    z=23;
   };
   Boundary("Sobekhotep II");
   };
     Difference("Duration of 1IP", "Mentuhotep II", "Start 1IP");
   };
```

Table 5.

	NEW KINGDOM MODELS										
	NKM1		NKM2		NKM3		NKM4		NKM5		NKM6	
	Accession (BC, 95%)		Accession (BC, 95%)		Accession (BC, 95%)		Accession (BC, 95%)		Accession (BC, 95%)		Accession (BC, 95%)	
	From	To	From	To	From	To	From	To	From	To	From	To
Start 17th Dynasty	1602	1572	1601	1541	1657	1634	1602	1571	1602	1572	1603	1576
Ahmose	1572	1542	1559	1539	1559	1537	1572	1541	1572	1543	1573	1546
Amenhotep I	1546	1517	1534	1515	1534	1512	1546	1516	1547	1518	1548	1521
Thutmose I	1525	1497	1512	1495	1512	1492	1525	1496	1525	1497	1526	1501
Thutmose II	1513	1485	1501	1484	1500	1480	1513	1484	1513	1486	1514	1489
Thutmose III	1499	1472	1498	1482	1497	1477	1499	1471	1500	1473	1501	1476
Queen Hatshepsut (Start)	1493	1467	1497	1481	1496	1476	1493	1466	1494	1467	1495	1470
Queen Hatshepsut (End)	1478	1452	1476	1461	1474	1455	1478	1451	1478	1453	1480	1456
Amenhotep II	1446	1421	1443	1427	1444	1424	1447	1420	1447	1422	1448	1425
Thutmose IV	1419	1394	1418	1402	1418	1398	1419	1393	1420	1395	1421	1398
Amenhotep III	1409	1384	1408	1392	1407	1388	1409	1383	1410	1385	1411	1388
Amenhotep IV	1371	1346	1371	1355	1370	1349	1371	1345	1372	1347	1373	1350
Neferneferuaten	1357	1332	1354	1338	1355	1334	1358	1330	1359	1332	1360	1336
Tutankhamun	1355	1330	1352	1336	1353	1332	1356	1328	1357	1330	1358	1334
Ay	1346	1321	1342	1325	1344	1322	1347	1319	1348	1321	1349	1325
Horemheb	1343	1317	1338	1321	1340	1318	1343	1315	1344	1317	1345	1321
Ramesses I	1315	1288	1311	1295	1312	1290	1330	1300	1316	1289	1318	1292
Sety I	1314	1287	1310	1293	1311	1288	1328	1299	1315	1287	1317	1291
Ramesses II	1299	1272	1299	1282	1297	1273	1314	1284	1301	1272	1302	1276
Merenptah	1233	1206	1234	1216	1231	1207	1248	1217	1235	1206	1236	1210
Amenmessu	1224	1195	1223	1205	1221	1196	1238	1207	1225	1196	1227	1200
Sety II	1221	1192	*	*	1219	1193	1235	1204	1222	1193	1224	1197
Saptah	1215	1186	1218	1200	1213	1187	1229	1197	1217	1186	1218	1191
Queen Tausret	1210	1180	1214	1196	1207	1180	1223	1191	1211	1180	1212	1185
Sethnakht	1208	1178	1212	1193	1205	1178	1221	1189	1209	1178	1211	1183
Ramesses III	1206	1175	1209	1190	1203	1176	1219	1186	1207	1175	1209	1181
Ramesses IV	1175	1144	1178	1160	1173	1144	1188	1155	1177	1144	1178	1149
Ramesses V	1169	1138	1172	1153	1166	1138	1182	1149	1171	1138	1172	1144
Ramesses VI	1166	1134	1168	1149	1163	1134	1179	1145	1167	1134	1169	1139
Ramesses VII	1159	1127	1161	1142	1156	1127	1172	1137	1161	1127	1162	1132
Ramesses VIII	1153	1120	1154	1134	**	**	1165	1130	1154	1120	1155	1125
Ramesses IX	1151	1116	1153	1133	**	**	1162	1127	1152	1117	1152	1122

NEW KINGDOM MODELS

	NKM1 Accession (BC, 95%)		NKM2 Accession (BC, 95%)		NKM3 Accession (BC, 95%)		NKM4 Accession (BC, 95%)		NKM5 Accession (BC, 95%)		NKM6 Accession (BC, 95%)	
	From	To	From	To	From	To	From	To	From	To	From	To
Ramesses X	1134	1098	1134	1114	**	**	1144	1109	1134	1099	1135	1104
Ramesses XI	1126	1089	1130	1110	**	**	1136	1099	1126	1090	1126	1095
Smendes	1096	1059	1101	1080	1096	1060	1106	1069	1096	1060	1096	1065
Amenemnisu	1071	1033	1076	1055	1070	1034	1081	1043	1071	1034	1071	1039
Psusennes I	1067	1029	1030	1009	1066	1030	1077	1039	1067	1030	1067	1035
Amenemope	1022	983	1028	1006	1020	984	1031	993	1021	984	1021	989
Osorkon the Elder	1012	974	1018	996	1011	975	1022	984	1012	975	1012	980
Siamun	1006	968	1012	990	1005	969	1016	977	1006	969	1007	974
Psusennes II	987	949	994	971	985	950	998	958	987	950	988	955

* Hornung *et al.* (2006) regard Amenmessu and Sety II as contemporaneous
** Kitchen (2000) does not stipulate accession years for Rameses VIII–XI

MIDDLE KINGDOM MODELS

	MKM1 Accession (BC, 95%)		MKM2 Accession (BC, 95%)		MKM3 Accession (BC, 95%)		MKM4 Accession (BC, 95%)	
	From	To	From	To	From	To	From	To
Mentuhotep II	2064	2019	2062	1998	2061	1992	2065	2019
Mentuhotep III	2012	1970	2010	1947	2010	1941	2013	1970
Mentuhotep IV	2003	1960	2001	1937	2000	1931	2004	1959
Amenemhat I	1998	1953	1994	1930	1994	1925	1999	1953
Senusret I	1971	1924	1977	1911	1975	1906	1972	1925
Amenemhat II	1929	1879	1936	1869	1934	1865	1929	1879
Senusret II	1895	1844	1903	1836	1901	1832	1896	1844
Senusret III	1889	1837	1894	1828	1894	1825	1890	1837
Amenemhat III	1851	1798	1877	1811	1876	1807	1852	1799
Amenemhat IV	1809	1754	1832	1767	1833	1763	1810	1755
Queen Sobekneferu	1801	1745	1825	1759	1825	1754	1802	1746
Wegaf	1797	1740	1822	1755	1822	1749	1798	1741
Sobekhotep II***	1791	1671	1818	1701	1816	1695	1793	1672

*** Hornung *et al.* (2006) place Amenemhet VII after Wegaf